Ideologies of History
in the
Spanish Golden Age

PENN STATE STUDIES
in ROMANCE LITERATURES

Editors
Frederick A. de Armas
Alan E. Knight

Anthony J. Cascardi

Ideologies of History
—— in the ——
Spanish Golden Age

The Pennsylvania State University Press
University Park, Pennsylvania

Publication of this book has been aided by a grant from The Program for Cultural Cooperation Between Spain's Ministry of Culture and United States' Universities.

Library of Congress Cataloging-in-Publication Data

Cascardi, Anthony J., 1953–
    Ideologies of history in the Spanish Golden Age / Anthony J.
Cascardi.
        p.   cm. — (Penn State studies in Romance literatures)
    Includes bibliographical references (p.   ) and index.
    ISBN 0-271-01667-1 (cloth : alk. paper)
    ISBN 0-271-01668-X (paper : alk. paper)
    1. Spanish literature—Classical period, 1500–1700—History and
criticism.   2. Literature and society—Spain.   I. Title.
II. Series.
PQ6066.C353   1997
860.9′003—dc20   96-31045
                                                           CIP

Contents

Acknowledgments

The present volume includes some of the work that I have done in Golden Age studies over the past ten years. Many of the chapters that are published here represent substantially revised and expanded versions of work that has appeared in print elsewhere during that time. An earlier version of Chapter 1 was first published as "The Old and the New: The Spanish *comedia* and the Resistance to Historical Change" in *Renaissance Drama* 17 (1986). Chapter 3 is based upon "Allegories of Power" in a volume entitled *The Prince in the Tower: Perceptions of La vida es sueño*, edited by Frederick A. de Armas (Lewisburg, Pa.: Bucknell University Press, 1993). A version of Chapter 4 was first published as an afterword to *Culture and Control in Counter-Reformation Spain*, a volume of *Hispanic Issues* edited by Anne J. Cruz and Mary Elizabeth Perry (Minneapolis: University of Minnesota Press, 1992). Chapter 5 is a revised version of "Gracián and the Authority of Taste," *Hispanic Issues* (Minneapolis: University of Minnesota Press, 1997). Chapter 6 incorporates some material that first appeared in "Don Juan and the Discourse of Modernism" in *Tirso's Don Juan: The Metamorphosis of a Theme* (Washington, D.C.: Catholic University of America Press, 1988). Chapter 7 is based upon my contribution to the volume *Cervantes and Psychoanalysis*, edited by Diana Wilson and the late Ruth El Saffar (Ithaca: Cornell University Press, 1993). Some of the material in Chapter 8 was first presented at a symposium organized by Marina Brownlee at the University of Pennsylvania and published in revised form as "History and Modernity in the Spanish Golden Age:

Secularization and Literary Self-Assertion in *Don Quixote*" in *Cultural Authority in Early Modern Spain: Continuation and Its Alternatives*, edited by Marina Brownlee and Hans Ulrich Gumbrecht (Baltimore: Johns Hopkins University Press, 1995). Chapter 9 is a much expanded version of "Instinct and Object: Subjectivity and Speech-Act in Garcilaso de la Vega," which appeared in the *Journal of Interdisciplinary Literary Studies* 6, no. 2 (1994). The nucleus of Chapter 10 was published as "Reason and Romance: The *Persiles* and the Disenchantment of the World" in *MLN* (March 1991). I am grateful to the editors of these various publications for their interest in my work.

I wish to thank Frederick de Armas for inviting this volume to be published as part of the Penn State Studies in Romance Literatures series, and Dian Fox, who so carefully read the entire manuscript and offered valuable suggestions for improvement. Philip Winsor and Sandy Thatcher at Penn State Press have provided invaluable assistance with this and numerous other projects.

The book is dedicated to my family, with whom it has grown and flourished over the years.

Introduction:
Historicizing the Golden Age

These essays constitute an attempt to historicize a category that has customarily been conceived in purely aesthetic terms. Whereas the notion of a "Golden Age" of Spanish literature and art has in the past been linked to the aesthetic productivity of this period, contemporary scholarship has increasingly reflected a historicizing ambition in the avoidance of the very term "Golden Age," favoring the designation "early modern Spain" instead. This descriptive change goes a long way toward breaking down claims that the works produced in Spain between the end of the fifteenth century and the end of the seventeenth must be understood in purely formalistic terms and suggests that Spanish culture of this period must be approached in relation to the larger questions of modernization and subject-formation in Europe. But the shift from the designation "Golden Age" to "early modern Spain" can too easily lead us to think that the work of historicizing this period is complete once we have succeeded in marking its chronological boundaries. My aim here is to suggest that the task of historicizing the Golden Age involves an investigation of the ways in which literature is shaped by tensions that are focused at the level of social structure; it is also, however, to investigate the ways in which literature is itself a social force, actively proposing solutions to historical conflicts that seem unresolvable by any other means or, conversely, resisting solutions to those conflicts.

One of the points of orientation in the historicizing of the Golden Age may be articulated in relation to what Américo Castro called the "axiology" of Spain's *edad conflictiva*. Another is provided by José

Antonio Maravall's description of a society of social estates (*esta-mentos*). By engaging the work of Castro and Maravall in relation to more recent theories of society whose roots lie in Marx, Max Weber, and Foucault, it is my aim to suggest that what may be truly polemical about the Golden Age is rooted in the clash of two incommensurable modes of social and historical orientation: the one based upon tradition-bound hierarchies associated with the values of caste; the other associated with the relatively more modern structure of social classes. We shall have ample opportunity in the chapters that follow to discuss the differences between the structures of social caste, which involve hierarchies that are relatively closed and racially bound, and the individual autonomy that is in principle possible in a society differentiated by classes. Castro's analyses, however, veered sharply away from the beginnings of a social order in Spain that was founded on the values of class. His work after *El pensamiento de Cervantes* remained wholly within the axiology of caste and its central concerns: the racial supremacy confirmed by purity of blood and personal honor as proved by social conduct and public repute.[1] But the point of the present volume is less a critique of Castro's views than a redescription of what was truly at issue about literature in the Golden Age. Above all, I suggest that the conflict between these two ways of structuring values socially was historical and that the prevailing historical orientations with respect to these axiologies were in turn ideological. This is foremost the case in those instances where literature takes a historical stance that denies the very contradictions underlying it. As we shall see, Golden Age writers often invented for themselves, and projected for others, a vision of history that looked either to the past or to the future as a way of suturing together the various contradictions that in their contemporary world could be attributed to the conflicting value-systems of caste and class. Indeed, the role of some of the most powerful "ideologies of history" at work in the Golden Age was to produce imaginary worlds in which historical conflict is itself eliminated.

In concrete terms, this imaginary "escape from history" provided potent fuel for the timeless "present" we associate with lyric poetry.[2] It

1. John Beverley has articulated a cogent criticism of Castro's views in his essay "Class or Caste: A Critique of the Castro Thesis," in *Américo Castro: The Impact of His Thought*, ed. Ronald Surtz (Madison: Hispanic Seminary, 1988), 141–49.
2. John Beverley's recent analysis of Garcilaso de la Vega's sonnet 23, "En tanto que de rosa y azucena" (While the colors f the rose and the lily) points out the ways in which

produces the nostalgic aestheticization of the past that we see in anonymous works like *El Abencerraje,* as well as in Lope de Vega's *El caballero de Olmedo.*[3] In a play like Calderón's *La vida es sueño* it leads to the advancement of a politics of virtue as a way to quell revolution and to avoid a more radical transformation of social structures. But, as I argue in relation to Cervantes, literature proves finally unable to deny its relationship to history. Especially in Cervantes, literature is the mode by which the present acknowledges its formation by and situation within the past, even as it seeks (as in the more idealizing *Novelas ejemplares*) to transcend the conflicts of the present.

The historical tensions visible in the literature of the Spanish Golden Age are easily perceived as incommensurable with those at play in the rest of Europe during this time. The case of Spain seems unique in part because it was the caste structure of medieval Spanish society rather than the economy of feudalism that played the major role in the social background to the period. But it is more important to note that a genre like the *comedia* responded ideologically to the question of historical change, very often by perpetuating the hierarchies of caste at a time when the influence of capitalism, which tended to reorient social differences along class lines, was becoming widespread elsewhere in Europe. As I argue in relation to *Fuenteovejuna* in Chapter 1, the *comedia* makes a turn away from modernity seem attractive by reconstructing historical narrative as a form of literary romance, which in turn occludes an awareness of those same modernizing factors that precipitate the agon or "conflict" of the play. Indeed, it would not be unreasonable to read the *comedia* as one of the imaginary (which is also to say, ideological) mechanisms through which Spanish society was able simultaneously to confront and to resist the social transformation that we can conveniently designate in terms of the conflictive historical

---

the dynamics of rose and lily, of stasis and change, also involve "the articulation of a historicism. The age of a perpetual present of sinless erotic gratification is the Golden Age, 'la alegre primavera.' This is the time before history, moral law, and the state, before writing—the time of *otium,* of a pastoral Arcadia. But this is also a time of perpetual infancy. History introduces the possibility of achievement and transformation, ripening and maturation, just as the linguistic composition of the poem sublimates and eternalizes its subject. This can lead, as in epic or religious narrative, to the possibility of a cultural apotheosis, but also to a loss of quality and a degradation, as in the ages of the lesser metals." *Literature Against Itself* (Minneapolis: University of Minnesota Press, 1993), 36.

3. See for example, Claudio Gullén's essay on "Literature as Historical Contradiction" in *Literature as System* (Princeton: Princeton University Press, 1971).

orientations of "old" and "new." The *comedia* often confronts a vision of the "modern" or the "new," yet it tends to reject that vision in favor of the stability to be achieved through the dominance of the "old." The utopian vision that it projects in a play like Lope de Vega's *Fuenteovejuna* is drawn from the past and consists in a vision of the perpetuation of that past in the form of an idealized political future.

The task of a historicized reading of *Fuenteovejuna* would be to deconstruct this vision by asking about the specific conflicts it effaces. It would begin by recording the concrete struggles represented literally or alluded to in the play: the conflicts between Fuenteovejuna and the Comendador, between the Order of Calatrava and Ciudad Real, and ultimately between the Catholic Monarchs of Spain and Alfonso V of Portugal. But it would proceed from there to an investigation of the factors at work behind these conflicts and to an analysis of the motives that drive the play's romantic and utopian passions. In this way, *Fuenteovejuna* as a structured whole can be seen as determined by the historical "crisis" outlined above, namely, by the exhaustion of one social order at a time when the newly emerging order was met with resistance and, quite possibly, with fear. It is because of this resistance to change that *Fuenteovejuna* and the *comedias* it most resembles can project a future that is continuous with the past, one in which the tradition-oriented system of racial castes and inherited professions, of "natural" social and political relations, is advanced as a way of protecting society against the pernicious effects of the Comendador's sexual aggressions. And insofar as the *comedia* may be seen as a strategy for the containment of these modernizing forms of existence and their ideological correlates, the genre may be described as the locus of a struggle between the traditional axiology that drew strength from the persistence in Spain of a system of social castes, and the more modernizing outlook of social class, which privileged the autonomy of individual subjects. Within this context, however, is located the "deep-structure" of the play, which consists in the struggle for recognition by a group (the *vulgo*) seeking to establish its identity within the context of historical change. For how long will it be possible to conceive the *vulgo* as the "vassals" of the Comendador or, indeed, the King? What are we to conclude about their need for recognition when the King declares at the conclusion of the play that they are his vassals? At what point must they be seen as the new subjects of the early modern state, collaborating in their own subjection? These are among the questions that a modern reader of the play may be drawn to ask, but that Lope deftly avoids.

In Chapter 2 I argue that the question of social and political legitimation is central to the formation of the *comedia* as a specifically national mode of literary expression during this period. My discussion of the transformation of the figure of the Cid in Guillén de Castro's *Las mocedades del Cid* represents an effort to clarify questions of legitimation in relation to the process of subject-formation. The figure of the Cid is reinterpreted within the historical context of the Golden Age in order to found the "new order" of society on the image of an original and self-defining whole, not, as traditional critics like Joaquín Casalduero would have it, in order to mirror an aristocracy's image of itself.[4] Rather, the appropriation of the figure of the Cid by Guillén de Castro is successful to the extent that the new theatrical public could imagine the process of their own historical emergence as legitimate because they could come to see it as continuous with the past. The "romantic" action of this play has as its endpoint the production of a hero capable of sanctioning the existing historical and social order by transforming the burdens of the epic past into the very foundations of the present age. This requires the development of the apprentice knight into the mature and fully empowered hero. The loyalty the Cid feels to his father Diego Laínez stands in tension with his passionate love for Ximena in such a way as to bring to light the phenomenon of passionate love as a distinctively modern mode of self-awareness and, in this instance, as one that appears irreconcilable with the demands of a traditional society. The issue marks a moment in the large-scale process that Norbert Elias has described as the "courtization of warriors," which was itself part of the process that transformed the coarse knight into a more refined object of amorous attachment. The conflicting demands of epic duty, which transmits patriarchal authority, and of *amor pasión*, which increasingly defines the intimate space of the subject-self, demonstrate the difficulty of creating the autonomous and interior space that would in principle allow for the individual's entrance into the new historical order. At the same time, such a reading of *Las mocedades del Cid* strengthens the claim that an underlying basis of the *comedia* lies in

4. Joaquín Casalduero, *Estudios sobre el teatro español* (Madrid: Gredos, 1962), 45–71.

literary romance, as witnessed both in the "marvelous" means through which the solutions to the conflicts in this play are produced and in relation to the question of the Cid's legitimacy, which also finds a solution in romance. The marvelous is at once the means through which the causality of events embodied in the plot can be suspended and a means of engaging an audience in such a way that it cannot resist the resolution of the plot. It is both structural and rhetorical in its function. Though apparently implausible, the marvelous is a way of gaining assent by appeal to the affects or, perhaps more accurately still, of substituting affect for belief.

The question of the affects and of the powers that control them is crucial to Calderón's *La vida es sueño,* which explores the question of power in both the aesthetic (theatrical) and the political domains. In my discussion of Calderón, I propose that the theatrical aesthetic of the *comedia* was invaluable in legitimizing and in strengthening the power of political absolutism in Spain. The response to the self-limiting crisis of absolutism was an effort to shore up sovereign authority by means of infusions of new forms of power, or by representing the old forms of power in a newly legitimized guise, such as the theater could provide. Especially in Calderón, however, this effort takes a specifically theatrical form, in which the preferred situation for investigating and "resolving" the crisis of authority involves the threat of the displacement of the sovereign from his position of power, either by jeopardizing his claim to the throne, or by raising questions about who will rightfully inherit it. The theater of Calderón thus allegorizes (in order to resolve) the crisis of power within the absolutist state. The threatened displacement of the sovereign is in turn mirrored in the polis itself, which in Calderón acknowledges the dislocation of human beings from one another and from nature and records acts of violence that define "nature" as an apparently lawless realm. Since Calderón imagines nature as a state in which human beings encounter the preexisting effects of power, it turns out that the need to "perfect" human nature must perforce be accomplished politically. In Calderón, as in Hobbes, the fundamental disgregation of individuals is engendered by nature's warlike—and deathlike—constitution. Again as in Hobbes, we begin from the premise that the inclusive order of nature has been destroyed and fragmented in such a way that social and political cohesion can only be achieved through some external operation performed upon it. The social bond must be maintained through an external force whose legitimacy is bound always to be in question. The problematic authority of the sovereign thus mirrors the problematic authority of the subject itself.

The drama of authority staged in Calderón's play takes a rather different form in Tirso de Molina's *El burlador de Sevilla*. The central dilemma of Tirso's play is rooted in the fact that the positions of patriarchal authority are *already* held by those who would seem to resist the modern transformation that is necessary for their re-occupation. In Tirso's play, the existing social regime is challenged when desire becomes driven by a mobile attachment to a constantly shifting series of objects. Perhaps even more so than in *Fuenteovejuna,* the representation of the erosion of the principles of social caste (lineage and honor) in *El burlador de Sevilla* amounts to the full-scale dramatization of modern desire as a threat to that structure. Indeed, Tirso's play suggests just how mistaken it would be to think that the *comedia* was incapable of representing desire in its mobile, modern forms. How is this desire bound? What place will this mobile form of desire be assigned within the *socius?* How it will be contained? In *El burlador de Sevilla,* Tirso recognizes that the authority that binds desire is itself desire-driven. Specifically, the conclusion of the play brings into relief the binding of desire as premised on the desire for the stability and wholeness of society itself.

My discussion of desire and authority in *El burlador de Sevilla* draws on the work of Gilles Deleuze and Félix Guattari, who can help us see that while all forms of social action, from the most basic rank orderings to the most elaborate search for recognition, are propelled by desire, desire must at the same time be contained if the social body is to function at all. The mobility of desire must be bound, and Deleuze and Guattari claim that the myth of Oedipus provides the model according to which this takes place. If this is so, then *El burlador de Sevilla* confirms this fact in a very unusual way by "deriving" what is in fact a very traditional form of authority (in this instance, that of the King) from the suppression of a much more mobile and modern form of desire. Indeed, if desire can be made to seem sufficiently boundless and threatening, then even the most traditional modes of authority may be adopted in response to it as if willed. In the case at hand, it is only through the wished-for binding of desire by a figure who stands in principle above desire that Tirso can move toward a conclusion in which society ignores the conflicts of history and continues to will the status quo. In its concluding moments, the play represents a historical gesture by which the *socius* perpetuates itself through a collective act of repression.

In turning from Tirso's play to the question of desire in Cervantes, Chapter 7 takes as its point of departure the insight of contemporary psychoanalysis that neither the thinking subject nor the literary/historical text can ever be accepted as fully "present" to itself, but that there invariably exists an absent and potentially troubling extension that history, text, and subject never eliminate. If *Don Quijote* invites us to pursue a psychoanalytic reading, it does not do so because its characters lend themselves to a diagnostic analysis, but rather because Cervantes places a particular emphasis on the visibility of the exclusions, gaps, and lacks that trouble this text. If *Don Quijote* presses us to move beyond the bounds of a psychoanalytic reading of the type that would simply decode a series of historically grounded signs and instead impels us to restore the text's potential for mobilizing desire, it does so because Cervantes's novel represents an exemplary instance of the refusal to be bound by either of two conceptually distinct, historically locatable structures of desire or by the corresponding structures of value described above. *Don Quijote* may be situated at a moment of historical conflict or transition to the extent that it articulates the eclipse of the "heroic" order of society idealized in the chronicles, the ballads, and the romances of chivalry, by a newer, relatively more mobile order oriented around the values of social class. The effects of Cervantes's refusal of these terms become apparent in the visibility, within the *Quijote,* of a series of culturally ambiguous or marginal groups (e.g., the *moriscos* and *pícaros*) whose identity cannot be located either within the social order that is in the process of being eclipsed or within the newly emergent order of things, but that is rendered problematic by the clash between them.

What bearing does Cervantes's engagement with such marginal social figures have on the question of his historical orientation? First and foremost, *Don Quijote* suggests that as long as we read literature with the aim of using history simply in order to fill in what remains unexpressed within a given discourse we shall have falsified and reduced the importance of desire-driven conflict, out of which history as a dynamic process is produced. Attempts to resolve the problematic ending of the Ricote episode in Part 2 by appealing to historical circumstances not mentioned explicitly in the text are a case in point.[5]

5. See, for example, Francisco Márquez-Villanueva, "El morisco Ricote o la hispana

But even the historicizing "correction" of quixotic idealism fails to see that the effort to locate meaning in historical terms may in fact reduce the disorienting effects of desire and may subject our reading to a series of monological strictures. As discussed in Chapter 7, the psychoanalytic concept of "archaeology" (specifically, an archaeology of desire) can prove useful in demonstrating how to avoid such a narrowing of our interpretive horizons. The premises of an archaeology of desire are that radical origins, once they have been concealed, are never fully recoverable, and that what we more commonly refer to as "history" provides substitutes for all the things that desire leaves hidden or eclipsed. Rather than think of desire as the ground of an absent satisfaction or as the basis for an audience-gratifying wish-fulfillment dream, as can be the case in romance-like *comedias,* we would do better to conceive of desire in Cervantes as the sign of an origin that can never be recuperated and as an indication that the text and its ideologies are not just historical, but historically plural. If we customarily imagine history as a means of orienting our relationship to the past, then a work like *Don Quijote* complicates that project and suggests that the "movement" of history toward the future is driven by the pressure of a potentially infinite desire for the origins we imagine to be located in the past. In this context, I propose that an investigation of the archaeology of desire in *Don Quijote* might also include a remapping of the historical displacement of the "old" by the "new" in terms of the strange productivity of "archaic" desires within a cultural space that believes itself to have overcome archaism through the processes of world-disenchantment, societal rationalization, and historical self-assertion.

In Chapter 8 I follow up these questions in relation to Lukács's claim that the origins of literary modernity as reflected in Cervantes's work may indeed be understood in terms of the process of secularization, provided that we regard "secularization" not just as the result of a change in the patterns of religious belief but as a master-trope for the problem of the transmission of authority. In this context, I modify certain standing presuppositions concerning the process of secularization so as to suggest that the attempt to represent the boundary between secularized and pre-secular modes of awareness initiates Cervantes's critique of the literary-historical rhetoric of self-assertion that was so

---

razón de estado," in his *Personajes y temas del Quijote* (Madrid: Taurus, 1975), 229–335. Needless to say, Márquez's interpretation of the Ricote episode is considerably more complex than this.

important for the culture of early modernity. I suggest that the process of secularization visible in a work like *Don Quijote* is not anything happening in culture external to literature, but that literary history itself, as an effort to reconcile the authority of the present and that of the past, is the best example of the "secularization" process whose consequences Lukács was attempting to describe in the *Theory of the Novel*. To conceive of literature in relation to the historical figure of "secularization" is also to recognize the power of modern literature to intuit its own status as both inside and outside of the traditional enclosures of "theology," "dogma," and "belief." When taken as a corrective to modernity's understanding of itself, the secularization process figured in Cervantes's text can lead us to a more complex understanding of literary history, and eventually to the conclusion that the peculiar productivity of literature in the modern age is a consequence of the impossible and unfulfillable desire to ground the present in the past.

Consider Cervantes's engagements with the poetry of Garcilaso, discussed in Chapters 8 and 9, in this light. For the characters of the *Quijote,* Garcilaso stands as the paragon of poetic power and authority. Yet for Cervantes's narrator it seems that the power of Garcilaso's verse must be understood as having been "always already" mediated and displaced in such a way that it cannot be made available apart from the literary history through which its reception was filtered. The inability to fulfill the fantasy of a poetic power over the world, the sustaining desire of which is both honored and criticized in Cervantes's text, yields the construction of "Garcilaso" as the object of a literary history with which a writer like Cervantes cannot escape involvement.

In Garcilaso's verse itself, by contrast, the question of poetic power is played out as part of the larger drama of subject-formation. Specifically, Garcilaso's verse raises a series of questions about the relationship between subject-formation and the first-person poetic voice. In addressing the issue of voice, I argue that Garcilasian subjectivity is a consequence or effect of the poet's failed attempt to reconstitute through speech a whole and original relationship to the objects of his (literary) desire, which are located in the past. Indeed, the Garcilasian "subject" that is produced in dealings with the lost or unyielding object of desire is one who repeatedly foregrounds the anxiety that attaches to his own powers of speech. The focus in Garcilaso's verse is not so much the objectivity of the object as the ability of the subject to create himself through a series of speech-acts whose strikingly modern discovery is their own performative inefficacy. I argue that the difficulty of crystallizing desire in the form of a durable object serves in Garcilaso to provide a set of terms against which the effect of lyric poetry can be tested and proved. Perhaps even more emphatically than for his Petrarchan model, Garcilaso's voice depends upon a beloved who escapes the poet's and his surrogates' powers; in signal instances, this voice articulates a prosopopeia that fails to animate its object. But this failure in turn opens a space in which the more daring project of lyric self-creation as a form of objectless enunciation can be put forth.

The availability of an inward voice in the lyric was intimately linked with the socialization of the subject-self. In addressing the question of social control in Counter-Reformation Spain (Chapter 4), I argue that while culture can indeed be defined in terms of its "control mechanisms" it is also necessary to ask who its subjects were and to investigate how they became *subject to* control. If we are to understand the complex question of ideology in Counter-Reformation Spain we shall need to articulate a series of questions about the relationship between the organized resources of power and the formation of the subjects of control. The question Who is in control? (which may be given a quick and easy answer by reference to the "ideologies" of the church and the state), must be supplemented by another, less readily answered series of questions, such as Who is controlled? and Why does the subject desire to be controlled? It is only in this way that we can use recent developments in our understanding of "ideology" to yield a nonreductive approach to the various modes of representation through which individuals adopted a social identity as subject-selves. By building upon the dynamics of subjectivity and subjection as seen in the plays of Lope de Vega and Calderón, it becomes essential to ask what, at the symbolic level of society, might have produced the desire for such control.

While my approach to such questions shares certain of the perspectives on the crisis-structure of the Spanish baroque first put forward by José Antonio Maravall, my principal thesis differs significantly from the one advanced by Maravall. Maravall regards the phenomenon of the Spanish baroque as bound up with the urbanization of life and with the creation of a mass culture that is dependent on the increasingly capitalistic environment of the sixteenth and seventeenth centuries.[6] Those who

6. See José Antonio Maravall, *La cultura del barroco* (Barcelona: Ariel, 1975); *The*

follow Maravall's thesis tend to agree that the culture of the Spanish baroque must be understood as a conservative formation whose ideological support of the status quo was produced in response to the economic crisis resulting from the transition from feudalism to capitalism. By contrast, I suggest that any attempt to align the ideological foundations of the Counter-Reformation with the stylistic practices commonly identified as "baroque" must turn first to the question of subject-formation; further, this attempt must incorporate into the questions of subjectivity and control the concept of *formation* that would satisfy the need to explain the culture of the baroque as an ongoing process that had a shaping power over those who became subjects within it. Moreover, by concentrating on the category of the "subject" and on the mechanisms of its formation, we may articulate the links between social power and artistic representation in a way that Maravall's focus on the "baroque" as a historical category does not always allow. We may in this way link large-scale transformations in historical structures with the changing modes of psychology and the shifting patterns of belief that shaped the nature of social relations.

A crucial site for addressing these issues is the notion of "taste" as elaborated by Gracián. Gracián has often been cited as central to the development of the modern discourse on aesthetics and, in this respect, as anticipating certain notions of subject-formation that became institutionalized in the writings of Kant. Both Gadamer and Arendt have seen Gracián in this way. I argue that, unlike Kant, who emphasized the disinterestedness of aesthetic pleasure, Gracián's notion of taste cannot be understood apart from the question of its sociogenesis, and that the peculiar authority of judgments of taste in the Golden Age depends upon the internalization of forms of authority that once were located elsewhere within the social sphere. Not only must Gracián's notion of taste be historicized in relation to the question of subject-formation, the "historicization" of taste can provide insights into taste's social roots. Gracián's notion of taste can in this sense be understood as a function of the displacement of the hierarchical and hereditary values of social caste, founded on the principles of purity of blood, by a system of values that would eventually be consolidated around the bourgeois

---

Culture of the Baroque: Analysis of a Historical Structure, trans. Terry Cochran (Minneapolis: University of Minnesota Press, 1986). See also Maravall, "From the Renaissance to the Baroque," in *Literature Among Discourses,* ed. Wlad Godzich and Nicholas Spadaccini (Minneapolis: University of Minnesota Press, 1986), 3–40.

principles of social class, which entail a suppression of the corporeal basis of social standing in the creation of a more abstract, transcendental subject. Gadamer's claims notwithstanding, Gracián's notion of social *Bildung* is not at all "independent" of the structures of social class. On the contrary, Gracián's discourse on taste points in the direction of the concepts of "good sense" and "common sense," which were among the most important discursive means by which the primacy of lineage was suppressed by the emerging middle class.

"Taste" (*gusto*) in Gracián marks a central moment in the history of the formation of the bourgeois values of social class: a moment at which a notion of the capacity for judgment or discrimination as inborn was displaced by the notion of aesthetic judgment as socially situated. In addition, the invention of "good taste" favored the goals of a society that could no longer justify its moral projects according to the hierarchical criteria of rank, while responding to the continuing need for discrimination among those whose interests had formerly been characterized as illegitimate or "vulgar" (see Lope's reference in the "Arte nuevo de hacer comedias" to the taste of the *vulgo*). In a period of radical social change, the notion of taste emerged to ground a form of social distinction that became necessary for the identification of "good society." In this way, the modern understanding of taste as a faculty that operates in concert with aesthetic disinterest was enhanced by the sociopolitical understanding of taste, which sees the exercise of aesthetic judgment as a necessary means for maintaining distinctions within the modern world. Thus Gracián regards the exercise of taste as one of the ways in which the individual can best achieve success in social and political life, provided of course that the individual first masters the art of *self*-control. The judgment of taste, which requires the assertion of individual differences within the context of universal agreement or assent, comes to represent not just a historical shift of preferences, but the self-correction of modernity's universalizing aims. In Gracián, taste joins dissimulation as a means to preserve and protect individual identity.

As I argue in Chapter 10, the project of reimaging or refashioning traditional values within the context of radical historical change is the burden of Cervantes's *Persiles*. For Cervantes, the desire for an escape from historical contradiction was entwined in the *Persiles* with a progressive moral stance. In this work, Cervantes rejects the *comedia*'s effort to stabilize the position of the modern subject-self within the dominant social order by means of an idealist reshaping of the past or the imposition of an archaic symbolic law. In the *Persiles,* Cervantes searches for a genre appropriate to his bold attempt to clear free from the rigidity of caste divisions in order to speak with a new moral voice. Central to this effort is the desire to adapt the marvel and wonder associated with the Greek romance to new social conditions and, in the wondrous moment, to recover the moral authority of the efficacious sign. One is indeed struck by the ways in which the marvelous persists in Cervantes's texts. Its presence suggests that the process of disenchantment that Lukács suggested was essential for the emergence of irony in the modern novel was never complete; rather, the romance places wonder in the service of aims that are not just aesthetic, but political and moral as well.

In attempting to re-institute the conditions of wonder in a world where the marvelous seems no longer to have a place, however, Cervantes would not have us believe that the "reenchantment" of the world could be achieved in any literal sense. Especially in the *Quijote,* Cervantes leads us to see that the conditions for wonder are themselves socially produced, just as the effects of wonder are conditioned socially.[7] As I discuss in connection with the episodes of Zoraida and Ricote in *Don Quijote,* history proves that there is no possibility of recuperating authentic wonder as a truly first form of knowledge, but only the possibility of a re-cognition that establishes wonder as the repetition of an "original" encounter with the world filtered through the subject's social self-consciousness. Likewise, there is never a complete or final re-naturalization of the sign, no return of its truly "original" aura or authenticity, but only its re-contextualization within new social conditions and the reinvestment of new forms of authority in it. As a complement to the literary discourse on wonder that circulates in and around the *Persiles,* the *Quijote* points to the ways in which wonder was central to the drama of historical transformation and subject-formation in the Spanish Golden Age.

The foregoing has suggested that my own approach to the task of "historicizing" the literature of the Spanish Golden Age proposes an investigation of diverse genres, that it focuses on issues of social struc-

---

7. As George Mariscal has recently pointed out, only some groups in seventeenth-century Spain were positioned so as to perceive the effects of wonder. See *Contradictory Subjects: Quevedo, Cervantes, and Seventeenth-Century Spanish Culture* (Ithaca: Cornell University Press, 1991).

ture, on tensions created within history and literature by the forces of desire, and on the process of subject-formation under the pressure of political absolutism. I appeal to contemporary Marxism in order to correct what I believe is Castro's exclusion of questions of social class, to Freud and Lacan on desire in reading the *Quijote,* and to Michel Foucault in assessing the impact of state control in Counter-Reformation Spain, just to name a few. In the process, I renounce the idea that there is a single critical method that can be privileged above all others for the interpretation of these literary texts. But rather than simply offer the diversity of these approaches as their own justification, I propose that each offers a distinct perspective on the historical conflicts at work in Golden Age Spain and that together they reveal the plurality of the "ideologies" implicit in the historical orientations of its texts. What we regard as "literature" in the Golden Age is situated within a social structure shaped by the polemical values of tradition and modernity, of "old" and "new," of caste and class. What is "ideological" about the historical role of literature in the Spanish Golden Age is that it is not merely shaped by these and similar tensions, but articulates a strongly inflected response to them.

1

The Spanish *Comedia* and the Resistance to Historical Change

Fear of the master is indeed the beginning
of wisdom.
—Hegel, *Phenomenology of Spirit*

The major enemy, the strategic adversary is
. . . the fascism in us all, in our heads and
in our everyday behavior, the fascism that
causes us to love power, to desire the very
thing that dominates and exploits us.
—Foucault, "Introduction" to Deleuze and
Guattari, *Anti-Oedipus*.

In a series of articles that first appeared in print two and three decades ago, historians E. J. Hobsbawm, H. R. Trevor-Roper, Pierre Vilar, and J. H. Elliott advanced the claim that the "modernization" of Europe was precipitated by a variety of circumstances that coalesced in the form of a "general crisis" during the seventeenth century.[1] Despite

1. An earlier analysis of the seventeenth-century crisis is that of Roland Mousnier in the *Histoire Générale des civilisations,* vol. 4 (Paris: Presses Universitaires de France, 1961). See also his "Trevor-Roper's 'General Crisis': A Symposium," in *The Crisis in Europe,* ed. Trevor Aston (New York: Basic Books, 1965), 97–104. J. H. Elliott's earliest study of "decline" (originally published in *Past and Present* 20 [1961]: 52–75, repr. in *The Crisis in Europe,* 167–73, also collected in Elliott, *Spain and Its World: 1500–1700* [New Haven: Yale University Press, 1989], 217–40, henceforth cited from the latter text as Elliott, "Decline") is anticipated by E. J. Hamilton, "The Decline of Spain," *Economic History Review* 8 (1938): 168–79. On the notion of "decline" as a historiographical

substantial disagreements among them, their work confirmed that a number of social, political, and economic transformations during this period led to the emergence of capitalist modes of production and exchange and also to the consolidation of the powers of the Absolutist State.[2] While there may have been manifestations of a nascent capitalism in Europe well before the seventeenth century, only at this time did social and economic pressures yield anything like a lasting change. Elaborating on Marx's view of the English Renaissance as a transitional stage between the dominance of the feudal aristocracy and that of the commercial bourgeoisie, Hobsbawm, for instance, recognizes that there may have been something at work to unsettle the feudal base of European society as early as the fourteenth century, but concedes that only in the seventeenth was there a full-scale recasting of the socioeconomic order.[3] The notion of "crisis" invoked both by Hobsbawm and by Trevor-Roper is already apparent among writers of the seventeenth century, as is the concept of "decline" that Elliott applies to the case of Spain in a series of essays on this subject.[4] Yet if a crisis is thought to indicate what Vilar describes as "the passage from an ascending conjuncture to one of collapse,"[5] then it is important to note

topic, see Randolph Starn, "Meaning-Levels in the Theme of Historical Decline," *History and Theory* 14 (1975): 1–31.

2. On absolutism in Spain, see Perry Anderson, *Lineages of the Absolutist State* (London: Verso, 1979).

3. See the essays and critical discussion of Maurice Dobb, *Studies in the Development of Capitalism* (London: George Routledge, 1946) in *The Transition from Feudalism to Capitalism*, by Rodney Hilton et al. (London: NLB, 1976). Lawrence Stone's work is useful for the case of England; see *The Crisis of the Aristocracy, 1558–1641* (Oxford: Clarendon Press, 1965). In connection with Shakespeare in particular, see Rosalie Colie, "Reason and Need: King Lear and the 'Crisis' of the Aristocracy" in *Some Facets of King Lear*, ed. R. Colie and F. T. Flahiff (Toronto: University of Toronto Press, 1974), 185–219, and Paul Delany, "King Lear and the Decline of Feudalism," *PMLA* 91 (1977): 429–40. Walter Cohen discusses both *King Lear* and *Fuenteovejuna* in detail from a Marxist perspective in *Drama of a Nation: Public Theatre in Renaissance England and Spain* (Ithaca: Cornell University Press, 1985), 322–56, which also contains a discussion of the rewritings of *Fuenteovejuna* by Cristóbal de Monroy and of *King Lear* by Nahum Tate (1681).

4. These are collected in part 4 of his book *Spain and Its World: 1500–1700*, 213–86, and include the above-referenced "Decline of Spain" as well as "Self-Perception and Decline in Early Seventeenth-Century Spain" (1977), and "Art and Decline in Seventeenth-Century Spain" (1983).

5. Vilar, "The Age of Don Quixote," *New Left Review* 68 (July–August 1971): 60. The essay originally was published as "Le Temps du Don Quichotte," *Europe* 34 (1956): 3–16.

that the crisis tendencies of the feudal order are seen as being finally *overcome* in the seventeenth century by the emergence of a new social paradigm. Seen from this vantage point, whatever factors might have continued to resist the newly consolidated modes of production and exchange are regarded as in some way limiting or "immobilizing" them. In the case of Spain, for instance, Trevor-Roper points to the survival of the ancien régime "as a disastrous, immobile burden on an impoverished nation."[6] And Hobsbawm more generally observes that "unless certain conditions are present . . . the scope of capitalist expansion will be limited by the prevalence of the feudal structure of society, that is of the predominant rural sector or perhaps by some other structure which 'immobilizes' both the potential labour-force, the potential surplus for productive investment, and the potential demand for capitalistically produced goods, such as the prevalence of tribalism or petty commodity production."[7]

The notion that certain political or social structures may have limited the expansion of capitalism may be useful in accounting for the unevenness of economic change across Europe, especially in the seventeenth century, but this still leaves much to be explained about the social and political consequences that early capitalism did have. Why, for instance, was the emergence of capitalism accompanied by a strengthening of absolutist forms of government? Why was the rise of the bourgeoisie not linked sooner and more directly to democratic individualism in the social order? Some provisional answers to these questions have been suggested by Maurice Dobb and Perry Anderson. In *Studies in the Development of Capitalism* and in the published debate surrounding that work[8] Dobb suggests that the embryo of bourgeois productive relations—the accumulation of small pockets of capital and the beginnings of class differentiation within an economy of small-scale producers—arose within a society that had been essentially feudal in its socioeconomic relations and that remained so. As we shall see in the case of Lope de Vega's *Fuenteovejuna,* however, it is more the hierarchical, caste structure of Spanish society than the economy of feudalism that provides the background relevant to early modern Spain, but still

6. Trevor-Roper, "The General Crisis of the Seventeenth Century," in *The Crisis in Europe,* ed. Trevor Aston, 95.
7. Hobsbawm, "The Crisis of the Seventeenth Century," in *The Crisis in Europe,* ed. Trevor Aston, 15.
8. See Hilton et al., *The Transition from Feudalism to Capitalism.*

it is worth noting that *Fuenteovejuna* addresses the problem of historical change by perpetuating traditional modes of consciousness at a time when the process of modernization was elsewhere in Europe firmly afoot. Numerous economic historians have suggested that the Spanish conquests in the New World may have supplied the initial capital necessary for the economic transformation that did indeed take place elsewhere in Europe, but as Perry Anderson rightly notes in *Lineages of the Absolutist State,* no other Absolutist State in Western Europe remained so resistant to bourgeois development. Thus if classical Marxism frequently comes to grief over the peculiar "lag" that occurs between any transformation in the modes of production and a corresponding transformation of social relations, these factors were exaggerated in the case of Spain to the degree where it would be more accurate to speak of a resistance to the culture of modernity than of the simple persistence of traditional values during early modern times.

＊　＊　＊

In considering the question of modernity in light of the specific case of Spain and in advancing some general notions about the ideological function of Lope's *comedia* as a genre during this period, one may begin with the observation that orthodox Marxism has itself been shown to conform to the shape of a literary "comedy" or romance, in which the various ends of secular and sacred narrative—familial harmony, the transcendence of the limiting consciousness of this world—are re-figured as a social version of the Utopian dream, in which mutual recognition among all members of society is finally achieved.[9] As we shall see,

---

9. Hayden White qualifies this in relation to the Comic structure of Hegel's vision, which Marx sets out to rewrite:

> Hegel's Comic conception of history was based ultimately on his belief in the right of life over death; "life" guaranteed to Hegel the possibility of an ever more adequate form of social life throughout the historical future. Marx carried this Comic conception even further; he envisioned nothing less than the dissolution of that "society" in which the contradiction between consciousness and being had to be entertained as a fatality for all men in all times. It would not, then, be unjust to characterize the final version of history which inspired Marx in his historical and social theorizing as a Romantic one. But his conception did not envisage humanity's redemption as a deliverance from time itself. Rather, his redemption took the form of a reconciliation of man with a nature denuded of its fantastic and terrifying powers, submitted to the rules of technics, and turned to the creation of a genuine community. (*Metahistory: The Historical Imagination in*

however, the Spanish *comedia* reinscribes this hopeful vision within the structure of a more complex set of social and historical relations; indeed, the Utopian telos of a play like *Fuenteovejuna* serves to occlude an awareness of the very factors that precipitate the agon or "conflict" of the play, the purpose of which may be identified as the production of social subjects by effacing the historical conflicts in which their subjectivity is embedded. In part because the Lopean *comedia* makes an appeal to the *vulgo* from the point of those social groups in power, it played a crucial role in fashioning social subjects, even if common people are not customarily its heroes.[10] If the progressive Marxist vision would regard the social changes at work in early modern Europe as in some way instrumental to the ultimate transformation of society, we would by contrast have to see a *comedia* like *Fuenteovejuna* as an imaginary means through which Spanish society was able simultaneously to confront and to resist that transformation, by presenting the process of recognition as having been achieved by a return to the hierarchies of the past. In this sense, the play may be regarded as rigorously historical, even if that fact is made most evident in its resistance to the struggles that drive historical change. Not only in *Fuenteovejuna*, the *comedia* seems to admit a vision of "new," "modern" modes of social awareness; yet with equal conviction it sacrifices that vision in favor of the stability to be achieved by the dominance of the "old." The Utopian vision projected in a play like *Fuenteovejuna* is drawn from the past and consists in the dream of the perpetuation of that past, and its imagined pastoral existence, in the form of a changeless future.[11] Thus a genre that Lope himself described in the "Arte nuevo

---

Nineteenth-Century Europe [Baltimore: Johns Hopkins University Press, 1973, 281–82])

The notion of romance as deliverance, and specifically as "deliverance from time," has been amply discussed in connection with Shakespearean drama by Northrop Frye. See *The Myth of Deliverance* (Toronto: University of Toronto Press, 1983).

10. On the question of the hero in the *comedia,* see Dian Fox, *Refiguring the Hero: From Peasant to Noble in Lope de Vega and Calderón de la Barca* (University Park: Pennsylvania State University Press, 1991). Fox in fact argues that the nobility and not the *villanos* are the heroes of the peasant plays. Nonetheless, there is room for moral censure of the nobility within her position; for example, she refers to Fernán Gómez as "the blackest of malefactors" (176).

11. On the subject of the pastoral as a mode for resisting history, see John Beverley's analysis of Garcilaso de la Vega's sonnet 23, "En tanto que de rosa y azucena" (While the colors of the rose and the lily), cited in the Introduction. I also anticipate here a contrast with the reading of Calderón developed in Chapter 3, "Allegories of Power," in

de hacer *comedias*" as responding to modern tastes is in practice marshaled in support of traditional forms of social recognition, that of honor as established by public repute and as sanctioned by the king. The mobile and individualist forms of behavior typical of modern society are limited by hierarchical social arrangements that leave little room for the autonomy of the self. And the motives that elsewhere in Europe were placed in the service of progressive political, economic, and philosophical individualism are made subservient to what Ortega y Gasset described as the "psychology of the masses" and to their desire for recognition within a hierarchical social order.[12]

To say this much is already to suggest that the process of modernization is Spain as it passed through the crisis of the seventeenth century was markedly different from that which occurred elsewhere in Europe. While feudalism per se was never as firmly established in Spain as it was in England or France, the social values of caste were deeply entrenched.[13] In part for this reason Spain did not easily consolidate a bourgeoisie or readily embrace bourgeois social values. Indeed, Martín González de Cellorigo complained in 1600 that the middle classes of the fifteenth and early sixteenth centuries had all but vanished. He wrote that "our Republic has come to be an extreme contrast of rich and poor, and there is no means of adjusting them to one another. Our

---

that Calderón seems unable to regard nature as a place of innocence. In *La vida es sueño* Calderón must grapple with history, moral law, the state, and writing, all because of the fact of a prior transgression in/of nature.

12. "The masses, by definition, neither should nor can direct their own personal existence, and still less rule society in general." José Ortega y Gasset, *The Revolt of the Masses* (New York: Norton, 1960), 11. For two attempts to read the *comedia* as a means for the "direction" of the masses, see José Antonio Maravall, *Teatro y literatura en la sociedad barroca* (Madrid: Seminarios y ediciones, 1972), and José María Díez Borque, *Sociología de la comedia del siglo XVII* (Madrid: Cátedra, 1976). On mass psychology, see Wilhelm Reich, *The Mass Psychology of Fascism*, trans. Vincent R. Carfagno (London: Souvenir Press, 1970).

13. Noël Salomon attempted to read the Lopean *comedia* and its glorification of peasant existence in terms of the perpetuation of older, feudal modes of production during such a period: "the monarchical-seigneurial society of 1600–1640 perpetuated in modern times . . . a mode of production (situated historically in between the system of indenture and the capitalist system) and all that derives from it" ("la société monarcho-seigneurial de 1600–1640 perpétuait dans les temps modernes . . . un système de production [placé historiquement entre le système esclavagiste et le système capitaliste] et tout ce qui en dérive"). *Recherches sur le thème paysan dans la "comedia" au temps de Lope de Vega* (Bordeaux: Féret et Fils, 1965), 744–54. But the play is for him an expression of genuine peasant insurgency, rather than the locus of a historical conflict in which the new is met with fierce resistance by the old.

condition is one in which there are rich who loll at ease or poor who beg, and we lack people of the middle sort, whom neither wealth nor poverty prevents from pursuing the rightful kind of business enjoined by natural law."[14] One consequence of this polarization of fortunes was the phenomenon that Pierre Vilar (in "The Age of Don Quixote") called the "irrationalism" of Spanish society—the paradoxical conjuncture of profligacy and miserliness, of consumption and waste, located within a single class or individual: "The rich man ate, was waited upon, entertained, gave, robbed, and allowed others to rob him. As a result of its situation and predicament . . . Spanish society of 1600, the antithesis of Puritan society, turned its back on saving and investment" (60).

Both Vilar and J. H. Elliott rightly abjure the standing notion of a Spanish "temperament" that may have been inhospitable to capitalism: "The Castilians, it is said, lacked that elusive quality known as the 'capitalist spirit.' This was a militant society, imbued with the crusading ideal, accustomed by the reconquista and the conquest of America to the quest for glory and booty, and dominated by those very ideals least propitious for the development of capitalism" (Elliott, "Decline," 232). Yet one must somehow account for the fact that Spain did relatively little to transform itself by the very same American gold and silver that, in all likelihood, provided the nuclear mass for economic expansion in the rest of Europe during the fifteenth and sixteenth centuries. Elliott points to the steady diversion of capital in Spain toward *censos* (personal loans) and *juros* (government bonds), which carried assured rates of return of between 5 and 10 percent. González de Cellorigo saw in the attraction to these relatively secure forms of investment the same "unproductiveness" that characterized the deployment of land and labor in Spain. Consider the following passage from the *Memorial de la política* (1600):

> For when the merchant, lured by the certain profits which the bonds will yield, gives up his business, the artisan his craft, the laborer his field, and the shepherd his flock; when the nobleman sells his lands in order to exchange the amount they are worth for five times that sum in Government bonds, then the real income from their patrimonies will be exhausted, and all the silver will vanish into thin air, at the same time as for his own

14. González de Cellorigo, as cited in Elliott, "Decline," 232.

needs, for those of the lord of the estate, the rentier, the tithe-collector, the tax-farmer and so many others who have some claim to make on the land. Thus, from the bottom of the scale to the top, one may calculate that the ratio of those who work to those who do nothing is of the order of one to thirty. . . . Wealth has not taken root because it has remained, and still does remain, etherealized in the form of papers, contracts, bonds, letters of exchange and gold or silver coinage, and not in the form of goods able to bear fruit and to attract wealth from abroad by virtue of the wealth within.[15]

On the subject of *censos* and *juros* and the lethargic climate of capital investment in Spain, Cellorigo and others did not go completely unheard. In 1617 the Council of Finance complained that there was no hope of a Castilian economic revival as long as the bonds offered higher rates of return than investments in agriculture, industry, or trade.[16]

It is in this respect instructive to compare the specific social form of Spanish traditionalism, the structure of social castes, with the emergent class structure of the rest of Europe and North America. Because a caste society forms its evaluations primarily along racial lines and construes social value in connection with lineage rather than individual wealth, there is little or no incentive to deploy economic capital toward the increase of value (profit) as a means to improve social standing. Indeed, the very notions of profit or the increase of value are alien to the axiology of caste, which functions in concert with social hierarchies that are racially fixed.[17] A caste society, it has been said, is overtly moral in its evaluations, but only covertly economic.[18] And because caste divi-

15. González de Cellorigo, as cited in Vilar, "The Age of Don Quixote," 66–67.

16. Archivo General de Simancas, Hacienda leg. 395–547, Consulta of 3 September 1617; as cited in Elliott, "Decline," 186.

17. The word "caste," which is Spanish in origin, did not carry the Hindu meaning, even though the Portuguese did later apply it to Indian society. See Américo Castro, *The Spaniards,* trans. Willard King and Selma Margaretten (Berkeley and Los Angeles: University of California Press, 1971), 51.

18. See Martin Green for this formulation in *Dreams of Adventure, Deeds of Empire* (New York: Basic Books, 1979). The late-fifteenth-century Spanish humanist Antonio de Nebrija defined caste as "good lineage." In the seventeenth century, Covarrubias explained that "caste means noble and pure lineage; he who comes from good family and descent, despite the fact that we say 'he is of good caste' or 'he is of bad caste.' . . . Those who are of good lineage and caste we call 'castizos.' " See Castro, *The Spaniards,* 51.

sions are racially based, they produce a hierarchy that is relatively "closed," especially when compared with the social mobility that is in principle available to members of a society differentiated by classes.[19] This fact remains true even where one understands Spanish society as defined by what José Antonio Maravall has called *estamentos* or "estates," which were structured according to a hierarchy of offices and professions.[20] The consequences of such an arrangement are a social sedimentation in which social status and the value accorded to professional functions are tightly circumscribed. The "traditional" order of society, which Maravall perceives to be "medieval" in character, is nearly identical to that which is put forward in neo-Scholastic terms by Calderón in his theological *comedias* and *autos sacramentales*. Consider what Maravall has to say about the ways in which the distribution of social roles into castelike divisions is seen as sanctioned either by nature or by God:

> Traditional society was founded on the idea that each person had a fixed and determined social function; that this carried with it a natural and proper mode of behavior for the possession and of enjoyment of economic goods, whose limits were not to be transgressed; that all this was determined by known procedures, and that in accordance with such circumstances, unchangeable in themselves, there belonged to each one a certain education and cultural heritage. . . . As the external projection of this conjuncture of personal facts, identifiable with a place in the fixed social order [*un emplazamiento estamental*], each one was to use his resources and to present himself before others in such a way that his place in the social hierarchy could be recognized immediately. (*Teatro y literatura*, 41–42)

19. Anthony Giddens makes a clear distinction between class societies and class-divided societies: "I use the term *class-divided society* as distinct from that of *class society*. A class-divided society is a society in which there are classes, a class relation always being inherently a conflict relation in the sense of opposition of interest; but it is not a society in which class analysis provides the key to unlocking all the most significant features of the institutional order." Giddens, *Central Problems in Social Theory: Action, Structure, and Contradiction in Social Analysis* (Berkeley and Los Angeles: University of California Press, 1979), 162.

20. See Maravall's description of the "sociedad estamental" in connection with the *comedia* in *Teatro y literatura*.

Ever since Américo Castro published his interpretation of the Golden Age in *De la edad conflictiva*,[21] it has been apparent that the Spanish *comedia* was in some special way indebted to the axiology of caste. In the strongest formulation that Castro offered, the preoccupation over honor in view of potential threats to the bloodline provided the theater of Lope de Vega and, indeed, the genre as a whole, with its very reason for being: "La presencia del motivo de la honra en el teatro de Lope de Vega y la razón de existir aquel teatro son dos aspectos de una misma conciencia colectiva" (49). As Lope himself remarked in the "Arte nuevo," honor plots were able to stir the emotions of every member of the audience: "Los casos de la honra son mejores, / porque mueven con fuerza a toda gente" (lines 327–38). Yet Castro never considered the possibility that the axiology of caste might have served an ideological function within the *edad conflictiva,* that this structure of social relations might have served to block the path toward modernization long after its original efficacy was past. And yet this is precisely the possibility that must be considered in view of the fact that during the time of the *comedia*'s greatest prestige, in roughly the period from 1580 until Calderón's death a hundred years later, the three castes of Spain were officially reduced to one (with the unresolved conflicts among them having been internalized, as in the struggles with the *moriscos*), thus reducing the visibility of caste divisions while still enforcing the value-structure and principles on which those divisions were founded.

I have suggested that the axiology of caste may have taken on an ideological function in the *comedia*. Yet it is not only Castro's understanding of the idea of caste that needs to be revised in this light but also Maravall's analysis of the social structure underlying the genre. On Maravall's reading, the "traditional" order of society envisioned by the Spanish drama is one that was imposed on it in the interests of maintaining the status quo, in much the same way, and through many of the same techniques, that a theology was "imposed" by the preachers

---

21. Castro is here radically revising his more conventional account of honor in the Golden Age published in "Algunas observaciones acerca del concepto del honor en los siglos XVI y XVII," *Revista de filología española* 3 (1916): 1–50, 357–86. See *De la edad conflictiva* (Madrid: Taurus, 1972), 49ff. Recall the fact that Aristotle reasons in the *Nicomachean Ethics* that honor cannot be a primary good. He argues (I.5) both that honor depends upon those who bestow honor rather than on the one who receives it and that honor can be no more than a secondary good because it depends upon something else that one is or does in order to merit it.

and moralists of the Counter-Reformation and the baroque.[22] In Maravall's judgment, Spaniards made use of the *comedia* in order to legitimate a structure of social relations founded on the domination of one group by another and, by so doing, to avoid the ethical questions that such situations of domination are bound to raise: "Los españoles emplearon el teatro para, sirviéndose de instrumento popularmente tan eficaz, contribuir a socializar un sistema de convenciones, sobre las cuales en ese momento se estimó había de verse apoyado el orden social concreto vigente el país, orden que había que conservar, en cualquier paso, sin plantear la cuestión de un posible contenido ético" (*Teatro y literatura*, 32–33). Yet this account offers only a partial view. As we shall see exemplified in *Fuenteovejuna*, it is precisely a moral opposition, that of good versus evil, that organizes the dramatic "content" of Lope's play. Morality ensures that the perfect closure offered by the binary oppositions of good and evil, right and wrong, self and other, function as what Fredric Jameson has called "strategies of containment,"[23] in this case as strategies for the containment of the modernizing threats to the traditional structure and hierarchy of Spanish society. In short, morality is not altogether avoided, as Maravall would suggest; it serves a function within the historical dynamic of social relations. As we shall see in greater detail, the force driving these relations was the search by an emerging social group for a form of recognition that they could best locate in terms of the social structures of the past.

It is not surprising to find that the social relations of the past seem to offer a desirable alternative to modern society. Marx and Engels wrote in *The Communist Manifesto* that

> the bourgeoisie, wherever it has got the upper hand, has put an end to all feudal, patriarchal, idyllic relations. It has pitilessly torn asunder the mostly feudal ties that bound man to his "natural superiors," and has left remaining no other nexus between man and man than naked self-interest, than callous "cash payment." It has drowned the most heavenly ecstasies of religious fervor, of chivalrous enthusiasm, of philistine sentimentalism, in the icy water of egotistical calculation. It has resolved

22. See Maravall's *Teatro y literatura* and also *La cultura del Barroco* (Barcelona: Ariel, 1975). I discuss this question at greater length in Chapter 4.

23. This notion is developed throughout Jameson's *The Political Unconscious* (Ithaca: Cornell University Press, 1982).

personal worth into exchange value, and in place of the number-less indefensible chartered freedoms, has set up that single, unconscionable freedom—Free Trade. In one word, for exploita-tion, veiled by religious and political illusions, it has substituted naked, shameless, direct, brutal exploitation. The bourgeoisie has stripped of its halo every occupation hitherto honored and looked up to with reverent awe.[24]

This passage suggests just how easy it is to be seduced by the wish for a time before capitalism, if only as a way to escape the "brutal exploita-tion" it brings.

One may nonetheless be surprised to discover a strategic conservatism in the *comedia* in light of the fact that the poetics of the genre, as conceived and articulated by Lope de Vega, are explicitly modernizing. Lope's "Arte nuevo de hacer comedias" seeks to locate the *comedia* in the very vanguard of artistic practice. Even in the title, the emphasis falls on what Lope considers to be the "*new way* of writing plays." As is common among vanguard aesthetics, and notwithstanding the fact that the "Arte nuevo" was commissioned by a Madrid academy, Lope's stance is anti-academic. In characteristically modernizing fashion, Lope speaks of his as a practice that is not simply innovative but wholly discontinuous with the recognized traditions:

> cuando he de escribir una *comedia*,
> encierro los preceptos con seis llaves;
> saco a Terencio y Plauto de mi estudio,
> para que no me den voces.
>
> (lines 40–43)

(when I must write a play, I lock up the rules with six keys; I throw Terence and Plautus out of my study so that they won't scold me.)

> Mas ninguno de todos llamar puedo
> más bárbaro que yo, pues contra el arte
> me atrevo a dar preceptos, y me dejo

24. Karl Marx and Friedrich Engels, *The Communist Manifesto,* trans. Samuel Moore (Chicago: Henry Regnery, 1954), 18–19.

llevar de la vulgar corriente, adonde
me llamen ignorante Italia y Francia.
(lines 362–66)

(But I can call none of these [writers] more barbarous than I,
since I dare to give precepts that contravene the rules, and I
allow myself to be carried by the common current, to where Italy
and France may call me ignorant.)

In terms of aesthetic practice, however, the *comedia* contradicts the
modernizing claims made for it in the "Arte nuevo." Whereas Lope
argues for the discontinuity of the *comedia* from known traditions, the
configuration of the genre in fact depends on the formation of highly
visible internal continuities. These are generated in part from its sources
in the chronicle and ballad traditions and are re-confirmed in ways that
are nearly formulaic. Thus Lope can refer to the elements of the *comedia*
as the parts of a generic narrative formula which, in theory at least, are
capable of infinite repetition: for example, "Dividido en dos partes el
asunto, / ponga la conexión desde el principio"; "En el acto primero
ponga el caso, / en el segundo enlace los sucesos" (divide the subject in
two parts, establish the connection from the beginning; place the
problem in Act One, tie the events together in Act Two) (lines 231–32,
298–99). The regulation of subject matter and form similarly becomes
a question of the interchange of nearly pre-programmed units (e.g., "las
décimas son buenas para quejas; / el soneto está bien para los que
aguardan; / las relaciones piden los romances" [Décimas are good for
complaints; the sonnet works well for those who wait; stories must be
told in ballad-verse], vv. 307–9).[25] At the same time, Lope's aesthetic of
continuity denies its own very obvious conventionality and instead
claims to rely upon the natural equivalence of style and form:

Si hablare el rey, imite cuanto pueda
la gravedad real; si el viejo hablare,
procure una modestia sentenciosa.
(lines 269–71)

25. On the generic repeatability of the *comedia,* see Díez Borque, 357ff. ("Una
estructura fija para unas funciones repetidas").

(If a king should speak, let him imitate insofar as possible the seriousness of a king; if an old man should speak, strive for an unassuming pithiness.)

> Remátense las scenas con sentencia,
> con donaire, con versos elegantes,
> de suerte que, al entrarse el que recita,
> no deje con disgusto el auditorio
> (lines 294–97)

(Finish off the scenes with wit and grace, with elegant verses, so that when someone comes on stage to speak, he will not leave the audience displeased.)

In pleading for the autonomy of the *comedia* from any recognized rules, Lope argues from a notion of taste (*gusto*) that is revealingly indicative of the place of the aesthetic object within a network of social relations that wants to assert itself as natural without relying upon rules. As we shall see in Chapter 5 in connection with Gracián, the notion of taste (*gusto*) played a central role in thinking about the social situation of subjects in this very respect. In Lope's case, however, justification of the aesthetics of the *comedia* also makes reference to a partly imaginary situation in which the *vulgo* is conceived as having an autonomy and authority based upon its economic power. Taste, as Lope understands it, refers principally to the preferences of the paying public: "como las paga el vulgo, es justo / hablarle en necio para darle gusto" (since the common people pay for these plays, it is just to speak to them injudiciously in order to please them) (lines 47–48). As Pierre Vilar remarked, the *comedia* was the only literary genre that "paid its way" in Golden Age Spain ("The Age of Don Quixote," 70). Yet by virtue of its mass appeal the *comedia* was also able to create the very conditions for the satisfactions of the desires it summoned up. Thus if the *comedia* can be seen to enact a conflict between tradition and modernity, old and new, caste and class, this is accomplished in such a way that the pressures of the modern are consistently masked; the fundamental conservatism of the genre acquires all the force of an ideology that is welcomed by the masses and willingly taken on by them insofar as they are able to imagine their desire for social recognition satisfied in it.

To view the *comedia* in such a way obliges us to locate it in history, where "history" is characterized not just by changing economic circumstances but by a dynamic relationship among those social interests that Raymond Williams called "dominant," "residual," and "emergent."[26] A play like *Fuenteovejuna* takes as its subject the conflicts between the aristo-military order (the Comendador of the Order of Calatrava) and the peasants (the townspeople of Fuenteovejuna), which resulted in a civil uprising and the murder of the Comendador in 1476. Yet the historical dimension of the play is apparent only in view of the value that Lope de Vega, writing during the "crisis" of the seventeenth century, ascribes to these historical events. The historical crisis of the seventeenth century was produced by the clash of an emergent (modernizing) culture with the entrenched authority of tradition, yet Lope transposes this crisis into the late fifteenth century (a distinctly premodern period) and draws on the archaic resources of Platonic idealism and myth in order to contain that crisis within acceptable bounds.[27] To read the Utopian tendencies of *Fuenteovejuna* and similar works in a historical light is thus to reverse the Platonizing readings that have been put forward in the leading formalist and stylistic interpretations of the genre, foremost among which are those of Leo Spitzer, Joaquín Casalduero, Karl Vossler, Alexander Parker, William McCrary, and Bruce Wardropper. All of these may be seen to repress historical conflict by framing their analyses so as to preclude any engagement of the concept of ideology or the possibility of a suppressed political struggle at work in the play. If one considers Spitzer's reading of *Fuenteovejuna* as a paradigmatic example of this work, it becomes apparent that such an approach not only dehistoricizes the play but, in so doing, leaves unquestioned the hierarchical social relations modeled in the trajectory of the work. Spitzer reads *Fuenteovejuna* as the fulfillment of a dream of universal harmony, as "the naive dream of a

26. Raymond Williams, *Marxism and Literature* (Oxford: Oxford University Press, 1977), 121–27.

27. The process is akin to that which Jonathan Dollimore has described as "containment," adopting Williams's rather than Jameson's sense: "Three aspects of historical and cultural process figure prominently in materialist criticism: consolidation, subversion, and containment. The first refers, typically, to the ideological means whereby a dominant order seeks to perpetuate itself; the second to the subversion of that order, the third to the containment of ostensibly subversive pressures." Dollimore, "Shakespeare, Cultural Materialism and the New Historicism," in *Political Shakespeare: New Essays in Cultural Materialism,* ed. Jonathan Dollimore and Alan Sinfield (Ithaca: Cornell University Press, 1985), 10.

Christian World Harmony, cherished by the Spanish poet of the Golden Age Lope de Vega."[28] His image of the village is of a place of beauty and innocence, outside of history, and his notion of Lope's accomplishment is that of having preserved an Arcadian or Utopian existence. Spitzer's strongly idealized reading of the play nonetheless ignores some of the traces of disharmony and imperfection that Lope himself attributes to the town of Fuenteovejuna prior to the action of the play. In lines 799–809, for instance, the Comendador insinuates that he knows of the promiscuity of the women, even if he makes the point in order to force Laurencia to yield to his advances. Similarly, the Comendador refers to the women of the town as "fáciles mujeres" (easy women) (lines 1083–84), suggesting that they have already fallen prey to such advances. Applauding Casalduero, who Spitzer says was the first to demonstrate that the play has "no political or revolutionary purpose . . . but treats a metaphysical or moral problem,"[29] yet faced with the fact that *Fuenteovejuna* does have an explicit political content, Spitzer explains politics in terms of the forces of demonic agency, "transient and dark forces of disorder":

> Lope worked, as it were, from the historical battle-cries, backward to their metaphysical source. By means of this projection he was able to lift the original village of Fuenteovejuna out of time and space as an island of metaphysical peace, the realization of the Golden Age in the midst of our age of iron, the locus of cosmic harmony in the midst of our world of chaos, at the same time an Arcadia and a Utopia. Thus the "political action" to which the villagers are forced to resort (and with which the drama is mainly concerned) is due only to a temporary and local invasion of that idyllic, timeless peace that is the principle of any "Fuenteovejuna," by transient and dark forces of disorder. ("A

---

28. Spitzer, "A Central Theme and Its Structural Equivalent in Lope's *Fuenteovejuna*," *Hispanic Review* 23 (1955): 192. See also *Classical and Christian Ideas of World Harmony* (Baltimore: Johns Hopkins University Press, 1963).

29. Casalduero's study was conceived as a reaction against Menéndez y Pelayo's nineteenth-century aesthetic, and marks the beginning of a Platonizing approach to the play from which Spanish criticism was long unable to clear free. See Casalduero, "*Fuenteovejuna*," *Revista de filología hispánica* 5 (1943): 21–44. Javier Herrero seeks to save the strictly political dimension of the play, but remains within the field of political theory rather than political praxis. See "The New Monarchy: A Structural Reinterpretation of *Fuenteovejuna*," *Revista hispánica moderna* 36 (1970–71): 173–85.

Central Theme and its Structural Equivalent in Lope's *Fuenteove-juna*," 209)

Even if the notion of romance as described above is able to accommodate a vision of the Comendador as an agent of historical change, Spitzer's reading is nonetheless guided by the same principle that Fredric Jameson saw in Northrop Frye's archetypal approach to romance: "his identification of mythic patterns in modern texts aims at reinforcing our sense of the affinity between the cultural present of capitalism and the distinct mythical past of tribal societies, and at awakening a sense of the continuity between our psychic life and that of primitive peoples" (*The Political Unconscious*, 130).

The thoroughgoing Platonism of Spitzer's interpretation of *Fuenteovejuna* serves to help reinforce the fact that this *comedia* relies on the strategies of literary romance, which Arnold Reichenberger saw as characteristic of the *comedia* as a genre.[30] The *comedia* moves, in Reichenberger's words, from "order disturbed to order restored," or in structural terms from agon to utopian resolution. The historical and political conflicts that shape the agon of romance are characteristically set in what has been called the "midworld," while there is at the same time a strongly teleological pull toward narrative and social closure. The telos is imagined in the form of a future that resists social conflict and historical change. If Fuenteovejuna the town is an example of uncorrupted nature, of the *locus amoenus,* then the Comendador may on one level be identified as the antagonist who disrupts its idyllic harmony, precipitating a nearly mythical "fall" from a state of innocence and grace, in whose wake there follows the rapid degeneration of everything that may be called "natural." The labors of the peasants, ordered in accordance with the cycles of nature, are violently disrupted, and the social cohesiveness of the town as a group begins to weaken. By the beginning of act 3, the town has been split from its leader and the lovers Laurencia and Frondoso are separated from one another. Indeed, nature itself has already begun to show signs of decadence in act 2, and there are auguries of a poor harvest for the coming year: "el año apunta mal, y el tiempo crece, / y es mejor que el susteno esté en depósito" (The

---

30. Reichenberger, "The Uniqueness of the *comedia*," *Hispanic Review* 27 (1959): 307.

harvest augurs badly and the year is wearing on; it is best to store up some food in case of need) (lines 863–64).

If one historicizes *Fuenteovejuna*, however, the manifest structural and thematic orderings of the plot (e.g., of plenty and decadence, of Comendador and town, of self-love and altruism, of amour propre and the general will) would have to be rewritten as the elemental constituents of a more essential romance, the principal condition of which is the historical one mentioned above: a moment of crisis or transition in which two competing structures of value uneasily coexist as "dominant" and "emergent" faces of a conflictive cultural moment. If this is so, then the Comendador would seem to function not just as the antagonist of romance, whose behavior is monstrously, and predictably, evil, nor simply as the demonic agent of history who disturbs Fuenteovejuna from what Spitzer imagines as the slumbers of its collective innocence, disrupting the idyll of its natural existence. Insofar as his relations with the town are determined according to a scale of quantitative pleasures and use-value, guided equally by arrogance and self-interest, he is both the decadent member of a caste of noble Christian warriors and the bearer of new forms of sexual and political acquisitiveness. Not unlike Don Juan, he seems to offer only false promises of the recognition that the townspeople seek.[31] Their relations with one another are, by contrast, determined according to a set of shared qualitative standards; similarly, their relationship to the products of their labor is seen as a reflection of the harmony of nature herself (compare Edward M. Wilson's confirming judgment that in the relationship between Casilda and Peribáñez: "the husband [sees] in Casilda the fruits of the earth which he cultivates").[32]

In Spitzer's and also in Casalduero's approach, the concrete historical conflict between the Comendador and the town is effaced by moralizing considerations. Specifically, the historical tensions underlying the action of the play are seen as the result of a moral defect in otherwise perfect human relations—where the standards of "perfection" are those of a

---

31. That *Fuenteovejuna* is not written against the nobility as a class is evident from the fact that Lope provides for the regeneration of the young Master of the Order of Calatrava, Rodrigo Téllez Girón. There is some possibility that Lope may have favored the Master because of political connections between the Girones and the Osunas, Lope's patrons.

32. Wilson, "Images et structures dans Peribáñez," *Bulletin Hispanique* 51 (1939): 134.

moral reciprocity mirrored in the order of nature. Thus it is often said that as feudal lord of the town the Comendador is obliged to look after the well-being of his vassals, and that he fails in his duty. The actions of the Comendador are abjured for the "irresponsibility" they demonstrate toward the town. As Comendador of Calatrava he is under obligation to protect the crown, yet he enlists the support of the Master of the Order in a plot to capture Ciudad Real, the ultimate implication of which is political treason. Indeed, the Comendador himself acknowledges the historical conflicts that form the ostensible subject of the action of the play, but he assumes a position of moral superiority with regard to his own actions:

> la cruz roja obliga
> cuantos al pecho la tienen
> aunque sea de orden sacro;
> mas contra moros se entiende
> (lines 465–68)

(even those who belong to holy orders are obliged to fight for the emblem of the red cross, provided that the war is against Moors.)

Moreover, his "failure" to protect the town takes the exceedingly violent form of sexual aggression against the women. There is, no doubt, poetic justice in the fact that the women later take a leading role in organizing the town as a whole to act against the Comendador. But Walter Cohen nonetheless suspects that the prominence of women in this play serves a "diversionary, obscurantist purpose"; for Cohen, "the transference of class conflict from economic struggle to the crime of rape enables the play to convert an irreconcilable opposition into an easy matter for moralism."[33] For Spitzer and those critics of the *comedia* who follow him, by contrast, the fact that the play trades on the conflicts between unequal social groups is largely ignored. Any moral imperfections in the relations between Fuenteovejuna and the Comendador are overcome by the powerful machinery of secular transcendence, which draws potent resources from romance. Indeed, the force of his reading is to suggest that an idyllic existence is in principle available

33. Cohen, *Drama of a Nation*, 323–24.

to any community that can purify its collective life of social and historical conflict.

If romance lends itself to the occlusion of historical conflict, this may indeed be because the oppositions that structure it are reducible to terms that are themselves essentially quintessentially moral in nature, the struggle of good and evil. As Nietzsche argued in *The Genealogy of Morals, Beyond Good and Evil,* and the fragments assembled as *The Will to Power,* such moral concepts may be nothing more than the sedimented remains of the concrete praxis of situations of domination. Nietzsche demonstrated that what is meant by "good" may simply be a reflection of one's position as an unassailable center of power, in terms of which the position of anyone who is radically different is marginalized as an "other" whose practices are then formalized in the concept of "evil." The Christian reversal of these circumstances in the revolt of the weak against the strong and the generation of the ideals of charity, care, and self-denial, such as we witness in *Fuenteovejuna,* are no less a function of a fundamental struggle for power than are the "ideals" of which they are supposedly the inversion.[34] Consider in this light the closing words of Esteban and the King in Lope's play; the laborers willfully submit themselves to the authority of an absolute monarch, while the King looks forward to the time when he will appoint a new feudal lord:

ESTEBAN: Señor, tuyos ser queremos.
     Rey nuestro eres natural.

     ....

REY: Y la villa es bien se quede
     en mí, pues de mí se vale,
     hasta ver si acaso sale
     comendador que la herede.
       (act 3, lines 2436–37, 2449–50)

(ESTEBAN: Sir, we wish to become your own. You are our natural king.

KING: It is right for the village to remain with me, since I am responsible for it, until such time as another comendador may inherit it.)

34. See Jameson's discussion of Nietzsche's "deconstruction" of ethics in *The Political Unconscious,* 114–17.

This moment, which is crucial to the resolution of the play, serves to establish kingly authority through the subordination of subjects under one who promises them recognition. What Francis Barker has written of *Hamlet* can help us understand what happens in *Fuenteovejuna*:

> the subjection at work here is not that modern form for which the ambitiously inappropriate name of "consciousness" is frequently used. Pre-bourgeois subjection does not properly involve subjectivity at all, but a condition of dependent membership in which place and articulation are defined not by an interiorized self-recognition . . . but by incorporation in the body politic which is the king's body in its social form. With a clarity now hard to recapture, the social plenum *is* the body of the king, and membership of this anatomy is the deep structural form of all being in the secular realm.[35]

What Barker does not say, however, is that this particular form of "subjection" substitutes one form of recognition (that granted by the king who "incorporates" his subjects) for another (that in which the subjects secure autonomy for themselves by recognizing one another). This substitution depends for its success on the erasure of the specific power relations that sustain the mode of recognition by which such subjection is achieved. And yet what is effaced or repressed invariably returns, most often in the form of a repetition. If this play seeks on one level to reproduce the consciousness of "mastery" in the "vulgar" subjects and thereby to "ennoble" them,[36] then on another level it succeeds in discovering subjection as an essential element in the historical process of subject-formation. It is for this reason that *Fuenteovejuna* provides crucial insights into the process of subject-formation in early modern Spain, in which it became necessary to invent mechanisms for the subjection of the *vulgo* to the "traditional" values enforced by the Absolutist State. That process occurs in this play by the formal "ruse" of romance, the magic of which allows subjection to appear as if it is desired or willed by the subjects themselves. Consider the prospect alluded to in the passage above, of *Fuenteovejuna* once again under the domination of a feudal lord. Or consider the fact that has long puzzled

35. Francis Barker, *The Tremulous Private Body: Essays on Subjection* (London: Methuen, 1984), 31.
36. See Dian Fox, *Refiguring the Hero: From Peasant to Noble in Lope de Vega and Calderón de la Barca.*

critics about the conclusion of Calderón's *El médico de su honra,* namely, that the protagonist Gutierre insists before the King that he may find his second wife unfaithful and that he may kill her just as he killed the first. As if to remind us of the remainders of power that will not be erased, even in a genre that strives so hard to achieve perfect closure (e.g., in the marriage of couples, the justice of God or of the King), there is at the end of *El médico* a bloody hand on Gutierre's door, and this blood will not be cleansed.

To the extent that the *comedia* may be seen as a struggle not simply of moral or metaphysical forces but of different social structures of value and of different ways of seeking recognition, it does indeed demonstrate affinities with the ideology of romance as described by Jameson in his essay in *The Political Unconscious* on the dialectical use of genre criticism ("Magical Narratives"). Yet when one assigns specific weights to the patterns of recognition that actually do come into conflict in the genre, it becomes clear that the *comedia* significantly modifies the historical role of romance outlined in that essay. On Jameson's account, the binary oppositions that form the manifest content of romance are characteristic of those periods of history sometimes designated as "times of trouble," times associated with the degenerate phases of epic society such as one might see reflected in Guillén de Castro's *Las mocedades del Cid,* or with the archaic forms of social instability and movement studied by Hobsbawm in *Primitive Rebels*—times when, in Jameson's words, "central authority disappears and marauding bands of robbers and brigands range geographical immensities with impunity" (118).[37]

---

37. Hobsbawm makes the following observation on the role of banditry, which helps shed light on its place in early modern Spain:

> The coming of the modern economy (whether or not it is combined with foreign conquest) may, and indeed probably will, disrupt the social balance of the kinship society, by turning some kins into "rich" families and others into "poor," or by disrupting the kin itself. The traditional system of blood-vengeance and outlawry may—and indeed probably will—"get out of hand" and produce a multiplicity of unusually murderous feuds and embittered outlaws, into which an element of class struggle begins to enter. (*Primitive Rebels: Studies of Archaic Forms of Social Movement in the 19th and 20th Centuries* [New York: Norton, 1965], 4)

The figure of Lope's *Pedro Carbonero* would repay further investigation in this light. See Avalle-Arce, "Pedro Carbonero y Lope de Vega: Tradición y *comedia,*" in *Dintorno de una época dorada* (Madrid: José Porrúa Turanzas, 1979), 353–69. For Hobsbawm, the "primitive rebel" is the genealogical antecedent of the bandit, a figure that comes into being with the existence of increasingly stratified societies:

> Tribal or kinship societies are familiar with raiding, but lack the internal stratification which creates the bandit as a figure of social protest and rebellion.

These are the times that give rise to figures like Roque Guinart, the legendary but historical Catalan bandit who makes an appearance in *Don Quijote,* part 2.[38] Romance of the type Jameson is discussing is seen as the historical engagement of the conflict that ensues when the rigidly binary mode of thinking often characteristic of such times is confronted by the consciousness of a group that has overcome its social and geographical isolation and has developed an awareness of itself as a universal "subject" of history. Romance would provide a means of "solving" the problem of that group's need for (political) recognition and for the legitimization of its power by subordinating the consciousness of another to its own. The result he posits is a "new kind of narrative, the 'story' of something like a semic evaporation. The hostile knight, his identity unknown, exudes that insolence which marks a fundamental *refusal of recognition* and stamps him as the bearer of the category of evil, up to the moment when, defeated and unmasked, he asks for mercy" (118–19; my emphasis). Yet insofar as *Fuenteovejuna* shows the emergence of anything resembling a "consciousness of class" among the *vulgo* it seeks to resolve such questions by remarkably different means. The demonic agent in *Fuenteovejuna* is eliminated rather than reassimilated into the social order, as would be the case according to the paradigm Jameson proposes, in which the dissidence of the rebel can be acknowledged and accommodated within the new order of things ("once his particular brand of deviation from the norm has been registered and classified by the culture industry, he belongs to it as the land reformer belongs to capitalism").[39] In *Fuenteovejuna,* in which the collectivity marks the resistance to the formation of a consciousness of class, the King can call the people of the town his "proper" vassals and can place himself above them as their natural

---

However, when such communities, especially those familiar with feuding and raiding such as hunters and pastoralists, develop their own systems of class differentiation, or when they are absorbed into larger economies resting on class conflict, they may supply a disproportionately large number of social bandits. . . . At the other end of historical development, modern agrarian systems, both capitalist and post-capitalist, are no longer those of traditional peasant society and cease to produce social bandits. (18–19)

38. It is worth noting that Roque encounters the legendary but fictional Don Quijote. Unlike many other characters in part 2 of the *Quijote,* Roque Guinart has not read the first part of the novel. But he nonetheless says that he knows Don Quijote by reputation.

39. The passage is from *Dialectic of Enlightenment,* trans. John Cumming (New York: Continuum, 1944), 132. See Jameson, *Late Marxism: Adorno, or, the Persistence of the Dialectic* (London: Verso, 1990), 69–70.

ruler. He is the source of any recognition they might need (e.g., "Y la villa es bien se quede en mí"; "Rey nuestro eres natural"). In so saying, the King only confirms what the townspeople had themselves already said in response to the Comendador: "¡Nuestros señores / son los Reyes Católicos!" (The Catholic Monarchs are our lords!) (lines 1885–86).

To suppose, as one might, that the ideological content of romance turns on the demand for recognition (or the refusal thereof) is also to imply that romance is deeply social and political, even if the politics that it advances depends in the case of the *comedia* on the effacement of modern, individual "subjectivity" in favor of the incorporation of the group into a social order controlled by the state. Indeed, the action of *Fuenteovejuna* consists largely in the effacement of a modern political self-consciousness—that of a collective "subject"—by purifying the motives of passion and self-interest that govern the "modern" individual. As Walter Cohen has said, *Fuenteovejuna* combines "the sympathetic portrayal of lower-class revolutionary insurgency with the concluding incorporation of that insurgency into a harmonious conservative resolution" (*Drama of a Nation*, 323). The resolution of the plot may indeed depend on the enunciation of a collective name ("Fuenteovejuna"); but this names the group whose admission of collective responsibility also subsumes the identity of all individual subjects (e.g., Mengo) within it: "Juntad el pueblo a una voz" (Join the town together in one voice); "Fuenteovejuna lo hizo" (Fuenteovejuna killed the Comendador) (lines 1808, 2107).

*   *   *

In dealing with such facts, one must seek a model that would acknowledge that recognition is promised in *Fuenteovejuna* to those who collectively work and serve. To the extent that this is so, the central social drama of the play asks to be read in the light of Hegel's account of the struggle for recognition. According to Hegel, bondsman and lord begin as radically unequal and fiercely opposed: the one is independent consciousness, whose nature is to be "for itself" (the Comendadores of *Fuenteovejuna* or *Peribáñez* and, to be sure, the King as well), while the other is dependent consciousness (the villagers, Peribáñez) whose essence is to live "for another." As part of the embracing project of consciousness to achieve recognition, each seeks to be acknowledged by the other; and since each must be willing to stake his own life on this pursuit, the dialectic of their relationship proceeds through a trial by death: "it is only through staking one's life that freedom is won. . . . The individual who has not risked his life may well be recognized as a person, but he has not attained the truth of this recognition as an independent self-consciousness. Similarly, just as each stakes his own life, so each must seek the other's death, for it values the other no more than itself."[40] The outcome of the struggle of master and slave is recognition but, as Hegel says, "a recognition that is one-sided and unequal" (para. 191). Both are, moreover, deeply unsatisfied: the slave remains dependent, and the lord achieves recognition from a consciousness that is dependent on, and not independent from, his own. Thus it may be said that "the truth of the independent consciousness is the servile consciousness of the bondsman" (para. 193) or, in more strictly Marxist terms, that "the truth of ruling-class consciousness (that is, of hegemonic ideology and cultural production) is to be found in working-class consciousness."[41]

The ironic discovery that the "truth" of the apparently ennobled consciousness of the *vulgo* lies in subjection is precisely what so often occurs in the *comedia*'s companion genre, the picaresque. Consider the final lines of the *Lazarillo*'s prologue, in which the anonymous author pretends humbly to present his work as a "pobre servicio" or "little offering" to his master, "Vuestra Merced":

> Suplico a vuestra merced reciba el pobre servicio de mano de quien lo hiciera más rico, si su poder y deseo se conformaran. Y pues vuestra merced escribe se le escriba y relate el caso muy por extenso, parecióme no tomarle por el medio, sino del principio, porque se tenga entera noticia de mi persona, y también porque consideren los que heredaron nobles estados cuán poco se les debe, pues la fortuna fue con ellos parcial, y cuánto más hicieron los que, siéndoles contraria, con fuerza y maña remando, salieron a buen puerto.

> (I beg Your Honor to receive this little gift from the author who would have written it better if his desire and skill had coincided.

40. Hegel, *Phenomenology of Spirit*, trans., with modifications, A. V. Miller (Oxford: Oxford University Press, 1981), para. 187.
41. Jameson, *The Political Unconscious*, 290.

Your Honor has written to me to ask me to tell him my story in some detail so I think I'd better start at the beginning, not in the middle, so that you may know all about me. I'd also like people who are proud of being high born to realize how little this really means, as Fortune has smiled on them, and how much more worthy are those who have endured misfortune but have triumphed by dint of hard work and determination.)[42]

In his 1948 introduction to the *Lazarillo*, Castro made the claim that the novel-like "realism" of the picaresque can be explained in terms of the moral autonomy of the work's characters, where the notion of "autonomy" is for Castro intimately linked to the principles of freedom and self-determination often attributed to the modern subject. Castro cites Lazarillo's episode with the Squire as confirming evidence of this claim. Here, he says, master and servant engage in "dignified expression . . . without trying to get the best of each other" (xi). In rejecting cynicism, self-interest, and despair, even momentarily, Lazarillo is said to establish himself as a free and autonomous moral subject, worthy of recognition: "the character does, in this instance, something unexpected: he changes the course of his behavior. Now his individual life is guided by a free decision, and not by hunger or by a set literary pattern; his life is not chained to a plot superimposed upon it. This autonomy of the literary character is what we call a novelistic feature, an indispensable condition for the future novel—a literary form which began in Spain with *La Celestina* and the *Lazarillo* and reached its plenitude with Cervantes' *Don Quijote*" (ibid.).

And yet, the notion that the protagonist of this picaresque novel is thus ennobled—achieves autonomy, independence, and freedom—is quite problematic when considered in relation to the specifics of this text, the boundless irony of which consistently reveals the dynamics of subjection to be at work, socially enforcing the authority of those in power long after their social standing had become suspect. Lazarillo remains structurally "dependent" not only upon "Vuestra Merced" but also upon the Squire, even if the Squire does not possess the economic means to be his master. Moreover, the conclusion of the novel, in which

42. *Lazarillo de Tormes*, ed. Everett W. Hesse and Harry F. Williams, introd. Américo Castro (Madison: University of Wisconsin Press, 1948), 4. Translations are taken from the version of Michael Alpert, in *Two Spanish Picaresque Novels* (Harmondsworth: Penguin Books, 1969), here 24.

Lazarillo "rises" to the post of town crier and is reasonably well fed while his wife regularly sleeps with the archpriest—all of which he describes quite ironically as being at "la cumbre de toda buena fortuna" (the height of good fortune)—argues strongly against any view that would see Lazarillo as morally autonomous and independent or of "noble" character. As Francisco Rico has shown, it is Lázaro's moral compromise that motivates the letter to "Vuestra Merced" that in turn initiates the work.[43] Without the articulation of subjection as "service," Lazarillo might have lived a life of humiliation and abjection; but it is the moral psychology represented by the topos of "service" that allows this story to be told, its message to be sent.

The problem of recognition in the *Lazarillo* is resolved, if at all, in the form of an irony that transforms the pain of desire into what Roland Barthes called the discursive "pleasure of the text." But this is a contradictory and ironic pleasure, to say the least; implicit in it is a demand for recognition that remains unsatisfied or incomplete. By contrast with the critical agenda of the *Lazarillo,* the *comedia* may be regarded as an effort to educate the *vulgo* in the enjoyment of their condition as subjects; they are "instructed" by the genre to derive pleasure from their social "service."[44] Thus while the powerful struggle for acknowledgment between masters and servants may not lead to complete satisfaction for either of the parties involved, the unhappiness generated therefrom is not entirely unmitigated. Indeed, even the "unhappy consciousness" in Hegel is not altogether unhappy: the slave will know moments of enjoyment, despite his subservience to the master, and may indeed come to find satisfaction in the self-alienating nature of his work. The *comedia,* for its part, proceeds toward a nearly obligatory "happy ending." Indeed, in the "Arte nuevo" Lope invokes the authority of the pleasure of the public as a legitimating criterion of the genre's success.

To take but one further example of these social dynamics, consider the fact that Lope's *Peribáñez* also stages a contest between the struggle for recognition and the will to subjection. The play has often been seen as moving from a state of inauthentic or "false" consciousness on the part of Peribáñez to a state of self-awareness. In the judgment of one

---

43. *La novela picaresca y el punto de vista* (Barcelona: Seix Barral, 1976).

44. For an illuminating discussion of this point, see Stanley Rosen, *G. W. F. Hegel: An Introduction to the Science of Wisdom* (New Haven: Yale University Press, 1974), chap. 7, "The Unhappy Consciousness."

modern critic, this process begins in Peribáñez's "loss" of self-awareness, a loss signaled most notably by his acceptance from the Comendador of certain gifts, including a set of expensive wall-hangings
embroidered with the Comendador's coat of arms.[45] But it seems clear
enough that these moments also mark Peribáñez's dependence upon the
Comendador. Moreover, the conclusion of the play may be seen to lie
not in the recovery of an "authentic" self-consciousness, as signalled by
Peribáñez's eventual rejection of those gifts, but simply in the transposition of his former relationship of subservience: Peribáñez and his wife,
though freed from the personal domination of the Comendador, come
willingly to accept for themselves the fact of their economic and social
"humility." Casilda offers an initial profession of faith in the virtues of
the peasant life:

> Más quiero yo a Peribáñez
> con su capa la pardilla
> que al Comendador de Ocaña
> con la suya guarnecida.[46]

(I love Peribáñez, with his humble brown cape, more than you,
Comendador, with your embroidered one.)

This profession is internalized by Peribáñez as he is forced to repress his
desire for the recognition bestowed upon him by the Comendador:

> Pienso que nos está bien
> que no estén en nuestra casa
> paños con armas ajenas:
> no murmuren en Ocaña
> que un villano labrador
> cerca su inocente cama
> de paños comendadores,
> llenos de blasones y armas.
> Timbre y plumas no están bien

---

45. See Donald Larson, *The Honor Plays of Lope de Vega* (Cambridge: Harvard
University Press, 1977), 67–68.

46. Lope de Vega, *Peribáñez y el Comendador de Ocaña*, ed. Federico Carlos Sainz
de Robles in *Obras escogidas de Lope de Vega*, vol. 1, *Teatro* (Madrid: Aguilar,
1969), 771a.

entre el arado y la pala,
bieldo, trillo y azadón;
que en nuestras paredes blancas
no han de estar cruces de seda.
(p. 776 a–b)

(I think it is wrong for us to have such cloths hanging in our
house, with someone else's arms on them. I would not have
Ocaña whisper that a peasant surrounds his humble bed with
noble hangings, covered with symbols of knighthood. Crests and
plumes go ill with plows and shovels, forks and hoes. Our
whitewashed walls should not be decorated with silk crosses.)

For Hegel, the dialectic of master and servant finds stabilization, if at
all, in the family. According to the *Philosophy of Right,* the state is an
extension of the family and of its ethical bonds. In the *comedia,* familial
relations are conspicuously absent because the issues that bind or
trouble the family (e.g., conjugal honor, cleanliness of blood) are *already*
one with those of the state. The literary and ideological closure that the
comedia is able to achieve depends, as in the final scenes of *Fuenteovejuna* and *Peribáñez,* on the authorization of recognition by those who
wield social power: the father, the feudal lord, or the perfected image of
these, the king. Yet this is precisely where the *comedia* most radically
transforms the dialectic that Hegel proposed, by resisting the process of
historical change wrought by the need of emergent social groups to gain
recognition for and legitimize themselves. Especially where the struggle
for recognition becomes effaced or is subsumed within existing power
relations that are left untransformed by it, the superiority of the ruling
master comes all too easily to depend on the willing submissiveness of
those who serve.[47]

Seen in such a light, the *comedia* is illuminating of a mode of
subjection all the more remarkable insofar as it offers resistance to the

47. On effacement and legitimization in connection with Renaissance drama, see
Dollimore: "Legitimization further works to efface the fact of social contradiction,
dissent and struggle. Where these things present themselves unavoidably they are often
demonised as attempts to subvert the social order. Therefore, if the very conflicts which
the existing order generates from within itself are construed as attempts to subvert it
from without (by the 'alien'), that order strengthens itself by simultaneously repressing
dissenting elements and eliciting consent for this action: the protection of society from
subversion" ("Shakespeare, Cultural Materialism and the New Historicism," 7).

transformative work of history by the most peremptory means; namely, by the cultivation of what Foucault described as the "fascism within," the desire of individual subjects to seek their own domination. Thus while the town of Fuenteovejuna is described as a disorganized and leaderless collectivity ("sin capitán," line 1845), it comes as no surprise to find that it wills its own submission to the authority of the King. It is from the search for recognition in the relatively closed and hierarchal structures of authority already in place that the *comedia* derives the rhetorical force with which Lope credits it in the "Arte nuevo," its ability to please the masses, to "mover con fuerza a toda gente." By elaborating only slightly on Lope's terms, one might describe the *comedia* as a practice designed to provide pleasure in the containment of the same social desires that it strategically summons up. If the formation of social subjects in the Golden Age involves the domination of the newly emergent masses by those already in power, then Lope's most important discovery was the fact that the psychology of the masses is ruled by the desire to gain recognition from those whose authority is unquestioned, and that the process of subject-formation could best be achieved by making this process a pleasurable experience, if not also a satisfying one.

2

Transformations of the Cid

In the previous chapter we began to see how the *comedia* offers a generic solution to problems posed by a shift in socially and historically ordered values within the period of early modern Spain. As a form of drama whose modernizing thrust is clearly announced in Lope's "Arte nuevo," *Fuenteovejuna* nonetheless embraces the ideology of the old, hierarchical order of society; it projects a direct and unmediated relationship between the new social classes and the central source of social authority. We have also seen that *Fuenteovejuna* is constrained in its attempt to imagine new social arrangements or indeed substantially to transform the old. *Fuenteovejuna* depends for its success instead on its ability to recast the old hierarchies in strongly idealized terms. This requires not so much the projection of a new order of things as a return to the heroic past, whose dominant features are purified and carried forward in the theatrical imagination as if they were an integral part of contemporary history. In a play like *Fuenteovejuna,* this "solution" to the problem of historical transformation is made possible by the plot-structure of literary romance. In Lope's use of romance, a return to the past becomes desired, not just imposed. But since a historical condition of Lope's use of romance as the grounding plot-structure of his play is the knowledge that there is in fact no possibility of a return to the past, the project to reshape the past as an object of desire must have a political and ideological significance, not just a social or historical one. If romance is indeed the genre of the "wish-fulfillment dream," then this particular form of *Wunschdenken* must itself be resituated within the framework of society and politics in Golden Age Spain, where new groups demanding recognition found themselves defined as subjects through a process of willed subjection to the authority of the state.

My discussion of the transformation of the figure of the Cid in Guillén de Castro's *Las mocedades del Cid* in the pages that follow explores the nature of this process as part of an effort to clarify questions of social and political legitimation in early modern Spain. As we shall see, the central conflicts of Guillén de Castro's play as focused in the demands that bear on the Cid—the loyalty he feels to his father Diego Laínez on the one hand, and his passionate love for Ximena on the other—are further manifestations of the tensions within early modern Spain between "old" and "new" modes of social awareness. More specifically, the seemingly irreconcilable demands of epic duty, which masks patriar-chal authority, and of passionate love (*amor pasión*), which increas-ingly defines the intimate space desired by the subject-self,[1] demonstrate the difficulty of creating the subject-space that would allow the individu-al's entrance into the emerging order of things. Indeed, this conflict leads us to ask whether the "individual" can ever be imagined as truly free from the conflicts in which its social and historical emergence was embedded, or whether subjective self-consciousness is not always marked indelibly by its inability to overcome the past. At the same time, a discussion of *Las mocedades del Cid* will allow me to strengthen and expand the case for the "romantic" bias of the *comedia,* as witnessed both in the "marvelous" means through which the above-mentioned historical conflicts are resolved, and in relation to the problematic legitimacy of the Cid himself, which is also resolved in "romantic"

1. The question of intimacy in modernity has recently been addressed by Anthony Giddens in *The Transformation of Intimacy* (Stanford: Stanford University Press, 1992).

terms. As I suggest, the importance of romance here depends not only on the overall shape of the plot or *mythos,* but also on the particular mechanisms through which the resolution of the plot is brought about; specifically, it is through magical moments that romance could be felt as an affective force.

* * *

The question of legitimation in its social and political dimensions may rightly be seen as central to the formation of the *comedia* as a specifically national mode of literary expression, and yet the relationship between the *comedia* as a public form of literature and the process of nation-building has only rarely been raised in connection with the literature of early modern Spain. In 1985, the issue was treated in a comparative context by Walter Cohen, who argued that the *comedia* was perpetuated by a state that served primarily the interests of the aristocracy.[2] Subsequently, in an essay entitled "Popular Culture and Spanish Literary History," Wlad Godzich and Nicholas Spadaccini examined several aspects of Golden Age literature in relation to the role of literary history and the formation of a national identity. Godzich and Spadaccini argued that the scholarly enterprise we have come to know as "literary history" may more accurately be understood as part of a project in which literature was embraced by the constituents of the modern state in order to secure its own political legitimation.[3] In the example they provide, the characteristically modern task of constructing a literary history that began in Germany in the late eighteenth and early nineteenth centuries served the interests of the emerging nation-state and was in turn dependent for its success on the existence of an autonomous "aesthetic sphere" of culture whose role was nonetheless central in defining national political goals.

In identifying the sphere of literary production and consumption as an autonomous domain within society, Godzich and Spadaccini take up

2. Cohen, *Drama of a Nation: Public Theatre in Renaissance England and Spain* (Ithaca: Cornell University Press, 1985).

3. Wlad Godzich and Nicholas Spadaccini, "Popular Culture and Spanish Literary History," in *Literature Among Discourses: The Spanish Golden Age* (Minneapolis: University of Minnesota Press, 1986), 41–61.

a problem common to Marxist aesthetics and Weberian social theory.[4] If Max Weber saw the segmentation of culture into separate value- or interest-spheres as itself an endemic feature of the modern world, the implication of this more recent work has been that the emergence of literature as a separate field within culture bears directly, if covertly, on questions of national identity and political legitimation. Outwardly, the distinction between literature as a form of aesthetic experience and politics as the arena of contested human interests was a sign of the differentiation of discourses within modern culture. Indeed, the differentiation of cultural spheres was reflected in the constitution of the category of "literature" as distinct from all other modes of cultural production and consumption. For Tacitus and Cicero, *literatura* simply meant writing or the alphabet; Quintilian used the term in reference to what for us would be grammar or philology. In the fully modern sense, however, literature is identified as part of an aesthetic sphere, the essential fate of which is to be divorced from the praxis of life.[5] If, as John Bender and David Wellbery note, the term "literature" once made reference to the grammatical production of texts and could legitimately claim to embrace all that was communicated by means of writing,[6] "literature" in the modern sense came to be associated with the production of pleasures of a specifically aesthetic or "disinterested" sort.[7]

While the spheres of politics and literature are separate on one level, they are on another level very deeply entwined. For example, a public genre like the *comedia* counted on an audience of spectators deeply invested in the project of self-legitimation (see Lope de Vega: "los casos

4. At the same time they situate themselves within a conceptual line that includes Theodor Adorno, Peter Bürger, Philippe Lacoue-Labarthe, Jean-Luc Nancy, and Terry Eagleton. See Adorno, *Aesthetic Theory,* trans. C. Lenhardt (London: Routledge and Kegan Paul, 1984); Bürger, *Theory of the Avant-Garde,* trans. Michael Shaw (Minneapolis: University of Minnesota Press, 1984); Lacoue-Labarthe and Nancy, *L'Absolu littéraire* (Paris: Seuil, 1978); and Eagleton, *The Ideology of the Aesthetic* (Oxford: Blackwell, 1990).

5. This subject has been treated by Jay M. Bernstein in *The Fate of Art: Aesthetic Alienation from Kant to Derrida and Adorno* (University Park: The Pennsylvania State University Press, 1992).

6. Bender and Wellbery, "Rhetoricality," in *The Ends of Rhetoric* (Stanford: Stanford University Press, 1990), 15. They duly note that "prior to the last decades of the eighteenth century, the concept of literature covered virtually all of writing; the breadth of its application was made possible by the overriding unity of rhetorical doctrine, which governed all of verbal production" (15).

7. The locus classicus for the definition of the aesthetic as a sphere of disinterested pleasures is Immanuel Kant, *Critique of Judgment,* "Analysis of the Beautiful."

de la honra son mejores / porque mueven con fuerza a toda gente";
[matters of honor are best because they move everyone forecefully]).[8]
And yet, for the social and political purposes of the modern state,
literature could hardly afford openly to acknowledge its existence as
autonomous and independent, for the very criterion that is used to
constitute literature as a realm apart—the criterion of "disinterestedness," the notion that all social, historical, or personal interests must be
bracketed or held in suspension—would presumably debar the aesthetic
response from galvanizing sentiments in the formation of the state. Nor
could the emergence of an autonomous aesthetic field within culture go
unchallenged in its claims to represent something wholly unprecedented
and new, for its efficacy as a form of legitimizing expression for the
emerging nation-state would thus be open to serious doubt. As long as
it is conceived as radically new, as truly modern, literature would be no
more "legitimate" than the emergent modern state.

If the autonomy of literature is a function of the differentiation of
spheres within early modern society, and if the fact of increasing
differentiation produces a greater need for community, then literature
often was forced outwardly to deny its own autonomy so as to assist in
the creation of a social or political whole. According to the arguments
put forward by Jean-Luc Nancy in *The Inoperative Community,* it is
precisely here that the notion of myth (and of literature as the myth of
a society that is otherwise bereft of myths) came to play a crucial role;
the recourse to myth offered a way in which literature could speak from
a position of authority even while acknowledging its existence within a
divided social world.[9] Similarly, it is within this context that the project
of literary *history* came to play a prominent role; by reconstructing a
literary past it was possible to imagine a form of expression in which
the aesthetic and the political were *originally* one. And it is here that
Spanish literature came to exert an extraordinarily powerful influence
on the shape of European literary history: the theatre, the ballads, the
books of chivalry, *Don Quijote,* and the epic of the Cid were all

8. It is a question of seeking the motives behind such a self-interpretation as the one
Lope proposed in the lines from the "Arte nuevo" just quoted rather than simply
accepting them as a reflection of a collective consciousness, as Castro and others have so
often done.

9. *The Inoperative Community,* ed. Peter Connor, trans. Peter Connor, Lisa Garbus,
Michael Holland, and Simona Sawhney (Minneapolis: University of Minnesota Press,
1991), esp. chap. 2, "Myth Interrupted."

taken as forms of expression whose achievement was the integral manifestation of a political spirit and national will. These works formed a literary-national myth that provided the image of a political and aesthetic community that later served as a model for the other emerging European nation-states. In his *Course of Lectures on Dramatic Art and Literature,* for instance, Schlegel saw this ideal as embodied in "romantic" art, which is said to have reached its apogee in Spain:

> If a feeling of religion, a loyal heroism, honour, and love, be the foundation of romantic poetry, it could not fail to attain to its highest development in Spain, where its birth and growth were cherished by the most friendly auspices. The fancy of the Spaniards, like their active powers, was bold and venturesome; no mental adventure seemed too hazardous for it to essay. The popular predilection for surpassing marvels had already shown itself in its chivalrous romaunts [romances]; when . . . their poets, standing on the lofty eminence of a highly polished state of art and society, gave [the theatre] the requisite form, breathed into it a musical soul, and refined its beautiful hues and fragrance from all corporeal grossness, there arose, from the very contrast of the matter and the form, an irresistible fascination.[10]

These observations, and the more general argument they are meant to support, hinge on an idealization of the "romantic" in art—a subject to which I shall return in connection with the particular version of the story of the Cid that Guillén de Castro adapts to the form of literary romance. In that context, we shall see some of the ways in which the idea of an absolute, epic past was appropriated in a "romantic" way within early modern Spain for the purposes of legitimizing a newly emergent social order under the guise of a national history that was transformed into myth.

But the analogy between Germany and Spain is of further significance: in the early histories of European literature, written for the most part by Germans who influenced and were in turn influenced by Hegel's *Lectures on Aesthetics,* the case of Spain was taken to be paradigmatic of literary history as such. Thus in Schelling's *Philosophy of Art* (which

---

10. August Wilhelm Schlegel, *Course of Lectures on Dramatic Art and Literature,* trans. John Black (1846; repr., New York: AMS Press, 1965), 500–501.

precedes Hegel) Spain is said to have provided the most fertile ground for the invention of "poetry" in the modern world. In Schelling's view, a writer like Cervantes found himself in a "thousandfold more favorable conditions than the German poet [Goethe]. He had the shepherds living in the open fields, a knightly nobility, the people of the Moors, the near coast of Africa, the background of the events of the age and of the campaigns against the pirates, and, finally, a nation in which poesy is popular."[11] As Godzich and Spadaccini point out, all literary histories would, on the model of Spain, be in search of a "classical," "golden," or "romantic" age, identified with "poetry," the literary or expressive qualities of which could be invoked in order to legitimize an emergent social order and the early modern state. Once understood in such "romantic" terms, literary evolution could be plotted according to a narrative that would tell of a national spirit coming to manifest itself in the way in which the Spanish character was asserted to have done, and all subsequent developments could be described in terms of the rhetoric of decline, with episodes of renewal and downfall marking the peripeteia of this historical course.[12] The union of literary excellence and national spirit was imagined to have occurred in its original form in Spain. By contrast, it would seem that the literary history of Germany was bound to pale; in Schelling's eyes it could at best represent a belated attempt to replicate what had occurred "originally" in Spain. Thus Schelling goes on to say that "what here [in Spain] *one* divine creation was able to execute and create from *one* mold, the German had to produce and create under totally unfavorable, fragmented circumstances" (235).

Schelling's arguments nonetheless elide the question of how a national literature and a national literary history were formed in early modern Spain out of elements from a factious past. Similarly, in adopting Spain as the model of an "original" confluence of literature and national identity, these arguments elide the question of romance as it contributes to the ligature of literary history and nationhood. To say this much is to suggest that the configuration of a "Golden Age" in Spain was itself an instance of the project that Philippe Lacoue-Labarthe has dubbed "national aestheticism."[13] Already in the Spanish Golden Age, this

11. Schelling, *The Philosophy of Art,* ed. and trans. Douglas W. Scott (Minneapolis: University of Minnesota Press, 1989), 235.

12. See Godzich and Spadaccini, "Popular Culture and Spanish Literary History," 45.

13. "National-aestheticism" names the desire to produce or create the community as a living artwork; it mirrors the wish of a people to erect itself as a *Gesamtkunstwerk,* to

project was dependent on the notion of an "originary" (read: mythical) literary and historical moment, one rooted in a belief in the presentness of the epic past. My argument here is that it is on the basis of the reappropriation of the epic of the Cid within the Spanish Golden Age that we can move from considerations about the ways in which Germany used the image of the Spanish Golden Age in the service of its own national-aesthetic project to an examination of the ways in which literature in the Spanish Golden Age itself appropriated an "epic" past in order to articulate a national identity and, in the process, to (re)define its own understanding of community.

The larger assumption that serves as a point of orientation for my reading of the Cid is thus that no moment of history—whether attached to epic or romance, the ancient or the modern—is in itself "original" or indeed ever fully present to itself, and that the transformation of the Cid from the epic *Poema* to Guillén de Castro's relatively "modern" play represents the evolution of a national literary myth in response to changes in a social structure that was at every stage comprised of conflicting interests, value-orientations, and ideals. Hence even within the framework of a literary historiography such as Américo Castro's, that aligns the emergence of the *comedia* with the particular social anxieties of a "conflictive" age,[14] it would be necessary to investigate the idealizing function of the story of the Cid within a framework of dominant, residual, and emergent interests, in order to see how the figure of the Cid provided a way of strongly remembering or reconstructing a past in which threats to the legitimacy of the present age could be forgotten or repressed.[15] Indeed, it is at this level that the historical and political functions of the *comedia* as a form of "romantic" self-imagining begin to make themselves clear; in seeking to fashion the figure of the hero according to the image of an original and self-present whole, Guillén de Castro attempts to resolve the contradictions among those historical elements of culture that Schiller described as embodying the virtues of Spanish or "romantic" poetry in general: "a loyal heroism, honour, and love."

---

produce itself as a collective entity represented by a leader who incarnates the entire community. See Philippe Lacoue-Labarthe, *Heidegger, Art and Politics: The Fiction of the Political,* trans. Chris Turner (Oxford: Blackwell, 1990), 58.

14. See Américo Castro, *De la edad conflictiva,* 3d ed. (Madrid: Taurus, 1972).

15. On the subject of the legitimacy of modernity in more general terms, see Hans Blumenberg, *The Legitimacy of the Modern Age,* trans. Robert M. Wallace (Cambridge: MIT Press, 1985).

The question at issue as we move from the Cid of the epic *Poema* to the hero of Guillén de Castro's play is the transformation of the Cid into a romance figure charged with the task of negotiating two distinct historical moments. It is here that we shall see that the "becoming literary" of the figure of the Cid served a function within Spanish culture analogous to that attributed to Spanish literature in the histories of the later Romantic age; that is, to bind together a relatively new and increasingly diverse group of popular, urban spectators who wished to imagine themselves as existing in a continuous relationship with the past. As a "romance," the story of the Cid provided a means by which a differentiated society came to invest heavily in the myth of the past to the point of establishing institutions such as "literature" for its safe-guard. As Wlad Godzich argues in his book with Jeffrey Kittay, *The Emergence of Prose*,[16] the continuation or revival of the old medieval heroes was a means by which literature was able to legitimize itself within an increasingly differentiated society. A figure like the Cid was able to answer this need, and came to represent an essential linkage between present and past. "As a consequence, the heroes do not disappear. . . . They remain, and on this new ground they can be, rather remarkably, freestanding again. . . . Guarded by an institution of literature that ensures that such texts are classified and visibly remain fictional, they can be taken back as story, if not history" (183–84).[17]

✳   ✳   ✳

An awareness of the *comedia*'s place within a history shaped by compet-ing social interests in an increasingly differentiated world is something that the analysis of the Cid by critics and historians like Ramón Menéndez Pidal and Américo Castro was bound to avoid. In addition, both Menéndez Pidal and Castro systematically excluded the question of the political legitimation from their concerns. In a work like *La España del Cid,* whose first edition was published in 1929, Menéndez Pidal moves in the direction of traditional historiography, away from

16. Godzich and Kittay, *The Emergence of Prose: An Essay in Poetics* (Minneapolis: University of Minnesota Press, 1987).

17. This is not of course to suggest that the Cid of the *Cantar* was factual while the Cid of Guillén de Castro's play was fictional. The point, rather, is that the figure of the Cid, already in the *Cantar* a mixture of fiction and fact, came to represent an essential link with the past.

the fictional and legendary representations of the Cid toward a recon-
struction of the factual circumstances of the "Cid's Spain." Yet he
remains firm in the belief that, in the case of a "founding" figure like
the Cid, history and poetry must be one. Thus he castigates his eigh-
teenth- and nineteenth-century predecessors as historiographers for
having failed to grapple with the Cid as a poetic figure: "La enorme
aberración con que la historiografía moderna vio la figura del Cid es una
última consecuencia de la progresiva negación de las fuentes poéticas,
negación que se viene trabajando desde el siglo XVII acá. Una vida
escencialmente excitadora de poesía, como la del Cid, acabó por ser
ajada con el mayor prosaísmo, incomprensivo, bronco o artero, en las
obras de Risco, Masdeu y Dozy" (the great aberration with which
modern historiography viewed the figure of the Cid is a final consequence of the progressive negation of poetic sources, a denial that has
been in progress from the seventeenth century onwards. A life that was
in its essence poetically stimulating, like that of the Cid, ended up
being spoiled by the most incomprehensive, prosaic, crude or cunning
treatment, in the works of Risco, Masdeu, and Dozy).[18]

Castro by contrast attempted to interpret the *comedia* as a historical
expression of the concerns of the inhabitants of the Spanish Golden
Age. But in the process he came to recapitulate the same view of it that
Lope de Vega expressed more than three and a half centuries earlier.
Writes Castro: "La presencia del motivo de la honra en el teatro de
Lope de Vega y la razón de existir aquel teatro son dos aspectos de una
misma conciencia colectiva" (the presence of the honor theme in the
theater of Lope de Vega and that theater's reason for existing are two
aspects of a single collective consciousness) (*De la edad conflictiva*, 49).
Moreover, Castro's understanding of the transformations of the Cid as
one moves from the *Poema*, the *Mocedades de Rodrigo*, and the
romances, to Guillén de Castro's play is that of an unbroken continuity
that embraces the notion of historical change only to reassert that
surviving such change is essential to feeling oneself a member of the
dominant caste. As such, Castro's analysis may itself be seen as an
attempt to ground literary history on a belief in the absolute self-

18. Menéndez-Pidal, *La España del Cid*, 3d ed. (Madrid: Espasa-Calpe, 1967), 40.
See Manuel Risco, *La Castilla, y el más famoso castellano* (Madrid, 1792); Juan
Francisco Masdeu, *Historia crítica de España, y de la cultura española*, 20 vols. (Madrid,
1783–1807); and Reinhart Pieter Anne Dozy, *Recherches sur l'histoire et la littérature
de l'Espagne pendant le moyen âge* (Leyden: E. J. Brill, 1881).

presence and continuity of the epic past. Although Castro existentializes history in speaking of what it meant to "feel oneself" to be an Old Christian, the values of that history remain essentially those of the epic:

> Las *Gestas,* el *Romancero,* la *Comedia* de Lope de Vega fueron modos mayores de expresión para la vida castellana, para los "hombres de fierro." . . . En el siglo XII cantaban que Mio Cid de Vivar nunca hizo una "deslealtanza." Y así sería en el trato con los de su casta. . . . Pasan siglos y Mio Cid se llama entonces Rodrigo. En él se encarna ya más la hombría que la "lealtanza." Aun muy mozo se negó a besar la mano del rey, a prestarle vasallaje; y por hombría mató al Conde de Gormaz, que había inferido a su padre graves ofensas. . . . Algo más tarde Lope de Vega proveyó de nuevas dimensiones las figuras representativas de la casta heróica, al concebir el trazado y arquitectura de su prodigiosa *Comedia.* Como era esperable, su discípulo Guillén de Castro no podía ya lanzar a Rodrigo como un neblí, en furia rauda y lineal. La conducta del caballero ha de caminar por vías que son vericuetos erizados de conflictos. Rodrigo tendrá que armonizar lo inarmonizable; matar al padre de Jimena sin perder la dulzura de su amor. . . . La hombría en la *Comedia* se hizo problemática, aunque seguía viva, apegada a su suelo y *sin despegarse de su pasado, porque éste y el horizonte del futuro coincidían en el vértice de sentirse existiendo como cristiano viejo, como casta totalmente española.*" (*De la edad conflictiva,* 42–44; my emphasis)

(The epic, the ballads, and the Lopean *comedia* were major modes of expression for Spanish life, for the "men of iron." . . . In the twelfth century they sang that Mio Cid never committed a disloyal act. And thus it would be in dealing with those of his caste. . . . Centuries go by and Mio Cid is then called Rodrigo. He incarnates manly courage rather than loyalty. While still very young he refused to kiss the King's hand, to render homage to him; and out of manly courage he killed the Conde de Gormaz, who had leveled grave insults at his father. . . . Somewhat later Lope de Vega gave the representative figures of the heroic caste new dimensions when he conceived the shape and architecture of his prodigious *comedia.* As was to be expected, his disciple

Guillén de Castro could no longer represent Rodrigo like a falcon, launched straight ahead in a torrent of rage. The conduct of the knight has to be directed along strange paths barbed with conflicts. Rodrigo will have to harmonize the irreconcilable; he will have to kill Jimena's father without losing the tenderness of his love. . . . Manly courage became problematical in the *come-dia*, even though it was kept alive, wedded to its roots and attached to its past, because the past and the horizon of the future came together in the vertex of the experience of feeling oneself exist as an Old Christian, as a completely Spanish caste.)

Indeed, the powerful historicism of Castro's remarks is in the final analysis undone by the fact that he is unable to countenance anything within Spanish culture that might contradict the fundamental values of caste; such a contradiction would in turn undermine his larger claims about the incommensurability of Spanish history and culture with respect to its European counterparts. In the specific case at hand, the central conflict of Guillén de Castro's play and the dramatic possibilities opened up by its romantic reading of the Cid are excluded from the field of his concerns.

Although Castro's specific historical thesis is unique, he is not alone in refusing to read *Las mocedades del Cid* historically or to see it as reflecting a conflict of values within early modern Spain. In general, criticism has failed to see that the transformation of the Cid may be described as part of the larger shift in which the structure and values of "traditional" society were submitted to the increasing pressures of modernization, as a system of evaluations based on the axiology of social class was brought to bear upon a social structure that had been formed according to the values of caste. The transition from "traditional" to "modern," and the shift in axiology this represented, is indicative of a far more complex social process by which the values of personal autonomy and self-determination were brought into contact with the hierarchical and largely static conception of self proper to a caste society, and in which a network of passionate drives anchored in the subjective ego came to displace the archaic ethos of the heroic world.

Quite remarkably, Hegel already questioned the image of the Cid as a fully autonomous and self-present individual. In his *Lectures on Aesthetics,* Hegel claimed that the ideal unity and integrity attributed to a figure like the Cid could not be taken for granted and that his autonomy could not be understood as long as we presuppose the identity of the hero and the head of state, the king. Hegel saw the Cid as a "free heroic character," and argued that his autonomy must be understood as a function of a breach in the unity between the hero and the king:

> the complete exemplar of this sort of thing [the king surrounded by "free heroic characters"] we find in the Cid. He too is a partner in a group, an adherent to the king, and has to perform his duties as a vassal; but over against this bond there stands the law of honor as the dominating mood of his individual personality, and the Castilian [the Cid] fights for its untarnished lustre, dignity, and fame. And so here too only with the counsel and assent of his vassals can the king pronounce judgement, make decisions, or wage war; if they object, they do not fight in his service and they do not submit to a majority of votes at all; each stands there by himself and draws from his own resources his will and his power to act.[19]

The further possibility for the development of an autonomous ego, which Hegel says is contained already within the epic of the Cid, can be located in the later part of the *Cantar*. Early on in the poem the Cid strives to win back Alfonso's good graces, but there is a subsequent shift in action and characterization. Rodrigo's greatly increased political and military power cause the King to strive to please the Cid. However, the Cid openly blames the King of the crime against his daughters (lines 2906–11) and goes armed to the King's court to seek justice (lines 3073–81). In *Las mocedades del Cid,* by contrast, the hero's sense of obligation and duty are placed in tension with strong new interests and with the forces of passionate desire. In Guillén de Castro's play this further development is staged in terms of a conflict between the "old," honor-driven order of things, and a new social world where the passion of love takes command of the ego and its drives. It is seen in at least two prominent ways: in the pressures that love as a realm of private desire and emotion places on honorable behavior, and in a reinforcement of the (extra)legal autonomy of the Cid that makes difficult

19. G. W. F. Hegel, *Aesthetics: Lectures on Fine Art,* trans. T. M. Knox (Oxford: Clarendon Press, 1975), 1:187.

demands on the "public sphere" that served for the arbitration of questions of law and right.[20] We shall later see that the Cid in the *comedia* must break the limits of any formal law, aligning himself with heroes such as Achilles, Aeneas, and David, who stand beyond the law. By so doing, the Cid of the *comedia* draws upon the incipient autonomy of the Cid of the *Cantar* in order to place the hero beyond the bounds of lawfulness.

The desire to establish the Cid's personal autonomy nonetheless flies in the face of the need to situate the drama of his emergence historically, and leads Guillén de Castro to envision a historical conflict that is resolved by the plot-magic of romance. Although the resolution may be quite different, the conflict dramatized by Guillén de Castro is analogous to that frequently imagined by Racine. In *Sur Racine*, Roland Barthes argued that the Racinian version of "classical" French tragedy was the reflection of a conflict between the desires created by two irreconcilable historical modes of awareness, which are brought together in such a way as to question the possibility of coherently structuring desires at all. To say that Racinian tragedy takes place in a "post-heroic" world is to say that Racine's characters are conscious of the historical distance between themselves and the "original" sources of value in the past. As Leo Bersani said, the parents of Racine's characters made history, while their children attempt to make love.[21] Barthes for his part asks how in Racine we can go from an old order (symbolized by the Father, the Past, and the Homeland) to a radically new or indeed a nonexistent social order, indicated by the individual whose identity has yet to be ascertained. Thus, for example, in a play like *Andromaque* we see a genera-

20. I place this term in quotes in order to indicate that there was not, properly speaking, a "public sphere" in medieval or Golden Age Spain equivalent to that which came into existence during the European Enlightenment. However, there is a structural similarity between them that allows a relationship to be drawn. On the "public sphere," see Habermas, *The Structural Transformation of the Public Sphere: An Inquiry into a Category of Bourgeois Society*, trans. Thomas Burger with Frederick Lawrence (Cambridge: MIT Press, 1991).

21. Bersani, *A Future for Astyanax* (New York: Columbia University Press, 1984), 47. In the Spanish Golden Age, the problem of the "children" who make love, not war, becomes particularly acute in a play like *El burlador de Sevilla*, in part because Tirso imagines that it may as a result be impossible for the new generation to inherit and occupy the values of the nobility. As Aminta says in act 3 of Tirso's play, "La desvergüenza en España / Se ha hecho caballería" (The shame of Spain has become its nobility) (lines 1928–29).

tion of post-heroic selves forced either to accept the authority of a past they cannot imitate, or to invent the future contexts in which their own historical legitimation will take place. By contrast, the contradictions that surround the Spanish *comedia* are either incorporated within a "romantic" action—by means of which they are also magically resolved—or are actively forgotten, as is the case with the legitimacy of the Cid himself.

To consider the latter of these two issues first, the question of legitimacy is central to the *Poema* insofar as the Cid's judicial demands against the Infantes de Carrión, based on the charge of *menosvaler,* imply that the accused are not entitled to the privileged status they hold because of the unworthy actions they have done: "¡por lo que les fiziestes—menos valedes vos!" (In doing this you have incurred infamy!) (line 3268).[22] Hence the Infantes respond with arrogant assertions of nobility that at the same time impugn the daughters of the Cid:

¡De natura somos—de condes de Carrión!
deviemos casar con fijas—de rreyes o de enperadores
ca non pertenecién—fijas de infançones.
Por que las dexamos—derecho fiziemos nós
(lines 3296–99)

(We are of the family of the Counts of Carrión!
We have a right to be married to daughters of kings and emperors;
The daughters of minor noblemen are not our equals.
We are right in deserting them.)

To aggravate these insults, the elder brother of the Infantes, Asur Gonçalez, undertakes to affront the Cid's social standing in verses that at least one recent critic has taken as an insult to his lineage as well:

¿Quién nos darié nuevas—de mio Cid el de Bivar?
¡Fuesse a Rio d'Ovirna—los molinos picar

---

22. I cite the *Poema de mio Cid* according to the text of Ian Michael, with facing translation by Rita Hamilton and Janet Perry, *The Poem of the Cid* (Harmondsworth: Penguin Books, 1975). Indications of caesurae are mine. Reference has also been made to the edition of Colin Smith (Madrid: Cátedra, 1972).

e prender maquilas—commo lo suele far!
¿Quíl' darié—con los de Carrión a casar?
(lines 3378–81).[23]

(Who ever heard of Mio Cid, that fellow from Vivar?
Let him be off to Rio d'Ovirna [Ubierna], to dress his millstones
and collect his miller's tolls, as usual!
Who would give him the right to marry into the Carrión family?)

The insinuation, on the strong reading of these lines, advanced by Joseph J. Duggan, is that the Cid is himself a miller, that is to say *descended* from one, and hence that one of his parents is not who was ordinarily supposed. The suggestion is that this insult is tantamount to a charge of illegitimacy or bastardy, which if proven would mean that the Cid would be unworthy to bear offspring of sufficiently high nobility to aspire to royal marriage.[24] The ending of the poem, in which the Cid's honor swells and his daughters are married *higher* than to the Infantes de Carrión, would be placed in serious jeopardy as a result:

¡Ved quál ondra crece—al que en buen ora nació
quando señoras son sus fijas—de Navarra e de Aragón!
Oy los rreyes d'España—sos parientes son,
a todos alcança ondra—por el que en buen ora nació.
(lines 3722–26)

(See what honor accrued to the Cid
when his daughters became Queens of Navarre and Aragon!
Today the kings of Spain are related to him,
and all gain luster from the fame of the fortunate Campeador.)

To what extent was the insinuation of bastardy recorded in subsequent literary memory? The suggestion of illegitimacy had not yet been eclipsed in the following verses from the *romancero*, which narrate the moment of the Cid's trial by his father:

---

23. See Joseph J. Duggan, "Social Status, Legitimacy, and Inherited Worth," in *The "Cantar de mio Cid"* (Cambridge: Cambridge University Press, 1989), 43–57.

24. Peter Berger and co-authors Brigitte Berger and Hansfried Keller have rightly pointed out the fact that individuals in modern societies have neither legal nor quasi-legal recourse against insults; see *The Homeless Mind* (New York: Random House, 1973).

Ese buen Diego Laínez
después que hubo yantado,
hablando está sobre mesa
con sus hijos todos cuatro.
Los tres son de su mujer,
pero el otro era bastardo,
y aquel que bastardo era,
era el buen Cid Castellano.[25]

(The good Diego Laínez
after having eaten,
is speaking at the table
with his four sons.
Three are by his wife,
but the other was a bastard,
and the one who was a bastard,
was the good Cid of Castile.)

The suggestion was reiterated in the *Crónica particular del Cid* (1521), and then later in Francisco Santos's *La verdad en el potro y el Cid resucitado* (1671).[26] But it is kept tellingly silent in Guillén de Castro's play, where any such threat would jeopardize the autonomy of the hero and undermine the project of a (literary) history founded on the absolute presence of the central hero of the epic past.

It may be true enough to say that in the epic, national history itself has not yet become a problem, or is not self-consciously dramatized as such. The conflict between Christians and Moors in the *Poema del Cid* is staging-ground for rivalries among the competing Christian clans as represented by the Cid and the Infantes de Carrión.[27] These conflicts may be resolved within a legal order already in place and in terms of the existing structure of social castes. In criticism of the legal aspects of

25. *Romancero del Cid*, ed. Carolina Michaelis (Leipzig: F. A. Brockhaus, 1871), 6–8; *Primavera y flor de romances*, ed. Ferdinand Wolf and Conrad Hofmann (Berlin: A. Asher, 1856); Duggan, The *"Cantar de mio Cid,"* 12.

26. For the material in the preceding passage, see Duggan, "Social Status, Legitimacy, and Inherited Worth," in The *"Cantar de mio Cid."*

27. See María Eugenia Lacarra, *El Poema de Mio Cid: Realidad histórica e ideología* (Madrid: Ediciones José Porrúa Turanzas, 1980), who claims that a purpose of the poem may have been to depict as reprehensible the Beni-Gómez, García Ordóñez, and Alvar Díaz—ancestors of the powerful Castro family—by the fierce rivals of the Castros, the Laras.

the *Poema* from that of Eduardo de Hinojosa in 1899 to María Eugenia Lacarra in 1980, and in the more recent work of Joseph Duggan (1989),[28] it has been demonstrated that the formal procedures represented in it correspond to the type of law that within aristocratic societies is both public and customary and is centered around the *corte extraordinaria* of the king.[29] It is within this context that the Cid's revenge against the Infantes de Carrión is carried out. Consider by contrast the following complaints of Ximena in Guillén de Castro's play. They represent unmistakable markers that kingly authority in this play is conceived as weak, but they also signal that Ximena's justice will have to be produced in a realm outside that of existing law:

XIMENA: Rey que no haze justicia
          no devría de reynar,
          ni pasear en cavallo
          ni con la Reyna folgar.
          ¡Justicia, buen Rey, justicia!"
                    (lines 1993–97)

(XIMENA: A king who does not do justice
          ought not to reign,
          or go about on horseback
          or sleep with the Queen.
          Justice, good King, justice!)

And again:

XIMENA: No hay en ti, para reynar, ni prudencia, ni razón,
          ni justicia, ni piedad.
                              (lines 2090–92)

(XIMENA: You have neither the prudence, nor the reason, nor the
          justice, nor the pity, to rule.)

28. Eduardo de Hinojosa, "El derecho en el *Poema del Cid,*" in *Homenaje a Menéndez y Pelayo* (Madrid: Librería General de Victoriano Suárez, 1899), 1:541–81; Lacarra, *El Poema de Mio Cid: Realidad histórica e ideología;* Duggan, "Social Status, Legitimacy, and Inherited Worth," in *The "Cantar de mio Cid."*

29. See Lacarra, *El poema de Mio Cid,* 69ff.; Eduardo de Hinojosa, "El derecho en el *Poema del Cid,*" 541–81; and Duggan, "Social Status, Legitimacy, and Inherited Worth," in *The "Cantar de mio Cid."*

Radical questioning of kingly authority and of the law in the *comedia* is characteristically determined by historical conflict, rather than by legal, moral, or metaphysical interests. In a play like *Fuenteovejuna,* for instance, the inability of the appointed royal judge to locate the culprits of the crime against the Comendador may be read as an indication of the internal contradictions that prevent any given historical order from achieving the permanence or transcendence it might wish for itself. In this case, the very presence of the King's deputy marks a relatively modernizing shift of the older principles of customary rule in a formal and bureaucratic direction and contains the implicit expectation that the requirements of judicial *process* will be met. And yet as is well known, the investigative process fails and the King's deputy resorts to force, a procedure long recognized as legitimate for investigative purposes. But not only is the new, procedural style of justice brought into conflict with the more direct imposition of force; here, procedural justice fails to satisfy the desire to produce an unmediated relationship between the newly constituted social body and the charismatic center of authority, the King himself. Hence the public must come, en masse and under a single name, to see the King:

JUEZ: A Fuenteovejuna fui
          de la suerte que has mandado
          y con especial cuidado
          y con diligencia asistí
             Haciendo averiguación
          del cometido delito,
          una hoja no se ha escrito
          que sea en comprobación;
             porque conformes a una,
          con un valeroso pecho,
          en pidiendo quién lo ha hecho,
          responden: "Fuenteovejuna."
             Trescientos he atormentado
          con no pequeño rigor,
          y te prometo, señor,
          que más que esto no he sacado.
             Hasta niños de diez años
          al potro arrimé, y no ha sido
          posible haberlo inquirido

ni por halagos ni engaños.
   Y pues tan mal se acomoda
el poderlo averiguar,
o los has de perdonar,
o matar la villa toda.
   Todos vienen ante ti
para más certificarte:
de ellos podrás informarte.
          (lines 2360–86)

(JUDGE: I went to Fuenteovejuna
as you asked
and with special care
and with due diligence your orders were obeyed.
   I made an investigation
into the crime committed.
Not a page has been written
that has not been verified.
   But down to a man,
courageously,
when I asked who did it,
they answered: "Fuenteovejuna!"
   I tortured three hundred
with no restraint
and I promise you, my Lord,
that I haven't learned anything more.
   I even stretched on the rack
children of ten years;
I accepted no flattery
and fell for no tricks.
   Since this matter
refuses to be found out
either you have to pardon them
or kill the entire town.
   They are all coming to see you
to prove what I say.
You can verify it for yourself.)

In Guillén de Castro's *Las mocedades del Cid,* the failure of established procedures of justice precipitates an extra-ordinary or "magical" solution, just as happens in *Fuenteovejuna*. And, just as in Lope's play that solution provided the means by which the *vulgo* was able to find a historical and political legitimation for itself as a collective and "heroic" body, so too in *Las mocedades* the Cid's charismatic actions outside the sphere of existing law (e.g., the Cid's defeat of four enemy kings, and his encounter with the beatific leper) provide a basis for the legitimation of the new classes of individuals who were being incorporated within the modern political state.

In light of the repression of the possible *il*legitimacy of the Cid in *Las mocedades*, however, one must fundamentally question those long-standing readings that, like Casalduero's, regard its conflicts in purely generational terms and that see in it the reconciliation of father and son rather than the more strategic appropriation of the ideology of honor by those classes who wished to find a means of social and political legitimation for themselves. Consider the way in which Casalduero succeeds in excluding history from his discussion of the play: "La obra empezaba haciéndole honor al hijo a causa del padre y terminará habiendo recobrado el padre a causa del hijo. Honor, alma individibles: vida de las generaciones. En el hijo se reintegra el padre de la dignidad perdida por el tiempo." (The work began by honoring the son because of the father and it will conclude with the father having recovered his honor because of his son. Honor and soul undivided: the life of the generations. The father recovers in the son the dignity that was lost with time.)[30] Here the central conflict of the play, which I have claimed is sociohistorical in nature, is absorbed into a biological conception of time, and this, according to the image of the epic as a closed or timeless form, taking place in what Bakhtin described as the "absolute past," is effectively dissociated from any consciousness of social change.

And yet not even claims for the strictly "literary" appropriation of the figure of the Cid by modern critics can occlude the fact that Guillén de Castro's romance-like play takes the matter of historical transformation—the juxtaposition of nonsynchronous moments of development or incongruous orders of value—as the very groundwork of its action. With regard to the conflicts that engage Rodrigo and Ximena, for instance, it can be seen that the introduction of a struggle that is wholly absent from the epic represents a historical process whereby a relatively modern and subjectivized form of love threatens the old order of honor, as a competing form of duty to which the self is bound. That

30. Casalduero, *Estudios sobre el teatro español*, 2d ed. (Madrid: Gredos, 1967), 72.

love is evident in its very passionate and sensory forms from the beginning, as Ximena is taken by the gallant young knight:

URRACA:	¿Qué te parece, Ximena, de Rodrigo?
XIMENA:	Que es galañ,
	—y que los ojos le dan (*Aparte*)
	al alma sabrosa pena.—
REYNA:	¡Qué bien las armas le están!
	(lines 16–20)

(URRACA:	What do you think about Rodrigo, Ximena?
XIMENA:	That he's handsome
	—and that his eyes give (*Aside*)
	my soul a pleasant pain—
QUEEN:	How well his armor becomes him!)

The introduction of such material reflects historical shifts in social values, and yet even a historically grounded critic like Menéndez Pidal could claim that the introduction of love as a principal theme in the story of the Cid was evidence of the "exhaustion of the values" of a heroic age, rather than the expression of an authentic historical possibility. As the social theorist Niklas Luhmann explained in *Love as Passion*, the development of a semantics of passionate love oriented ultimately toward marriage was bound up with a large-scale transformation in the nature of social relations, as part of the increasing differentiation and autonomy of individuals within early modern society.[31] Whereas the success or failure of marriage was at one time a matter of public determination, it was increasingly up to individuals to decide whether a marriage would endure.[32] And while the code of *amor pasión* that accompanied the differentiation of social relationships was at first

31. See Luhmann's *Love as Passion,* trans. Jeremy Gaines and Doris L. Jones (Cambridge: Harvard University Press, 1986).

32. Historically, the consent of the partners in marriage can be traced to the Roman prescription "Nuptias non cucubitus sed consensus facit." Howard Bloch, in citing this source, claims that "it was not until the twelfth century that the Church, in extending its jurisdiction over all issues having to do with marriage, also asserted the power of the partners to choose." *Etymologies and Genealogies* (Chicago: University of Chicago Press, 1983), 161. The point to be made in connection with *Las mocedades* is the tension created when consent (or choice) is grounded in passion.

directed against marriage as a traditional and conservative social institution, passion was gradually incorporated into the vision of an institution founded by the lovers themselves. For Menéndez Pidal, the literary transformation of the Cid is the story of the "contamination" of epic material by increasingly privatized concerns and indicates the separation of matters of historical importance from purely private concerns: "llega un tiempo en que la poesía heróica comienza a perder su imperio en las regiones apartadas de la vida política y social en que su dominio es siempre débil; entonces se refugia en el amor como en un apacible retiro, buscando allí el consuelo de su pérdida. Llegó un tiempo, en efecto, en que el amor . . . entró al fin también en la leyenda del Cid" (there comes a time when heroic poetry begins to lose its power over the separate regions of political and social life, where its power is always weak; this is when it takes refuge in love as in a peaceful retreat, seeking there consolation for its loss. There came a time, in effect, when love finally entered into the legend of the Cid).[33] But it would in these terms be difficult to explain why such an extraordinary pressure is exerted at precisely the point where the will to marriage and the conjugal mingling of blood is limited by allegiance to the engendering powers of the father and to the honor which must be avenged on his behalf:

CID: ¿Qué haré, suerte atrevida,
      si él es el alma que me dio la vida?
      ¿Que haré (¡terrible calma!),
      si ella es la vida que me tiene el alma?
      Mezclar quisiera, en confiança tuya,
      mi sangre con la suya,
      ¿y he de verter su sangre? . . . ¡brava pena!
      ¿yo he de matar al padre de Ximena?
                 (lines 526–33)

(CID: What shall I do—cruel fate!—
      if he is the soul who gave me life?
      What shall I do—oh, terrible calm!—
      if she is the life that sustains my soul?
      Secretly, I would like to mix

33. Ramón Menéndez Pidal, *La epopeya castellana a través de la literatura española* (Madrid: Espasa-Calpe, 1945), 93–94.

my blood with hers,
but must I spill her blood? . . . what fierce sorrow!
Must I kill the father of Ximena?)

In verses such as these, one can read the conflict of honor and love as the struggle of two distinct modes of historical awareness and of the corresponding obligations they entail. In *Las mocedades del Cid*, the prominence of passionate love marks a moment in the large-scale process that Norbert Elias described as "the courtization of warriors," which was itself a part of the "civilizing process."[34] Love is, in this context, the result of a maturation of the knight's "original" warlike instincts. On Elias's account, this process was centered in the great royal courts of Europe:

> In tracing the sociogenesis of the court, we find ourselves at the centre of a civilizing transformation that is both particularly pronounced and an indispensable precondition for all subsequent spurts and counter-spurts in the civilizing process. We see how, step by step, a courtly nobility is replaced by a tamed nobility with more muted affects, a courtly nobility. Not only within the Western civilizing process, but as far as we can see within every major civilizing process, one of the most decisive transitions is that of *warriors to courtiers*. But it need scarcely be said that there are widely differing stages and degrees of this transition, this inner pacification of a society. In the West the transformation of the warriors proceeds very gradually from the eleventh or twelfth centuries until it slowly reaches its conclusion in the seventeenth and eighteenth centuries.[35]

In Corneille, the emergence of love as passion generates a psychic immobility in the hero. It is the source of the psychological double bind that Corneille expresses rhetorically in the form of the paradox. In Guillén de Castro's play, such blockages may be taken as signs that the

---

34. The anxiety felt by critics like Menéndez Pidal over the fate of the epic has to do with the worry that the introduction of love might jeopardize the hero's ability to serve as a worthy exemplar of national values.

35. Norbert Elias, *The Court Society*, trans. Edmund Jephcott (New York: Pantheon, 1983), 259.

past has come to constitute something more complex than the purely imaginary point of reference for the legitimacy of the present age. The idealized image of an epic past enables the self-assertion of the present age, but it is also a burden, an order from which these characters must clear free if they are to have any future at all. Hence the contradictory and potentially tragic nature of historical transformation as dramatized in this play: the past is both that which would legitimize the present constitution of society and also that which must be overcome if the new order of society is to be viable at all. Hence Ximena's cry: "¡Ay, honor, cuánto me cuestas!" (Oh, honor, how dearly you cost me!) (line 2057).

"Romance" may in this context be read as supplying imaginary solutions to the problems posed by that strong form of memory which is history itself, in this case by contravening both the order of nature and the order of existing law. With regard to the principal action of the play, for instance, it can be seen that the central dilemma of duty-bound honor versus passionate love is resolved by a romantic plot, the magical workings of which would not be outdone by any of the theatrical marvels to which Schlegel referred. At the conclusion of the play the Cid appears as if miraculously returned form the dead, his heroic qualities and Christian virtues having been confirmed in a sphere that circumvents, or perhaps more accurately, *transcends*, the lawfulness embodied in society and court. Yet the apparent miracle, the "ocasión tan peregrina" (most strange occasion) in which Ximena finds justice in receiving the head of the Cid, but in which the Cid nonetheless remains alive, also provides a means of legitimizing their marriage, which is to say that it is used to sanction a lawful social state of the kind that would be taken as meaningful by the popular audience of the *corral*. To be sure, critics of the *comedia* have not been reluctant to point out the genre's ability to reconcile conflicting demands and to generate visions of pastoral harmony and social peace. Casalduero's and most other idealizing interpretations of *Las mocedades del Cid* read the play as a way of balancing youth and old age, or of reconciling public honor and the heart's command, and see in it those same expression of religion, honor, heroism, and love that Schlegel classified as typical of the Spanish national character. Yet it should by now be apparent that the situation is somewhat more complex than this, for romance depends for its generic configuration not only on the "happy ending" but on the production of such an ending by seemingly unnatural, unlawful, or marvelous means. The marvels of romance might thus more accurately be understood as ways of establishing the lawfulness or legitimacy of society by necessary transgressions of the law.

This is also to say that the "romantic" action of this play is written into a metanarrative of social and political legitimation, the telos of which is the production of a hero capable of sanctioning the social order by transforming the burdensome duties of memory demanded by the epic past into the necessary foundations of the present age. This larger narrative takes as its basis the development of the mature and fully empowered hero out of that adolescent figure which the Conde Lozano describes as the "novel caballero," the novice or apprentice knight.[36] In the opening scene of the play, the question is who should serve as the tutor of this young knight and, in particular, whether Don Sancho is worthy of the charge. The larger question it raises is whether, and how, it is possible for a youth to enter into manhood. (This question becomes particularly acute in works like Tirso's El burlador de Sevilla and Ruiz de Alarcón's La verdad sospechosa, where those who occupy positions of patriarchal authority are themselves either corrupt or effete.)

In Guillén de Castro's Las mocedades, the hero's transformation, through a process of extraordinary self-proving, ultimately contradicts the modern individualism it might seem to represent. Indeed, the task of the play is to redeem the Cid as a hero in spite of his remarkably "modern" autonomy and his amorous attachment to Ximena. In Las mocedades del Cid the development of the mature Cid as a heroically autonomous individual presupposes a rigorous obedience to the father. As such the play enables the collective appropriation of the past, its authority and its rules, for present social and political ends. If questions of legitimacy in the Poema were controlled by customary forms of behavior and if, in the heroic society the Poema represents, such questions could be formally arbitrated at the cortes of the king, here social legitimacy is not guaranteed by any formalized means. Instead, it is produced in the figure of a hero who entirely transcends the law. By

---

36. In Tirso's El burlador de Sevilla, Don Juan is the apprentice knight gone astray. His uncle, Don Pedro Tenorio, is charged with looking after him early in act 1, but to no avail. Don Juan gains the sympathy of his uncle (and also implicates the older nobility): "mozo soy y mozo fuiste; / Y pues que de amor supiste, / Tenga disculpa mi amor" (I am a young man and so were you; / And since you knew love, / Forgive my act of love) (lines 62–64).

reimagining the hero as "incommensurable" rather than socially or morally autonomous, the literary transformation of the Cid provided the theatergoing public of the Golden Age with access to an absolute or mythic past. The story of the Cid's maturation, his near-miraculous transformation and triumph over conflict, responds to the desires of those relatively new classes of individuals whose desires for legitimation could best be satisfied by the strategic appropriation of history as myth. As I have suggested here, the transformation of the Cid from the *Poema* to the *comedia* was inseparable from the need for legitimation of those groups of individuals whose presence in the *corrales* was essential for their incorporation into the early modern Spanish state.[37]

37. See Noël Salomon and Maxime Chevalier, "Creación y público: para una socio-logía de los siglos de oro," in Francisco Rico, *Historia y crítica de la literatura española,* vol. 3, *Siglos de Oro: Barroco,* ed. Bruce Wardropper et al. (Barcelona: Editorial Crítica, 1983), 75–86.

3

Allegories of Power in Calderón

El dosel de la jura, reducido
a segunda intención, a horror segundo,
teatro funesto es, donde importuna
representa tragedias la fortuna.
—*La vida es sueño*

(The throne room,
split by duplicity and horror,
becomes again the grisly stage where
urgent fate enacts its tragedies)[1]

Allegories are, in the realm of thoughts,
what ruins are in the realm of things.
—Walter Benjamin, *The Origin of German
Tragic Drama*

In *Lineages of the Absolutist State,* Perry Anderson observes that of all early modern European states, it was Spain that provided "the general character of Absolutism in the West." While recognizing significant differences in the form of absolutism in all the Western European countries, Anderson nonetheless returns to the position that the rise of Hapsburg Spain as an absolutist monarchy was not just an isolated episode within a set of more or less comparable experiences of state-construction. It was an exemplary model, a "determinant of the whole set as such."[2]

1. Translations make reference to the English versions of *La Vida es sueño* by Edwin Honig (New York: Hill and Wang, 1970), here 87; and by Edward and Edith Huberman, in *Spanish Drama,* ed. Angel Flores (New York: Bantam, 1962).
2. *Lineages of the Absolutist State* (London: Verso, 1979), 60. The entire chapter on Spain (60–84) is relevant. See also J. H. Elliott, "The Court of the Spanish Hapsburgs:

To what causes can Spain's preeminence in this regard can this be attributed? How can the paradigmatic importance of Spanish absolutism be explained? What, if any, is the relationship between the Hapsburgs' absolutist rule and what seems to be the relatively tardy or uneven development in Spain of a bourgeois "public sphere"?[3] Anderson ventures two principal reasons to explain the overwhelming success of Spanish absolutism. First, he suggests that the Spanish ruling house benefitted more than any other in Europe from the compacts of dynasty-marriage. Shrewd arrangements in this area gave the Hapsburgs a range of territory and influence unrivaled in Europe. Second, the colonial conquest of the New World supplied Spain with a seemingly limitless stream of precious metals, and provided it with a treasury that few of its counterparts could match. Presumably because this wealth was not widely disseminated, Anderson reasons that absolutism took particularly strong hold in Spain, where it fostered social and political conditions inimical to bourgeois social and economic development. Indeed, Anderson suggests that the massive fortune derived from Spain's control of the mines in America proved a disincentive to the growth of manufacturing at home and provided no impetus to the development of a mercantile enterprise within Spain's own European empire. Spain itself was said to have become "colonized" by the many foreign goods that were increasingly being imported from abroad. Indeed, the colonies that Spain had dominated seemed as if to dominate Spain, at least in economic terms. "The cry went up: *España son las Indias del extranjero:* Spain has become the Americas of Europe, a colonial dumping-ground for foreign goods. . . . The productive potential of Castile was

A Peculiar Institution?" in *Politics and Culture in Early Modern Europe: Essays in Honor of H. G. Koenigsberger,* ed. Phyllis Mack and Margaret C. Jacob (Cambridge: Cambridge University Press, 1987), 5–24; reprinted in Elliott's *Spain and Its World: 1500–1700* (New Haven: Yale University Press, 1989), 142–61. The importance for the Versailles court has been shown by Norbert Elias in *The Court Society,* trans. Edmund Jephcott (New York: Pantheon, 1983).

3. The claim for the paradigmatic status of the Spanish court is countered by claims that it was among the least representative of European countries in developing a "bourgeois public sphere" crucial to the culture of the Enlightenment. Thus Jürgen Habermas proposes the case of Britain as paradigmatic of this development, and offers France and Germany as comparative references, but makes no mention of Spain whatsoever in *The Structural Transformation of the Public Sphere: An Inquiry into a Category of Bourgeois Society,* trans. Thomas Burger with Frederick Lawrence (Cambridge: MIT Press, 1991).

being undermined by the same Empire which was pumping resources into the military apparatus of the State for unprecedented adventures abroad" (*Lineages of the Absolutist State,* 73). At the same time, Anderson suggests that the sprawling nature of the Hapsburg empire overextended its capacity for social and political integration and helped to block the process of administrative modernization in Spain. Tellingly enough, the Inquisition remained the one unitary "Spanish" institution on the peninsula; the Cortes by contrast were an assembly of an occasional nature and of indefinite duration.

Thus while Spanish absolutism may be taken as representative, even paradigmatic of absolutism in early modern Europe, Anderson's analysis suggests that there may have existed a flaw, or perhaps more accurately a series of flaws, within the political and economic structure of Spanish absolutism that prevented it from following the "natural" course of historical development of other early modern nation-states in Europe. Spanish absolutism worked against itself, but not so directly or thoroughly as to bring the structure crumbling down. Rather, its limitations served to obstruct the transformation toward a fully constituted society of social classes that was beginning elsewhere in Europe. The question Anderson does not stop to ask is how Spanish absolutism was sustained politically and supported culturally, even in the face of these structural flaws or weaknesses. Any political system depends for its efficacy and power on the way in which it is able to represent itself culturally. Indeed, it would not be too much to suggest that an aesthetic basis can be found for every political regime even if it is one that classical political theory would prefer to ignore.

In this chapter, I argue that in the case of Spanish absolutism these "aesthetic" modes of representation were invaluable first in legitimizing and then in strengthening the power of the state. In one of its dimensions at least, the theater of the Golden Age (and especially the theater of Calderón), thematizes in an "allegorical" way the crisis of power within the structure of the Absolutist State. It shows that the response to the self-limiting crisis of absolutism was an effort to shore up sovereign authority by means of infusions of new forms of power, or by re-presenting the old forms of power in a newly legitimized guise. Especially in Calderón, this effort takes a dramatic form in which the preferred situation for investigating and "resolving" this crisis is the displacement of the sovereign from his position of power, either by jeopardizing his claim to the throne, or by raising questions about who will rightfully inherit the throne.[4] As we shall see, the displacement of the sovereign and the crisis of authority it figures is mirrored in the polis itself, which reflects a displacement among human beings, both from one another and from the natural world. This displacement is rooted in acts of transgressive violence that constitute an apparently lawless realm, which Hobbes would redefine for political theory as the "state of nature" itself.[5] Since Calderón imagines the state of nature as not at all inherently "natural" and good, as critics accepting a providential view of it tended to assume,[6] but as one in which human beings encounter the pre-existing effects of power, it turns out that the need to "perfect" human nature is best accomplished politically.[7] Under

4. Not surprisingly, Franco Moretti draws support for a related view of Shakespeare from Calderón. See "The Great Eclipse: Tragic Form as the Deconsecration of Sovereignty," in *Signs Taken for Wonders* (London: Verso, 1988), 42–82.

5. Schelling is one among many who accept the manifest interpretation of transgression in Calderón as a form of sin: "The primary feature and the foundation of the entire edifice of his art Calderón has, of course, received from the Catholic religion, whose view of the universe and of the divine order of things essentially requires that there be *sin* and sinners so that through the mediation of the church God may prove his grace. This introduces the general necessity of sin, and in Calderón's piece under discussion [*La devoción de la Cruz*] the entire element of fate develops out of a kind of divine providence." *The Philosophy of Art*, trans. Douglas W. Scott (Minneapolis: University of Minnesota Press, 1989), 273.

6. See, for example, Peter Dunn, who writes that for Calderón "nature was not merely the visible world outside ourselves, waiting to be observed and catalogued. Nor was it the Nature of the Romantics like Coleridge or Schopenhauer, a universal energy perpetually realizing itself, in which we are swept impersonally along, and which mocks our faith in will and reason. In the traditional view, Nature is a sign of God's providence, abundant, generous. But the abundance does not hide an orderliness in which each created thing has its place and its function. Men could, indeed should, learn from Nature." Introduction to *El alcalde de Zalamea*, ed. Peter N. Dunn (Oxford: Pergamon, 1966), 18. Roberto González Echevarría refers to this as the "correct" view in "Calderón's *La vida es sueño:* Mixed-(Up) Monsters," in *Celestina's Brood* (Durham: Duke University Press, 1993), 254 n. 20. For a more complex account of related issues in Shakespeare, see John F. Danby, *Shakespeare's Doctrine of Nature: A Study of King Lear* (London: Faber and Faber, 1948). Danby unfortunately goes to the extreme of seeing *Lear* as a "dramatization of ideas," among which the central one is "Nature."

7. Stephen Rupp brings out the allegorical nature of Calderón's effort here in *Allegories of Kingship: Calderón and the Anti-Machiavellian Tradition* (University Park: Pennsylvania State University Press, 1996). See, for example, 27: "Calderón locates the antidote to secular politics in the traditional princely virtues because he maintains that the Christian king can amend the state by aligning its actions and institutions with the due order that providence has established for human affairs. . . . These techniques illustrate the complexity of Calderón's allegorical practice and the central place of allegory in his conception of history."

conditions where there can be no return to the state of nature in its plenitude and its goodness, morality is subsumed under politics. This may suggest why the need to mend the faults of absolutism were so urgently felt. In Calderón, the result of this need is what I would call an "allegory of power," whose basis is not to be found anywhere in nature, nor in the primacy of a system of natural signs, but which is instead referred back to the *loss* of faith in nature's fundamental goodness. This particular form of allegory, I shall argue, leads to a political imperative consistent with the interests of absolutism. This is indeed remarkable given the generally anti-Machiavellian bias of political theory in Golden Age Spain. As Dian Fox has pointed out, Spanish commentators of Machiavelli's work waged a theoretical counterattack against Machiavelli's pragmatic political science and insisted emphatically on the principle of the people's supremacy over the head of government.[8]

The basis for the peculiar set of allegorical relationships we see in Calderón has best been described by Walter Benjamin in his study of the baroque *Trauerspiel*. At several points in *The Origin of German Tragic Drama,* Benjamin cites Calderón as having produced the most perfect example of the "drama of mourning" or *Trauerspiel* that came to prominence in Europe during the period of the baroque. Unlike Germany, where the *Trauerspiel* was preoccupied with the potential hopelessness of the earthly condition when considered with respect to salvation, where Lutheran moralism attempted to bring together the transcendence of faith and the immanence of everyday life without recourse to a system of external mediations, and where the bourgeois vocational ethic tended to deny the possibility of a conflict between the worldly predicament of the hero and the princely will on which the action of so much Counter-Reformation drama in Spain depends, the drama of Catholic Spain allowed for the incorporation of a figure of transcendence, albeit in an abbreviated, or as Benjamin says, "miniaturized" or "crystallized" form, within the secular realm. According to Benjamin, the development of the *Trauerspiel* is dependent on a process of secularization that is nearly, but not totally, complete. Thus in *La*

8. This "allegory of absolutist power" is remarkable given what is generally assumed to be Calderón's support, as a Catholic writer, for anti-Machiavellian political views. See Fox, *Refiguring the Hero: From Peasant to Noble in Lope de Vega and Calderón* (University Park: Pennsylvania State University Press, 1991), 52. See also Fox, *Kings in Calderón: A Study in Characterization and Political Theory* (London: Tamesis Books, 1986), and Rupp, *Allegories of Kingship.*

vida es sueño Calderón begins—in Segismundo's opening monologue and in Rosaura's initial complaint—with a vision of subjective self-consciousness as produced by a disruption in the essential order of nature; and yet we find salvaged what Benjamin describes as "a totality worthy of the mystery-play, in which the dream stands over waking life like the vault of heaven." Benjamin concludes: "Nowhere but in Calderón could the perfect Baroque *Trauerspiel* be studied. The very precision with which the 'mourning' [*Trauer*] and the 'play' [*Spiel*] can harmonize with one another gives it its exemplary validity."[9]

In so saying, Benjamin takes up a fundamental tenet of German Romanticism, whose principal proponents were unstinting in their praise for Calderón as a universal mythmaker whose art draws on the resources of a symbolism that had been gradually eclipsed with the advent of modern, Protestant culture.[10] Yet a thinker like Schelling also views Protestantism as a "necessary" historical development, intimately connected to the Enlightenment, which makes the mystical Catholicism of Calderón's work seem all the more impressive:

> this is also the subject of the modern world, namely, that all that is finite in it is transient, and that the absolute is infinitely removed. Here everything is subordinated to the law of the finite. According to this law a new mass has thrown itself between the world of art in Catholicism on the one hand, and the present age on the other: Protestantism was born and was historically necessary. . . . One need only recall that the Freethinkers and the Enlightenment cannot claim even the smallest poetic accomplishments in order to see that they are, both of them, fundamentally nothing more than the prose of the new age, applied to religion.[11]

As articulated by Fichte in his *Ethics,* the problem posed by the breach between Protestantism and Catholicism is whether (religious) symbols should be taken in the "Catholic" sense as themselves essentially and ultimately true, or whether the symbols in question should instead

9. Benjamin, *The Origin of German Tragic Drama,* trans. John Osborne (London: NLB, 1977), 81.

10. Schelling's *Philosophy of Art,* for instance, asserts that the only playwrights worthy of comparison to Calderón were Shakespeare and Sophocles. Schelling anticipates Benjamin in arguing that the subject of modern drama is a finite and the transient world from which the absolute has lost integral connection.

11. Schelling, *The Philosophy of Art,* 70, 71.

be taken in the "Protestant" sense, "counterfactually," that is, as a substitute for what is, in the spiritual realm, essentially real.[12] Schelling, for his part, criticizes "the imbecilic representatives of the Enlightenment" while also holding that Catholicism could not in and of itself provide "a modern poesy and mythology." He still, however, grants that Catholicism provided an important protection for the universal power of myth: outside Catholicism "one can expect *only* subordination to content, forced movement without serenity, and mere subjective usage," an event in which "mythology degenerates into an object for *use*."[13]

As Benjamin understands it, the formation of the *Trauerspiel* depends on a thesis about the "original form" in which this debate over the meaning and efficacy of symbol and myth occurred. This takes the form of a transition from the archaic *mythos* to the modern (and implicitly historical and enlightened) *logos* that in turn provides the basis for a distinction between *Trauerspiel* and ancient tragedy.[14] Additionally, Benjamin's understanding of the difference between *Trauerspiel* and tragedy is dependent on a claim about the allegorical nature of the system of signs and meaning out of which the *Trauerspiel* is built. As in Schelling, this allows for the modern poet to continue to function as a mythmaker in a world that is increasingly demythologized as it becomes

12. See Fichte, *Science of Ethics,* trans. A. E. Kroeger (New York: Harper and Row, 1970), 258. The centerpiece of Calderón's *autos,* the Eucharist, was the focal point of this debate. Although it is for both sides a symbol, it is also what W. D. Winnicott calls a "transitional object": "I think I am right in saying that for the Roman Catholic Community it *is* the body, and for the Protestant community it is a *substitute,* a reminder, and is essentially not, in fact, actually the body itself." *Playing and Reality* (London: Tavistock, 1971), 6.

13. Schelling, *Philosophy of Art,* 67, 72–73.

14. Benjamin writes of the *Trauerspiel* that "historical life, as it was conceived at that time, is its content, its true object. In this it is different from tragedy. For the object of the latter is not history, but myth, and the tragic stature of the *dramatis personae* does not derive from rank—the absolute monarchy—but from the pre-historic epoch of their existence—the past age of heroes" (62). Benjamin's approach to allegory in the *Trauerspiel,* which sees it as a thoroughly historical phenomenon, is on the whole far more illuminating and fruitful than the blanket claim that, in contrast to the literature of the Middle Ages, Renaissance art and art theory simply de-allegorize. Compare, for example, Agnes Heller, who writes that in the Renaissance, "art theory de-allegorizes. We need only to compare the illustrations which adorn the scientific and philosophical literature with works of art proper, full of life and independent: while the illustrations reveal an ever more complicated allegorical mode of representation, art proper is almost untouched by it." *Renaissance Man,* trans. Richard Allen (New York: Schocken Books, 1978), 408.

ever more "enlightened."[15] The crucial difference is that the modern mythmaker's art will necessarily be historical and political. Although the *Trauerspiel* may not in every instance deal with historical issues at the thematic level, the conditions of its existence ("its content, its true object," as Benjamin says) are those of nature understood as subject to historical contingency and change.[16] So too the characters of the *Trauerspiel* are "subjects" in the sense that they internalize the historicity of their existence in some strikingly self-conscious ways. What is mourned in the *Trauerspiel* is not (or not only) the death of the king or prince, but something that might be more accurately described as the loss of nature to history. "The word 'history' stands written on the countenance of nature in the characters of transience. The allegorical physiognomy of the nature-history, which is put on stage in the *Trauerspiel,* is present in reality in the form of the ruin. . . . In this guise history does not assume the form of the process of an eternal life so much as that of irresistible decay" (Benjamin, *The Origin of German Tragic Drama,* 177–78). While the Aristotelian precepts required the tragic hero to be of sufficiently high stature so that his downfall would be a cause not only for pity but for admiration or wonder as well, the tragic stature of the dramatis personae of ancient tragedy was nonetheless independent of any historical notion of social change and in Benjamin's opinion derived from the "pre-historic" (read as "mythical") nature of these characters. They are drawn from what Benjamin calls the "past age of heroes" (62), which we may understand as a realm akin to the "absolute past" Bakhtin ascribed to the epic.[17]

Regardless of whether or not any such an age ever existed in fact, the notion is important as a way of locating the peculiarly modern myth that these were not just times past, but times immune to time. The formation of the *Trauerspiel* depends by contrast on the essential, constitutional historicity of all persons, objects, and events that enter

15. Schelling argues that the novelist in turn takes this task upon himself in reflecting the world: "The novel should be a mirror of the world, or at least of the age, and thus become a partial mythology. . . . Don Quixote and Sancho Panza are mythological persons extending across the entire cultivated earth, just as the story of the windmills and so on are true myths or mythological sagas" (*The Philosophy of Art,* 232, 234).

16. The relationship between allegory, history, and metaphysical decay has been treated in relation to ancient rhetoric and contemporary critical theory by Gordon Teskey in "Irony, Allegory, and Metaphysical Decay," *PMLA* 109 (1994): 297–408.

17. See Bakhtin, "Epic and Novel," in *The Dialogic Imagination,* trans. Caryl Emerson and Michael Holquist (Austin: University of Texas Press, 1981).

into it. Indeed, Benjamin claims that the form of the *Trauerspiel* had the power to disclose everything that was "unsuccessful," "untimely," or "sorrowful" about historical reality itself (166).[18] This fundamental historicity is epitomized in the vulnerability of the sovereign, whom Benjamin describes as "the principal exponent of history," as its "incarnation": "the sovereign is the representative of history. He holds the course of history in his hand like a sceptre" (65), but also as the one who most dramatically suffers history's effects in the course of his tragic-like deconsecration. For Benjamin, it is in this combination of absolute power and subjective fragility that we find the essence of the baroque, and it is this that gives rise to a uniquely secularized form of allegory: "Everything about history that, from the very beginning, has been untimely, sorrowful, unsuccessful, is expressed in a face—or rather in a death's head. . . . This is the form in which man's subjection to nature is most obvious and it significantly gives rise not only to the enigmatic question of the nature of human existence as such, but also of the biographical historicity of the individual. This is the heart of the allegorical way of seeing, of the baroque, secular expansion of history as the Passion of the world; its importance resides solely in the stations of decline" (166).

It may further be said that the historical world of the *Trauerspiel* corresponds to that of modern allegory insofar as in it the decipherment of the essential meaning of the world has become a "hermeneutical" task, one that consists in reading signs (in Calderón, hieroglyphics and horoscopes) whose intent may be uncertain, or interpreting a script whose meaning may be unclear.[19] Ideally, such a process would involve not only interpreting signs, but resurrecting and enacting a meaning whose original force lies buried in the past, thus *animating* signs tinged with death; it is this dream of life in a dead or dying world that the

18. The "sadness" of the *Trauerspiel* can thus be contrasted to the "happiness" that Lukács attributes to the "integrated civilizations" of the epic world in *The Theory of the Novel*, trans. Anna Bostock (Cambridge: MIT Press, 1971).

19. On allegory in this respect, see Edwin Honig, *Dark Conceit: The Making of Allegory* (Evanston: Northwestern University Press, 1959). See also Frederick A. de Armas, *The Return of Astraea: An Astral-Imperial Myth in Calderón* (Lexington: University of Kentucky Press, 1986). For a discussion of tendencies in the Renaissance both toward and away from the notion of allegory as involving the figuration of dark truths, with particular reference to Spain (and to Cervantes), see Diana de Armas Wilson, *Allegories of Love: Cervantes's "Persiles and Sigismunda"* (Princeton: Princeton University Press, 1991), chap. 3, "Some Versions of Allegory," especially 53–62, "Renaissance Notions of Allegory."

allegory of the *Trauerspiel* suggests. Allegory in its baroque, Benjaminian sense depends neither on the possibility of establishing any direct correspondence between these desacralized signs and a fixed order of original meaning, nor on the possibility of drawing universally valid moral conclusions from the interpretations we may in fact give to them. Instead, the allegory that Benjamin discusses takes as its point of departure the fundamentally secular premise that the commanding authority of nature as the primary ground or locus of meaning and interpretation has been withdrawn.[20] It roots in the realization that, as Benjamin says, "nature has always been subject to the power of death" (166). Thus in the plays of the Spanish baroque that best conform to Benjamin's description, epitomized in *La vida es sueño,* we may discover an initial reversion to the conditions of nature's original brutishness. Indeed, we may even encounter a world tainted by a kind of death-in-life: Rosaura describes Segismundo as inhabiting "una prisón oscura / que es de un vivo cadáver sepultura" (a gloomy prison / which is the sepulcher of a living corpse [lines 93–94]).[21] Yet at the same time the actions of the principal characters—especially, in this case, the astrologer-king—carry out a search for a meaning, an attempt to read nature's

20. Compare the relationship between allegory, scriptural interpretation, and psychoanalysis proposed by Angus Fletcher: "Scriptural exegesis interprets Holy Writ in historical terms, as being capable of foretelling the future and explaining the past and present, by assuming that the prophets were divinely inspired through voices from God or his angels. The method absolutely requires a belief in daemonic agency and inspiration. The psychoanalyst therefore differs from the exegete in the values he places upon the truth of oracular messages and occult signs. The findings of psychoanalysis are borne out further by the uses to which oracles are put in the poetry of the ancient world, where they authorize given lines of conduct." *Allegory: The Theory of a Symbolic Mode* (Ithaca: Cornell University Press, 1964), 297.

21. See Javier Herrero, "*Vivo cadáver:* Segismundo in the Shadow," in *The Prince in the Tower: Perceptions of "La vida es sueño,"* ed. Frederick A. de Armas (Lewisburg: Bucknell University Press, 1993), 183–214. One might well compare the *vivo cadáver* to the death-in-life effect of still-life painting in the baroque. See Jean Rousset's description of "a little coffin containing the absolute" in baroque architecture in *La littérature de l'âge baroque en France* (Paris: Corti, 1953), 171. Gilles Deleuze relates it to Leibnitz's monads: "For ages there have been places where what is seen is inside: a cell, a sacristy, a crypt, a church, a theatre, a study, or a print room. The Baroque invests in all of these places in order to extract from them power and glory. . . . The monad is a cell. It resembles a sacristy more than an atom: a room with neither doors nor windows, where all activity takes place on the inside." Gilles Deleuze, *The Fold: Leibnitz and the Baroque,* trans. Tom Conley (Minneapolis: University of Minnesota Press, 1993), 27–28. In Calderón, the question is whether (and, if so, how) the platonic-Christian light can enter this windowless cell and enliven/enlighten the "vivo cadáver" dwelling there.

signs (Segismundo's horoscope), that would in turn secure the order of the secular-political realm.[22] What remains to be seen is not so much whether the signs of nature can be reanimated—for that is a possibility accepted as lost—but how a secular order can be restored.

✳   ✳   ✳

In both its historical and its allegorical dimensions the emergence of the *Trauerspiel* is symptomatic of the processes that, during the Renaissance and early modern periods, lead to the questioning of what Roberto Mangabeira Unger has called the "naturalistic thesis" about society and the self. The naturalistic thesis takes a particular form of social life as "the context of all contexts—the true and undistorted form of social existence." As Unger goes on to say, "the natural context of social life may pass through decay or renascence, but it cannot be remade. Nor is there, in this view, any sense in which the defining context of social life can become less contextual—less arbitrary and confining. It is already the real thing. . . . This authentic pattern of social life can undergo corruption and regeneration. But it can never be rearranged."[23] Understood in a broad, philosophical and sociological sense, the displacement of the naturalistic thesis can be read both as the great achievement and as the inescapable fate of modern European cultures. The optimistic and progressive narratives of modern philosophy may be read as both a cause and a consequence of it, just as we shall see that Calderón's invocation of the Platonic and Aristotelian models of natural and moral order is for its part meant to re-establish a grounding in the "natural context" believed essential for the security and cohesion of the state. The question of whether Calderón's humanist-prince has nobility at heart, or whether nobility is learned through a process of education, is

---

22. See especially Frederick A. de Armas, *The Return of Astraea: An Astral-Imperial Myth in Calderón,* especially chaps. 5 and 6. The horoscope motif in the play has been treated by Peter N. Dunn in "The Horoscope Motif in *La vida es sueño,*" in *Critical Studies of Calderón's Comedias,* ed. J. E. Varey (Westmead, Farnborough, Hants: Gregg International, 1973), 117–31. Among the background sources Dunn mentions are the story "El pronóstico cumplido," in Alonso de Castillo Solórzono's *Noches de placer* (1631), and Castillo's source in the *Cento novelle* of Francesco Sansovino (Giorno 4, no. 5), said to have been copied word for word from a collection entitled *I compassionevoli avvenimenti di Erasto,* published in Venice in 1558. Dunn in turn traces this story's links to the group of folk tales known as the *Seven Wise Masters of Roma.*

23. Unger, *Social Theory: Its Situation and Its Task* (Cambridge: Cambridge University Press, 1987), 23–24.

in the end eclipsed by Calderón's attempt to marry humanism with the naturalistic thesis it sought to displace.

Calderón's response to the conditions of emergent modernization is marked by the fact that the historicization of the natural world is concealed by the figuration of a power whose scope and basis, though finite, appears to supplant that of nature—by a power that is, in this sense, "absolute." Because the historical world is radically conflictive, Calderón draws near a vision that resonates with French classical tragedy as described by Lucien Goldmann in *The Hidden God*. In Goldmann's view, tragedy comes to counterpose "against a world composed of fragmentary and mutually exclusive elements a demand for totality that inevitably becomes a demand for the reconciliation of opposites. For the tragic mind, authentic values are synonymous with totality."[24] For figures like Descartes and Hobbes, this "absolutism" is primarily a discursive and theoretical demand articulated against a disenchanted historical world, although for Hobbes its relationship to political absolutism is also fairly direct. At the theoretical level, reason appears and acquires its force by requiring that every valid social or political assertion derive an absolute authority from and re-create a form of sovereignty within the subjects themselves. "Reason" perpetuates itself absolutely and ideologically in the "disenchanted" historical world out of the need to establish a community of subjects where none in fact naturally exists.[25]

In Calderón we consistently find a series of neo-Aristotelian and Platonic ideas used to buttress political absolutism in its philosophically "legitimate" form. Consider as one example the question of Rosaura's beauty, which appears to inspire Segismundo to recognize Truth. What may appear in this instance to be a revival of a Neoplatonic philosophy in fact allows Segismundo to submit himself to his father's authority, and so ideologically supports that version of subjectivity on which political absolutism rests: subjection to a sovereign will. Benjamin posits as a central problem of his *Trauerspiel* book the question of whether truth an do justice to beauty.[26] The answer Calderón would seem to give is that the convergence of beauty and truth is possible (e.g., in Segismundo's recognition of Rosaura), but only within the confines of

24. *The Hidden God*, trans. Philip Thody (New York: Humanities Press, 1964), 57.
25. See Alan F. Blum, *Theorizing* (London: Heinemann, 1974), 157.
26. *The Origin of German Tragic Drama*, 31.

representation, and only in the service of the state.[27] The absolutist state in turn can be seen as the ground of a power that is allegorical in the modern, Benjaminian sense: having first destroyed the authority of nature as that which is *originally* beautiful and true, absolutism goes on to reclaim nature's power as the legitimizing basis of its own. Absolutism supplants nature with what might be described as a series of quasi-aesthetic "power effects," whose artificial origins and historical contingency it attempts at the same time to conceal. As we shall see in conclusion, these effects go to prove the theatrical nature of power itself.[28]

In contrast to Calderón, where the thrust of this effect is politically conservative, consider how in the *Meditations,* the *Discourse on Method,* and the *Rules for the Direction of the Mind,* Descartes works systematically to claim for the philosophical subject the authority and autonomy required to reject the doctrine of natural essences. Consider how this rejection is represented as "progressive" by reducing history to the category of error:

> regarding the opinions to which I had hitherto given credence, I thought that I could not do better than undertake to get rid of them, all at one go, in order to replace them afterwards with better ones, or with the same ones once I had squared them with the standards of reason.[29]

27. Benjamin all but articulates representation as the specific difference between truth and beauty when he says that "this relationship between truth and beauty shows more clearly than anything else the great difference between truth and the object of knowledge, with which it has customarily been equated, and at the same time it provides an explanation of that simple and yet unpopular fact that even those philosophical systems whose cognitional element has long since lost any claim to scientific truth still possess contemporary relevance. In the great philosophies the world is seen in terms of the order of ideas." *The Origin of German Tragic Drama,* 31–32. Through Benjamin one can read Nietzsche's famous comment that existence and the world are justified only as an "aesthetic" phenomenon as an expression of the pathos of Platonism. The issue of representation is taken up explicitly and at some length in the "Epistemo-Critical Prologue" to Benjamin's work, though not with reference to the context of absolutism.

28. Nicholas Spadaccini and Jenaro Talens argue that, in the culture of seventeenth-century Spain, fiction became a mechanism of power and cultural control insofar as it was a form of "alienated theatricality." See *Cervantes and the Self-Made World* (Minneapolis: University of Minnesota Press, 1993), 133–36.

29. Descartes, *Discourse on Method,* II in *The Philosophical Writings of Descartes,* trans. John Cottingham, Robert Stoothoff, and Dugald Murdoch (Cambridge: Cambridge University Press, 1984), 117.

> I will suppose then, that everything I see is spurious. I will believe that my memory tells me lies, and that none of the things that it reports ever happened. I have no senses. Body, shape, extension, movement and place are chimeras. So what remains true? Perhaps just the one act that nothing is certain. (*Meditations*, in *Philosophical Writings*, 2:12)

Indeed, Descartes works to suppress and exclude the essential historicity that Benjamin flagged as central to the baroque. As these passages also suggest, Cartesian doubt is in the service of a larger, progressive project of "self-assertion" that calls for the rejection of the wisdom of the past and the accumulated experience of prior generations in favor of those truths of reason that can be certified by the self-reflective mind. Beginning with Descartes, history is no longer a reflection of preexisting norms and no longer supplies examples worthy of imitation. This is confirmed in the first part of the *Discourse on Method*, where Descartes classifies historical writings together with the fables of the past:

> I thought I had already given enough time to languages and likewise to reading the works of the ancients, both their histories and their fables. For conversing with those of past centuries is much the same as travelling. It is good to know something of the customs of various peoples, so that we may judge our own more soundly and not think that everything contrary to our own ways is ridiculous and irrational, as those who have seen nothing of the world ordinarily do. But one who spends too much time travelling eventually becomes a stranger in his own country; and one who is too curious about the practices of past ages usually remains quite ignorant about those of the present. Moreover, fables make us imagine many events as possible when they are not. And even the most accurate histories, while not altering or exaggerating the importance of matters to make them more worthy of being read, at any rate almost always omit the baser and less notable events; as a result, the other events appear in a false light, and those who regulate their conduct by examples drawn from these works are liable to fall into the excesses of the knights-errant in our tales of chivalry, and conceive plans beyond their powers. (*Philosophical Writings*, 1:113–14)[30]

30. On the Cartesian critique of historiography, see Lucien Lévi-Bruhl, "The Cartesian

And yet it remains nonetheless clear that Descartes's progressive project of self-assertion cannot fully account for or comprehend the process of its own historical origination. Thus already in the early *Rules for the Direction of the Mind,* when Descartes sets himself the task of a fully rational critique, he invokes the notion of a *prior* division of history and reason (where reason is seen as "science"); this is a division of which reason is unable to give an account. In the *Rules* Descartes says that "all the arguments of Plato and Aristotle" would not constitute true knowledge: "what we would seem to have learnt [in studying them] would not be science but history" (*Rules,* III, in *Philosophical Writings,* 1:13).

But rather than say categorically that history is eliminated from such an account of reason, it would be more accurate to claim that the past is rendered unintelligible or illegible by it: reason renders the past unreadable, which is to say that it demands a new allegoresis if it is to be interpreted at all. Thus, Descartes introduces a skeptical narrative designed to stage the emergence of reason in history as if it were not just "rational" but also "natural." The narrative of skepticism provides the means through which the otherwise unreasonable and unnatural emergence of reason on the historical plane can be imagined as taking place. Similarly, since Descartes cannot *a priori* assert the priority of consciousness over nature, he must allegorize its emergence in terms of the production of a "new world," created as if by a surrogate god or demiurge: "I decided to leave our world wholly for them to argue about, and to speak solely of what would happen in a new world. I therefore supposed that God now created, somewhere in space, enough matter to compose a world" (*Discourse,* V, in *Philosophical Writings,* 1:132). So seen, the founding of Cartesian "science" is a historical project whose origins are allegorized in terms of the creation of the world out of chaos. But because it can at best explain itself in terms of a narrative of skepticism, its claim to represent the world accurately and truthfully is also a reflection of the willfulness of its own powers of self-formation.[31]

The political consequences of such a project become more fully apparent in the work of Hobbes, whose position on the "disenchanted"

Spirit and History," in *Philosophy and History: Essays Presented to Ernst Cassirer,* ed. Raymond Klibansky and H. J. Paton (Oxford: Clarendon Press, 1936), and A. J. Cascardi, "Genealogies of Modernism," *Philosophy and Literature* 11 (1987): 207–25.

31. Jay M. Bernstein makes a related argument in *The Philosophy of the Novel: Lukács, Marxism and the Dialectics of Form* (Minneapolis: University of Minnesota Press, 1984), 179.

state of nature radicalizes what was merely latent in Descartes and makes explicit what is most feared in Calderón's reaction. Notwithstanding Hobbes's explicit criticisms of Descartes, he shares the project of "self-assertion" in which the accomplishments of reason are seen as self-justifying insofar as they reflect the successful actualization of human aims, intentions, and designs. The key to their interpretation is power: "Good successe is Power . . . which makes men either feare him, or rely on him."[32] By laying bare and criticizing previously authoritative beliefs, a work like the *Leviathan* proposes a true and final (which is also to say, nonallegorical) interpretation of political life. Hobbes begins from the crucial modern verity that no essential order—neither history, nor nature—binds men from the origin to the end of all things. For Hobbes, the proof of this truth lies in the new, self-justifying allegoresis of reason, which takes the form of progress itself: "Time, and Industry, produce every day new knowledge. . . . Long after men have begun to constitute Common-wealths, imperfect, and apt to relapse into disorder, there may, Principles of Reason be found out, by industrious meditation, to make their constitution (excepting by externall violence) everlasting" (*Leviathan*, part 2, chap. 30, p. 378). Hobbes's principles of politics constitute an interpretation of progress inasmuch as they result in the "constitution everlasting" of an absolute state.[33] The place of reason with respect to history is fully revealed only when it is seen that reason is not in fact independent of history or emergent from it but rather that progress in history—as the allegory of power, rather than as the mere coming to be and passing away of human things or as an expression of the radical instability of nature—validates reason as the true measure of human events.

In Hobbes's view, subjects are not directly the agents of this progress. Rather, they must respect the temporal authority and visible power of the rational state in a way that is directly proportionate to their capacity for fear. The passion of fear, which is only heightened by an awareness of the breakdown of falsely "natural" social hierarchies, leads to an awareness of one's immersion in the war of all against all, hence to a realization of one's dependence on others and need for recognition. Fear itself is the beginning of reason insofar as it provides a knowledge of one's own weakness and of the need for the protections of the state.[34]

32. Hobbes, *Leviathan*, ed. C. B. Macpherson (Harmondsworth: Penguin, 1968), part 1, chap. 10, p. 151.

33. See Barry Cooper's chapter on Hobbes in *The End of History* (Toronto: University of Toronto Press, 1984), especially 26–29, and 39–40.

34. See Cooper, *The End of History*, 39.

✳ ✳ ✳

Not unlike Hobbes, Calderón asks us to imagine what it would be like to exist in a "state of nature." And yet it seems that in *La vida es sueño* the state of nature can never quite be imagined as "natural." If nature was once regarded as a realm of lawfulness,[35] it is now the place of the transgression of the law. Indeed, the "state of nature" seems always to be infected by some prior human transgression, which introduces a fundamental distortion of its order. Instead of a realm of fixed and stable essences, or a well-ordered hierarchy, "nature" for Calderón is figured as generating "monsters" that allegorize the conflictive social and political forces at work in it.[36] Hence Rosaura describes her arrival to Poland on a most unnatural animal, the hippogriff, and explains how together they leave traces of blood on the sand:

> Hipogrifo violento
> que corriste parejas con el viento,
>   ¿dónde, rayo sin llama,
> pájaro sin matiz, pez sin escama,
>   y bruto sin instinto
> natural, al confuso laberinto
>   destas desnudas peñas
> te desbocas, arrastras y despeñas?
> ....
>   Mal, Polonia, recibes
> a un extranjero; pues con sangre escribes
>   su entrada en tus arenas.
>   (lines 1–8, 17–19)

35. This is Kant's description of nature in, among other places, the *Prolegomena to Any Future Metaphysics*, trans. Paul Carus, rev. James W. Ellington (Indianapolis: Hackett, 1977).

36. On monsters in Calderón, see Roberto González Echevarría, "Calderón's *La vida es sueño:* Mixed-(Up) Monsters." Ruth El Saffar has proposed a reading of the play that raises the question not just of lawfulness, but of what it takes, and costs, to sustain the law: repression, constant vigilance, the exclusion of passion and the feminine other, which she locates in the figure of Violante. She writes that "Violante is the name for that part of the psyche permanently locked out of consciousness, permanently consigned to the realm of abandon in *La vida es sueño.* Though silent and absent, she is nonetheless a potent presence from which the male characters seek to keep a healthy distance." See "Violante: The Place of Rejection," in *The Prince in the Tower: Perceptions of "La vida es sueño,*" 168.

(Wild hippogriff,
running swiftly with the wind,
      flash without flame,
bird without color, fish without scales,
      beast with no natural instinct,
where are you running wildly
      through the intricate labyrinth
of these bare cliffs?

....

      How rudely indeed
you welcome a stranger, Poland;
you inscribe her arrival on your sands with blood.)

From the very beginning of the play, nature is presented as already rife with the conflicts of passion and will that lead directly to social and political struggle. The "state of nature" in this play is a condition in which the passions, as shaped by society and culture, provoke the war of all against all. Indeed, that "war" is something that Calderón imagines as duplicated within subjective self-consciousness itself. This is the burden carried by Segismundo's opening monologue in the play:

SEGISMUNDO: ¡Ay mísero de mí
            Ay infelice . . . !
            Apurar cielos, pretendo
            ya que me tratáis así
            ¿qué delito cometí
            contra vosotros naciendo?"
                        (lines 103–6)

(SEGISMUNDO: Heavens above, I cry to you
            in misery and wretchedness,
            what crime against you did I commit
            by being born, to deserve
            this treatment from you?)[37]

37. There is a possible echo for this passage in Sophocles' *Oedipus at Colonus:* "not to be born prevails over all meaning uttered in words; by far the second-best for life, once it has appeared, is to go as swiftly as possible whence it came"; as Hannah Arendt observes of that play, Theseus lets us know that "it was the *polis,* the space of men's free deeds and living words, that could endow life with splendor." See Arendt, *On Revolution* (New York: Viking, 1965), 285.

The original dis-order found in the state of nature seems to be reflected in the alienation of self-consciousness from itself. The alienation Segismundo experiences is brought about by something that pre-exists him but is nonetheless transmitted through him. Specifically, it is due to a violent dislocation in the structure of authority that in traditional, patriarchal societies is meant to pass from father to son. At one level, *La vida es sueño* is the representation of a grand Oedipal conflict displayed upon the political stage, and the crisis of consciousness Segismundo experiences duplicates that struggle. As Segismundo explains, his father transgressed both the natural and the social order in raising his son as a beast:

> Mi padre, que está presente
> ....
> . . . me hizo
> un bruto, una fiera humana;
> de suerte, que cuando yo
> por mi nobleza gallarda,
> por mi sangre generosa,
> por mi condición bizarra
> hubiera nacido dócil
> y humilde, sólo bastara
> tal género de vivir,
> tal linaje de crianza,
> a hacer fieras mis costumbres.
> (lines 3168–80)

> (My father who is here before us . . .
> made of me a brute, a half-
> human creature, so that
> even if I'd been born gentle
> and sweet-tempered, despite my noble
> blood and inbred magnanimity,
> such bizarre treatment, such upbringing,
> would have been enough to turn me
> into a wild animal.)

Segismundo is the "beastly" product of his father's rule and, for that reason, the son who cannot succeed his father. But he is also the son who, it is feared, would enact the Oedipal drama most literally and usurp his father's place.[38] What hangs in the balance in the conflict between Basilio's "old" wisdom and the rising star of the new humanistic learning represented by his son is the order of the state itself. Seen from Basilio's point of view, this can only generate a fear of displacement by the "new" order signified by his son:

BASILIO: Yo, acudiendo a mis estudios,
            en ellos y en todo miro
            que Segismundo sería
            el hombre más atrevido,
            el príncipe más cruel
            y el monarca más impío,
            por quien su reino vendría
            a ser parcial, y diviso,
            escuela de las traiciones
            y academia de los vicios;
            y él, de su furor llevado,
            entre asombros y delitos,
            había de poner en mí
            las plantas, y yo rendido
            a sus pies me había de ver.
                        (lines 708–22)

(BASILIO: I discovered everywhere I looked
            that Segismundo would be
            the most imprudent of men,
            the cruelest prince, the most ungodly
            monarch, through whom this kingdom
            would be split and self-divided,
            a school for treason, academy
            of all vices, and he,
            swept by fury and outrageous crimes,

38. As Walter Cohen has pointed out, the opposition between father and son, which ultimately issues in the comic resolution of the Oedipal conflict, was not uncommon in Counter-Reformation drama, even though Calderón's earlier attempts to deal with this structure issued in tragic outcomes. See *Drama of a Nation: Public Theatre in Renaissance England and Spain* (Ithaca: Cornell University Press, 1985), 398. Once Calderón could imagine the political form in which a comic outcome to the conflict was possible, he never again found it necessary to return directly to the theme.

would trample on me, and while I lay
prostrate before him (what an effort
for me to say this!), would see
this white beard on my face
become a carpet for his feet.)

Whereas the usurpation of the father's place is a necessary part of the struggle to secure a modern form of authority, *La vida es sueño* forecloses that struggle, or resolves it in favor of the father's authority, which is nonetheless made contingent upon the magnanimity or *générosité* of the subject-son.[39]

In Calderón, the understanding of nature as a realm of conflict is set directly in tension with a conception of the state of nature as that *social* condition in which everyone fears dishonor and so must strive to establish his honor and prestige by any available means. In the Hobbesian or "liberal" version of absolutism, the hierarchical criteria of nobility, privilege, status, and caste that we find at stake in the theater of the Golden Age—and the vision of "natural order" on which these principles draw—are seen as irrelevant to considerations of moral, legal, or political personhood, which are founded on the right to represent and to be represented and to make contracts of association in the open marketplace. Insofar as civil society is embedded in the economic relations of the market, it recognizes no prior substantive restrictions on the terms of the agreements we may make. Calderónian drama is by contrast subtended by a social context in which the leveling effects of the city and the market presented an imminent threat to the dominant paradigm of patriarchal values, which were still in force at court. Thus the restoration of political order in the play, which depends on the possibility of recuperating an inherent nobility that has been placed in eclipse, but never entirely lost, closely mirrors the political reality of life at court:

BASILIO: Hijo, que tan noble acción
            otra vez en mis entrañas
            te engendra, príncipe eres.

39. Calderón's understanding of Segismundo's virtue represents a revision of Aristotle's notion of *megalopsuchia* that approaches Descartes's distinctively modern understanding of *générosité*. It focusses strongly on the will, though it does not make virtue subordinate to the will, or to the will alone.

A ti el laurel y la palma
se te deben; tú venciste;
corónete tus hazañas.
                    (lines 3244–49)

(BASILIO: My son—because your noble deed
             has re-engendered you in me—
             you are a prince indeed!
             The laurel and the palm belong to you.
             You've won the day. Your exploits crown you.)

At the same time, we see that the eclipse of the idea of an essential order of nature, on which the conception of intrinsic nobility rests, comes to generate a desire for what might best be called "pure prestige," as reflected in the competition between Astolfo and Estrella for the throne. As Norbert Elias and others have noted, the desire for prestige was particularly intensified at court. In the absence of a secure belief in a "natural ground" for social relations, the purely social desire for prestige can never fully be satisfied; but it can nonetheless be terminated by what amount to surreptitiously violent means when the "rightful" (i.e., "natural") heir is restored to the throne and when everyone (including Segismundo) can be induced to invest a single higher authority with a monopoly of power in the realm. This is to say that none of the "political" operations necessary to the restoration of Basilio's rule can be made successful unless his reign can be made to appear "popular" and not just "natural."[40] It must be popular in the broad sense because it must not threaten to advance the prestige of any one individual or group over any other. In this way, the competition for power and prestige among members of the court and pretenders to the throne can be put to rest. (As in *Fuenteovejuna,* the popular solution is one that represents a way of reinforcing the principles of honor while circumventing the hereditary nobility in favor of a direct alliance

40. Dian Fox has aptly pointed out the fact that Basilio's initial tyranny is a function, not just of his own actions, but of his courtiers, and especially of Clotaldo, who carries out his plan. (See *Kings in Calderón,* esp. 103–18.) Hence it is appropriate that the restoration and transformation of his rule should reflect a change in his subjects. Indeed, one could well argue that the (concealed) "subject" of this play—what is at stake in it—is not so much the King or Prince but the subjects themselves, in *their* relation to nature. The process of subject-constitution is, of course, a matter of history, and not of nature.

between the populace and the throne.) In *La vida es sueño*, the project to legitimize power requires proof: first, that Segismundo is the ally of a collective, popular cause; and second, that Segismundo agrees to pardon his father the King, thus reversing by an act of subjective will the willful and violent acts that had engendered disorder in the natural world. When news of Segismundo's popular revolt reaches Basilio, the King's reaction is to stay and risk death. But this risk is well worth it, since it turns out that Segismundo is inclined to re-establish his father's rule:

SEGISMUNDO: Señor, levanta.
                Dame tu mano; que ya
                que el cielo te desengaña
                de que has errado en el modo
                de vencerla, humilde aguarda
                mi cuello a que tú te vengues:
                rendido estoy a tus plantas.
                        (lines 3238–43)

(SEGISMUNDO: Rise, Sire,
                and give me your hand. Now
                that Heaven's disabused you
                of the illusion that you knew the way
                to overcome it, I offer
                myself up to you. Take
                your vengeance. I kneel before you.)

This is also to say that the identification of Segismundo's pretensions not with the desire for pure prestige characteristic of courtly society but with the "popular" consciousness and desire for order is justified in terms of Segismundo's neo-Scholastic "prudence"; as Rosaura says, "¡Qué discreto y qué prudente!" (What prudence and wisdom!) (line 3299). But the reestablishment of the political order nonetheless rests upon a troubling alliance between subjectivity and subjection. In this specific case, the result of Segismundo's revolution is not the modern, liberal form of "freedom," in which subjection is disguised under the authority or self-discipline of the subject-self, but a restructuring of patriarchal authority, minus many of the anxieties of prestige common at court. Thus the crowd cries for their freedom and for their (new) king:

Todos (*unos*):   ¡Viva nuestro invicto rey!
    (*otros*):   ¡Viva nuestra libertad!
Clarín: ¡La libertad y el rey vivan!
                (lines 3038–40)

(All: [*some*]:   Long live our unconquerable king!
    [*others*]:   Long live our freedom!
Clarín: Long live freedom and the king!)

Because the allegorization of nature's original authority as the sovereign's absolute power is a phenomenon with rigorously historical roots—because the sovereignty of the absolute monarch is itself a consequence of the becoming historical of the natural world—Calderón's recourse to ancient philosophy (e.g., to the Aristotelian doctrine of prudence and to the Platonic conception of beauty as the sensuous manifestation of an immutable realm of Ideas) does not represent a freely chosen philosophical or "theoretical" position. Rather, it represents a position of ideological resistance with respect to the problem of history itself. Because the traces of this problem are also figured in the form of an allegory in the *autos sacramentales* it may be useful to sketch some of the differences here. In *El gran teatro del mundo,* which was written for the Corpus Christi stage, the self-consciousness of dramatic representation is less a sign of the fundamental uninterpretability of historical phenomena than an indication of a residual faith in the possibility of attributing a fixed moral meaning to the contingencies of earthly life. For A. A. Parker, allegory in this *auto* takes the form of "an analysis of human life in terms of social classes: an analysis of the relation of social classes to each other and to the final end of human existence, and of the nature of a moral life in terms of individual social status. It is thus not primarily a 'philosophical' but a 'sociological' *auto*" (*The Allegorical Drama of Calderón,* 113). But by virtue of the fact that the social inequalities among human beings are seen as *merely* contingent, allegory enables the dramatist and his public to conceal the role of power in configuring the differences that do exist. The point is not so much that there is not a moral level on which the King and the Pobre (Poor Man) are equal, but that the moral allegory tends to explain away the traces of power that govern the differences between them. As Parker writes, "during Calderón's lifetime there was being vigorously expounded and adopted in countries less reactionary than Spain the doctrine, destined to have such revolutionary and world-wide consequences, that 'man's self-love is God's providence' and that the pursuit of economic self-interest is the law of nature. Calderón could not conceive of individual morality as being distinct from social morality. His traditional Christianity is the antithesis of the puritan and liberal individualism which came to lay all stress on an individual morality, on the individual's acquisition of the economic virtues to the disparagement of the significance of the social structure" (*The Allegorical Drama of Calderón,* 150–51).

What Parker forgets to notice is that such a position virtually required a faith in the legitimacy of the status quo. Although any example of social inequality could serve to make the point, the case is strikingly true in the case of the Poor Man, where Calderón's interpretation carries forward staunchly traditional attitudes. Describing those attitudes, José Antonio Maravall said that "the resigned and submissive poor man was a necessary and important figure in medieval society: in principle he was an example of great Christian virtues. . . . Poverty revealed itself in the Middle Ages as a pillar of resistance, which supported the socio-economic structure of traditional society. Religious faith and poverty go together in the doctrines that were preached from medieval pulpits."[41] But since changes in the social structure made it difficult to continue simply to presuppose the moral value of poverty, it was necessary to bolster the idea that social inequality provided an opportunity for proving Christian virtue. And it was here that the allegorical idea of theater became central. In *El gran teatro del mundo,* the allegorical motif of theater itself serves fundamentally conservative social purposes by referring the conditions of social inequality to the justice of a higher moral order; the work promotes a vision of social disorder supplanted and replaced by moral order on the transcendental plane.

In *La vida es sueño,* however, we find the more complex phenomenon of resistance to the effects of the historicization of the natural world. This resistance shows up in the form of a drama that attempts to disavow the fully contingent nature of the events with which the *Trauerspiel* or modern tragedy must deal. Whether or not this work or any other *comedia* can in fact be called a "tragedy" has been a subject

41. "El pobre resignado y sumiso era una figura importante y necesaria en la sociedad medieval: en principio era ejemplo de grandes virtudes cristianas. . . . La pobreza se revela como un resistente pilar en el que se apoya la estructura económico-social de la sociedad tradicional." José Antonio Maravall, *La literatura picaresca desde la historia social (siglos XVI y XVII)* (Madrid: Taurus, 1986), 23, 25.

of heated discussion among critics since at least A. A. Parker's 1962 article on the subject of Calderónian tragedy.[42] For the most part, critics engaging in this debate have been preoccupied with a series of issues that are themselves indebted to a neo-Aristotelian and ahistorical perspective. Parker, for instance, accepted the principle of "poetic justice" as a veritable tenet of the Golden Age theater. But none of these studies confronted the possibility of tragedy in the Golden Age in a truly historical light and none saw that the function of Calderónian drama is to enact first the destruction and then the reconstitution of the theocratic paradigm of the culture in which it is embedded. Deconsecration is precisely the function Benjamin attributes to the *Trauerspiel*, and it is a position that Lukács similarly identified when he argued that "tragedy destroys the hierarchy of the higher worlds; in it there is no God and no demon."[43] Calderón acknowledges the imminent possibility of tragedy from the very beginning of *La vida es sueño*, where Segismundo's imprisonment and the conditions of Rosaura's dishonor signal a crisis in the order of succession to the throne that in turn reflect a crisis in the dominant paradigm of authority. As a result of these crises, it is no longer apparent that the underlying political order can be made legitimate at all.

La vida es sueño opens itself to the possibility of tragedy only to foreclose it in the end. The play concludes with a triumphant restoration of order that could well be viewed as overdetermined. And yet the issue is not so simple as it might appear; Calderón's attempt to foreclose or avoid tragedy fails to seal off the effects of history once and for all. In Ruth El Saffar's phrasing, comedy in Calderón is simply tragedy postponed.[44] In *La vida es sueño* the traces of history show up through power's indelible effects. In marking these effects, I would first point out that the rebel soldier who frees Segismundo from the dungeon is in

42. See Alexander A. Parker, "Towards a Definition of Calderonian Tragedy," *Bulletin of Hispanic Studies* 39 (1982): 227–37; Edwin S. Morby, "Some Observations on 'Tragedia' and 'Tragicomedia' in Lope," *Hispanic Review* 11 (1943): 185–209; and A. Irvine Watson, "*El pintor de su deshonra* and the Neo-Aristotelian Theory of Tragedy," in *Critical Essays on the Theatre of Calderón*, ed. Bruce Wardropper (New York: New York University Press, 1965).

43. Lukács, *Theory of the Novel*, 87. Moretti echoes the Lukácsean view when he writes that "tragedy disentitled the absolute monarch to all ethical and rational legitimation. Having deconsecrated the king, tragedy made it possible to decapitate him" (*Signs Taken for Wonders*, 42).

44. El Saffar, "Violante: The Place of Rejection," in *The Prince in the Tower*, 170.

turn imprisoned by the magnanimous prince; this is an episode that offers sufficient evidence of the inability of absolute power to conceal its own violent basis. More specifically, the rebel soldier's fate is a reminder of the violence that the system of absolutism cannot eliminate. As a sign that the new regime is not unsullied by violence, we might well expect him to be an occasion of horror, which Julia Kristeva associates with various impurities and remainders: "remainders are residues of something but especially of someone. They pollute on account of incompleteness."[45] And yet there is little horror associated with this figure in Calderón's play, and certainly none of the *phobos* that Aristotle designated as necessary for tragedy. On the contrary, the punishment of the rebel soldier is a sign of the repression of tragedy in Calderón. Second, I would signal the fact that the avoidance of tragedy in this play allows sovereign power to be sustained through a series of controlled theatrical effects. As a signal instance, consider the fact that the Platonic "recognition" of Rosaura's beauty, which makes possible Segismundo's "aesthetic education" over the course of the play (literally, his education through sense experience), is a function of the feeling of wonder or awe (*admiratio*) that is produced in him. But Segismundo's wonder is not the response to a nature seen in its "original" condition; on the contrary, it is a function of his re-cognition of Rosaura. If the originary force of beauty was "lost" with the passage from nature to history, then Segismundo's response to Rosaura is equivalent to an allegorical repetition of an originary awe. As Segismundo responds to Rosaura's beauty, he becomes a surrogate for the spectator-subjects of the play, who are meant to be enlightened politically as they too are held in awe. Moreover, this process of awe-provoking recognition, which is not originary, destroys the closure and finality that *La vida es sueño* might otherwise achieve and threatens to become mere repetition:

> Con cada vez que te veo
> nueva admiración me das,
> y cuando te miro más,
> aun más mirarte deseo.
>   (lines 223–35)

45. Julia Kristeva, *Powers of Honor: An Essay on Abjection*, trans. Leon S. Roudiez (New York: Columbia University Press, 1982), 76.

(Each time I look at you
the vision overwhelms me
so that I yearn to look again.)

The wonder and awe with which Segismundo sees Rosaura here are direct counterweights to the horror provoked by Segismundo's "monstrous" condition at the opening of the play; in "educating" the monstrous beast, Calderón attempts to replace horror by wonder.

At the same time, the theatrical effect of Segismundo's recognition of Rosaura serves to distance Calderón from those forms of allegorizing that simply attempted to represent some form of the Great Chain of Being, in part by showing that mind, or self-consciousness, is inevitably affected by or infected with some form of "matter."[46] Already in Plotinus's *Enneads,* in Macrobius's *Commentary on the Dream of Scipio,* and in the Neoplatonic traditions that Calderón must have known, there was a recognition that the "imprinting of beauty" on the soul could not occur entirely in the abstract, but must occur through some visible language or script. Indeed, it is only for this reason that nature could be "read." By Calderón's time, the materiality of the process of inscription had already become a conventional topic of literature, in which the literality of the writing of beauty was widely acknowledged also to stand for literature; literature, by assimilation to this script, was thought to stand for beauty itself. Consider, for example, Garcilaso's sonnet 5: "Escrito 'sta en mi alma vuestro gesto / y cuanto

46. Mary Gaylord provides a compelling account of the strictly idealizing and orthodox view that I am suggesting is problematic in Calderón when she writes that "in these ideal arrangements, according to which the role of each part in service to the whole is determined by its position on the Great Scale of Being, man's superior faculties preside over his baser parts, legislating their subordination in service to his (and the whole's) higher ends. For Aristotle and his Scholastic followers in Golden Age Spain, this paradigm incarnated nothing less than the order of nature and was, naturally, used as a blueprint not only to structure the body politic from household to empire but also to describe (or prescribe) the structure of knowledge and experience. And that structure simultaneously informs the very structure of consciousness, which in turn is a sort of consciousness of the structure in question, that is, *an awareness of the rule of mind over matter.*" See "The Whole Body of Fable with All of its Members: Cervantes, Pinciano, and Freud," in *Quixotic Desire: Psychoanalytic Perspectives on Cervantes,* ed. Ruth Anthony El Saffar and Diana de Armas Wilson (Ithaca: Cornell University Press, 1993), 132; my emphasis. An overview of these and related notions of world-order can be found in Leo Spitzer, *Classical and Christian Ideas of World Harmony,* ed. Anna Granville Hatcher (Baltimore: Johns Hopkins University Press, 1963) and in A. O. Lovejoy, *The Great Chain of Being* (Cambridge: Harvard University Press, 1971).

yo escribir de vos deseo: / vos sola lo escribistes; yo lo leo" (Your visage is written on my soul, / and also all that I wish to write about you / you alone write it; I read it) (lines 1–3).[47]

And yet in Calderón it is clear that "beauty" means nothing if it is not affiliated with political power. Correspondingly, power must acknowledge its dependence on aesthetic modes of presentation, including those cultivated in the theater. This is the thought that explains why Calderón's plays cannot simply be deciphered "philosophically" but must be interpreted theatrically and aesthetically. Just as "nature" for Calderón is neither an originary place of goodness and beauty, nor, as some have suggested, a term that anchors a set of conventional "ideas" about goodness and beauty, but a historically produced and rhetorically articulated phenomenon incorporating the prior fact and occasion of transgression, so too sovereignty in this play sustains itself not on the basis of what can be claimed of "nature," nor on the basis of any explicit moral or philosophical beliefs, but rather through the transformation of its very power into an aesthetic effect.[48] In this case, what can be said for power can be said for morality as well: the moral quality of the exemplary character, who is meant to compel belief, takes on theatrical proportions as Segismundo calls attention to the affective impact of "staged" events:

SEGISMUNDO: Sirva de ejemplo este raro
espectáculo, esta extraña

47. In England, Philip Sidney plays with these figures liberally in *Astrophil and Stella*.

48. Compare Angus Fletcher, who argues that the authoritarian base of allegory became prominent during the Renaissance, where the meaning of the term "cosmos" as "ornament" was powerful enough to embrace all forms of adornment and dress: "Nowhere is this authoritarian base more evident than during that period when rhetoricians most vigorously developed the concept of the 'garment of style,' which I take to be the common *generalized* form of the theory of *kosmos*. During the Elizabethan period it is apparent that the Court, with its real political power on the one hand and its ideal, moral, and aesthetic sanctions on the other, could set the standard of 'dress' that would be the pattern for rhetorical as well as actual costume" (*Allegory*, 136–37). Fletcher goes on to claim for the English masque what could be claimed for the *autos* of Calderón, provided one recognizes that the interests Fletcher attributes to the secular state in England would have to be redescribed in order to fit the theocratic Spanish context: "The Renaissance drama actually develops a type of dramatic literature which is based on the 'cosmetic' use of ornament. The masques, designed and presented in the most lavish richness of decor, are intended to praise and reinforce the high standing of leaders of the state. They do this both verbally and visually. The words of the masque are allegorical and in effect explicate the costuming, the dancing, and the background scenery which give a dazzling aesthetic surface to this art form" (138).

admiración, este horror,
este prodigio; pues nada
es más, que llegar a ver
con prevenciones tan varias,
rendido a mis pies un padre,
y atropellado a un monarca.
(lines 3224–31)

(SEGISMUNDO: Let this strangest
of spectacles, this most amazing
moment, this awesome, prodigious scene
serve as an example. Because
nothing better shows how,
after so much had been done
to prevent its happening,
a father and a king lies subject
at his own son's feet.)

In *La vida es sueño* the allegory of absolute power built on the edifice of a disenchanted, historicized, and violently social nature is theatrically sustained. It is here that Calderón's theater responds, perhaps unwittingly, to the anti-Machiavellian political theorists of the time, such as Pedro de Rivadeneira and Diego de Saavedra Fajardo.[49] In Calderón, the theater itself becomes an aesthetic vehicle through which absolute power attempts simultaneously to perpetuate itself and to avoid recognition of itself as a thoroughly aesthetic form. At the same time, Calderón suggests that Segismundo's subjectivity—as measured by the increasing self-consciousness he gains throughout the play—is of a piece with his subjection to his father's sovereign authority. As I have shown, the process of allegorization that attempts to mask the absolutism of sovereign power represents a form of the subject's "subjectivity." It is a process that allows us to see that once the essential order of nature is imagined as withdrawn, then power—in Calderón's case, an absolute and aesthetic power—rushes in to fill any gaps that may remain.

---

49. See J. A. Fernández-Santamaría, *Reason of State and Statecraft in Spanish Political Thought, 1595–1640* (Lanham, Md.: University Press of America, 1983).

4

The Subject of Control in Counter-Reformation Spain

In a 1946 essay entitled "An Introduction to the Ideology of the Baroque in Spain," Stephen Gilman advanced the view that the artistic style characteristic of the late sixteenth and early seventeenth centuries in Spain was the reflection of a series of doctrinal premises that had come into power beginning roughly with the Council of Trent. The "ideological" force of the baroque style could best be measured by the degree to which the art of that period succeeded in communicating the Counter-Reformation orthodoxy to the public at large.[1] For evidence of his views, Gilman drew on some of the more dramatic representations of Counter-Reformation ideology in Spanish baroque literature and thought. Looking at the controversial area of the theology of free will

1. Gilman, "An Introduction to the Ideology of the Baroque in Spain." *Symposium* 1 (1946): 82–107.

and grace (as exemplified in the *de auxiliis* debate), as well as at the literature of asceticism as represented in the works of authors like Malón de Chaide (*La conversión de la Magdalena*), Luis de Granada (*Guía de pecadores*), Ignacio de Loyola (*Ejercicios espirituales*), and Hernando de Zárate (*Discursos de la paciencia cristiana*), Gilman described how the "ideological" invocations of a sacred infinity and eternity exerted a disorienting pressure on representations of space, time, and substance, transforming the placid Renaissance landscapes of Garcilaso's swains into a baroque cosmos of grand theological drama, promising eternal salvation but also threatening spiritual doom and gloom. As critics from Heinrich Wölfflin to Jean Rousset and Gilles Deleuze have all noted, the baroque is marked by sharp divisions of space, but this division is never clear or clear-cut, in part because the spiritual principle underlying it is never as absolute as one might wish. The realm of the spirit, though in principle separated from the temporal and secular world, continues to exert a visible pressure on the realm of inner-worldly values; in the paintings of an artist like El Greco these are manifestly distorted in its light.[2] Turning finally to the literature of moral repentance and to the figure of the "caído en la cuenta," Gilman described the spiritual model of the Spanish baroque as "ascetic" in the sense that it idealized a repressive "victory over self" in the moral battle of the soul against the seductions of the world. The point is not lost on Calderón's Segismundo, who says in act 3 of *La vida es sueño:*

> Pues que ya vencer aguarda
> mi valor grandes victorias,
> hoy ha de ser la más alta
> vencerme a mí.
> (lines 3251–54)

(Since my courage now awaits great victories, the greatest one today will be the victory over myself.)

Insofar as the fundamental asceticism that underlies this interest in self-control leads in Calderón to a distinctive other-worldliness, the

2. Wölfflin, *Principles of Art History,* trans. M. D. Hottinger (New York: Holt, 1932); Jean Rousset, *La littérature de l'âge baroque en France* (Paris: Corti, 1953); Gilles Deleuze, *Le Pli: Leibnitz et le Baroque* (Paris: Minuit, 1988), trans. as *The Fold; Leibnitz and the Baroque,* by Tom Conley (Minneapolis: University of Minnesota Press, 1993).

spirituality characteristic of Counter-Reformation Spain could be placed in contrast both to the inner-worldly asceticism that developed in conjunction with the Protestant ethic described by Max Weber, as well as to the measured worldliness of the French *honnête homme,* for whom meaningful intercourse with the world could be rationally regulated by the principles of decorum, and the seductions of the senses thereby resisted and controlled.[3]

Already in 1946 Gilman recognized the poverty of the concept of "ideology" when taken in its literal sense, as the analysis of ideas and their cultural consequences. In place of "ideology" Gilman proposed to substitute a study of what in German is called "effective [*Wirklich*] history," which for Gilman was oriented in terms of the life-experience (*Erlebnis*) of an individual:

> No rigid sequence of cause and effect can be traced between the religious movement and its ultimate artistic expression, since innumerable economic, sociological and political changes interweave themselves into the texture of the period. ("Introduction to the Ideology of the Baroque," 83)

> By [ideology] I mean not only a system or complex of ideas but also a cohesive system of values. This latter, alone, could perhaps be referred to by using the technical term "axiology," but this, also, would not carry the full meaning desired. Actually the thought lying behind "ideology" is something corresponding to the German *Erlebnis,* that is to say, a living totality of points of view, attitudes toward life, and patterns of thought occurring in those generations of *men actively partisan to the Counter-Reformation.* ("Introduction to the Ideology of the Baroque," 98; my emphasis)

---

3. The baroque is often seen as marked by a series of specific dualisms and divisions. In *The Fold,* for instance, Deleuze describes the complex dualism characteristic of the baroque in the following terms (his own and Leibnitz's): "the Baroque differentiates its folds in two ways, by moving along two infinities, as if infinity were composed of two stages or floors: the pleats of matter, and the folds in the soul. Below, matter is amassed according to a first type of fold, and then organized according to a second type, to the extent its part constitutes organs that are 'differently folded and more or less developed.' Above, the soul sings the glory of God inasmuch as it follows its own folds, but without succeeding entirely in developing them, since 'this communication stretches out indefinitely' " (1). The references to Leibnitz are to the *Monadology* (sect. 61).

And yet, as this final phrase perhaps all too clearly reveals, an awareness of the depth to which ideology penetrates all levels of cultural life and, similarly, any strongly defined notion of Counter-Reformation culture in relation to the problems of ideological power or cultural control, remained external to his approach. Indeed, Gilman himself abandoned his interest in "ideology" in exchange for the views of Américo Castro on the decisive importance of caste values in the formation of Spanish culture. And perhaps equally as important for assessing the direction of this work, the study of "ideology" was conceived as constituting the merely preparatory labor necessary for the kind of biographical and existentialist criticism whose supervening goal was to uncover the relationship between the artist qua individual and the social values that provided the "vital context" for the creative act. As Gilman's reconstructive biography of Fernando de Rojas makes clear, history plays a role in this picture only insofar as it is biographically relevant.[4]

It is only in relatively recent years that a new understanding of ideology has made its way into studies of the history and literature of the Spanish baroque. In part through the work of critics associated with the journal *Ideologies and Literatures* and, more recently, with the regularized publication of *Hispanic Issues,* ideological analysis of the culture of the Golden Age has moved increasingly to the fore.[5] The difference between the understanding of "ideology" reflected in this recent work and that of Gilman's 1946 essay, however, is clear. Whereas the concept of "ideology" functioned for critics of Gilman's generation largely as a means to relate the doctrinal pronouncements of the Catholic bishops at Trent concerning the issues of free will, salvation, and the theology of grace, to a series of stylistic tendencies prevalent in art and literature during subsequent years in Spain, the work of more recent critics has been strongly shaped by an awareness of the fact that ideas do not, in and of themselves, play a causal role in culture and so can of themselves serve as the basis for interpretive claims of a relatively limited scope. For those historians of Spanish culture who have come to take their bearings by Marx, Max Weber, and Foucault, the challenge is rather to understand the role of ideology, which works through the

---

4. *The Spain of Fernando de Rojas* (Princeton: Princeton University Press, 1972).

5. See also the volume edited by Wlad Godzich and Nicholas Spadaccini, *Literature Among Discourses: The Spanish Golden Age* (Minneapolis: University of Minnesota Press, 1986), and also Antonio Gómez-Moriana, *Discourse Analysis as Sociocriticism: The Spanish Golden Age* (Minneapolis: University of Minnesota Press, 1993).

symbolic articulation of power, within culture as a whole. By focusing on shifts in economic modes of production (as in Marx), on the mediating power of social institutions (as in Max Weber), and on practices directed toward the body (as in Foucault), these critics allow us to see ideology as involving all the varied means through which symbolic forms of power are brought to bear on cultural life.

It is thus not altogether surprising to see that contemporary interests in the study of ideology have turned toward the questions of culture and control in Counter-Reformation Spain, if only because of all the phenomena associated with the Spanish Golden Age none offers so varied and dramatic a demonstration of the social, political, and aesthetic means through which the symbolic effects of power were brought to bear on material life, and none offers so many challenges to the views that would see Spanish culture of the Counter-Reformation as the simple reflection of the conservative doctrinal positions originally mapped at the Council of Trent. The collection of essays assembled by Anne J. Cruz and Mary Elizabeth Perry entitled *Culture and Control in Counter-Reformation Spain* is a case in point.[6] While attempting to bridge the disciplinary gap between the fields of history and literature by placing the work of historians alongside that of literary critics sensitive to the social and cultural embeddedness of texts, these essays aim to redefine our understanding of the Counter-Reformation in Spain by a re-reading of culture in terms of the "control mechanisms" that govern human behavior and, I might add, that serve to direct power's material effects.

On the one hand, these essays suggest that cultural control in Counter-Reformation Spain was produced by the inscription of orthodox beliefs in the public at large, in such a way that material culture served to reinforce a series of canonical church positions. For instance, Jean-Pierre Dedieu argues that the growing concern of the church for religious education served to promote an orthodox ideology among the masses and thus to "socialize" a heterogeneous population.[7] Religious "education" thus becomes a more or less direct mechanism for the

6. *Culture and Control in Counter-Reformation Spain* (Minneapolis: University of Minnesota Press / *Hispanic Issues*, 1992). See also *Cultural Encounters: The Impact of the Inquisition in Spain and the New World*, ed. Mary Elizabeth Perry and Anne J. Cruz (Berkeley and Los Angeles: University of California Press, 1991), and Mary Elizabeth Perry, *Gender and Disorder in Early Modern Seville* (Princeton: Princeton University Press, 1990).

7. Dedieu, " 'Christianization' in New Castile: Catechism, Communion, Mass, and Confirmation in the Toledo Archbishopric, 1540–1650," in *Culture and Control*, 1–24.

enforcement of theocratic power. Sara T. Nalle shows how the municipal government and the cathedral of Cuenca used baroque celebrations of power in order to popularize the cult of Saint Julian, which had been all but abandoned since medieval times; in the process she leads us to recognize that these celebrations served not just as expressions of belief but also as ways of directing beliefs.[8] Jaime Contreras for his part stresses that the most powerful and threatening organ of control of all, the Inquisition, marginalized New Christians by excluding them from positions at all levels of power.[9] Yet it is precisely in the face of examples such as these, where the evidence for control is so explicit and direct, that the constellation of problems described under the heading of "culture and control" is vulnerable to the effects of a telescoping of theoretical terms by prematurely identifying Counter-Reformation culture with its basis in orthodox religious belief.[10] At the very least, such a conception of control suggests a more or less unquestioned faith in the relationship between religious doctrine and the patterns of behavior that such doctrine was used to encourage and support. If this is the case, then the notion of ideology as a kind of hidden but nonetheless systematic distortion at work within culture proves superfluous for historical analysis; one need not account for a hidden source of power, or for a power that masks itself in its effects, but only for the mechanisms by which a power in one sphere of society (e.g., the religious) exerts control upon another (e.g., the literary).

The work of critics and historians like Alison Weber, Gwendolyn Barnes-Karol, and Jorge Klor de Alva suggests that a historical analysis of culture must be supplemented, first, by an understanding of culture's symbolic basis and, second, by an investigation of the psychological mechanisms of control and of power's subversive and sometimes contradictory effects.[11] For instance, Klor de Alva suggests the ways in which

8. Nalle, "A Saint for All Seasons: The Cult of San Julián," in *Culture and Control,* 25–50.

9. Contreras, "Aldermen and Judaizers: Cryptojudaism, Counter-Reformation, and Local Power," in *Culture and Control,* 93–123. On the failure of Inquisitorial authority in the New World see J. Jorge Klor de Alva, "Colonizing Souls: The Failure of the Indian Inquisition and the Rise of Penitential Discipline," in *Cultural Encounters: The Impact of the Inquisition in Spain and the New World,* 3–22.

10. See, for example, Werner Weisbach, *Der Barock als Kunst der Gegenreformation* (Berlin: P. Cassirer, 1921).

11. Alison Weber, "Santa Teresa, Demonologist," in *Culture and Control,* 171–95; Gwendolyn Barnes-Karol, "Religious Oratory in a Culture of Control," in *Culture and Control,* 51–77; J. Jorge Klor de Alva, "Colonizing Souls: The Failure of the Indian

religious practices came to exercise a subtle psychological control over New World subjects where more direct Inquisitorial methods failed. And Weber suggests how in the case of Saint Teresa the conditions of an authoritarian and patriarchal culture produced a contradictorily rational defense of the authenticity of mystical experience. To wit, Weber describes Saint Teresa as a "dissident demonologist" within an orthodox culture and, in this respect, as occupying for strategic reasons a position that was both conservative *and* marginal with respect to the dominant discourses of her day.[12] In Weber's analysis, Saint Teresa adopts a full-blown skepticism toward mystical claims in order to *preserve* a confidence in women's capacity to identify and experience a genuinely mystical spirituality. As these and other examples suggest, it would be hazardous indeed to form direct or categorical associations between particular modes of consciousness (whether orthodox in the doctrinal sense, mystical, or demonic) and any particular class or gender of individuals, even within a culture as apparently authoritarian and closed as that of Counter-Reformation Spain. Moreover, if Counter-Reformation Spain was in fact a culture of remarkably uniform authoritarian control, then it would not be altogether surprising to find that those who may have been most marginalized within it might also have been most strongly motivated to find ways of resisting its mechanisms of control.

In what follows here, I suggest that an analysis of any culture's "mechanisms of control" requires a corresponding analysis of the "subjects of control." For if culture can indeed be studied in terms of its "control mechanisms" then it is necessary also to ask, Who were its subjects and how did they become *subject to* control? What at the symbolic level of society would suggest their desire for such control? I would suggest that if we are to understand the complex question of the ideology of the baroque in terms of the relationship between "culture" and "control" in Counter-Reformation Spain we shall need to voice a series of questions about the relationship between the organized re-

---

Inquisition and the Rise of Penitential Discipline." See also María Helena Sánchez Ortega, "Woman as Source of 'Evil' in Counter-Reformation Spain," in *Culture and Control*, 196–215. She shows how the frequent association of women with the devil created an atmosphere of fear and dread whose effects were at least as disturbing as the allegedly demonic powers attributed to women.

12. Compare Mary Elizabeth Perry's analysis of Saint Teresa in *Gender and Disorder in Early Modern Seville*, 84–89.

sources of power and the formation of the (social, historical, psychological) subjects of control. The question Who is in control? (which may be
given a summary answer by reference to the "ideologies" of the church
and the state), must be supplemented by another, less easily answered
series of questions: Who is controlled? and Why does the subject desire
to be controlled? It is only by locating the links between cultural
control and the matter of self-control that we can use recent shifts in
Hispanism's understanding of "ideology" as a way to go beyond the
tasks of locating the material consequences of ideas or of describing
the various mechanisms of psychological control to a less reductive
understanding of the various modes of representation through which
individuals adopted a cultural identity as subject-selves.

＊　＊　＊

While my approach to these issues shares certain of the perspectives on
the crisis-structure of the Spanish baroque first put forward by José
Antonio Maravall (and taken up by, among others, John Beverley and
Mary Elizabeth Perry),[13] my principal thesis differs from Maravall's in
significant respects. Maravall regards the phenomenon of the Spanish
baroque as bound up with the urbanization of life and with the creation
of a "sociedad de masas" that was dependent on the increasingly
capitalistic environment of the sixteenth and seventeenth centuries.[14]

13. John Beverley, "On the Concept of the Spanish Literary Baroque," in *Culture and Control*, 216–30; Perry, *Gender and Disorder in Early Modern Seville*, describes the Counter-Reformation as a crisis of the patriarchal structure of Spanish (or at least Sevillian) society, a period in which "officials had to respond to a growing central government, an expanding empire, developing capitalism, increasing population, external attacks on the Church, an intensification of ecclesiastical attempts to impose orthodoxy, and a changing local economy tied every more strongly to imperial interests." She goes on to say that "their response was to strengthen their authority through a political system that was closed to women, through guild regulations that multiplied to restrict the economic activities of women, and through more careful enclosure of women in convent, home, or brothel." She concludes that "for officials of this period, restoration of the social order required the sword of authority repaired and the wandering woman restrained" (13).

14. José Antonio Maravall, *La cultura del barroco* (Barcelona: Ariel, 1975); *The Culture of the Baroque: Analysis of a Historical Structure*, trans. Terry Cochran (Minneapolis: University of Minnesota Press, 1986). See also Maravall, "From the Renaissance to the Baroque," in *Literature Among Discourses*, 3–40. For a skeptical review of Maravall's work from the perspective of a more traditional historian, see J. H. Elliott, "Concerto Barroco," *New York Review of Books* (9 April 1987): 26–29.

Those who follow Maravall's thesis most closely tend to agree that the culture of the Spanish baroque must be understood as a conservative formation whose ideological support of the status quo was produced in response to the economic crisis resulting from the transition from feudalism to capitalism. Beverley sees the baroque, not implausibly, as Janus-like, with one face turned toward the "sunset of feudalism," the other looking out onto the "dawn of capitalism"; and Maravall himself argues that "the baroque was a culture . . . consisting in the response given by active groups within a society that had entered into a severe crisis in association with *critical economic fluctuations*" (*The Culture of the Baroque,* 19). Maravall's understanding of the "baroque" depends on a thesis about the dynamic interaction between historical and cultural epochs. For him, the "crisis-structure" of the baroque derives its significance from a prior moment of "expansion" more or less equivalent to a "Renaissance" whose autonomy cannot be presupposed.[15] (In the long essay "From the Renaissance to the Baroque: The Diphasic Schema of a Social Crisis," Maravall explains that this diphasic model is patterned after the work of the economic historian Kondratieff.) By contrast, I would suggest that any attempt to align the doctrinal groundwork of the Counter-Reformation with the cultural practices commonly identified as "baroque" in order to account for the lasting influence of Counter-Reformation ideas must articulate the problem of cultural control in terms of the question of subject-formation in early modern Spain. Most emphatically, it must incorporate into the questions of subjectivity and control the concept of *formation* that would satisfy the need to explain the culture of the baroque as an ongoing process with direct implications for our understanding of the relationship between Spanish culture and modernity, and not just as one that developed out of or responded to a prior "Renaissance." To introduce the category of subjectivity in this debate is not to suggest that we should return to a theory of the individual as freely constituting the world, or that we should once again analyze the problem of self-consciousness in relation to the history of ideas; indeed, it is precisely such notions that a concept of subject-*formation* would be used to argue against. Moreover, by focusing on the category of the "subject"

15. For example, Maravall considers the Spanish Renaissance a "Renaissance by emulation" or by "imitation." See his *Estudios de historia del pensamiento español* (Madrid: Cultura Hispánica, 1983).

and on the mechanisms of its formation, we may be able to articulate the links between power and representation in a way that Maravall's concentration on the baroque as a historical category may not allow. And in addressing subjects as formed we may be able to link large-scale transformations in historical structures with the changing modes of psychology and the shifting patterns of belief that determined the nature of social relations in early modern Spain.

The crisis of subjectivity in early modern Spain can be described as the product of a familiar *structural* conflict between two distinct value-systems, each with its own psychology and each with modes of representation proper to it. On the one hand a hierarchical society, in which actions were legitimized according to a series of naturalistic principles, and in which social functions and roles were sedimented into near-static patterns, was confronted with modes of thinking, feeling, acting, and evaluating based on the premises of a psychologizing "individualism," in which the social order was dominated by what Weber described as "rationalized" structures, and in which the dominant cultural ethos was that of auto-regulation or *self*-control. In what are sometimes taken as the paradigmatic instances of subject-formation in early modern Europe—in England, Germany, and France—the conflict between these two value-structures is generally conceived as having been "successfully" resolved. At the very least, what Hans Blumenberg called the "legitimacy of the modern age"[16] is staked on claims of the independence of the subject from the historical questions that this category may in fact have been invented to answer. Elsewhere I have argued that this understanding lends a semblance of false necessity to the pattern of modernization taken as representative for the West.[17] Here I would point out that the particular case of Spain is inherently more complex than a large-scale analysis of European modernity can represent, and also that the powers at work in the process of subject-formation in early modern Spain were unique. Social conditions in early modern Spain were not particularly amenable to the formation of individuals who

16. See Hans Blumenberg, *The Legitimacy of the Modern Age,* trans. Robert M. Wallace (Cambridge: MIT Press, 1983).
17. See A. J. Cascardi, *The Subject of Modernity* (Cambridge: Cambridge University Press, 1992), for a correction to the views expressed in Blumenberg, *Legitimacy.* The term "false necessity" is drawn from Roberto Unger, *False Necessity: Anti-Necessitarian Social Theory in the Service of Radical Democracy* (Cambridge: Cambridge University Press, 1987).

could be "hailed" as modern subject-selves.[18] As Barnes's study of religious oratory helps makes clear, however, practices derived from Counter-Reformation beliefs nonetheless counted on the existence of subjects who would be responsive to relatively "modern" methods of psychological persuasion and control directed at the subject's intimate and interior psychological space.[19] Thus when the Inquisitorial methods failed to produce sufficient numbers of conversions among New World subjects, for instance, the church turned to more subtle methods of coercion. Drawing on the work of Foucault in *Discipline and Punish,* Jorge Klor de Alva writes that

> an effective proselytizing strategy had to go far beyond violent or physical coercion, the performance of baptisms, or the teaching of the rudiments of the Christian doctrine. It had to penetrate into every corner of native life, especially those intimate spaces where personal loyalties were forged, commitments were assessed, and collective security concerns were weighed against individual ambitions. Thus, "the invasion within" could not be done by scare tactics . . . but rather by shifting the moral gears to produce social and political effects that favored the interests

18. The notion of the subject as "hailed" is Louis Althusser's. George Mariscal treats this process at length and with specific reference to the Althusserian theory of "interpellation" in *Contradictory Subjects: Quevedo, Cervantes, and Seventeenth-Century Spanish Culture* (Ithaca: Cornell University Press, 1991).

19. Miguel Herrero García cites a stunning passage from Fray Angel Manrique that explains the ways in which the control of conscience depended upon the internalization of the power of the preacher's living voice:

> Oiréis un Sermón a un predicador, y paréceos tan bien que no juzgáis palabra por perdida ni hay cosa que dejar en todas sus razones. Aficionado de él y de ellas, pedís el papel y leéis, y no os parece la mitad de bien que cuando le oísteis. ¿En qué está eso? En que el predicador daba vida a lo que decía con la voz, con las acciones, con el modillo de decir, con los meneos; pero en el papel es imposible escribirse nada de esto.

> (You will hear a preacher's Sermon, and it seems so fine that you consider no word to have been wasted nor anything to be lacking in all his proofs. Fond of him and of his words, you ask for the paper and read it, and it does not seem half as good as when you heard it. Why is this so? The preacher animated what he said with his voice, with his actions, with his style of preaching, with his movement; but it is impossible to put any of this down on paper.)

Herrero García, *Sermonario clásico* (Madrid: Escelicer, 1947), lvii. I draw this reference and translation from Barnes-Karol, "Religious Oratory," 71.

in stability and productivity of those in power. An operative indoctrination that could produce such results had to begin with the widespread, but localized, imposition of a constant regime of moral calisthenics through corporal and magical punishments (like the threat of the fires of Hell). These exercises, backed by the threat of the provisors, had to have as their aim the retraining of the individual in order for him or her to internalize a Christian form of self-discipline that would ultimately make external force secondary or unnecessary.[20]

The production of self-discipline through religious-ascetic practices must in turn be understood in the context of a restructuring of interests that were originally quite revisionary, even "modernizing," and sometimes heterodox, in nature. For example, it is often forgotten that the "original" context for Christianity's individualist asceticism was anti-institutional. But as Henry Chadwick pointed out in his work on the formation of Christianity, asceticism was taken as a serious threat to the institutional authority of the bishops in the early church. In particular during the fourth century, what was perceived as the secularization and corruption of the church prompted some of its members to withdraw from the institution in order to pursue their spiritual goals independent of any institution and outside any orthodoxy.

Just as the cross was God's triumph over the powers of evil, so the martyr shared in his triumph in his own death. The ascetics continued this spirit after the persecutions were past. They strove to achieve the same self-sacrificing detachment from the world. The evangelical demand for sacrifice, however, was fused with attitudes toward frugality and simplicity inherited from the clas-

20. Klor de Alva, "Colonizing Souls," 15–16. The reference to the "invasion within" is to James Axtell, *The Invasion Within: The Contest of Cultures in Colonial North America* (New York: Oxford University Press, 1985); see also Klor de Alva, "Spiritual Conflict and Accommodation in New Spain: Toward a Typology of Aztec Responses to Christianity," in *The Inca and Aztec States, 1400–1800: Anthropology and History*, ed. George A. Collier, Renato I. Rosaldo, and John D. Wirth (New York: Academic Press, 1982); "Sin and Confession among the Colonial Nations: The Confessional as a Tool for Domination," in *Ciudad y campo en la historia de México*, ed. Richard Sánchez, Eric Van Young, and Gisela von Wobester (Mexico City: Instituto de Investigaciones Históricas, Universidad Nacional Autónoma de México, 1990); and "Contar Vidas: La autobiografía confesional y la reconstrucción del ser nahua," *Arbor* 515–16 (1988): 49–78.

sical past. The Monastic movement had room not only for simple folk but for men educated in the tradition of Plato and his ideal martyr, Socrates, in the cynic principle of self-sufficiency, and in the stoic doctrine that happiness lies in suppressing the desire for anything one cannot both get and keep, and therefore demands the suppression of the passions for a life of right reason.[21]

No doubt, a strong connection can be found between this sense of the ascetic life and the Christian humanist ideal evidenced in, among other places, Fray Luis de León's *Vida retirada*.[22] But the humanist interpretation of asceticism was, relatively speaking, already a fully socialized and normative phenomenon, no matter how threatening it may have seemed within the context of an absolutist state. By the time of the Counter-Reformation, ascetic practices and beliefs had come to form such an integral part of the Christian tradition that they could easily be reincorporated as part of the institution's dominant ideology.[23] Indeed, if one follows the analysis of Michel Foucault, the Council of Trent brought about a series of new procedures for the training, disciplining, and purifying of ecclesiastical personnel: "Detailed techniques were elaborated for use in seminaries and monasteries, techniques of discursive rendition of daily life, of self-examination, confession, direction of conscience and regulation of the relationship between director and directed. It was this technology which it was sought to inject into society as a whole, and it is true that the move was

---

21. *The Early Church* (Harmondsworth: Penguin Books, 1967), 177. See also Geoffrey Galt Harpham, *The Ascetic Imperative in Criticism and Culture* (Chicago: University of Chicago Press, 1987). Perhaps the strongest critique of asceticism is that offered by Nietzsche in *The Genealogy of Morals*. Nietzsche proposes that the ascetic ideal was the only means that human beings ever had to give meaning to life.

22. The transformation of solitude into a virtue demonstrates one of the many ways in which Christian writers such as Fray Luis had succeeded in modifying the classical tradition. The ancestor of our word for solitary (hermit) is *erēmos:* while for Christianity the life of a hermit could be exemplary in a moral fashion, it would have been regarded as deficient in fifth-century Athens. As Alasdair MacIntyre notes, in Greek and especially in Athenian culture, friendship, company, and a city-state were essential components of humanity. See *After Virtue,* rev. ed. (Notre Dame: Notre Dame University Press, 1984), 135.

23. The figure of the ascetic hermit stands at the center of Mira de Amescua's *El esclavo del demonio* and of Tirso de Molina's *El condenado por desconfiado.* On the hermit and the beggar as fundamental to ascetic practices, see Georg Simmel on "Ascetic Poverty" in *The Philosophy of Money,* 2d ed., trans. Tom Bottomore and David Frisby, ed. David Frisby (London: Routledge, 1990), 251–54.

directed from the top downwards."[24] Moreover, Foucault argued that the tendency to transform religion into an institution that operates through an elaborate technical apparatus is somehow natural to Christianity. And, as the case of Fray Luis once again illustrates, within the church ascetic practices were part of a more general structure of power that could be described as "pastoral." The specific traits of "pastoral power" can be explained in the following terms, drawn from Foucault, which demonstrate its relevance for the process of subject-formation:

> [The Christian Church] postulates in principle that certain individuals can, by their religious quality, serve others not as princes, magistrates, fortune-tellers, benefactors, educationalists, and so on, but as pastors. However, this word designates a very special form of power.
>
> 1) It is a form of power whose ultimate aim is to assure individual salvation in the next world.
>
> 2) Pastoral power is not merely a form of power which commands; it must also be prepared to sacrifice itself for the life and salvation of the flock. Therefore, it is different from royal power, which demands a sacrifice from its subjects to save the throne.
>
> 3) It is a form of power which does not look after just the whole community, but each individual in particular, during his entire life.
>
> 4) Finally, this form of power cannot be exercised without knowing the inside of people's minds, without exploring their souls, without making them reveal their innermost secrets. It implies a knowledge of the conscience and an ability to direct it.[25]

It bears noting nonetheless that the cumulative effect of the ascetic psychology of the Counter-Reformation and the exercise of pastoral power was contradictory. On the one hand asceticism tended to close off the very same resources of subjectivity it seemed to open up, in

24. Foucault, "The Confession of the Flesh," in *Power/Knowledge: Selected Interviews and Other Writings, 1972–1977*, ed. Colin Gordon, trans. Colin Gordon, Leo Marshall, John Mepham, and Kate Sopher (New York: Pantheon, 1980), 200.

25. Michel Foucault, "The Subject and Power," in *Michel Foucault: Beyond Structuralism and Hermeneutics*, by Hubert Dreyfus and Paul Rabinow, 2d ed. (Chicago: University of Chicago Press, 1983), 214.

effect reinforcing a theocentric essentialism by creating in subjects a willingness for subjection to the principles of a "higher" rule.[26] But on the other hand, this asceticism was crucial in the large-scale project of *asujétissement* or subject-formation by means of subjection during the early modern age in Spain. As we shall see in the case of Gracián, the internalization of authority was crucial in allowing the modern subject also to represent itself as autonomous and free.[27] Indeed, the crucial problem of political legitimation could not be resolved without a consideration of the psychological mechanisms necessary for the control or *asujétissement* of subjects: given the weakening of "naturalistic" premises about the social world, the state could depend only on its ability to establish a willingness for subjection among those who were submitted to its rule. To understand the effects of the Counter-Reformation in terms of the process of *asujétissement* may thus enable us to locate what Maravall calls the "motivating factors" (*resortes*) that allowed the proponents of a conservative religious program to secure a position of dominance and control, in part because the crisis of subjectivity—as reflected in the Counter-Reformation's drama of free will, sin, salvation, and grace—provided the means through which the state was able to defend itself against the modernizing "threats" to its legitimacy presented by the desires and wills of those same subject-selves. As I also suggest, these considerations will enable us to move from a description of the means and mechanisms of control as imposed to a calculation of the motives by which a heterogeneous "public" came willingly to submit to the state's political force.[28]

26. Compare Lope de Vega, who supplies this authority when he addresses the audience of his plays in the "Arte nuevo de hacer comedias": "como las paga el vulgo, es justo / hablarle en necio para darle gusto" (since the common people pay for them, it is right to address them injudiciously if that will please them) (lines 47–48).

27. When Max Weber describes the asceticism of Protestantism, he characterizes it as "inner-worldly." By contrast, Spanish asceticism was for the most part "other-worldly." And yet the self-discipline required of all human beings when confronted with a world of appearances (as happens for instance in Gracián) shows how rapidly this distinction can break down.

28. As Maravall's translator, Terry Cochran, points out, the issue of the *resorte* (mechanism) is of crucial theoretical importance. Literally, the term *resorte* refers to the mechanical action of a coil-spring, where the act that "moves" the spring is itself already a reaction to the energy reserved in the coil itself. When taken as a figure for social action, as is the case in Maravall's text, the term *resorte* points equally to the motivations of individuals and to what motivates them. In Cochran's formulation, the spring came to represent the model for all social activity, including the posing of political hegemony and counterhegemony ("The Translating Mechanism," in *The Culture of the Baroque*,

✳   ✳   ✳

To continue these arguments, I turn back to the question of the Counter-Reformation's philosophical and intellectual basis; as Gilman's essay exemplifies, it is with reference to a certain orthodox set of beliefs that the Counter-Reformation is customarily conceived as having had regressive ideological effects in Spain. For example, it is often argued that what became visible as a "Counter-Reformation" ideology had its origins in Spain's theocentric reaction to the progressive philosophical rationalism emergent in England and France during the late Renaissance and early modern age. Indeed, literary critics and historians of ideas have long argued that while philosophy outside of Spain took a decisively modern and rationalist turn, the climate of opinion in Spain remained theocentric, in large measure because it remained subordinate to the premises of neo-Scholastic belief. It is often pointed out that while the *Disputationes metaphysicae* (1597) of the Spanish Jesuit Francisco de Suárez played a decisive role in the development of modern subjectivity insofar as they served to stimulate the thinking of Descartes, the Spanish response to skepticism took a theocentric, rather than a rationalist or empiricist turn.[29] In the face of evidence like this, a series of comparative questions inevitably come to mind. Given prevailing tendencies to relocate the centers of consciousness, agency, and value in the rational capacity of the subject-self, what can explain persistence of neo-Scholasticism in early modern Spain? Given the strategic linkages between an emergent capitalism and liberal political theory elsewhere in Europe, what can account for the continuing Spanish defense of the Absolutist State?[30] In works like Suárez's *De legibus ac Deo legislatore* (1612) and Quevedo's *Política de Dios y gobierno de Cristo, nuestro señor* (1626), the discourse of legitimation proceeds from a defense of

xvii–xviii). The concept of the *resorte* thus helps to resolve the antinomy of subject and structure addressed by social theorists like Anthony Giddens. See Giddens, *Central Problems in Social Theory: Action, Structure, and Contradiction in Social Analysis* (Berkeley and Los Angeles: University of California Press, 1979).

29. See, for example, Etienne Gilson, *Etudes sur le rôle de la pensée médiévale dans la formation du système Cartésien* (Paris: J. Vrin, 1951).

30. I hasten to add that these questions are in one respect false, as they fail to recognize the covert links between subjectivity and subjection—between the psychology of the free and autonomous "modern" self and the authority of the liberal state—as a recurrent problem of modernity. They would better be exchanged for questions about the particular modes of subjectivity and the particular discourse of legitimation characteristic of Counter-Reformation Spain.

the *religious* basis of the absolute monarch's power, rather than from a recognition, as in Hobbes, of absolutism's "rational" core. The decision outlined in the *Leviathan* to invest all power in a single center so as to avoid the war of all against all can be regarded as a "legitimation" of absolutism. But one must place the term "legitimation" in quotes in order to recognize that what Hobbes offers is also a rationalization of absolute power, one ultimately based on control of the interests of those subjects who submit to its control. What differs in England and Spain are the mechanisms of cultural control through which the wills of social subjects in what Maravall describes as a *sociedad de masas* were shaped.

If we are to address the issue of subject-formation we shall nonetheless need to abandon the idea that the role of ideology in Counter-Reformation Spain was simply to enforce a series of orthodox religious beliefs. To be sure, it might initially seem that Counter-Reformation beliefs presented a reaction against the kind of subjective self-consciousness that developed elsewhere in Europe during the sixteenth and seventeenth centuries. Counter-Reformation culture was indeed authoritarian and repressive in certain of its methods of control. But the customary description of early modern Spain in terms of the power of its reactionary position with respect to modernizing institutions and ideas underestimates the relationship between subjectivity, the mechanisms of subjection through which it was produced, and the psychology of the will that came to the fore during this period. Indeed, the thesis of a fully autonomous subject-self (whether sacred or secular, masculine or feminine), wholly free from control and empowered by an autonomous will, must itself be recognized as an "ideological" construct of the early modern world, belief in which leads at best to a systematic denial of the individual's political position as *subject to* an external authority or rule. Moreover, it may conceal the ways in which the disciplinary techniques learned in Counter-Reformation Spain were subsumed and incorporated by writers like Gracián as part of the psychology of *self*-control, which was later assimilated to the European discourse on taste.[31]

In the case of Spain, the effect of Counter-Reformation beliefs was to align a neo-Scholastic understanding of the nature of the will with a series of hierarchical principles about social values couched in terms of

---

31. The importance of Gracián to the discourse on taste has been noted by both Gadamer and Arendt; see Chapter 5.

the accessibility of the good to those who could prove themselves to be of truly noble character. The neo-Scholastic philosophy invoked to reinforce Counter-Reformation practices and beliefs customarily identified the innate faculties of memory, understanding, and the will and related each to a particular dimension of the human soul. The final goal of such philosophy, as witnessed for example in the development of Segismundo over the course of Calderón's best-known play, was to integrate and balance these faculties in the service of the moral will, thus producing through the mechanism of self-control a subject who could confirm the legitimacy of the state. In the neo-Scholastic reading, which takes *La vida es sueño* as the structural mapping of this moral psychology, Segismundo's opening complaint represents the action of memory, as the prince recalls his vexed origins and recognizes the conditions of his own spiritual displacement from the world: "¡Ay, mísero de mí, y ay, infelice! / Apurar, Cielos, pretendo, / ya que me tratáis así, / ¿qué delito cometí?" (Oh, miserable and unhappy me! You heavens above, I demand to know, since you treat me this way, what crimes I've committed against you) (lines 102–5). Segismundo's famous second monologue is in turn seen to display the work of the reflective intellect or "understanding," as he comes to recognize remarkable transformations in his material circumstances: "pues reprimamos / esta fiera condición, / esta furia, esta ambición" (let us repress this beastly nature, this fury and ambition) (lines 2148–50). This second speech demonstrates the skepticism characteristic of one who has experienced the full force of the Counter-Reformation's ascetic warnings against the deceit of the senses and who has come to adopt an ethical denial of the external world. And yet the point of this reading would be lost if it were not also said that neither memory nor the understanding when taken without the will can lead to the kind of moral action expected of the truly "noble" soul.

The process of moral development as imagined by Calderón culminates in the creation of the "magnanimous prince," whom we may provisionally describe as an essentialist, neo-Scholastic version of the "generous soul"[32] described in Covarrubias's *Tesoro de la lengua castel-*

---

32. Rosaura addresses the prince as "generoso Segismundo" in act 3 (line 2690). On this subject, see Edwin Honig, *Calderón and the Seizures of Honor* (Cambridge: Harvard University Press, 1972), 158–75 ("The Magnanimous Prince and the Price of Consciousness: *Life Is a Dream*").

lana as being of impeccable lineage.[33] Indeed, the neo-Scholastic interpretation of Calderón's play takes it as crucial to show that the work of memory and the understanding would remain incomplete without the intervention of the will, which begins with self-control. As the events of act 3 suggest, the structural allegory of Segismundo's moral development only can be made complete and the moral "profit" of the inherited Counter-Reformation lessons about the contingency of life fully received, when the prince freely renounces his own circumstantial power and agrees to restore his father's rule. Calderón's hero puts the point well when he remarks that the course of events overwhelms the powers of his intellect and virtually *requires* the intervention of the will: "Cielos, si es verdad que sueño, / suspendedme la memoria, / que no es posible que quepan / en un sueño tantas cosas" (Heavens, if indeed I'm dreaming, suspend my memory, for in a dream so many things could not occur) (lines 2918–21). The will serves thus to "complete" what memory and understanding could not by themselves bring to perfection.

And yet it might be more accurate to say that the will also represents the inscrutable and ultimately unrepresentable object of baroque persuasion and control. Indeed, all the more overt and explicit mechanisms

33. Sebastián de Covarrubias, *Tesoro de la lengua castellana o española*, ed. Martín de Riquer (1611; Barcelona: S. A. Horta, 1943), s.v. *generoso:* "El hombre ilustre, nacido de padres muy nobles, y de clara estirpe, conocida por el árbol de su descendencia. Este es generoso por linage." Compare Descartes, who writes in *Les passions de l'âme* that

> Those who are generous . . . are naturally led to do great deeds, and at the same time not to undertake anything of which they do not feel themselves capable. And because they esteem nothing more than doing good to others and disregarding their own self-interest, they are always perfectly courteous, gracious and obliging to everyone. Moreover they have complete command over their passions. In particular, they have mastery over their desires, and over jealousy and envy, because everything they think sufficiently valuable to be worth pursuing is such that its acquisition depends solely on themselves; over hatred of other people, because they have esteem for everyone; over fear, because of the self-assurance which confidence in their own virtue gives them; and finally over anger, because they have very little esteem for everything that depends on others, and so they never give their enemies any advantage by acknowledging that they are injured by them. (*The Passions of the Soul*, 156; in *Philosophical Writings*, trans. John Cottingham, Robert Stoothoff, and Dugald Murdoch [Cambridge: Cambridge University Press, 1985], 1:385)

The passage reveals the ways in which the "generous soul" has learned to refashion the asceticism characteristic of the baroque according to the principles of self-sufficiency of the new rationalism.

of "control"—whether in religious oratory, meditative practice, or catechesis—are directed toward this elusive faculty. Hence Calderón's recourse in other plays to the intervention of wonder-working magicians, to near-miraculous conversions, and to the astonishing power of the saving angels of the Lord—none of which succeeds in representing the will as such, but all of which are calculated to have effects upon it. Moreover, in the experience of the *arrebatos* of wonder and "disbelief" the subject also comes to experience the will aesthetically *as will*. In this same context one might note the Counter-Reformation's effort to represent in demonic forms those powers that could act *upon* the will. Hence Loyola's effort to represent the will, in meditation, as under control. All of these efforts, and many more, were designed to make explicit and confirm what remained in fact the unpresentable element within persuasion itself.

Whether the will is ultimately imagined in philosophical or moral terms as "free" or "bound," there can be no doubt that it was socially and culturally controlled. And it seems equally clear that a work like *La vida es sueño* amounts to something still more complex than a reflection of the Counter-Reformation attempt to represent what is unpresentable in the work of persuasion itself, albeit fortified by the intervention of a neo-Scholastic interpretation of the progress of the soul toward the moral good. While the moral teleology of the play lies in the production of the virtuous prince, Segismundo's development begins from a subjective psychology that this orthodox reading finds difficult to accommodate. More accurately, Calderón mirrors the crisis of subjectivity in Spain by staging the encounter of neo-Scholastic perspectives about the innate faculties of the soul with a series of relatively "modern" discoveries about the contingent existence of the self. In the process, he allows us to uncover the genealogy of the "moral psychology" of absolutism and to understand the crisis of legitimation in a society of increasingly disgregated individuals, albeit "resolving" the latter in favor of a neo-Scholastic defense of the inherent goodness of order, authority, and control. In a writer like Calderón, the purpose of glossing a fundamentally political action in moral terms, or of turning secular plots *a lo divino,* as in the *autos sacramentales,* was to integrate neo-Scholastic moral psychology with absolutist politics, and by so doing to model the formation of subjects who would in principle be unable to resist control. In this context, the confirming power of orthodox beliefs was to bridge moral psychology and politics in order to present the image of culture as a unified, seamless whole. In the process, the resistance to subjectivity became an essential ingredient in the task of political subjection, and so served to help legitimize the Absolutist State.

Phrased in other terms, Calderón's view of Segismundo not simply as the subject of an ideal moral itinerary but as *subject to* the "passions of the soul" mirrors a crisis of subjectivity that leads to a vision of the self as *requiring* a form of self-control that is also political. Indeed, it could be said that a work like *La vida es sueño* provides one of the best examples of the ways in which an encounter of the inherited principles of psychology with the problem of the legitimacy of authority leads to manifestly political (and, in this case, conservative) ends: what is ultimately at stake in Calderón's play can best be described in terms of the relationship between Segismundo's subjective self-consciousness and the need to restore authority in his father's state. Counter-Reformation "ideology" served even at this historical distance as the means by which the state could reassert, reassure, and legitimize its rule, not so much by dominating subjects as by producing subjects who would not wish to escape its control.

As we have already seen in Chapter 3, the problem of subject-formation in early modern Spain begins with the discovery, characteristic of the antinaturalism of the baroque, that the existing political order is no longer entitled to draw on the legitimizing authority of nature itself. Calderón thematizes the excruciating "difficulty" of Segismundo's situation in terms of the moral psychology of sin, guilt, and free will.[34] Not unlike the pilgrim-hero of Góngora's *Soledades*, and not unlike Hamlet, whose time is "out of joint," Segismundo believes that the order of nature has been rendered inscrutable to the human gaze and that his own condition has been rendered unintelligible and seemingly without cause in naturalistic terms; accordingly, it requires interpretation in psychological ways:

> . . . si nací, ya entiendo
> qué delito he cometido;
> bastante causa ha tenido

---

34. The "difficulty" of baroque style, which Beverley associates with an anti-foundationalist conception of politics and power, may be understood as an attempt to reproduce conditions of alienation in the subject-spectator of the play—organized in such a way, however, that the subject might come eventually to welcome the imposition of order and control.

> vuestra rigor,
> pues el delito mayor
> del hombre, es haber nacido.
> Sólo quisiera saber,
> para apurar mis desvelos
> —dejando a una parte, cielos,
> el delito del nacer—,
> ¿qué más os pude ofender,
> para castigarme más?
>
> (lines 107–18)

(I know that to have been born is an offense, and with just cause I bear the rigors of your punishment, since just to have been born is man's worst crime. I only want to know, in order to relieve my doubts—leaving aside the crime of birth—what greater crime could have offended you so to have punished me more?)

Whereas his father Basilio could once employ "subtle calculations" ("matemáticas sutiles") in order to fathom the "difficulty" of the world, Segismundo's task is to recover—and if not to recover, then to invent or impose—the "reason of nature" through the resources of prudence, *ingenio,* and the will. Given the confrontation of neo-Scholastic beliefs about the innate capacities of the soul with the "anti-naturalistic" perspectives characteristic of the baroque, it was perhaps to be expected that a vision of the subject as shaped by the desires or "passions," and of desires as requiring political direction and control, would emerge as central elements in the formation of the subject-self.[35] Ostensibly, the

---

35. The erosion of strictly "naturalistic" premises about society and the self contributed in fairly direct ways to the political discourse of the baroque. On the one hand, the antinaturalism of the baroque reflects a new confidence in the human capacity to transform and supplement the natural world by human artifice; as such, it may be related to a series of hopeful pronouncements about the salutary consequences of human intervention in political affairs. Maravall cites the *Nueva filosofía de la naturaleza del hombre* of Miguel Sabuco (1587), and in particular Sabuco's "Coloquio sobre las cosas que mejoran este mundo y sus repúblicas" (Discourse about the things that improve this world and its republics) (*The Culture of the Baroque,* 22) as but one example of the new optimism in political affairs, but I think we miss the point unless we see the state as itself the largest "supplement" of nature in the baroque. Indeed, there were no guarantees that the human supplement of nature would not worsen the existing state of affairs, or that political conditions could not be blamed on the failures of human artifice. As one of

baroque hero's work is to find a solution to the problem of subjective self-consciousness, a problem that is mirrored as a crisis in the reason of nature itself. Since, however, the subject discovers that the authority of nature has been withdrawn, he is confronted with the imperative of a reactionary political task, one that requires the reinforcement of the father's rule as legitimate and just, but that recognizes as well that any authority must be heterogeneous to nature, external to the subjects, and so *imposed*. The hero's development must include the moral and political work of self-repression and control, as he pardons his father and imprisons the rebel soldier. In this respect, Segismundo is not unlike Tirso's Don Juan, who exemplifies the distinctively modern problem of a desire that must be repressed if the subject is to be incorporated into social life. But though it was only through a repressive politics that the baroque crisis of subjectivity could be resolved, this process had to be staged as a form of personal growth. Segismundo's moral "progress" only begins with the Counter-Reformation's work of ascetic self-repression: for example, "reprimamos / esta fiera condición" (let us repress this bestial nature) (lines 2148–49). As we shall see in relation to Gracián, that self-repression becomes part of a more "rationalized" model of the self.

In describing the subjects of early modern Spain as existing within the context of a "guided culture" (*una cultura dirigida*) and a "mass culture" (*una cultura masiva*) Maravall has also argued that it was increasingly "bourgeois." "It is absurd to deny the baroque a bourgeois character," Maravall says, "simply because it failed to exhibit a complete process of rationalization" (*The Culture of the Baroque*, 63). Indeed, the same can be said of the psychological "subject" of early modern Spain, whose development has been portrayed as damaged, truncated, regressive, or incomplete with respect to the seemingly homogeneous models of "rational" self-consciousness theorized by thinkers like Descartes, Hobbes, and Locke. In Don Juan's case, as in Segismundo's, the psyche is better seen as internally split rather than undeveloped. It is cleaved metaphysically between the attractions of the finite *siglo* and

---

Philip IV's advisers, in all probability González de Cellorigo, wrote of the nation's political decline, "The negligence of those who rule is without a doubt the author of misfortune and the door through which enter all the ills and injuries in the republic, and in my mind no republic suffers greater misfortune than ours because we live with neither suspicion nor fear of catastrophe, trusting in a lackadaisical confidence" (cited in Maravall, *The Culture of the Baroque*, 22).

the moral threats of the everlasting world, and it is split psychologically, between the conditions of subjective desire and the various resistances to desire that we have begun to see above. Not least important, it is divided historically, between the "seignorial" values of nobility and prestige on the one hand and a newly mobile individualism on the other.

As Maravall notes, the fundamental problem with a mass culture is the heterogeneity of the masses with respect to their origin or estate: "individuals act outside the limits of the traditional group to which they belong, and they are united in functional and impersonal forms of behavior extending beyond differences in profession, age, wealth, and beliefs" (*The Culture of the Baroque*, 102). In other words, the heterogeneity of the masses presents a problem for society as a whole insofar as it came to generate anxieties about the terms in which social "subjects" might identify themselves and be recognized by others. The protocols of behavior developed at court mirror this problem in myriad ways. On the one hand, the baroque court incorporates the "naturalistic" principles of social distinction characteristic of a hierarchical society. But on the other hand the increasing "psychologization" of behavior, the continual testing of moral psychology against observations drawn from "experience," required principles of differentiation that a hierarchical structure could not easily provide. Accordingly, there arose a series of procedures designed to control and regulate (on the basis of "psychological" rules) the experience of increasingly heterogeneous subject-selves. But unlike the empirical psychology that later took shape in the writings of Locke and Hume, the art of courtly conduct took as its object a self that had not yet come to conceive of itself as detachable from its social effects.[36]

Because of the central role of court society in establishing rules of conduct and consent, the members of the court came to be aligned with an ethical norm. By virtue of the identification of "court society" with "good society," they perceived themselves on an exclusionary moral basis as elites, thus adopting in moral terms a principle of social distinction that could find no basis in the natural world. Indeed, the "courtization" of society has been seen by cultural historians like Norbert Elias as essential to the civilizing process insofar as it springs from the ascription of an ethical value to the taming of "natural" aggression or, what amounts to

---

36. Wlad Godzich and Nicholas Spadaccini make a related point in *Literature Among Discourses* when they argue that art and politics in the Golden Age did not necessarily constitute separate activities.

the same thing, the sublimation of "subjective" desires and the transformation of the self into an object of psychological self-control: "In the midst of a large populated area which by and large is free of physical violence, a "good society" is formed. But even if the use of physical violence now recedes from human intercourse, if even duelling is now forbidden, people now exert pressure and force on each other in a wide variety of different ways."[37] Elias's conclusion is that the court is, if not the first, then certainly among the most important centers of systematic social regulation and control. Insofar as the various modes of this control bring an increase in self-discipline (which, following Weber, he labels "rationalization"), the courtization of society in the baroque is of a piece with the "psychologization" of the early modern subject-self; "psychological" analysis and observation develop in this context as techniques of self-mastery and as means of self-discipline.

✳   ✳   ✳

In addressing these issues, and in anticipation of matters to be taken up at greater length in Chapter 5, I turn to briefly to the case of Gracián, who elevates the "subjective" virtues of sincerity and authenticity into the basis of a new decorum, one that represents a new social rationality: for example, "Creer al corazón. . . . Nunca le desmienta, que suele ser pronóstico de lo que más importa" (Believe your heart. . . . Never contradict it, for it usually predicts what matters most about the future).[38] Indeed, Gracián provides matchless examples of the authority of self-control within early modern Spain, demonstrating what might best be described as an internalization of the control mechanisms that had been inherited from the Counter-Reformation world. In Gracián the privileged place of control is not the church, but the society of the court and the psyche of the subject. The authority of control in force at court has been transferred to the subject-self, in such a way that what acquires value in the emergent discourse of the self is the relatively "rationalized" psychology of self-control.

A writer like Gracián is faced with the task of finding a new standard

37. Norbert Elias, *Power and Civility*, trans. Edmund Jephcott (New York: Pantheon, 1982), 270–71.

38. Baltasar Gracián, *Oráculo manual y arte de prudencia*, ed. Arturo del Hoyo (Barcelona: Plaza y Janés, 1986), trans. Christopher Maurer, *The Art of Worldly Wisdom: A Pocket Oracle* (New York: Doubleday/Currency, 1992), no. 178, p. 43.

of conduct for the self where two once-available models have been rendered inaccessible. The first of these is represented by the figure of the common man (*el hombre vulgar*), repeatedly characterized as incapable of self-control and therefore as "base" (cf. *Oráculo*, no. 28, "En nada vulgar," p. 370 [In no respect vulgar] and also no. 69, "No rendirse a un vulgar humor. Hombre grande el que nunca se sujeta a peregrinas impresiones," p. 387 [Do not give in to vulgar passions. A great man is one who never subjects himself to transitory impressions]).[39] The second is the aristocratic individual or "noble soul," whose desire for social recognition (in the form of honor) has been rendered "inessential" or transmuted into aristocratic vice. Gracián transforms *sprezzatura* into the psychology of self-control (e.g., *Oráculo*, no. 3, "El jugar a juego descubierto ni es de utilidad, ni de gusto," p. 359 [To play an open game is neither useful nor fun]). In place of the courtier's *sprezzatura* or the common man's vulgarity Gracián fashions the image of the "prudent" man (*el discreto*). The ideals of the *discreto* are characterized first of all by his rational asceticism, otherwise known as self-imposed moderation and restraint (cf. *Oráculo*, no. 82, "A la moderación en todo redujo la sabiduría toda un sabio," p. 393 [A wise man reduced all wisdom to moderation in all things] and no. 117; "Nunca hablar de sí. O se ha de alabar, que es desvanecimiento, o se ha de vituperar, que es poquedad," p. 406 [Never refer to oneself. Either one must praise oneself, which is pride, or one must condemn oneself, which is cowardice]). In his pursuit of self-control, Gracián's *discreto* has learned to reduce (and in this sense, to "rationalize") the contradictory passions experienced by figures like Segismundo and Don Juan. The prudent man, by contrast, embodies the "modern" value of social tact: "Sin mentir, no decir todas las verdades. No hay cosa que requiera más tiento que la verdad, que es un sangrarse del corazón. Tanto es menester para saberla decir como para saberla callar" (no. 181, p. 432 [Without lying, not to speak all the truths. There is nothing that requires more tact than truth, which is like a bloodletting from the heart. Just as much is required to know how to speak the truth as to know how to silence it.]). In the process, Gracián helps us see how "psychological" observation came to represent something more than a mechanism of

---

39. See also nos. 206 ("Sépase que hay vulgo en todas partes," p. 442 [Know that there is vulgarity everywhere]) and 209 ("Librarse de las necedades comunes," p. 443 [To free oneself from common foolishness]).

control; in his own terms, it afforded a means of self-regulation through self-understanding: "One cannot be master of oneself," Gracián writes (no. 89), "if one does not first understand oneself. There are mirrors for the face, but not the soul; let prudent self-reflection serve this purpose" ("No puede uno ser señor de sí, si primero no se comprehende. Hay espejos del rostro, no los hay del ánimo: séalo la discreta reflexión sobre sí," p. 386). In conceiving of truth in such terms, Gracián provides a framework for the modern subject's vision of itself as "in control."

With the example of Gracián we shift from a concept of "control" as modeled in the discourses of pulpit, confessional, and prayerbook— where the response to authority is by nature always inadequate, where the effects of persuasion can never be sufficiently willed, and where the action of the will remains inscrutable to mortal eyes—to a social discourse in which the ethical basis of relations is social tact, and in which the allegiance to external authority is represented as having been radically reduced. And yet it would be wrong to think that Gracián somehow represents a decisive break with the psychology of control in Counter-Reformation Spain. It would be more accurate to say that the increasingly "rational" model of psychology evident in Gracián both incorporates and subsumes the psychological models developed during the Counter-Reformation. In the process, the Counter-Reformation's methods of authoritarian control were transformed into the principles of auto-regulation or "self-control" used to govern social relations in the "modern" world. While Gracián's *discreto* may have received his cultural training at court, he was formally "educated" and historically "schooled" in the Counter-Reformation's methods of control. Thus rather than think of the Counter-Reformation as having presented an obstacle to the process of subject-formation in early modern Spain, it might be better to reflect on its surprising historical success, as having marked a central moment in the process of subject-formation in the early modern age. For in a writer like Gracián we can see how the Counter-Reformation's teachings came to yield not only a new source of authority, but also a new logic of truth and a personal psychology whose strongest belief was that all authority originated from within the subject-self. As we shall see in Chapter 5, the subject's psychology depends on the awareness that the subject inhabits a social world that cannot be grounded in any a priori form of truth. As the discourse of taste that begins with Gracián amply reveals, the subject of "reason" and "truth" came increasingly to be recognized as socially formed.

5

Gracián and the Authority of Taste

It has long been recognized that the category of taste was crucial in the formation of the modern subject. What role did social thought in the Spanish Golden Age play in this process? In the opening chapter of *Truth and Method* (1960), Hans-Georg Gadamer described the work of Gracián as standing at the very beginning of the modern discourse on taste, which articulates a link between the capacities of the intellect and the experiences of the body.[1] Posed in its paradigmatic modern form,

---

1. Gadamer, *Truth and Method* (New York: Continuum, 1975). See Joan Corominas, *Diccionario crítico etimológico castellano e hispánico* (Madrid: Gredos, 1954–57), s.v. *gusto*: "*buen gusto*, 'sentido estético justo' parece haber nacido en España, donde ya lo empleaba Isabel la Católica." Gracián's importance for the eighteenth-century conception of "taste" is developed in Karl Borinski, *Baltasar Gracián und die Hofliteratur in Deutschland* (Halle an der Saale: Nachdruck Tübingen, 1971). See also Emilio Hidalgo-Serna, *Das Ingeniöse bei Baltasar Gracián: Der 'concepto' und seine logische Funktion* (Munich: Wilhelm Fink, 1985), especially chap. 5, "Die Vorrangstellung des ingeniösen

the question of taste is as follows: If knowledge involves cognition, then how can we validate the claims we make in response to feelings of pleasure and pain, which are derived from the body?[2] As Gadamer went on to say, it might initially seem doubtful that one could speak of "knowledge" with respect to such judgments at all, since these are not made according to concepts; it remains nonetheless clear that judgments of taste do indeed contain the idea of universal agreement or assent, even if this agreement is sensuously and not conceptually grounded. Perhaps for this reason, Gadamer located the most instructive aesthetic claims in the form of judgments about "tasteless" objects, or in claims about objects offensive to "good taste":

Taste really seeks, not what is tasteful but what does not offend it. . . . Taste is practically defined by the fact that it is offended

'guten Geschmacks'—*buen gusto*. Seine Bedeutung und Funktion." To be sure, there are contrary views. Concerning the priority of Gracián in the history of the concept of "taste," in *A History of Modern Criticism* (New Haven: Yale University Press, 1955) René Wellek, for instance, cites passages from Guez de Balzac (1645) and Ludovico Zuccolo (1623)—by way of Benedetto Croce—and draws the conclusion that "the widely held view that 'taste' comes from Spain and particularly from Balthasar Gracián is thus untenable." He grounds his claim in a passage of a letter by Guez that includes the phrase "Puisque vous *goûtez* mes derniers Ecrits, et que vous avez *le goût* extrêmement bon" (reproduced in E. B. O. Borgerhoff, *The Freedom of French Classicism* [Princeton: Princeton University Press, 1950], 14). Croce cites Zuccolo on *buon gusto* as "una certa potenza superiore, unita insieme con l'occhio e con l'orecchio, forma un cotal giudicio: la qual potenza tanto meglio conosce, quanto ha più d'accutezza nativa o più di perizia nell' arti, senza però valersi di discorso" (*Dialoghi* [Venice, 1625], 67–68), in *Storia dell' Età barocca in Italia* (Bari: G. Laterza, 1957), 166. I should thus clarify that the question is not so much one of priority as of the particular inflection Gracián gives to the notion of *gusto* in relation to questions of social change. But there is a second challenge as well, which concerns the relationship between taste and aesthetics. Frances Ferguson claims that "the aesthetic, in the process of becoming defined as something distinct from taste as a particularly demanding version of consumption, becomes less important as a social and sociological phenomenon and more important for representing a distinct kind of experience. The aesthetic, as Kant outlines it, prefigures and justifies Heidegger's later suggestion (in *Kant and the Future of Metaphysics* [sic]) that the imagination should be promoted to the standing of a separate faculty, on the order of reason or the understanding." *Solitude and the Sublime: Romanticism and the Aesthetics of Individuation* (New York: Routledge, 1992), 6.

2. The Kantian formulation, drawn from the opening of the *Critique of Judgment,* is as follows: "If we wish to discern whether anything is beautiful or not, we do not refer the representation of it to the Object by means of understanding with a view to cognition, but by means of the imagination . . . we refer the representation to the Subject and its feeling of pleasure of displeasure. The judgement of taste, therefore, is not a cognitive judgement, and so not logical, but is aesthetic—which means that it is one whose

by what is tasteless and thus avoids it, like anything else that threatens injury. Thus the idea of "bad taste" is not an original counter-phenomenon to "good taste." The opposite of the latter is to have "no taste." (*Truth and Method*, 35)

The grounding of judgments of taste in the sensuous experiences of pleasure and pain is nowhere more apparent than in Freud, who describes the originary identification of the ego as taking the form of a corporeal judgment:

> Expressed in the language of the oldest—the oral—instinctual impulses, the judgment is: "I should like to eat this," or "I should like to spit it out"; and, put more generally: "I should like to take this into myself and to keep that out." . . . The original pleasure ego wants is to introject everything into itself that is good and to eject from itself everything that is bad.[3]

Along with Freud, more recent social theorists like Pierre Bourdieu have argued that the experiences of pleasure and pain form the very basis of modern aesthetic theory, even if it is a basis that such theory would prefer to renounce: " 'Pure taste,' " writes Bourdieu, "purely negative in its essence, is based on the disgust that is often called 'visceral' (it 'makes one sick' or 'makes one vomit')"; "Kant's principle of pure taste is nothing other than a refusal, a disgust—a disgust for objects which impose enjoyment and a disgust for the crude, vulgar taste which revels in being represented comfortably to nature without destroying all aesthetic delight, and consequently artistic beauty, namely, that which excites *disgust*."[4]

---

determining ground *cannot be other than subjective*." Kant, *Critique of Judgment*, trans. James Meredith (Oxford: Oxford University Press, 1986), 41–42.

3. "Negation," in *The Standard Edition of the Complete Psychological Works of Sigmund Freud* (London: Hogarth Press, 1953–74), 237. As Freud goes on to say, "judging is a continuation, along lines of expediency, of the original process by which the ego took things into itself or expelled them from itself, according to the pleasure principle" (239).

4. Pierre Bourdieu, *Distinction: A Social Critique of the Judgment of Taste*, trans. Richard Nice (London: Routledge and Kegan Paul, 1984), 486, 488. Compare Hannah Arendt, who reminds us that for Kant "the true opposite to the Beautiful is not the Ugly but 'that which excites disgust.' " She goes on to remind us that "Kant originally planned to write a Critique of Moral Taste" (i.e., instead of the *Critique of Judgment*). Hannah Arendt, *The Life of the Mind* (New York: Harcourt Brace, 1978), 2:266. Kant's remarks on disgust (*Ekel*) can be found in sect. 48 of the *Critique of Judgment*.

For Gadamer, the notion of an individual capacity for taste, rooted in the ego, is subsumed into the collective, social body—the community—such that taste becomes its faculty of collective reason, its "sense." Specifically, Gadamer maintains that writers beginning with Gracián show us that "the true sense of community . . . is taste" (*Truth and Method,* 33). And yet it seems that it is not enough simply to identify the sense of community or the "community sense" (*sensus communis*) with taste as such. As in Kant, the validation of taste as a "foundational" concept for the community also requires limiting the concept of taste to judgments about what is beautiful or not.[5] In other words, the community's need for foundations can be addressed not just by restricting the concept of the sense of community to that of taste—as if what were at stake were simply the movement from the empirical singularity of the individual's corporeal experiences of pleasure and pain to the supposedly reasoned generality of judgments that can be validated by everyone—but also limiting the application of taste to the objects we would judge beautiful; that is, to works of art, which over time become identifiable as such within the social world. Accordingly, it is not just that aesthetic judgments serve the "foundational" needs of the community but that the founding of community in taste is dependent on the (prior) existence of works of art. Thus it is not surprising to find that we can uncover a residue of the transition from the physical reactions of the sensuous and material body to the reasoned response of the "social body" or the "body politic" in the faculty of aesthetic judgment.[6]

By the same token, artworks came eventually to be seen as sublimating or subsuming the particularity of sensuous aesthetic experience into occasions of universally acceptable and communicable judgments. Taste

5. For Kant, of course, the question is one of delimiting and thereby purifying judgments of taste (judgments of the beautiful and the sublime) by excluding everything that is not sufficiently pure.

6. The strict delimitation of taste to works of art was the concern of French neoclassical theorists. In Kant, the application of judgments of taste extends equally to nature and to art. In the preface to the *Critique of Judgment* Kant writes that "it is chiefly in those estimates that are called aesthetic, and which relate to the beautiful and sublime, whether of nature or of art, that one meets with the above difficulty about a principle [of judgment]." Howard Caygill, *Art of Judgment* (Oxford: Basil Blackwell, 1989) argues that the adaptation of taste constituted a gesture of aristocratic dissent against the Royal Academy (39). See also Remy G. Saisselin, *The Rule of Reason and the Ruses of the Heart: A Philosophical Dictionary of Classical French Criticism, Critics, and Aesthetic Issues.* (Cleveland: Case Western Reserve University Press, 1970).

has its origins in the sensuous experiences of pleasure and pain, but the exercise of taste can appear to hide the genealogy of the aesthetic in sensuous reality just as the development of culture by and through taste can seem to conceal the animal origins of human nature. This situation is duplicated in the notion of the *sensus communis* which, like taste, has sometimes seemed not really to be a sense at all, or to be only a sense of form: it is neither the particular nor the general, but rather what makes it possible to assimilate the particular to the general, an individual to a pattern, the self to the social or political world. Reflecting on this tendency, Gadamer relies on Gracián in order to explain the process by which the bodily origins of taste are desensualized. Indeed, Gadamer quotes Gracián to say that the development of taste represents a "spiritualization of animality."[7] Gracián here echoes the Aristotelian distinction between the human and the animal and, within the human, the idea of an ascent from sensation to the intellect; in *De sensu et sensato* (443b), for instance, Aristotle had said that only human beings are sensitive to the differences between agreeable and disagreeable odors, noting that animals do not shun the disagreeable, properly speaking, but only the noxious, which harms them physically or taints their food (445a).[8] But insofar as the formation of the "sense of community" depends not just on the laws of human reason, but also on the existence of artworks around which to develop judgments of taste, the modern understanding of this issue hides the problematic role of taste in "raising" mankind out of sensuous reality; clearly if such artworks exist then humanity is no longer in an uncultured state.[9] (As

7. It would perhaps be more accurate to say that the development of taste *preserves* the contradiction implicit in the notion of a "spiritualized animality." Bourdieu offers a fascinating commentary on the "overcoming" of barbarism by "pure" taste: "If one follows through all the implications of an aesthetic which, in accordance with the logic of Kant's 'Essay on Negative Magnitudes,' has to measure virtue by the magnitude of the vices overcome and pure taste by the intensity of the impulse denied and the vulgarity refused, then the most accomplished art has to be recognized in those works which carry the antithesis of civilized barbarism, contained impulse, sublimated coarseness, to the highest degree of tension" (*Distinction*, 490).

8. See David Summers, *The Judgment of Sense: Renaissance Naturalism and the Rise of Aesthetics* (Cambridge: Cambridge University Press, 1987), 56.

9. Pierre Bourdieu provides a very forceful critique of the Enlightenment's rejection of the sensuous basis of taste: " 'Pure' taste and the aesthetics which provides its theory are founded on a refusal of 'impure' taste and of *aisthesis* (sensation), the simple, primitive form of pleasure reduced to a pleasure of the senses, as in what Kant calls 'the taste of the tongue, the palate and the throat', a surrender to immediate sensation which in another order looks like imprudence. At the risk of seeming to indulge in the 'facile

we also shall see, it similarly obscures the aporia of the social education of taste.) Gadamer nonetheless suggests that Gracián's understanding of the problem of taste can be of particular importance in this regard. If we can recover from Gracián's work an understanding of the civilizing role of taste with respect to sensuous, material reality, then we can move from an understanding of political community as founded directly in sensuous reality—not on the basis of desire, but of need—to the notion of politics as founded on judgments, even if these, like aesthetic judgments, do not necessarily conform to a priori concepts.

✳ ✳ ✳

There are, nonetheless, difficulties with Gadamer's account of the origins of taste in Gracián. First, in addressing the question of taste, Gadamer favors the notion of the beautiful at the expense of the sublime. Additionally, Gadamer's attempt to recuperate aesthetic pleasure for social ends does not sufficiently take into account the ways in which communities may constitute and transform themselves by the systematic exclusion of what they cannot represent. In Kant, for instance, it is the fear of exclusion and unrecompensed sacrifice that is so strongly rendered in the sublime. If taste is in principle founded on agreement, then artworks are bound to be pressed into the service of the "common sense." Where then is the possibility for the kinds of resistance to agreement that works of art so often provoke? Furthermore, Gadamer asserts that the origins of taste lie in sensuous reality, but he begins his discussion with the claim that Gracián demonstrates how taste was originally a moral concept. To say the very least, the route from sensuous reality to morality in Gracián—where taste is deemed to play a crucial role—is unclear. In Gadamer's view, Gracián configures taste itself as an "ideal of genuine humanity" whose broad accessibility is nothing short of remarkable when compared with the philosophical Scholasticism whose earlier prudential ideals were the province of the privileged few.[10] Gracián starts from the view that while

---

effects' which 'pure taste' stigmatizes, it could be shown that the whole language of aesthetics is contained in a fundamental refusal of the *facile*, in all the meanings, which bourgeois ethics and aesthetics give to the word" (*Distinction*, 486).

10. Gracián frequently makes reference to "la sindéresis," or "law of understanding which contains the precepts of natural law, which are the first principles of human action" (*Summa Theologica*, I–II, q. 94a, I ad 2). See the note in *El héroe*, ed. Arturo del Hoyo Martínez (Barcelona: Plaza y Janes, 1986), 116.

the sense of taste may be the most animal and inward and in this respect the most common of our faculties, it nonetheless contains the beginnings of the discriminations we are all said to make in our "higher" reflective and moral judgments (cf. Gracián: "No hay perfección donde no hay delecto" [There is no perfection without discernment]).[11] The sensuous judgment of taste, by which we seem to accept or reject things as if by instinct, is not *merely* an instinct, because it subordinates our instinctual reactions to the "freedom" of reflective judgment: "*Cultura y aliño. Nace bárbaro el hombre; redímese de bestia cultivándose. Hace personas la cultura; y más, cuanto mayor*" (*Oráculo manual,* 87, p. 395). (*Culture and refinement.* Man is born a barbarian. Culture raises him above the beast. Culture turns us into true persons: the more culture, the greater the person [*Art of Worldly Wisdom,* 49].) Taste is instinct transformed. More accurately, it is the mark of a "natural" refinement. As Andrée Collard observed, "en su aplicación crítica, *buen gusto, gusto* designa la reacción espontánea de un individuo frente a tal o cual obra, e implica cierto natural refinamiento, cierto sentido innato del decoro."[12] At the same time, it is through the exercise of choice and judgment that taste is conceived as being able to gain us a "humanizing" distance from the natural world. Perhaps this is why the exercise of taste may appear to be a moral faculty of the spirit or soul; indeed, there are moments in Gracián when its relationship to a perfectionist ethics seems to be all but direct.[13] The overcoming of instinct by aesthetic judgment is said to provide evidence that there is cultivation (*cultura*) not only of the faculties of the mind (*ingenio*), but of *gusto* itself. As Gracián remarks in *El héroe,* "Hay cultura de gusto, así como de ingenio" (*El héroe,* Primor V, p. 122). He takes up the theme again in the *Oráculo manual,* under the heading "*Gusto relevante*": "Cabe cultura en él, así como en el ingenio" (sect. 65, p. 385) (*Elevated taste.* You can cultivate it, as you can the intellect) (*Art of Worldly Wisdom,* 36).

11. Gracián, *Oráculo manual* (abbreviated *OM*), ed. Arturo del Hoyo Martínez (Barcelona: Plaza y Janés, 1986), 51, p. 380. Trans. Christopher Maurer, as *The Art of Worldly Wisdom: A Pocket Oracle* (New York: Doubleday/Currency, 1992), 29.

12. "In its critical understanding, 'good taste,' 'taste' designates the spontaneous reaction to a given work, and implies a certain natural refinement, a certain innate sense of decorum." Andrée Collard, *Nueva poesía: conceptismo, culteranismo en la crítica española* (Madrid and Waltham, Mass.: Editorial Castalia and Brandeis University, 1967), 63–64.

13. On the question of perfection in Gracián, see Monroe Hafter, *Gracián and Perfection* (Cambridge: Harvard University Press, 1966).

Gadamer's interpretation of Gracián's importance for the history of the concept of taste follows more or less in the line of Romantic notions about the formation of an "aesthetic state." His account of the role of taste in society can be located as part of a tradition that goes back at least as far as Schiller's *Letters on the Aesthetic Education of Man*. By implication, Gadamer positions Gracián as the forerunner of this same line. As Gadamer claims, the notion of *gusto* is the starting point for Gracián's ideal of an education that is itself aesthetic, even if it is not directly controlled by works of art. For Gracián, "good taste" (which is also to say, educated taste) is essential to the constitution of "good society." As we shall also have occasion to discuss, Gracián's ideal of education is that of preparation for life in the social world; as such, it may be understood as a modern version of the ideal of the Christian courtier, one that looks forward to the reorientation of taste not according to virtue but according to the values of social class. It represents a sociological interpretation of the prudential ideals characteristic of Scholastic thought. Perhaps with reason, Hannah Arendt credits Gracián in her lectures on Kant's political philosophy as having been instrumental in developing the sense of taste as a faculty of judgment.[14]

On Gadamer's account, however, the ideal of aesthetic education is understood as occurring independent of the class-construction of social reality. In his view, Gracián's educational ideal is "remarkable in the history of Western ideals of Bildung for being *independent of class*. It is the ideal of a society based on Bildung" (*Truth and Method*, 34; my emphasis). But at the same time Gadamer remains convinced that taste is a historical idea. As he goes on to say, "the ideal of social Bildung, while independent of class, seems to emerge everywhere in the wake of absolutism and its suppression of the hereditary aristocracy. Taste is not only the ideal created by a new society, but we see this ideal of 'good taste' producing what was subsequently called 'good society.' Its criteria are no longer birth and rank but simply the shared nature of its judgments, or, rather, its capacity to rise above the narrowness of interests and private predilections to the title of judgment" (34).

In response to what may seem like Gadamer's contradictory stance, I argue that Gracián's notion of taste must be historicized in relation to

14. Hannah Arendt, *Lectures on Kant's Political Philosophy,* ed. Ronald Beiner (Chicago: University of Chicago Press, 1982); see esp. 64, 66.

the question of the formation of the psychology of the "individual" as a relatively new social phenomenon in early modern Spain. Additionally, the "historicization" of taste can provide access to an understanding of taste's social genesis, even if this is not the genesis that a thinker like Gadamer imagines for it. This is to say that the historical specificity of Gracián's notion of taste must be located in relation to the ways in which the individual's feelings of pleasure and pain were subsumed as part of the social structuring of experience in early modern Spain. This process can best be understood in terms of the displacement of the hierarchical and hereditary values of social caste by a system of values that would eventually consolidate themselves around the principles of social class, which entails a suppression of the corporeal basis of social value.

In Alasdair MacIntyre's view, an individual in "traditional" society is a member of a variety of social groups that all together provide the keys to personal and social identity: "I am brother, cousin and grandson, member of this household, that village, this tribe. These are not characteristics that belong to human beings accidentally, to be stripped away in order to discover 'the real me.' They are part of my substance, defining at least partially and sometimes wholly my obligations and my duties. Individuals inherit a particular space within an interlocking set of social relationships; lacking that space, they are nobody, or at best a stranger or an outcast."[15] It is on the basis of a direct contrast with the principles of traditional society that the problem of taste can be understood. Gadamer's assertion notwithstanding, Gracián's notion of social *Bildung* is not at all "independent" of notions of social class; on the contrary, Gracián's notion of taste point in the direction of the psychology of "good sense" and "common sense," which were some of the philosophical foundations by which the primacy of lineage was suppressed by the emerging middle class. (Cf. Descartes, whom we shall have occasion to engage at greater length below: "Good sense is the best distributed thing in the world: for everyone thinks himself so well endowed with it that even those who are the hardest to please in everything else do not usually desire more of it than they possess.")[16] In

15. *After Virtue*, revised ed. (Notre Dame: Notre Dame University Press, 1984), 33–34.

16. Descartes, *Discourse on the Method*, I, in *The Philosophical Writings of Descartes*, trans. John Cottingham, Robert Stoothoff, and Dugald Murdoch (Cambridge: Cambridge University Press, 1985), 111.

response to Gadamer, it would be more accurate to say that Gracián's notion of taste marks a moment in the prehistory of the values of social class—a moment at which the notions of social relations as fixed and the capacity for judgment as inborn were displaced by the notion of aesthetic judgment as socially formed. The invention of "good taste" served the aims of a society that could no longer legitimize its ethical and moral projects (not to speak of its aesthetic ones) according to the aristocratic criteria of rank, while at the same time serving the continuing need for discrimination among those whose interests had formerly been characterized as illegitimate or "vulgar" ("el gusto del vulgo"). In a period of social change, taste (and especially "good taste," *buen gusto*) emerged to ground that particular form of social distinction that was crucial for the redefinition of "good society." In this way, Gadamer's "enlightened" understanding of taste as a faculty that operates at a distance from social interests must be set beside the sociopolitical understanding of taste, which sees the exercise of taste as a necessary means for maintaining distinctions within the modern world, for it is largely through the process of distinction that societies are formed.

The question of taste as posed by Gracián nonetheless poses a theoretical problem for an understanding of the changing sociohistorical order of which it is a part. While taste proves essential for the (re)constitution of social order within a period of historical change, it turns out that the constitution of society seems always to *precede* the formation of judgments of taste.[17] In one respect, the question of taste in early modern Spanish society is a version of the issue of "foundations" encountered in all societies. Aristotle recognized that education in

17. Howard Caygill—who likewise places Gracián in the line that leads up to Kant's Aesthetics—relates the question of such nonfoundational judgments to the paradigm of production: "Like Hobbes, who saw productive judgment as the creation of illusion, Gracián resolved the formative moment of taste into the production of appearance. In the *Oráculo Manual Y Arte De Prudencia* (1647) taste finds itself between reticence and dissemblance, applying judgement to the shaping of appearances. It is an unknowable faculty, present in the subject in an inexplicable way, and exercised intuitively. The object of its formative activity is the subject as appearance, the prudent one 'who realises that he is being observed, or will be observed' (1647 Sec. 297). Much of the pathos of Gracián's writing arises from the necessity of the prudent to dissemble, to represent themselves as appearance, to 'Cultivate a happy spontaneity.' But what if the object of taste is not the subject itself, but a different object? A similar conclusion follows: the object exists only as appearance, only in so far as it has been produced by taste. And yet this formative activity of taste cannot know itself; it is only discernible through the pleasures of producing and manipulating appearances" (*Art of Judgment*, 39).

political life required possession of the same virtues that participation in political life would cultivate; in the *Nicomachaean Ethics,* for instance, he wrote that "any one who is to listen intelligently to lectures about what is noble and just and, generally, about the subjects of political science must have been brought up in good habits."[18] Gracián's understanding of the education of taste mirrors this same aporia, but does so more dramatically because it is articulated during a period of radical social change. Insofar as Gracián's understanding of taste centers around the cultivation of the individual's distinctive individualism, it offers a way to resist the tendency of existing social reality to dictate the limits of human action. But since the pre-existing social world cannot be rejected *tout court,* Gracián comes to regard the exercise of taste as one of the ways in which the individual can best achieve success, given the constraints of social and political life. The exercise of taste, which requires the assertion of individual differences within the context of universal agreement or assent, comes to represent not just a historical shift of preferences, but a "moral" correction of modernity's universalizing aims. In this respect, taste joins dissimulation as a means to preserve and protect individual identity, which is taken as a strategic moral project. Gracián: *"Entrar con la ajena para salir con la suya.* Es estratagema del conseguir; aun en las materias del Cielo encargan esta santa astucia los cristianos maestros. Es un importante disimulo, porque sirve de cebo la concebida utilidad para coger una voluntad" (*OM,* 144, pp. 416–17) (*Enter conceding and come out winning.* This is a strategy for getting what you want. Even in heavenly matters, our Christian teachers recommend this holy craftiness. It is an important sort of dissimulation and you use it to capture someone else's will) (*Art of Worldly Wisdom,* 81).[19]

18. *Nicomachaean Ethics,* I.4, trans. David Ross, rev. J. L. Ackrill and J. O. Urmson (New York: Oxford University Press, 1980), 5.

19. In moments such as these, Gracián approaches La Rochefoucauld. Nonetheless La Rochefoucauld's *Maxims* often lack the impulse toward moral command that runs through Gracián. For example, La Rochefoucauld states as if it were a fact that "in order to succeed in the world people do their utmost to appear successful." La Rochefoucauld, *Maxims,* trans. Leonard Tancock (Harmondsworth: Penguin Books, 1959), 56, p. 44. Or again, La Rochefoucauld states that "hypocrisy is a tribute vice pays to virtue" (218, p. 65). Emilio Hidalgo-Serna comments briefly on the relationship between Gracián and both La Rochefoucauld and Madame de Sablé in *Das Ingeniöse bei Baltasar Gracián,* 24. See also G. Hough, "Gracián's *Oráculo manual* and the 'Maximes' of Madame de Sablé," *Hispanic Review* 4 (1936): 68–72.

* * *

Gracián's ideas of taste and of the education (*cultura*) of taste emerge in the context of the crisis of values created by the weakening of the hereditary aristocracy in Spain, one of the consequences of which was a corresponding crisis in the authority of judgments of all kinds. As Norbert Elias and others have amply noted, the crisis of the hereditary aristocracy was widespread throughout Europe and may help account for the extraordinary resonance of Gracián's work outside of Spain. As Elias points out, the *Oráculo manual* went through approximately twenty editions in France alone during the course of the seventeenth and eighteenth centuries under the title *L'Homme du Cour;* it came to be regarded as the first handbook of courtly psychology in the same way that Machiavelli's *Il Principe* was recognized as the first handbook of courtly-absolutist politics.[20] On the account I would propose, the context for the emergence of Gracián's notion of taste was that of an encompassing shift from a world in which judgments of value (including, increasingly, judgments of moral and aesthetic value) were supported by the notion of a fixed social hierarchy, to a world in which grounds for discrimination among values could no longer be aligned with the notion of an inherent hierarchy of social ranks. As the social basis of the hereditary aristocracy weakened, it became increasingly difficult to sustain the idea that "good taste" was aligned in any fundamental way with nobility of birth or purity of blood. And yet, as is all too clear from the literary controversies of the late sixteenth and early seventeenth centuries, as it is from a work like the *Oráculo manual,* the need to provide a grounding for social values through notions like taste (*gusto*) remained urgent.

One can read Gracián's work as a sign of the continuing need to assert the possibility of making discriminations of taste in the absence of a hierarchical social basis for such judgments. To say that the social context for Gracián's understanding of *gusto* is one in which the privilege of making discriminations of taste was no longer guaranteed by claims of nobility of birth is not to say that Gracián writes out of a context where the traces of social difference had been eradicated. Rather, it is to suggest that the authority of those making such distinctions could no longer be explained in terms of lineage, heredity, or other

20. See Norbert Elias, *Power and Civility* (New York: Pantheon, 1976), 358.

"natural" traits. Indeed, even when Gracián recognizes the ordering principle of distinction that seems to be fundamental to most conceptions of social reality, he avoids any explanation that would rely on the criteria of inborn rank:

> Hay sujetos que son buenos para mandados, porque ejecutan con felicísima diligencia, mas no valen para mandar, porque piensan mal y eligen peor, tropezando siempre en el desacierto. Hay hombres de todos géneros, unos para primeros y otros para segundos. (*El discreto,* 21, p. 330)

> (There are some subjects who are good for carrying out orders, because they do so with pleasure and diligently, but they are not good for giving orders, because they do not think well and make worse judgments, always making mistakes. There are all kinds of men, some who lead and some who follow.)

It is clear that social distinctions remained in place even after the erosion of the hereditary nobility. Indeed, some of these distinctions are seen as categorical, and some are as unfathomable in Gracián's mind as the distance that separates man from beast: "Hay, a veces, entre un hombre y otro casi otra tanta distancia como entre el hombre y la bestia; si no en la substancia, en la circunstancia; si no en la vitalidad, en el ejercicio della" (*El discreto,* p. 240) (Sometimes there is as much distance between one man and another as there is between man and beast; if not in substance, then in circumstances; if not in vital power, then in the exercise of it). But since it was not immediately clear just how distinctions could continue to be made in the absence of criteria that depended solidly on the principles of lineage, there arose a need to "invent" the (aesthetic) circumstances within which they might occur. The emergence of the styles of *culteranismo* and *conceptismo,* which were purposefully difficult and so served to create a social elite, can be understood in this light. So too Gracián's own aesthetic, where the capacity to produce and comprehend difficulty is valued as a sign of the ability to make discriminations: "*No allanarse sobrado en el concepto. Los más no estiman lo que entienden y lo que no perciben lo veneran. Las cosas, para que se estimen, han de costar; será celebrado cuando no fuese entendido*" (*OM,* 253, p. 460) (*Don't express your ideas too clearly.* Most people think little of what they understand, and venerate what they do not. To be valued, things must be difficult: if they can't understand you, people will think more highly of you) (*Art of Worldly Wisdom,* 143).

If difference is ineradicable—indeed, if the need to recognize and mark difference is the constitutional basis of the social—the question then becomes how to sustain the authority required by a notion like *buen gusto,* which is at the heart of Gracián's understanding of social differentiation. Similarly, one might ask how the different levels of accomplishment or perfection in evidence in society could be judged (Gracián: "Hay perfecciones soles y perfecciones luces," *El héroe,* Primor V, p. 122) (Some perfections are dazzling, others sparkle brilliantly). In one respect, the answers to all these questions are to be found in Gracián's concept of the individual—perhaps one should say, in the *individualism* that underwrites Gracián's conception of the individual—especially if one considers the fact that the notion of the "individual," and the principles of social differentiation based on such a notion, are categories that could only have emerged after the weakening of the value-base of the hereditary aristocracy had taken place. But since Gracián also thinks of taste as a quality that must be cultivated through social action, and not as something that is simply exhibited as a function of social status, it might be more accurate to say that the "individual" is for him the name for those calls to social action that were generated by the erosion of the notion of authority as hereditary.

It is no great surprise to find that Gracián's conception of the individual is subject to the same paradox that marks the social education of taste. On the one hand, individualism names a quality that is necessary for achieving the right relationship to the praxis of life; on the other hand, individualism is the quality that results from having successfully achieved such a relationship. Ideally, individualism describes a kind of self-sufficiency that would be independent of social reality: "Bástese a sí mismo el sabio" (*OM,* 137, p. 413) (The Wise are sufficient unto themselves) (*Art of Worldly Wisdom,* 76). And yet the individual who exercises "good taste," such as the "hombre de buena elección," must by definition also validate social norms. Insofar as taste occupies a central place in the *ethos* of the individual cultivated by Gracián, it is at once the occasion of a certain independence from the social body and also a confirmation of the primacy of the social body. Ideally, it is the sign of an ability to establish and reproduce one's own standards. In principle, it marks an ability to fashion oneself independent of the imitation of models, which appears to be inextricably bound up with the aporias of social education described above. The "individual" sets his own standards and goals: "Grande excelencia es una intensa singularidad, cifrar toda una categoría y equivalerla" (*El héroe*, Primor VI, p. 125) (Great excellence is an intense singularity, to mark off an entire category and be equal to it). Imitation, by contrast, is seen as a thanklessly difficult and doomed procedure, one that threatens to absorb and exhaust the individual: "Son tenidos por imitadores de los pasados los que les siguen; y por más que suden, no pueden purgar la presunción de imitación" (*El héroe*, Primor VII, p. 127) (They who follow past examples are deemed imitators of the past; and no matter how hard they might work, they cannot purge the presumption of imitation). And yet it remains equally true that the individual's individualism, especially as it is achieved through the exercise of taste, would have no standing were it not for the validation offered by society. "Taste" is the mark of the individual, but it also marks the incorporation of the individual into the social body.

Not surprisingly, perhaps, it proved difficult to articulate the principles of such new values. While Gracián puts forward a series of generic figures who represent recognizable character types (e.g., "el hombre de buena elección," "el discreto," "el hombre en su punto") he never quite succeeds in laying bare the sources of the ability to choose well. It is clear that "good taste" cannot be cited directly as evidence of one's incorporation into "good society." This is because one must first be educated into good taste. And yet it remains unclear just how society can accomplish this task. A critic like Gadamer simply does not notice that the antinomy of taste yields a paradox in which society requires for its foundation a process of education that it must at the same time produce. Likewise, he seems not to notice that taste is a faculty that requires an education that is always insufficient to it and that it is always required to surpass. (Gracián: "Supone el buen gusto y el rectísimo dictamen, que no bastan el estudio ni el ingenio," *El héroe*, Primor VII, p. 127) (You need good taste and an upright judgment; intelligence and application are not enough).[21] This paradox is especially sharp where Gracián rejects the imitation of models as a paradigm of cultural education.[22] In the case of "el discreto," for instance, Gracián

---

21. The ideal of "social education" must at the same time be considered in relation to Gracián's sometimes quite un-social understanding of human nature. See, for example, *Oráculo manual*, 167, on "self-reliance" ("saberse ayudar").

22. This is yet another instance in which Gracián prefigures Kant in the *Critique of Judgment*.

holds as an ideal that of someone who, on his own, achieves the proper freedom and distance from life and society, and who is thus able to make choices and distinctions from a superior position. But Gracián does not (or perhaps cannot) say whether it is distance that enables good judgment or whether such distance is already the result of having been educated into the habits of good judgment. So too for the man who "knows how to choose," the "hombre de buena elección":

> *Hombre de buena elección.* Lo más se vive della. Supone el buen gusto y el rectísimo dictamen, que no bastan el estudio ni el ingenio. No hay perfección donde no hay delecto; dos ventajas incluye: poder escoger, y lo mejor. Muchos de ingenio fecundo y sutil, de juicio acre, estudiosos y noticiosos también, en llegando al elegir, se pierden, cánsanse siempre con lo peor, que parece afectan el errar. Y así este es uno de los dones máximos de arriba. (*Oráculo manual,* 51, p. 380)

> (*Know how to choose.* Most things in life depend on it. You need good taste and an upright judgment; intelligence and application are not enough. There is no perfection without discernment and selection. Two talents are involved: choosing and choosing the best. There are many people with a fertile, subtle intelligence, rigorous judgment, both diligent and well informed, who are lost when they have to choose. They always choose the worst, as though they wanted to show their skill at doing so. Knowing how to choose is one of heaven's greatest gifts.) (*Art of Worldly Wisdom,* 29)

The cultivation of the faculty of taste is essential to the development of the personality of each of the figures Gracián imagines. And yet the cultivation of taste seems also to indicate the prior completion of this moral development. One must exercise taste in order to reach perfection, and yet the exercise of taste is also seen as providing evidence of perfection achieved:

> *Hombre en su punto.* No se hace hecho; vase de cada día perfeccionando en la persona, en el empleo, hasta llegar al punto del consumado ser, al complemento de prendas, de eminencias. Conocerse ha en lo realzado del gusto, purificado del ingenio, en

lo maduro del juicio, en lo defecado de la voluntad. Algunos nunca llegan a ser cabales: fáltales siempre un algo; tardan otros en hacerse. El varón consumado, sabio en dichos, cuerdo en hechos, es admitido, y aun deseado, del singular comercio de los discretos. (*OM*, 6, p. 362)

(*Reach perfection.* No one is born that way. Perfect yourself daily, both personally and professionally, until you become a consummate being, rounding off your gifts and reaching eminence. Signs of the perfect person: elevated taste, a pure intelligence, a clear will, ripeness of judgment. Some people are never complete and are always lacking something. Others take a long time to form themselves. The consummate person—wise in speech, prudent in deeds—is admitted to, and even desired by, the singular society of the discreet.) (*Art of Worldly Wisdom*, 3–4)

In a study of the aesthetics of individuation, Frances Ferguson identifies a closely related paradox in the eighteenth century. Referring to the work of Edmund Burke, she suggests that "even if [his] is a 'scientific' account of taste, an analysis of the kinds of social testimony that people give in expressing what looks like individual preference, it describes taste not by explaining individual tastes as relationships toward aesthetic objects but rather by redefining what it might mean to give an explanation of taste. Explaining taste turns out to be pointing to other tastes like this one, admitting, that is, that one cannot give a very good explanation of individual taste but can show that there is more (i.e., collective taste, in the form of the social, the class, the local, etc.) where it came from. . . . Individual taste appears merely a mystification of the social" (*Solitude and the Sublime*, 63).[23]

In Gracián, where the historical context is quite different, the cultivation of the individual's individualism is also a substitute for a certain

23. Compare Gracián, who elevates *gusto* to the level of a "science": "Un modo de ciencia es éste que no le enseñan los libros ni se aprende en las escuelas; cúrsase en los teatros del buen gusto y en el general tan singular de la discreción. Hállanse unos hombres apreciadores de todo sazonado dicho y observadores de todo galante hecho. . . . Estos son los oráculos de la curiosidad y maestros de la *ciencia del buen gusto*" (*El discreto*, Discurso V, "Hombre de plausibles noticias: Razonamiento académico" [n.b. this title duplicates that of the *Oráculo manual*, 22, which nonetheless does not mention the "ciencia del buen gusto"]). *El discreto*, ed. Luys Santa Marina (Barcelona: Planeta, 1984), 63.

kind of social prestige that, under other circumstances, could be guaranteed by claims to nobility of birth. Similarly, taste is a quality of character whose principal trait is itself the ability to render judgments of quality: "Tanta diferencia e importancia puede caber en el cómo" (*El discreto*, Discurso XXII, p. 125) (Just as much difference and importance can depend on the "how"). It is of particular importance to members of social groups whose economic means were substantial and who could thus enjoy the luxury of pretending to have overcome their "natural" needs. According to the account proposed by Elias,

> A compulsive desire for social prestige is to be found as the primary motive of action only among members of classes whose income under normal circumstances is substantial and perhaps ever growing, and at any rate is appreciably over the hunger threshold. In such cases the impulse to engage in economic activity is no longer the simple necessity of satisfying hunger, but a desire to preserve a certain high, socially expected standard of living and prestige. This explains why, in such elevated classes, affect-control and self-constraint are generally more highly developed than in the lower classes: fear of loss or reduction of social prestige is one of the most powerful motive forces in the transformation from constraints through others into self-restraints. Here, too, as in many other instances, the upper-class characteristics of "good society" are particularly highly developed in the courtly aristocracy of the seventeenth and eighteenth centuries, precisely because, within its framework, money was indispensable and wealth desirable as a means of living, but certainly not, as in the bourgeois world, the basis of prestige as well. Membership of courtly society means to those belonging to it more than wealth. (*Power and Civility*, 268)

✳ ✳ ✳

If Elias is right, then it is no surprise to find that the category of *gusto* emerges in its specifically aesthetic sense in the debates surrounding *conceptismo* and *culteranismo* in poetry,[24] as well as in discussions of

---

24. Andrée Collard writes that "aside from arguments about changes in practice and custom that cause change in art, the notion of *good taste* becomes generalized, which occupies a preeminent place in the criticism of culteranism and in critical language in

the aesthetic principles underlying the *comedia* as a form of entertainment designed for the *vulgo,* and not just in the writings of Gracián; it was in all these areas that one could witness the suppression of "natural" needs by the "social" refinements of culture. By comparison, in a work like the *Lazarillo,* where the "natural" passion of hunger is figured as standing at the root of all desire (including the preeminent social desire for prestige that dominates the Escudero and, presumably, "Vuestra Merced" as well), the concept of "taste" does not yet have the aesthetic standing it would acquire later in the Golden Age. This is because "nature," and natural needs, had not yet been conclusively overtaken by the new configuration of social values evident in seventeenth-century Spain; needs (e.g., the need to satisfy hunger) and desires (e.g., for social standing) are equally forceful factors in that work. By the early seventeenth century, things had changed in radical ways. Sancho Panza's experiences in governing the island of Barataria in *Don Quijote,* part 2, are determined by the need to temper his "natural" inclinations and appetites so that he might "civilize" himself. But since Sancho's experience on Barataria is of course staged by the Duke and the Duchess, it also seems reasonable to assume that the "civilizing" desire to overcome nature was also quite self-consciously felt among the courtly aristocracy.[25]

Although Elias is certainly right to suggest that the desire for social prestige was intensified at court, it would be mistaken to think that the validity of the concept of taste was limited to this context. Especially in debates surrounding the legitimacy of the pleasures and preferences of the masses *(el vulgo),* it is clear that the newly emergent notion of taste played a decisive role in establishing a basis for discrimination among works of art where the "natural" (read: hereditary) basis for distinction had been eroded. Consider in this regard the positions of Cervantes and Lope de Vega on the role of the *vulgo* in fashioning taste. In *Don Quijote,* part 1, the Canon of Toledo inveighs against the *novelas de caballerías* insofar as they cater to the *gusto del vulgo,* whose unedu-

---

general. Herrera uses it already with reference to the pleasure that is derived from the reading of some beautiful pages: the ancients "travajaron por el gusto y aprovechamiento de todos" (*Nueva poesía,* 20). The reference to Herrera is to the *Anotaciones* to the poetry of Garcilaso de la Vega, in Antonio Vilanova, *Garcilaso de la Vega y sus comentaristas* (Madrid: Gredos, 1972), 581.

25. At the same time, one must recognize that Sancho's abandonment of his governorship represents a rejection of these "civilizing" pretenses and a "return" to the "natural" world of needs.

cated interest in reading for pleasure is said to outweigh the intellectual interests of learned readers. Regarding the contemporary *comedias,* he says that taste is not in itself sufficient to guarantee the quality of the works being judged. This is because, while taste must be educated, the *vulgo* brings uneducated opinion to bear on these works:

> . . . el vulgo las oye con gusto, y las tiene y las aprueba por buenas, estando tan lejos de serlo, y los autores que las componen y los actores que las representan dicen que así han de ser, porque así las quiere el vulgo, y no de otra manera, y que las que llevan traza y siguen la fábula como el arte pide, no sirven sino para cuatro discretos que las entienden, y todos los demás se quedan ayunos de entender su artificio, y que a ellos les está mejor ganar de comer con los muchos, que no opinión con los pocos. (Part 1, chap. 48, p. 568)

> (. . . the crowd enjoy seeing them, and approve of them and reckon them good, when they are so far from being so; and if the authors who write them and the managers who put them on say that they must be good, because the crowd likes them like that way and not otherwise, and that the authors who observe a plan and follow the story as the rules of drama require only serve to please the three or four men of sense who understand them, while all the rest are left unsatisfied and cannot fathom their subtlety.) (trans. Cohen, 427)

For Don Quijote, the issue of taste is somewhat more difficult to resolve. Especially in part 2 of the novel, Don Quijote rejects both the "progressive" view of taste as the forerunner of social change, and the "conservative" view of taste as requiring the confirmation of preexisting social groups. He represents the view that there is a nobility of taste that reaches "beyond" conservative and progressive postures, a "true nobility" that cannot be defined in any social terms, a nobility that produces a hierarchy of taste all its own and that is not determined by social standing at all. In his defense of poetic taste in response to the Caballero del Verde Gabán he seeks to "overcome" the traces of both the individual and the social body in the work of art. But rather than simply reject the affiliation of taste with the individual body, he interprets good taste as a form of bodily purity. And once the body is introduced it seems that even an idealizing defense of poetry is bound to be the defense of *particular* literary tastes; in the case at hand, it amounts to a rejection of modernizing tendencies in art in favor of more traditional poetic values:

> La poesía . . . es como una doncella tierna y de poca edad, y en todo estremo hermosa, a quien tienen cuidado de enriquecer, pulir y adornar otras muchas doncellas, que son todas las otras ciencias, y ella se ha de servir de todas, y todas se han de autorizar con ella; pero esta tal doncella no quiere ser manoseada, ni traída por las calles, ni publicada por las esquinas de las plazas ni por los rincones de los palacios. Ella es hecha de una alquimia de tal virtud, que quien la sabe tratar la volverá en oro purísimo de inestimable precio; hala de tener, el que la tuviere, a raya, no dejándola correr en torpes sátiras ni en desalmados sonetos; no ha de ser vendible en ninguna manera, si ya no fuere en poemas heroicos, en lamentables tragedias, o en comedias alegres y artificiosas. No se ha de dejar tratar de trujanes, ni del ignorante vulgo, incapaz de conocer ni estimar los tesoros que en ella se encierran. Y no penséis, señor, que yo llamo aquí vulgo sola- mente a la gente plebeya y humilde; que todo aquel que no sabe, aunque sea señor y príncipe, puede y debe entrar en número del vulgo. (Part 2, chap. 16, p. 155)

> (Poetry . . . is like a tender, young, and extremely beautiful maiden, whom other maidens toil to enrich, to polish and adorn. These maidens are the other sciences; and she has to be served by all, while all of them have to justify themselves by her. But this maiden does not care to be handled, or dragged through the streets, nor to be shown at the corners of the market place, or in the antechambers of palaces. She is formed of an alchemy of such virtue that anyone who knows how to treat her will transform her into purest gold of inestimable price. Her possessor must keep her within bounds, not letting her run to base lam- poons or impious sonnets. She must be exposed for sale only in the form of heroic poems, piteous tragedies, or gay and artificial comedies. She must not let herself be handled by buffoons, nor by the ignorant vulgar, who are incapable of recognizing or appreciating her treasures. Now do not imagine, sir, that by

vulgar I mean only the common and humble people; for all who are ignorant, even if they are lords or princes, can rightfully be included under the name of vulgar.) (trans. Cohen, 568–69)

For Gracián, likewise, the *vulgo* is scorned for its lack of wisdom and independence; in *El Criticón,* part 2, Crisi 5 ("Plaza del populacho y corral del vulgo"), it is said that "los sabios son pocos, no hay cuatro en la ciudad, los ignorantes son los muchos, los necios son los infinitos" (wise men are few, there are not four in the city; the ignorant are many, the fools are infinite).[26] But in *El Criticón* at least, it is not the *taste* of the crowd that is at stake. Indeed, Gracián elsewhere sees the exercise of taste as a sign and symbol of modernity. Taste does not just rely for its validity on the fact that there are other tastes like it, as in the case of Burke. The power of taste is validated because it is a forerunner of social change, which it in turn validates. As Gracián writes in *El discreto,* "Siempre va el gusto adelante, nunca vuelve atrás; no se ceba en lo que pasó, siempre pica en la novedad; pero puédesele engañar con lo flamante del modillo" (*El discreto,* Discurso XXII, pp. 334–35) (Taste always runs ahead, it never turns back; it does not feed on what has already happened, it always snacks on novelty; but it can be bedazzled by the latest fashion).[27]

*   *   *

In contrast to the quixotic understanding of the unchanging aristocracy of certain tastes, Gracián's conception of taste is more closely allied to notions of common sense. On the one hand, his understanding of *gusto* as a form of judgment represents a transformation of the Scholastic ideal of prudence.

> *De la gran sindéresis.* Es el trono de la razón, base de la prudencia, que en fe della cuesta poco el acertar. Es suerte del cielo, y más deseada por primera y por mejor: la primera pieza

---

26. Gracián, *El Criticón,* ed. P. Ismael Quiles (Madrid: Espasa-Calpe, 1964), 179. From Gracián's scorn of common ignorance to Flaubert's great fear of *bêtise,* which culminates in a work like *Bouvard et Pécuchet,* is but a short step.

27. But compare the following passage from *El discreto:* "es lisonja la novedad, hechiza el gusto, y con solo variar de sainete, se renuevan los objectos [*sic*], que es gran arte de agradar" (*El discreto,* Discurso XXII, p. 335).

del arnés, con tal urgencia que ninguna otra que le falte a un hombre le denomina falto; nótase más su menos. Todas las acciones de la vida dependen de su influencia y todas solicitan su calificación, que todo ha de ser con seso. Consiste en una conatural propensión a todo lo más conforme a razón, casándose siempre con lo más acertado. (*OM, 96,* p. 398)

(*Good common sense.* It is the throne of reason, the foundation of prudence, and by its light it is easy to succeed. It is a gift from heaven, highly prized because it is first and best. Good sense is our armor, so necessary that the lack of this single piece will make people call us lacking. When least present, most missed. All actions in life depend on its influence, and all solicit its approval, for all depends on good sense. It consists of a natural inclination to all that conforms most to reason, and to all that is most fit.) (*Art of Worldly Wisdom,* 53–54)

But perhaps more important than its Scholastic affinities, taste, as a form of "common sense," bears striking resemblance to the modern, Cartesian notion of "good sense." When seen in relation to "good sense," what Gracián calls *gusto,* and especially *buen gusto,* is not at all a form of reason *manqué.* Rather, it represents a kind of judgment that anticipates the form of critical reason that was systematized in modern philosophical discourse.[28] For Descartes,

Good sense is the best distributed thing in the world: for everyone thinks himself so well endowed with it that even those who

28. See Robert Klein, "Judgment and Taste in Cinquecento Art Theory," in *Form and Meaning: Writings on the Renaissance and Modern Art* (Princeton: Princeton University Press, 1981), 161–69. In *The Judgment of Sense* David Summers provides a succinct conceptual genealogy of "common sense" in which there are striking connections between ancient philosophy and early modern thought: "The modern notion of common sense retained its connection with spirit, embracing the Stoic notions of *oikeiosis* [an implanted feeling or affinity, not a product of custom or habit], the self-evident principles of human society and of *koinos nous,* common reason undisfigured by sophistication, combining them with the Stoic *koinai ennoiai* (or common notions, which Locke rejected as 'innate'), and 'common conceptions of the mind,' as writers of the Middle Ages had called the axioms of Euclidean geometry. The philosophy of the common sense school incorporated these traditional elements. . . . The 'common conceptions' were supplemented by the newly self-evident principles of modern natural science, which in turn magnified and solidified the authority of the common sense as a criterion. In these ways common sense grew closer to reason, from which reason might proceed" (328–29).

are the hardest to please in everything else do not usually desire more of it than they possess. In this it is unlikely that everyone is mistaken. It indicates rather that the power of judging well and of distinguishing the true from the false—which is what we properly call "good sense" or "reason"—is naturally equal in all men, and consequently that the diversity of our opinions does not arise because some of us are more reasonable than others but solely because we direct our thoughts along different paths and do not attend to the same things. For it is not enough to have a good mind; the main thing is to apply it well. The greatest souls are capable of the greatest vices as well as the greatest virtues; and those who proceed but very slowly can make much greater progress, if they always follow the right path, than those who hurry and stray from it.[29]

The problems faced by Descartes in moving from the "good sense" that is plentiful in the world but so often insufficient or simply wrong, to critical reason, which is far less common but unimpeachable, are not so different from those encountered by Gracián in formulating the notion of *buen gusto*. What links Gracián and Descartes is the need to account for the authority that is invested in the judgments of "good taste," even if the answers suggested by these two writers take somewhat different forms. The question What is the authority of taste? in Gracián is parallel to the question What is the authority of critical reason? in Descartes because both are derived from a common basis in a form of "good sense" that must finally validate itself. As is well known, the confirmation of the authority of reason for Descartes involves a derivation of the truth of pure self-reflection through the overcoming of skepticism that calls mere "good sense" into question; it relies on and confirms a categorical distinction between the individual, corporeal self and the disembodied rational subject. Indeed, Descartes formulates the authority of the subject through an overcoming both of the errors of sense experience and of the social authority of commonly distributed "good sense." Accordingly, the voice of authority that speaks in the *Meditations* and the *Discourse on Method* is taken to represent more than the voice of authority of René Descartes. It achieves a "generalization" of the authority of that voice by "calling away" all the particulari-

29. *Discourse on the Method*, I, 111.

ties of body that might locate it in physical, social, or historical space and time.

The problem of the authority of taste is "resolved" in a similar fashion. Especially in the *Oráculo manual*, where matters of taste seem to move us directly from the arena of social conduct to the moral domain, Gracián's maxims present themselves as authoritative insofar as they are spoken by an anonymous, generalized, and disembodied voice. "Don't outshine your boss"; "associate with those you can learn from"; "don't make yourself disliked"; "don't talk about yourself"; "be known for your courtesy"; "live practically." These and many other maxims like them are articulated by a voice that refuses to be positioned exclusively either on the side of the individual or on the side of society. Indeed, its authority stems from its ability strategically to refuse either of these positions, the better to negotiate the difference between them. In Gracián's maxims, it is no longer the voice of the individual or of society that speaks, but rather the voice of a secular conscience, which is to say, the voice of that peculiar, internal form of authority that governs conduct where no "external" authority is in sight.[30] It is a surprisingly short step from Gracián's aesthetically oriented maxims to Kant's conception of what a moral "maxim" is (namely, one that could be willed as a universal law).[31] If it is true, as Alasdair MacIntyre claims, that Enlightenment morality requires on the one hand a stock of maxims and on the other hand a conception of just what a rational test for a maxim must be,[32] then Gracián's importance is to demonstrate the relevance of judgments of taste for the history of morality insofar as the internal, inner voice of the individual, the voice that internalizes and reproduces society's "universal" commands, provides an anticipatory semblance of what Kant will later indicate as the "rational" basis of morality, that is, the strict universalizability of its commands.

30. Several recent studies point out the ways in which various forms of interior speech came into play in the *asujétissement* of New World subjects. See especially Jorge Klor de Alva, "Colonizing Souls: The Failure of the Indian Inquisition and the Rise of Penitential Discipline," in *Cultural Encounters: The Impact of the Inquisition on Spain and the New World,* ed. Mary Elizabeth Perry and Anne J. Cruz (Berkeley and Los Angeles: University of California Press, 1991), 3–22. Some of this work has recently been brought to bear on Peninsular texts, such as Cervantes's *El celoso extremeño.* See James D. Fernández, "The Bonds of Patrimony: Cervantes and the New World," *PMLA* 109 (1994): 969–81.

31. Kant, *Foundations of the Metaphysics of Morals,* trans. Lewis White Beck, ed. Robert Paul Wolff (Indianapolis: Bobbs-Merrill, 1969), 23.

32. See *After Virtue,* 44.

*   *   *

In addressing the question of the foundations of the social community in relation to the authority of judgments of taste, we encountered the structural dilemma wherein judgments of taste and social community seem at once to create and to presuppose one another, such that the idea of a social education into "good taste" seemed at best aporetic. While the aporia of taste may be widespread within the culture of modernity, the solutions for it are historically specific. They become especially apparent at moments of social change, when the principles by which society is ordered are themselves called into question. In the instance of a social world governed by the traditional principles of caste, for instance, the solution to the aporia of taste takes the form of an assumption that there is something inborn but nonetheless transmissible, something prior to the social and to any faculty of judgment— something, indeed, that is prior to the individual itself—that is constitutive of social values and that authorizes judgments of taste. In such a context, judgments including those of taste can be seen to derive from and reflect back directly upon the existing social order, reconfirming it and conferring upon it the authority of a moral order. Within the changing social climate of early modern Spain, however, where the hereditary aristocracy had grown weak and where the principles of *limpieza de sangre* were beginning to be placed in doubt, it began to appear that the authority of taste was no longer supported by social norms and no longer carried its former moral force. (Indeed, if the literature struggling with the principles of caste can be taken as any indication, it would seem that aesthetic practice had long been running considerably ahead of the authority of social norms.) It was such a dilemma that the quasi-moral notion of "good taste" was meant to resolve. Like the notion of the *sensus communis,* "good taste" was not conceived of primarily as a physical "sense," but rather as a supplementary sense, a sense of form, and especially for Gracián a sense of "good form." As such, it was a particularly powerful tool in forming social cohesion while preserving the need for social distinction. Moreover, taste was not itself conceived as having an authority in the conventional sense; it was the indication, rather, of a social authority that was absent or displaced. In part by resolving the problem of authority, the discourse of taste made it possible for the newly emergent individual, as a particular body, to imagine himself (or, less often, herself) as standing in relation to a social body that was in the process of reconstituting itself. As Gracián's writings suggest, social authority was not dissolved in the process; rather, it was reconstituted by the workings of a seemingly anonymous voice onto subjects who accepted its insistent commands.

6

Desire and Authority in the Spanish Golden Age: Oedipus and Don Juan

> Oedipus begins in the mind of the father.
> —Deleuze and Guattari, *Anti-Oedipus*

"Is Oedipus universal, . . . the great paternal catholic symbol, the meeting place of all the churches?" Or is the Oedipal paradigm of desire and authority merely a contingent historical phenomenon, specific to certain cultures and localizable at particular times and places? Gilles Deleuze and Félix Guattari raise these questions in the course of an attempt to explore the boundaries of the Oedipal paradigm in their influential study, *Anti-Oedipus: Capitalism and Schizophrenia.*[1] As with any large questions such as these, the interesting issues arise not just in the conflicts between the principal positions—in this instance, between psychoanalysis (Freud, Jones, Lacan) and anthropology (Malinowski,

---

1. Deleuze and Guattari, *Anti-Oedipus: Capitalism and Schizophrenia* (hereafter cited as *A-O*), trans. Robert Hurley, Mark Seem, and Helen R. Lane (Minneapolis: University of Minnesota Press, 1983), 171.

Róheim, Ortigues)—but among the factions on each side. On the side of "universal Oedipus" there are at least two divergent positions. One views Oedipus as a natural affective matrix or constellation of the psyche, and argues that the Oedipal paradigm derives from a real event in history whose effects have been transmitted throughout the ages by the process of phylogenetic heredity. The other denies any possibility of locating the origins of the Oedipal conflict within the natural history of the human species at all and in fact finds such an effort to be symptomatic of a desire for the "real" that is itself Oedipally controlled.[2]

For Guattari and Deleuze, these either/or's are best understood as neither/nor's. On their view, the particular complex of desire that establishes masculine authority in its most general and abstract form by killing off the father and reoccupying his place has its roots neither as an archaic affect, nor as a universal structure of human (un)consciousness, nor as a purely contingent historical phenomenon. Rather, *Capitalism and Schizophrenia* constitutes an attempt to show that thinking of Oedipus as either universal *or* historical places constraints upon the free discharge or "flow" of desire that drives human action, and that this leads us merely to reinscribe, rather than understand, criticize, or liberate desire in its Oedipal form. For this reason, Deleuze and Guattari refuse to see Oedipus either as the product of a specific system of social and psychic laws (those associated with capitalism) or as a universal structure of desire that remains always and everywhere the same. Instead, they suggest that Oedipus is the privileged mode, within capitalism, of maintaining social order by limiting or constraining the mobility of human desire—"privileged," they argue, because this particular means of constraint underwrites the specific configuration of desire within which all representations of reality and all "real" transactions take place. In their language, Oedipus is the principal means that modern Western cultures have of "coding the uncodable, of codifying what eludes the codes, or of displacing desire and its object, a way of entrapping them" (*A-O*, 173).

2. The Oedipal nature of this desire lies in the wish to possess the secrets of the ancestors as the earliest, most original, form of the real. Add to these debates the claims of Jean-Pierre Vernant that what Freud discovered in Oedipus could not have been part of the original Greek myth. See Vernant and Pierre Vidal-Naquet, *Myth and Tragedy in Ancient Greece*, trans. Janet Lloyd (Cambridge: Zone Books, 1988), especially Vernant, "Oedipus Without the Complex," 85–111. Vernant is writing in direct opposition to the claim advanced by Didier Anzieu that Oedipus is pervasive throughout Greek culture and myth.

To be sure, it is tempting to read their effort to challenge the Oedipal paradigm simply as an attempt to step across the bar of repression in order to recuperate a freedom otherwise lost to modern Western culture. There is indeed something transgressive about *Anti-Oedipus,* but Deleuze and Guattari are considerably more subtle and intricate than this in their arguments. In order to appreciate the force of their position, it is important to recall that Deleuze and Guattari imagine that all societies are driven by various forms of production, including desiring-production, social production, and economic production. Each of these constitutes the condition of possibility or "limit" of the others. For instance, "desiring-production," which originates in what they call energy-flows, is situated at the limit of social production, which binds the energy-flows.[3] All forms of social production, from the crudest rank-orderings to the most elaborate drama of recognition, are propelled by desire; at the same time, however, desire must be limited, contained, or bound, if the social body is to function at all. Especially in capitalism, which operates on the basis of an unusually mobile form of desire, desire must be structured or constrained, and Deleuze and Guattari claim that the figure of Oedipus provides the model according to which this takes place. (Whether Oedipus models this binding work *only* for capitalist societies is something that remains to be seen.) Relative to precapitalist economic formations, capitalism is a form of economic production that both requires and helps reproduce a desire that circulates with apparent freedom; nonetheless, capitalist production is in fact governed by the figure of Oedipus as the one who enforces the invisible law of the father, whose limitations allow for the circulation and exchange of desires. More accurately phrased, Oedipus transforms desire into a contradictory law that makes the killing of the father and the repossession of his authority the means through which a semblance of order is possible for the children. Deleuze and Guattari thus see the figure of Oedipus not so much as the essence of capitalism (which on their account has only a "displaced essence") but as its condition of possibility, its "limit."

---

3. They write: "Desiring-machines are binary machines, obeying a binary law or set of rules governing associations: one machine is always coupled with another. The productive synthesis, the production of production, is inherently connective in nature: 'and . . .' 'and then . . .' This is because there is always a flow-producing machine, and another machine connected to it that interrupts or draws off part of this flow (the breast—the mouth). . . . Desire causes the current to flow, itself flows in turn, and breaks the flows" (*A-O,* 5).

In their understanding, the notion of a "limit" has implications both theoretical (or structural) and historical. Theoretically or structurally viewed, Oedipus represents the particular form of authority within capitalism that makes possible the free circulation of desire by constraining it in determinate ways. But Deleuze and Guattari suggest that the configuration of every society is also historically limited. At some point, every society is bound to experience the foreboding sense of its own finitude as "the real form in which the limit threatens to arrive, and which it wards off with all the strength it can command" (A-O, 176). It is to the desire on the part of societies to gain some protection against this historical "limit" that Deleuze and Guattari credit the obstinacy with which the formations preceding capitalism tended to restrict the development of their essential social and economic functions, in the hope of preventing accumulations of capital from gaining the momentum that might destroy the structures underlying them.[4]

The case of the Spanish merchant class in the Golden Age provides a good illustration of this point. By the sixteenth century this class had accumulated substantial wealth in money and other assets, such that it had to be reckoned with *as* a class. In 1585 the Spanish merchant fleet rivaled the Dutch, doubled the German, and trebled the English and the French.[5] But over the long term this class resisted transformation.[6] Why was this so? Contemporary explanations make the ideological nature of this resistance immediately clear. In the opinion of Pedro de Valencia, for instance, gold, silver, and money were all "poison for cities and republics": "People think money is what provides for their subsistence, and this is not true. The inheritance of well-tended fields, herds, and fisheries, that is what feeds cities and republics. Each man ought to work his share of the land. And those who subsist on the income of the money they invest are idle and useless, only there to eat what others have sown and nurtured."[7] A similarly ideological attachment to agri-

4. See A-O, 176.
5. Hamilton, "The Decline of Spain," *Economic History Review* 8 (1938): 168. The figures assume that one includes the Portuguese fleet as part of the Spanish.
6. Extensive work has been done on the Spanish merchant class. See for instance Basas Fernández, *Mercaderes burgaleses en el siglo XVI* (Burgos: Boletín del Instituto Fernán González, 1954), and Ruth Pike, *Aristocrats and Traders: Sevillian Society in the Sixteenth Century* (Ithaca: Cornell University Press, 1972).
7. Pedro de Valencia, *Escritos sociales* (Madrid: Vinas Mey, 1945), 36–37, as cited in Pierre Vilar, "Les primitifs espagnols de la pensée économique," in *Mélanges offerts à Marcel Bataillon* (Bordeaux: Féret et fils, 1962), 283.

culture as a means of resisting social change shows up in the emphasis on pastoral virtues and in the topos of the *alabanza de aldea,* in which the fecundity of the earth is aligned with the symbolic, whole, productive, body.[8] At the same time, the attempt to preserve existing social and economic functions, which I have described in connection with *Fuenteovejuna* as part of an active resistance to social and historical change, represents an effort to ward off the anxiety with which a culture would only naturally respond to the prospect of its own demise. The anxiety of a sonnet like Quevedo's "Miré los muros de la patria mía," in which the fatherland is portrayed as in a state of moral and physical decline, can be seen more as registering the fear of historical finitude than as exemplifying the *desengaño* that was the stock-in-trade of the poets of the baroque. The sometimes desperate political rhetoric of "decline" that marks the difficult accommodation of capitalism in early modern Spain, as studied by J. H. Elliott, was provoked by an awareness of the historical limitations of Spain's precapitalist social and economic base, as were its counterparts, the practical optimism of the *arbitristas* and the encouragements offered by writers like Miguel Caxa de Leruela, whose *Restauración de la abundancia de España* (1631) offered a series of symbolic arguments for the reinvigoration of agriculture as the means to restore prosperity to Spain.[9]

We shall return to the question of the resistance to the desires characteristic of capitalism in the discussion of Don Juan. The point to be noted from Deleuze and Guattari is that, regardless of whether or not the Oedipal paradigm is determined to be specific to Western cultures, only in modern Western capitalism did it become fully "occupied." Even the financial and mercantile capitalism characteristic of Western societies in the early modern age left the Oedipal paradigm truncated or only incompletely filled. Capitalism did not fully take root, and the Oedipal paradigm did not fully take hold within the subconscious steering mechanisms of society, they argue, until production was completely and directly controlled by capital, which is to say until financial and merchant capital became functions of the global

---

8. On the fecundity topos, see Edmond Cros, *Theory and Practice of Sociocriticism,* trans. Jerome Schwartz (Minneapolis: University of Minnesota Press, 1988), 190–207 ("Social Formations and Figurative Discourse in Mateo Alemán's *Guzmán de Alfarache*").

9. See the modern edition of Leruela by Jean Paul le Flem (Madrid: Instituto de Estudios Fiscales, 1975).

expropriation of labor-power. For when labor-power is governed by a detached transcendent object one enters the self-sustaining circle of desire and production that brings about the peculiar form of reality that they describe as "the production of productions, the production of recordings, and the production of consumptions" (A-O, 226). (Compare Marx, who wrote of the "self-expansion of existing capital," and who described capitalist production as driving toward "unlimited expansion of production, to production as an end in itself, to an unrestricted development of the social productive powers of labour.")[10] In capitalism, they argue, the field of social production is independent of familial reproduction. Social production in capitalism is not dependent upon the network of kinship structures that in "primitive" societies place strict limits upon desire in relation to its objects.[11] Capitalism is not dependent upon the regulations necessary to keep bloodlines pure, nor is it compelled to make reference to immediate bodily needs. (On the contrary, capitalism works to suppress the body as the locus of labor-power.) Similarly, the desire for commodities in capitalism is never direct; it is always mediated by another desire. Moreover, capitalism admits the free circulation of desire in its "dirtiest" and most protean possible form: money is the "filthy lucre" that touches everything and that everyone can touch, but that has no use-value in itself and whose origins cannot be traced back to any source. Little surprise to find that money is so often thought of as a threat to those precapitalist societies structured around the values of social caste.[12]

Whereas societies oriented around the axiology of caste are governed by the racial phantasm of "pure blood," the mode of social production characteristic of capitalism attempts to repress the question of racial purity. It honors instead a transcendent detached object, which is the imaginary possession of the res cogitans. In addition, the rise to dominance of the power of the transcendent detached object (the phallus) brings about a reduction of the social field of the non-phallic or feminine "other" to the familial field. Hence the increasing confinement of

10. Karl Marx, Capital, trans. David Fernbach (New York: Vintage Books, 1981), 3:358.

11. See in this regard Marc Shell's analysis of Measure for Measure in The End of Kinship (Stanford: Stanford University Press, 1988).

12. Simmel makes the related argument that money is perceived as a threat and a danger to ascetics and hermits. See The Philosophy of Money, 2d ed., ed. David Frisby, trans. Tom Bottomore and David Frisby (London: Routledge, 1990), 251–54.

women to the home in capitalist society, where the spheres of "home" and "work" were held increasingly apart. (Recent historicist work in Renaissance studies, some of it centering on Cervantes, has confirmed this very fact.)[13] Hence also the reduction of the colonial "other" to those traits most easily encapsulated in his or her identity as a member of an "extended family" (race, kinship group, and so forth).[14] Indeed, for Deleuze and Guattari, it is colonization that "causes" Oedipus to exist, or is a precondition of its existence, in the sense that it assures that "these Savages are deprived of the control over their own social production, that they are ripe for being reduced to the only thing they have left, the familial reproduction imposed on them" (A-O, 179).

And yet it is clear that even the analysis of the "full occupation" of the Oedipal paradigm in capitalism cannot avoid reference to certain archaisms that are borrowed from so-called primitive socioeconomic formations.[15] If the figure of Oedipus stands as the "limit" of capitalism, coding desire in such a way that the *socius* is able to reproduce itself in an apparently seamless fashion and without any grave anxieties about its own historical origins in precapitalist formations, the figure of Oedipus was certainly not born with capitalism. Oedipus is a truth of modern, capitalist society not because it originates in or was discovered by capitalism, but because Oedipus is a formation of the unconscious that succeeded by "assembling the parts and wheels of its apparatus from elements of the previous social formations" (A-O, 175). Deleuze and Guattari give the example of the position of the transcendent object, which has a place within both capitalist and precapitalist economies,[16] but there are other "borrowed archaisms" that are equally important.

---

13. See, for example, Mary Elizabeth Perry, *Gender and Disorder in Early Modern Seville* (Princeton: Princeton University Press, 1990), and James D. Fernández, "The Bonds of Patrimony: Cervantes and the New World," *PMLA* 109 (1994): 969–81, which concentrates on "El celoso extremeño."

14. As Marc Shell notes, the notion of "universal brotherhood" that became prevalent in the early modern period was the source of numerous contradictions, many of which were registered within early modern Spain. See "Marranos (Pigs), or from Coexistence to Toleration," *Critical Inquiry* 17 (1991): 306–35, and *The End of Kinship*.

15. Various writers have commented on the increasing scholarly aversion to the term "primitive," including Mary Douglas in *Purity and Danger: An Analysis of Concepts of Pollution and Taboo* (New York: Praeger, 1966).

16. The difference between the two apparently lies in the degree to which this transcendent object is detached. Learning to live in capitalism involves learning to accept the increasing distance of this object. The phenomenon of the "hidden God" could well be understood as a function of it.

For instance, Marx linked the "mystical" element in commodity-formation directly to fetishization.[17] Drawing on the nineteenth-century religious and anthropological discourse about fetishes,[18] Marx wrote at length about the ways in which commodification reflects a process whereby certain material things came to stand for *more* than what they are materially.[19] Similarly, Norman O. Brown drew a number of parallels between the religious and ritualistic bases of archaic and modern money.[20] "If we recognize the essentially sacred character of archaic money," he wrote, "we shall be in a position to recognize the essentially sacred character of certain specific features of modern money—certainly the gold standard and also the rate of interest. . . . Measured by rational utility and real human needs, there is absolutely no difference between the gold and silver of modern economy and the shells or dogs' teeth of archaic economy. . . . That the imaginary value placed on gold and silver in the modern economy is derived from the domain of the sacred is a point already fully recognized by Keynes in the *Treatise on Money*."[21]

The question of these and other "residual" or "archaic" elements is particularly relevant to the case of early modern Spain, where it is

17. See Marx, *Capital*, trans. Ben Fowkes (New York: Vintage Books, 1977), 1:165–66.

18. See William Pietz, "Fetishism and Materialism," in *Fetishism as Cultural Discourse*, ed. Emily Apter and William Pietz (Ithaca: Cornell University Press, 1993), 128–33; and Jack Amariglio and Antonio Callari, "Marxian Value-Theory and the Problem of the Subject: The Role of Commodity Fetishism," ibid., 186–216.

19. Marx explains that this begins in the materialization or objectification of sense impressions ("the impression made by a thing on the optic nerve is perceived not as a subjective excitation of that nerve but as the objective form of a thing outside the eye"), but with the attachment to the physical nature of the commodity effaced, so that the commodified thing stands ready to be reinvested with a supernatural value. Marx goes on to say that in order to understand commodity fetishism "we must take flight into the misty realm of religion. There the products of the human brain appear as autonomous figures endowed with a life of their own, which enter into relations both with each other and with the human race. So it is in the world of commodities with the products of men's hands." Marx, *Capital*, 1:165.

20. There are significant differences between "primitive" and "archaic" money. Perhaps most important is that primitive money (feathers, shells, dogs' teeth, stones) is unstamped, while archaic money (ancient coinage) is stamped.

21. *Life Against Death* (Middletown: Wesleyan University Press, 1959), 246–47. Compare Mateo Alemán, who includes gold and silver among those fruits of the earth among the things necessary to satisfy human desire: "[la tierra] nos da las piedras de precio, el oro, la plata y más metales, de que tanta necesidad y sed tenemos" (The earth gives us precious stones, gold, silver, and other metals, which we need and thirst after). *Guzmán de Alfarache*, part 2, book 2, chap. 1.

generally agreed that the passage into the world of capitalism did not follow the pattern established by other European nations. As noted in the discussion of *Fuenteovejuna* in Chapter 1, economic historians are largely in agreement that the transformation of early modern Spain was "aphasic" when compared with the rest of Europe. But despite this general agreement on the historical issues, many questions of interpretation remain. Does the social and economic history of early modern Spain seem unusual only from hindsight, because capitalism in its paradigmatic, industrial, form was slow to take root? Are these contradictions then resolved if we grant that the economy of early modern Spain was one of commercial and financial (i.e., mercantile), rather than industrial, capitalism? If so, then why did industrial capitalism not take root? How could it have been that the "success" of the Spanish colonial enterprise, which brought increased quantities of gold and silver into Spain, led to a resistance to capitalism and to a renewal of support for agricultural and the traditional ideologies of social caste?

More than half a century ago, E. J. Hamilton set out to explain the exact nature of the link between the influx of American bullion into Europe, the general rise in prices in the sixteenth century, and the contemporaneous transformations of social and economic relations.[22] Within the framework of this question, he advanced the influential view that Spain trailed behind the rest of Europe in developing industrial capitalism because the chief cause of industrial progress in the West— the incentive to investment created by an increase in revenues from rising prices relative to wages that did not grow so fast, precipitated by an influx of Mexican and Peruvian silver—was not nearly so pronounced in Spain as it was elsewhere in Europe.[23] While Spanish cities boomed and the population grew throughout the sixteenth and seventeenth centuries, it appeared that the gap between prices and wages in Spain narrowed as early as 1530. Accordingly, Hamilton took it as no surprise to find that Spain remained principally a producer of raw materials but not a manufacturer of value-added products, exporting olive oil, wine, and wool in return for foreign goods.[24]

22. I draw also on the review of Hamilton's work by Pierre Vilar, "Problems in the Formation of Capitalism," *Past and Present* 10 (1956): 15–38.

23. Hamilton, "The Decline of Spain," 168. For a critical review of this and other theories of the development of capitalism with special reference to Spain, see Pierre Vilar, "Problems of the Formation of Capitalism."

24. Hamilton, "The Decline of Spain," 169; Vilar, "Problems," 17.

On close inspection, the central thesis supporting Hamilton's interpretation of Spain turns out to be an extension of claims that had already been advanced by Marx. In an 1847 lecture, Marx suggested that

> In the sixteenth century the amount of gold and silver in circulation in Europe increased as a result of the discovery of American mines, richer and easier to exploit. The result was that the value of gold and silver diminished in relation to that of other commodities. The workers continued to be paid the same money-wage for their labour-power. Their *money-wage* remained stable, but their *wage* had fallen, for in exchange for the same amount of money they now received a smaller amount of goods. This was one of the factors which favoured the growth of capital, the rise of the bourgeoisie in the sixteenth century.[25]

Needless to say, however, Hamilton did not share Marx's critical perspective on capitalism. Hamilton's research and the studies that followed from it took capitalism as normative and, in seeking to explain the situation of early modern Spain, failed to relate capitalism to the economic formations preceding it or to the modes of desire propelling it. Rather than pursue an economic analysis of the society of Golden Age, I would suggest that the cultural contradictions of Golden Age Spain were the consequence of a deeper set of historical conflicts, in which the forms of desire and authority crucial for the development of capitalism were in tension with competing ones not fundamentally capitalist at all. At the same time, however, the case of early modern Spain helps nuance our understanding of the drives at work in the early stages of capitalism by revealing the presence of authoritarian elements that were "residual" or "archaic" within what was to become the capitalist norm. To expand upon the arguments of Deleuze and Guattari, who remind us of the "archaic borrowings" of capitalism, it can be shown that the Oedipal paradigm was indeed central to the caste-based structure of values in the Spanish Golden Age. The issue in Golden Age Spain was not just whether Oedipus would control desire but which version of Oedipus would be in control: a "primitive" one in which desire is governed by attachment to the presence of the father and to the transmission of his authority after his death by the law of

25. Marx, *Wage-Labour and Capital* (1847), as cited in Vilar, "Problems," 18.

clean blood, or a more "modern" version of Oedipus, in which the law of desire allows society to install the authority of the father in a relatively abstract and ultimately institutionalized form.

In this connection, I would amplify the thesis argued elsewhere in this book—that cultural production in Golden Age Spain was dominated by a conflict between the "old" social formations of caste and the relatively "new" formations based on the capitalist values of social class—by showing that the value-structures of "caste" and "class" could not be so easily kept apart. As a case in point, Tirso de Molina's dramatization of the myth of Don Juan in *El Burlador de Sevilla* can be read as a representation of the conflict between the modes of desire and authority characteristic of "caste" and "class." In Tirso's play, the challenge is to represent the crisis in authority that results when desire is driven by a mobile attachment to a constantly shifting series of objects, and then to represent that crisis as resolved by imagining the authority that binds and limits desire as itself desire-driven. Read in this way, the play also allows us to nuance the analyses of Deleuze and Guattari by representing (Oedipal) authority not only as that which limits desire, but as itself derivable from the desires it would limit.

✳   ✳   ✳

Tirso's play is perhaps the best place to explore the relationship between desire and authority in Golden Age Spain because the figure of Don Juan so clearly represents an attempt to unleash free flows of desire that disrupt the established social codes. Tirso's play shows that it would be wrong to read even a dominant genre like the *comedia* as structurally unable to represent desire in its mobile, modern form. What remains to be seen is what place this mobile form of desire will be assigned within the sphere of the social, that is, how this desire will be bound. In the case of Tirso's *El Burlador de Sevilla*, the staging of "threats" to the structure of desire founded upon the principles of social caste amounts to the full-scale dramatization of a modern alternative to that structure. *El Burlador* stages the paradigmatic variability of modern desire, its constantly shifting attachments to a sometimes bewildering variety of objects. Don Juan is the model of desire as a labile force that would transgress the system of social ranks founded on the principle of purity of blood. The play credits the mobility of desire with the power to disrupt established hierarchies and codes. But it also imagines the regulation and transformation of desire into a structure of authority that must in the end be willed by those who have witnessed its disruptive effects.

When viewed in its historical context, the figure of Don Juan reflects a shift in the patterns in which desire was controlled. In Tirso's play, the Don Juan myth is projected along the axis defined by the features of "traditional" and "modern" societies and their respective codings of desire: on the one hand a traditional culture in which desire is a form of attachment to one particular thing, in which order is determined by kinship ties and by bloodlines, where actions are evaluated according to an ethos in which word and deed are in principle one and the same, and in which social functions and roles are sedimented into near static hierarchies; on the other hand, a more modern, capitalist culture in which the circulation of desire is free of attachment to any particular thing, in which the full exercise of authority requires that power be established as independent of the one who immediately wields it, and in which the desiring subject relinquishes attachment to any predetermined end.[26] (Recall Kierkegaard's pointed critique of modern, bourgeois culture: "purity of heart is to will just one thing.")[27]

The drama of Don Juan may be situated along these lines to the extent that it consistently appears to admit a vision of desire that circulates among a great diversity of objects, while at the same time seeming to support the wish to limit desire by the forms of authority characteristic of the "traditional" world.[28] The tension at the center of

26. For a thinker like Georges Bataille, the nature of "primitive" society is aligned to a thesis about the nature of societal rationalization as seen in the contrast between a bivalent archaic "sovereignty" and the bourgeois attachment to objects: "In archaic society, rank is tied to the consecrated presence of a subject whose sovereignty does not depend upon objects but integrates things into its movement. In bourgeois society, it still depends on ownership of objects that are neither sacral nor sovereign." I owe this reference to Habermas, in *The Philosophical Discourse of Modernity,* trans. Frederick Lawrence (Cambridge: MIT Press, 1987), 226. For a thinker like Jean-François Lyotard, the difference between "modern" and "primitive" societies with respect to the question of desire is itself illusory. See *Economie Libidinale* (Paris: Minuit, 1974), esp. 148–55.

27. Kierkegaard's book of this title bears the subheading "Spiritual Preparation for the Office of Confession." The substitution of a concern for a quasi-religious, subjective, "spiritual" purity for a concern over racial purity in Kierkegaard's writing is worth noting.

28. In the Mozart–Da Ponte version of the myth, the heterogeneity of desire is signaled in Don Giovanni's "catalogue" aria, in which he claims to have seduced "a thousand and three" women. But it is reflected as well in the vacillations of female desire, in the women who yield while defending themselves ("vorrei e no vorrei").

the myth of Don Juan is that between the mobile flows of desire characteristic of modern, capitalist societies on the one hand and the more limited circulation of desire possible in a hierarchical society on the other. An appropriate model for the study of the Don Juan myth would be one in which the discrepancies between these two codings of desire is "resolved" not just by a resistance to the free circulation that desire within the context of modern capitalism permits, but by a derivation of the authority through which desire is finally bound as a willed response to that very mobility.

To be sure, it would be easy to read the story of Don Juan as a drama of raw male aggression and female victimization, as the story of pure phallic power and its assaults, or as a domestic allegory of colonization. Some musicologists, for instance, have tended to construct the desire of the women in Mozart's *Don Giovanni* as themselves functions of masculine power; the women surrounding Don Giovanni, and above all Donna Anna, have sometimes been seen as hysterical figures *desiring* rape. But as Catherine Clément has shown, this is not only to misread feminine desire, it is to misinterpret the meaning of Don Juan as well. On her reading, Don Giovanni's central signifiers undermine or negate the full (meaningful) body of the precapitalist world; they are the hollowed-out signs of cultural authority and social standing; the women he deceives are "entrapped by a figure, a cloak, a hat."[29] His desire is "good for seducing, good for identifying, good for locating oneself with empty images," foremost among which are "empty clothes," but proves useless for providing the authority that the *socius* demands. For what are the possibilities of social order where there is only "fear, threat, and the great, shadowy silhouette hiding in the dark" (*Opera*, 35)? Don Juan reveals the potential power of an unmasterable desire; he stands for a mode of desire that cannot be satisfied or "filled up" and that, if left unbound, would reveal itself as nothing more than the "emptiness of soul behind the cape and cloak" (*Opera*, 36), or a quantum of energy in circulation.

Rather than simply stage desire as mobile and disruptive, however, *El burlador de Sevilla* strives to imagine social order as the consequence of a need for authority produced by desire itself. And rather than simply reinforce the principles of virtue, honor, kinship, and rank into which

---

29. Catherine Clément, *Opera; or, the Undoing of Women,* trans. Betsy Wing (Minneapolis: University of Minnesota Press, 1988), 35.

the authority of the father is so easily read, the myth of Don Juan may more accurately be seen as advancing the values of traditional, patriarchal society as a means to reestablish the authority that mobile, modern desire may unconsciously want. Indeed, if one considers seventeenth-century Spanish society as open to conflicting configurations of the relationship between desire and authority, then the myth of Don Juan need not be seen either as representing a form of desire that cannot be mastered by existing modes of social control, or as a purely reactionary function of those interests devoted to the maintenance of the status quo and to the assurance of the power of those in whose hands it had already come to rest. Instead, the function of the myth can be explained in terms of the need to imagine social control as a willed response to the increasing fluidity of desire and a loosening of the constraints on the attachment of desires to preestablished ends. Without a mechanism such as this, it would be nearly impossible to account for those features of the play that critics like José Antonio Maravall have described as particular to the theater in seventeenth-century Spain, most notably its ability to control and direct those who stood least to gain from its conservative stance, the *vulgo*.[30]

This particular understanding of the relationship between desire and authority in turn has consequences for our conception of the desiring subject in early modern Spain. While it may never be entirely legitimate to associate specific patterns of desire with particular social configurations, one may grant at least heuristic validity to the proposition that traditional societies are supportive of relatively fixed, even rigid structurings of desire, while the historical process of modernization and the development of capitalism was made possible by the formation of an ego that, in its attachment to shifting objects of desire, was relatively mobile and easily displaced.

If the "traditional" hero upholds the social order by remaining faithful to a series of preestablished values or codes, then Don Juan seeks by transgressing lines of distinction to undermine the social forms through which the values of traditional society are expressed. As the mechanism through which desire begins to circulate freely, he represents

30. On Maravall's reading, the "traditional" order of society is one that was imposed on it in the seventeenth century in the interests of maintaining the status quo, in much the same way, and through many of the same techniques, that an orthodox theology was "imposed" by the preachers and moralists of the baroque. See Maravall, *La cultura del barroco* (Barcelona: Ariel, 1975).

an early form of the paradigm that Deleuze and Guattari describe as characteristic of capitalism. This form of desire is opened up by a particularly mobile disposition of the ego, and it is reinforced by the promises offered to the women whom Don Juan seduces. Don Juan is very much unlike the heroes of many serious Spanish *comedias,* who seek to assert themselves through unswerving allegiance to the principles of heroic virtue, of bloodline, and of *honor,* the formulation of which is given in the near-talismanic slogan of epic derivation that refuses to expropriate the phallus, "I am who I am" ("soy quien soy").[31] Moreover, Don Juan destroys the unity of self-consciousness emblematized in the (epic) integrity of word and deed. He is, in this respect, an example of the "schizophrenia" that Deleuze and Guattari associate with capitalism in *Anti-Oedipus.* Indeed, the closural strength of this play—in which this freely circulating and potentially disruptive form of desire is restrained by Christian virtue and justice, all authorized by the King—must be measured against the broken promises that precede it, notwithstanding that the promised pleasures must finally be repressed. The psychological mobility of Don Juan, which is perceived as a threat to the foundations of traditional society, is overcome once it is discovered that within it lies an extreme concern for honor, which is the very basis of self-consciousness in a "traditional" world. Consider, for instance, the following exchange between Don Juan and the "Stone Guest":

GONZALO: ¿Cumplirásme una palabra como caballero?
DON JUAN: Honor
            Tengo, y las palabras cumplo,
            porque caballero soy.
GONZALO: Dame esa mano; no temas.
DON JUAN: ¿Eso dices? ¿Yo, temor?[32]

(GONZALO: Will you keep your word as a gentleman?

31. This phrase translates the Vulgate Bible's "Ego sum qui sum," which is in turn an ontologizing translation of the original Old Testament's mysterious formula, "ehyeh ascher ehyeh," in which the absence of the name of God stands out. Luther translated "Ich werde sein, der ich sein werde," or "I will be who I will be," registering the fact that the Hebrew verb *haya* has no present tense form. See Hans Blumenberg, *Work on Myth,* trans. Robert M. Wallace (Cambridge: MIT Press, 1985), 224.

32. Except for slight modifications, I follow the translation of Eric Bentley, in *The Classic Theatre,* vol. 3 (Garden City: Doubleday, 1959). I follow the Spanish text of Joaquín Casalduero (Madrid: Cátedra, 1977), here lines 2434–43.

DON JUAN: I am a man of honor, and I keep my word, because I am a knight.
GONZALO: Then give me your hand on it. Don't be afraid!
DON JUAN: What! *Me* afraid?)

As we shall have occasion further to note, the play meets the demand to bind or limit desire through what is in essence a double ending: the first, adapted from classical tragedy, provides for the sublimation of those "illicit" desires that have been vicariously invested in Don Juan, while the second conforms to the patterns established by romantic comedy, and specifically to what is known as "new comedy,"[33] where the elimination of some central obstructing force permits the ordering of social relations in the form of institutional marriages, or in the case of Isabela in this play, in what amounts to a remarriage:

REY: ¡Justo castigo del cielo!
        Y agora es bien que se casen
        todos, pues la causa es muerta,
        vida de tantos desastres.
OCTAVIO: Pues ha enviudado Isabela,
        quiero con ella casarme.
                        (lines 2852–56)

(KING: Just punishment from Heaven has been dealt!
        Now let them all be married, since the cause
        Of all their harm is dead.
OCTAVIO: Since Isabela has been widowed now, I wish to marry her.)

The fact that the myth of Don Juan is predicated upon a crisis of authority is thrown into bold relief by Don Juan's situation in Tirso's play as an orphaned or nameless man ("un hombre sin nombre") within a society that otherwise takes its bearings from figures of absolute self-possession and self-mastery, the king, the father, and above all the noble *caballero,* the knight. By contrast with these father figures, Don Juan introduces us into the world in which men are eternally boys, attempting to avoid the recognition of their own destiny toward fatherhood. As Don Juan says to his uncle Pedro after being discovered with Isabela,

33. See Northrop Frye's early essay "The Argument of Comedy," in *English Institute Essays, 1948,* ed. D. A. Robertson Jr. (New York: Columbia University Press, 1949).

DON JUAN: Tío y señor,
             mozo soy y mozo fuiste;
             y pues de amor supiste,
             tenga discupla mi amor.
                              (lines 61–64)

(DON JUAN: My uncle and my lord,
             I'm still a lad, as you were once;
             such loves you had,
             so don't blame me.)

In this world, the real is exchanged for a substitute; promises and contracts, which can be endlessly broken or deferred, stand in the place of the "thing in itself."[34] Hence Don Juan's repeated effort to postpone his encounter with the "limit" of his desire through a seemingly endless deferral of his meeting with the figure of the father, whose place he seemingly renders null. What he calls "trust," which is in fact a false promise, is built upon this potentially endless deferral of meaning: "¡Tan largo me lo fiáis!" (Trust me a while longer!). Like Ruiz de Alarcón's Don García in *La verdad sospechosa*, for whom the contractual promise becomes a veritable parody of the knight's sacred vow, Don Juan promises what he cannot deliver and gives what is not his own. In this way he violates the principles of reciprocal exchange and anticipates the endless circulation of desire characteristic of the commodity production and of the modern (capitalist) world.[35]

What appears in Tirso's *El burlador* as universal expropriation—that is, as the refusal of the proper, or of the principles upon which it rests—forms the basis of what Marx described as "alienation" in commodity capitalism. Consider Marx's claim that when we buy in order to sell we enter a relationship in which a great leap *(salto mortale)*

34. See Shoshana Felman, *Le scandale du corps parlant*, trans. Catherine Porter as *The Literary Speech Act: Don Juan with Austin, or Seduction in Two Languages* (Ithaca: Cornell University Press, 1983).

35. See the sections on the commodity, money, and exchange in *Capital*, vol. 1. See also Michel Serres's analysis of Molière's *Dom Juan*, "The Apparition of Hermes: *Dom Juan*," in *Hermes: Literature, Science, Philosophy*, ed. Josué Harari and David F. Bell (Baltimore: Johns Hopkins University Press, 1982), 3–14; and also Shoshana Felman, *Le Scandale du corps parlant* (Paris: Seuil, 1980). In *Economie Libidinale* Jean-François Lyotard raises the interesting question of whether, from the perspective of desire, the concept of "traditional society" has any force.

immediately takes place in the transformation of a commodity into money: "if the leap falls short, it is not the commodity which is defrauded, but rather its owner";[36] the circuit continues at the moment of purchase, when money is again transformed into a commodity. At the hinge of this relationship stands money as "the absolutely alienable commodity, because it is all other commodities divested of their shape, the product of their universal alienation. It reads all prices backwards, and thus as it were mirrors itself in the bodies of all other commodities" (*Capital*, 1:205). Moreover, unlike the direct exchange of products, the effects of alienation do not disappear once the commodities have themselves been exchanged. Rather, capitalism allows money to proliferate as "absolute alienation" throughout society as a whole. The circulation of money as capital becomes itself an end, and establishes the "real" as increasingly independent of any "objective" telos.

And yet it would be wrong to center the problem of desire in this play as an issue for Don Juan alone. Consider, for example, the episode with Tisbea the fisherwoman. Tisbea claims immunity from Don Juan's seductions by appeal to the power of her own authority to resist his advances. Tisbea's initial claim is to be so self-possessed that she can close off the possibility of desire altogether:

TISBEA: Yo, de cuantas al mar,—
           pies de jazmín y rosa,—
           en sus riberas besa
           con fugitivas olas,
           sola de amar esenta,
           como en ventura sola,
           tirana me reservo
           de sus prisiones locas.
                     (lines 375–82)

(TISBEA: Of all whose feet the fleeting waters kiss,—as the breezes kiss the rose and jasmine, —of the fishers' daughters and longshore maidens, of all those I am the only one exempt from Love, the only one who rules in sole, tyrannical contempt the prisons which he stocks with fools.)

36. *Capital*, 1:200–201.

But by the time Don Juan falsely promises to marry her (lines 929–30), she has already given in to him (line 920: "tuya soy" [I am yours]). As Tisbea's impassioned rhetoric of resistance and the equally passionate seduction that follows both display, no desire can be *absolutely* self-controlled. None is powerful enough to achieve perfect mastery over itself; every desire seeks control (and in a certain sense, mastery) by another desire. The need for authority follows directly from it. In the specific case at hand, we can see that Tisbea's initial resistance to desire is tantamount to a wishful denial of authority, but that this is a form of self-deception that ends only in enslavement or domination:

TISBEA: Yo soy la que hacía siempre
de los hombres burla tanta;
que siempre las que hacen burla
vienen a ser burladas.
Engañóme el caballero
debajo de fe y palabra
de marido, y profanó
mi honestidad y mi cama.
(lines 1013–21)

(TISBEA: I was the one that ever made fun of men and cheated them; then came a knight to sever the thread, and by base stratagem destroy and kill my honor dead by swearing marriage as his bait, enjoy me and profane my bed.)

The question of the relationship between desire and authority is made all the more acute where desire is fundamentally mobile and authority cannot be located in a single exemplary figure (e.g., the father, the prince, the king, or the noble knight). Where authority is diffuse, and the possibility of satisfying desire is no longer available within the order of society as it stands, the task of deriving authority from desire proves all the more difficult to fulfill. With regard to the ending of Tirso's play, it now can be seen that it contains two distinct ways of bounding, limiting, or containing desire, which is successful only to the degree that this containment can be represented as the function of another desire, hence as willed. The first ending of the play seeks categorically to suppress the mobility of desire by moving toward stillness (as we see, for example, in the figure of the Stone Guest), and ultimately toward death. The second seeks the containment of desire through the power invested in social institutions, rules, and codes, as sanctioned by the King, who emerges as the fatherly figure of authority that these characters want. The King is the figure who legitimizes desire; but as the virtually bodiless voice of uncontested authority, he is also the figure in whom all desires come to an end.

In the meeting with the Stone Guest, Don Juan would seem to demonstrate the consciousness that Hegel ascribes to the superior individual or noble-spirited soul, that is, to the one who seeks above all the certification of his honor in the struggle for recognition by another desiring consciousness. In light of Don Juan's display of honor, though, two important qualifications must be made. The first is that while Don Juan seems to possess a deep-seated nobility, he is not in fact a knight but an aristocratic courtier; he is by any account a degenerate transformation of the noble warrior whose true standing must be confirmed in the struggle for recognition in the trial by death. His fluent discourse throughout the play is an example of the attempt to defer death by rhetoric. But the drama of desire and authority will not tolerate this evasion. The nobleman's willingness to risk everything in the fight to the death, emblematized in the play's first, tragic-like ending, allows for the triumphant emergence of the consciousness of the slaves, who see themselves as "victorious" over the master. In Tirso's play, this permits the comic-romantic closure of the play and the refounding of society under the sign of a socially coded and controlled desire, in which the appearance of the King conceals that theirs is indeed the desire of the "slave." All the figures who appear in the play's "second ending" have suffered degradation or dishonor at the hands of Don Juan. They have been rendered "base," "unworthy," or "unclean" because of violations against the principle of cleanliness of blood. Provided that they can subordinate their own desires to the authority of a truly noble-spirited soul who is in principle above the need for recognition, however, they are uniformly redeemed, made whole and pure.

Considered in this light, Don Juan's encounter with the "Convidado de Piedra" may be seen to have implications that reach well beyond the poetic justice of the defeat of a mobile ego by a man made of stone, just as Tirso's recourse to the authority of the King goes beyond the simple containment or immobilization of the mobile modern ego by the top-down imposition of an archaic form of authority. Rather, the conclusion of the play presents an instance in which a traditional form of authority appears to be derived from a much more mobile and modern form of desire. As is well known, the order of traditional society is typically confirmed in moments of ritual and symbolic exchange, such as occur on the occasions of duels, banquets, and wedding feasts. On such occasions the knight seeks to reconfirm his self-mastery and self-possession by gaining the recognition of another desiring consciousness; but if this effort is not to result in the very social upheavals that brought "traditional" society to an end, the exchanges accomplished and the recognitions achieved must be reciprocal. There must be a desire-driven conflict with no net gain or loss, no profit or risk, which in Tirso's play is ensured by the principle of retributive justice. As Don Gonzalo de Ulloa repeatedly asserts, "Quien tal hace, que tal pague" (You must pay for what you've done). The banquet scene with the Stone Guest neatly inverts the occasion of Don Juan's seduction of Aminta at the wedding feast, magically transforming him into a noble and honorable (which is also to say, self-possessed) knight. As a result, the encounter with the Stone Guest, which stills and immobilizes subjective desire, may be said to generate the very phenomenon that Max Weber called the consciousness of traditional society. In Tirso's play, this is a product of the mobility of modern desire.

When seen from the perspective of modern capitalist society, this particular derivation of authority from desire might well appear to be "reactionary" or "archaic." From the vantage point of Tirso's play, however, we can see that the willed transformation of desire into authority—through the wished-for binding of desire by a figure who stands in principle above the need for recognition, hence above desire as well—allows us to move beyond what would be the impasse of tragedy to what is the true conclusion of the play, the ending in which society maintains a placid demeanor as it goes about its normal business and perpetuates itself under the aegis of the King.

7

The Archaeology of Desire
in *Don Quijote*

The foregoing analysis of Tirso's Don Juan was meant to suggest that what we commonly call "desire" has a specifically historical face and, likewise, that what we call "history" is driven by different, often competing configurations of desire. What is the relationship between history and desire in the *Quijote*? This chapter takes as its point of departure the assumption that Cervantes's text engages two modalities of desire and two ways of reading texts that are historically quite distinct. On one level, the *Quijote* may be situated within the shifting historical field we have discussed in preceding chapters to the extent that it articulates the eclipse of the "heroic" order of society dominated by the values of caste by a newer, functionally differentiated order controlled by the values of social class. But beyond this, Cervantes locates substantial conflicts within each of these structures of desire, revealing each to be contingent upon a desire for the other one, which of course neither can sustain. At its extreme, this means that "modern" desire in the *Quijote* is fueled by a desire for those social structures that are located in the past, while those desires that Cervantes's characters associate with the past are reconfigured as discontinuous, heterogeneous, and surprisingly modern in nature. Throughout the *Quijote*, Cervantes represents the large-scale transformation that I have described above in relation to the social and historical conflict between the "old" and the "new" in terms of the difficulties of finding a stable representation of desire. In Cervantes, the historical and existentialist ways of configuring desire both ignore the mediated nature of desire, including our desire for the past.[1] As I suggest in this chapter and the next, Cervantes's awareness of the mediated nature of desire corresponds to his recognition of the inaccessibility of a past whose authority nonetheless continues to haunt the present age. It raises the question of the role of literature in our relationship to the past.

✳ ✳ ✳

Let us begin from the proposition that desire is what drives social action and, correspondingly, that social codes are the public forms in which desire tends to coalesce. What happens when desire shifts and social codes undergo significant change? In early modern Spain, we witness the emergence of a series of culturally ambiguous, displaced, or "marginal" groups (such as the *moriscos, conversos, pícaros,* and of course women) whose identity cannot be located either in terms of the social order that has been eclipsed or in terms of the emergent order of things. Cervantes's representation of many of these groups has become prominent in recent scholarly debates.[2] Second, this shift in social codes is written

---

1. René Girard's work on mediated desire in the *Quijote* is well known. See *Deceit, Desire, and the Novel,* trans. Yvonne Freccero (Baltimore: Johns Hopkins University Press, 1965). Girard focuses more on the desires of the characters than on the role of literature in the mediation of desire.

2. See, for example, E. Michael Gerli's discussion of race, marginality, and resistance in the Captive's tale, in *Refiguring Authority: Reading, Writing, and Rewriting in Cervantes* (Lexington: University Press of Kentucky, 1995), 40–60. Gerli draws on earlier dicussions of the *moriscos* in Cervantes, such Francisco Márquez-Villanueva's discussion of the Ricote episode in *Personajes y temas del "Quijote"* (Madrid: Taurus, 1975). The question of women in Cervantes (and the Golden Age in general) was the subject of much of Ruth El Saffar's work. See, for example, *Beyond Fiction: The Recovery of the Feminine in the Novels of Cervantes* (Berkeley and Los Angeles: University of California Press, 1984).

into the moral conflicts between Don Quijote and the other characters of Cervantes's work. Whereas Don Quijote construes every opposition as some manifestation of the hierarchical division of society into two groups—the worthy and the unworthy, or the noble and the base—the others are apt to find themselves positioned within a network of relationships defined by the circulation of desires, including the desire for upward mobility promised by a system of "free" economic exchange. Thus in contrast to Don Quijote, a figure like Teresa Panza desires the economic means to improve her family's situation in society and to better her lot. Sancho's desires, which are modeled on those of Don Quijote, remain opaque to her. Consider Teresa's exchange with Sancho at the conclusion of part 1:

> "¿Qué bien habéis sacado de vuestras escuderías? ¿Qué saboyana me traéis a mí? ¿Qué zapaticos a vuestros hijos?"
>
> "No traigo nada deso," dijo Sancho, "mujer mía, aunque traigo otras cosas de más momento y consideración."
>
> "Deso recibo yo mucho gusto," respondió la mujer; "mostradme esas cosas de más consideración y más momento, amigo mío. . . . ¿Qué es eso de ínsulas, que no le entiendo?"

> ("What profit have you got out of your squireships? Have you brought me a skirt? Or some pretty shoes for the children?"
>
> "I haven't brought any of that, wife," said Sancho, "although I bring other things of greater value and importance."
>
> "I'm very glad of that," replied his wife. "Show me these things of greater value and importance, my friend. . . . But tell me, what is this about isles? I don't understand you.")[3]

This passage may stand as an example of the ways in which two distinct modes of historically conditioned desire contend with one another in the *Quijote*. And yet the attempt to align specific historical structures with particular modes of desire does not quite do justice to the complexity of Cervantes's text. On the contrary, *Don Quijote* suggests that as long as we look to history in order to make explicit what seems unexpressed within literary discourse we shall have underes-

---

3. I cite *Don Quijote* according to the edition of Luis Murillo (Madrid: Castalia, 1978), here part 1, chap. 52, pp. 602–3. Translations are those of J. M. Cohen, *The Adventures of Don Quixote* (Harmondsworth: Penguin Books, 1950).

timated the predicament of the modern writer, who is forced to recognize the disorienting presence of forms inherited from the past. How can we respect the historicity of Cervantes's text while still coming to terms with Cervantes's predicament as an early modern writer?

I propose that the complex relationship between history and desire indicated by Cervantes's text can be understood in terms of the psychoanalytic concept of archaeology.[4] If the notion of archaeology suggests, on Freud's account, an investigation into concealed origins,[5] then the premises of an archaeology of desire must be that origins, because concealed, are never fully recoverable and that desire tends to gather around a series of substitutes for what has been hidden or eclipsed, although not entirely lost.[6] Rather than think of desire merely as the ground of an absent satisfaction, we would do better to think of desire as the motive force of history and of history as the source of those imaginary objects around which a desire in search of origins tends to coalesce. If customarily we think of the discourse of "history" as a means for locating ourselves with respect to the past, then a work like *Don Quijote* complicates that picture and suggests that the "movement" of history toward the future is driven by the pressure of a desire for

4. Paul Ricoeur provides a lengthy discussion of this concept in *Freud and Philosophy: An Essay on Interpretation,* trans. Denis Savage (New Haven: Yale University Press, 1970), 439–52.

5. See Freud's lengthy comparison, in *Civilization and its Discontents,* of the psyche to the archaeological remains of ancient Rome, where he concludes that "what is past in mental life *may* be preserved and is not *necessarily* destroyed." *Civilization and Its Discontents,* trans. James Strachey (New York: Norton, 1961), 20. Even more interesting is Freud's analysis in *Delusion and Dream* of the archaeologist Dr. Norbert Hanold, a fictional character from Wilhelm Jensen's *Gradiva* (1903) who suffers from a lack of desire for living women, and who regards them all as objects of marble and bronze. In his love for Gradiva, Hanold's desire congeals around an object that substitutes for something archaic that has been hidden or eclipsed, but not entirely lost; in a dream that takes place in old Pompeii on the day of the eruption of Vesuvius, he sees Gradiva stretched out on the steps of the temple, where she becomes covered by a rain of ashes; her face turns as white as marble and comes to resemble a bas-relief. Gradiva turns out to be Fraulein Zoë Bertgang, the archaeologist's childhood sweetheart. On Freud's account, Hanold's dream represents a "disappearance plus preservation of the past." *Delusion and Dream and Other Essays,* trans. Harry Zohn, ed. Philip Rieff (Boston: Beacon, 1956), 73. My thanks to Diana Wilson for the reference to *Delusion and Dream.*

6. By an extension of this logic, then even what we may perceive as the most archaic moments of consciousness or culture are best viewed as forgotten or repressed, and therefore as having the power to demonize or haunt the present, just as the romances of chivalry have demonized Don Quixote.

origins that are suppressed, concealed, or lost. History then appears not so much as the framework in terms of which the deep-structure of a given text may be made explicit, but rather as the source of those displacements whose effects can be glimpsed in the form of the text's discontinuities, inconsistencies, or gaps. In the case of *Don Quijote*, I propose that an investigation of the archaeology of desire might best proceed by remapping the historical displacement of the "old" by the "new" in light of the strange productivity of "archaic" desires within a culture that believed itself to be overcoming archaism through the processes of world-disenchantment, societal rationalization, and historical self-assertion.[7] The success of such an investigation will nonetheless depend on our own ability to resist the static models of desire in terms of which the historical distinction between "old" and "new" has customarily been understood.

※　※　※

By way of contrast, I first consider the links between a historical analysis of some of the central problems posed in the *Quijote* and an existential understanding of desire; that is, one that centers principally around the qualities of personal agency and character. A historical analysis of *Don Quijote* may lead quite plausibly to a series of conclusions about the nature of personality having largely to do with the impossibility of satisfying heroic desires in the modern, disenchanted world. Don Quijote "remembers" epic society as the place where it was possible to invoke the principles of virtue and justice and to make judgments according to unambiguous moral criteria. Accordingly, Don Quijote attempts to "re-read" the modern world in terms of the categorical oppositions between good and evil, the noble and the base. His own claims of virtue and exemplarity are counterbalanced by his repeated, categorical condemnations of his enemies as unworthy, ignoble, or vile. In addition, he imagines the possibility of existence in a world of unambiguous values, faithfully transmitted through the chronicles, the ballads, and above all the romances of chivalry.

When seen from the perspective of an existential understanding of

7. For further discussion of historical self-assertion in relation to the problem of modernity, see Hans Blumenberg, *The Legitimacy of the Modern Age*, trans. Robert M. Wallace (Cambridge: MIT Press, 1985), and A. J. Cascardi, *The Subject of Modernity* (Cambridge: Cambridge University Press, 1992).

desire, it would appear that heroic society may offer its members the security of a stable identity and the "metaphysical comfort" of values derived as if from first principles. But this model of desire, although historical, meets with a series of internal limitations, ones that *Don Quijote* rapidly forces us to take into account. First, it seems that "heroic" society severely restricts the mobility of desire in the construction of personality and therefore limits the possibilities of what the self may be. The controlling institutions of such a society remain closed to the majority of its ordinary members, who cannot aspire to the condition of nobility that heroic action requires. In light of the comic, deflationary impulse of *Don Quijote,* it seems also that "epic" society sets for its heroes a series of extraordinary goals whose contingencies it chooses to ignore. Such heroes may be momentarily exalted, and the ordinary members of this society may find themselves temporarily ennobled and empowered by the hero's exemplary deeds. But the hero is bound eventually to be deflated, and the nonheroic individuals of this society may well find themselves deceived when they discover that the hero is not in fact an ultimate source of empowerment but a human artifact who expresses in a contingent way their own interests, desires, and fears. In the judgment of at least one critic, these members of society would have done better to seek this empowerment through the criticism and revision of their ordinary experiences, beliefs, and practices, rather than in the pursuit of heroic ideals.[8]

When seen from an existentialist point of view, *Don Quijote* represents a successful correction of the heroic ideal insofar as Cervantes is compelled to redirect his hero's failures and succeeds in transforming these into sources of authentic self-creation. Thus for a critic like Américo Castro, who existentializes Ortega's doctrine of the circumstance, "*Don Quijote* shows us that the reality of existence consists in receiving the impact of all that can affect man from without, and in transforming these influences into outwardly manifest life processes. The illusion of a dream, devotion to a belief—in short, the ardently yearned for in any form becomes infused in the existence of him who dreams, believes, or longs; and thus, what was before transcendency without bearing on the process of living becomes embodied into life."[9]

8. Roberto Mangabeira Unger, *Passion: An Essay on Personality* (New York: Free Press, 1984), 56. Cervantes's supreme awareness of this danger stands at the heart of his ambivalence toward the theater of his day, especially that of Lope de Vega.

9. Castro, "Incarnation in Don Quijote," in *An Idea of History,* ed. and trans. Stephen Gilman and Edmund L. King (Columbus: Ohio State University Press, 1977), 26.

As it later takes shape in what Lukács describes in *The Theory of the Novel* as the "novels of disillusionment," the existential correction of the heroic ideal comes under the pressure of an extreme skepticism about the possibilities for the satisfaction of desire and the achievement of human virtue in the modern world. Indeed, it would seem on this account that the controlling anxiety of the novel as a genre is dominated by a permanent loss of faith in the existence of an "original" context for desire, rather than by the hope for its recovery.

When evaluated as an experiment in existential projection, however, it seems that works of modern fiction in general, and *Don Quijote* in particular, are powerless to reorient desire from within. At best, characters in the novel experience an ambiguous *desengaño* that leads them to positions of self-irony or, in the case of Don Quijote, to a normalized relationship with the world that can be achieved only at death. This evidence suggests that the existentialist interpretation of desire in *Don Quijote*—in terms of which Castro construes Cervantes's postheroic protagonist as justified and redeemed by his own free self-assertion—has in some ways failed to come to terms with the ways in which desire and its consequences are represented in the text. Moreover, it appears that Cervantes is troubled less by the success or failure of the heroic ethos, by the disappearance of the conditions of heroism from the modern world, or by the outcome of the struggle between the pressures of normalcy and heroic ideals, than he is concerned with finding an alternative to the self-destructive and potentially sacrificial forms of desire that may be pursued in the name of heroic ends. (I argue in Chapter 10 that the *Persiles* represents Cervantes's idea of a solution to this same problem.)

Not only in Don Quijote, but also in the figures of Fernando and Dorotea, and in the tale of the "Curioso impertinente," Cervantes takes as the object of his concern the potentially violent, self-sacrificing forms of desire characteristic of a social order predicated on the replication of hierarchical distinctions and on the preservation of such distinctions through notions of racial purity or "cleanliness of blood." Recall that at the conclusion of her tale Dorotea represents herself as having been sacrificed to the requirements of society's unyielding law of honor. To transgress boundaries in Dorotea's world is to allow oneself to be touched by alien matter and to experience abjection. Because she has been "defiled" by Fernando, Dorotea must exile herself and deny both herself and her parents any hope for reconciliation: "es tanta la vergüenza que me ocupa sólo el pensar que, no como ellos [mis padres] pensaban, tengo de parecer a su presencia, que tengo por mejor desterrarme para siempre de ser vista que no verles el rostro, con pensamiento que ellos miran el mío ajeno de la honestidad que de mí se debían de tener prometida" (I am so overwhelmed by shame at the mere thought of appearing in their presence, so different from the daughter they had supposed me, that I think it would be the lesser evil to banish myself for ever from their sight rather than look them in their face and know their thoughts. For they will consider that I have lost the honor they had the right to expect of me) (Part 1, chap. 29, p. 359). Seen in "existential" terms, with Castro, Dorotea's task is to find a place for herself within the order of society as it stands.[10] Yet it would seem equally important to say that Cervantes rejects the attempt simply to reproduce the existing social order through a resolution of crises such as Dorotea and her family suffer. Indeed, Cervantes seems to suggest that what is suffered by Dorotea is like a wound that cannot be repaired, at least not within the framework of the existing historical or social world; accordingly, Dorotea more closely resembles those "marginal" groups whose desires cannot be accommodated within the framework of social relations as they exist.

Similarly, Cervantes resists attempts to situate the self in relation to the dominant social order through an idealist reshaping of the past or the resurrection of an archaic symbolic law, as the *comedia* and its sacrificial code of honor attempted to do. Consider in this regard the "Curioso impertinente," which compels us to associate the structure of violence and sacrifice with the *comedia*-like patterns of desire that lead to self-destructive suspicion and jealousy. Camila, Lotario, and above all Anselmo resemble certain *comedia* characters who are caught in sacrificial patterns of desire. Though not all Golden Age honor plays involve sacrificial violence, much less condone it, Cervantes responds powerfully to the ways in which the obsessive desires of certain characters reach disastrous ends. Anselmo refers to the way in which he has fashioned his own dishonor, describing himself at the conclusion of the tale in *comedia*-like terms as the "fabricador de mi deshonra" (maker of my own dishonor) (Part 1, chap. 35, p. 445). Hierarchical systems of desire organized around the values of caste tend to increase the occa-

10. See "La ejemplaridad de las novelas cervantinas" in *Hacia Cervantes* (Madrid: Taurus, 1967), 451–74.

sions for violence by establishing clear lines of demarcation around desire's possible objects and by demanding that certain of these objects be valued more highly than the rest. "Camila es finísimo diamante" (Think of Camila as a rare diamond), says Lotario. He continues:

> "Mira que no hay joya en el mundo que tanto valga como la mujer casta y honrada, y que todo el honor de las mujeres consiste en la opinión buena que de ellas se tiene."

> "La honesta y casta mujer es arminio, y es más que nieve blanca y limpia la virtud de la honestidad."

> "Es asimesmo la buena mujer como espejo de cristal luciente y claro; pero está sujeto a empañarse y escurecerse con qualquiera aliento que le toque. Hase de usar con la honesta mujer el estilo que con las reliquias: adorarlas y no tocarlas. Hase de guardar y estimar la mujer buena como se guarda y estima un hermoso jardín que está lleno de flores y rosas, cuyo dueño no consiente que nadie le pasee ni manosee; basta que desde lejos y por entre las verjas de hierro gocen de su fragrancia y hermosura." (Part 1, chap. 33, p. 409)

> ("There is no jewel in the world so precious and chaste as a virtuous woman, and the whole honor of women lies in their good reputation."

> "The chaste and virtuous woman is an ermine, and the virtue of chastity is whiter and purer than snow."

> "A good woman is also like a mirror of clear and shining glass, which is liable to be stained and dimmed by every breath which touches it. A chaste woman must be treated like holy relics, which are to be adored but not touched. A good woman must be guarded and prized like a beautiful garden full of flowering roses, whose owner does not allow anyone to walk in it or to touch them; enough that they enjoy its fragrance and beauty from far off through its iron railings.")

The objects of desire in such instances are not simply exalted; they are exalted as part of a sacrificial logic, which is to say that they are elevated *in order to be excluded or destroyed*. This economy of desire depends on their destruction. This is paradigmatically the case with women like Camila, who are positioned (typically by men) as the supreme repositories of "value"; they become "heterogeneous" in Bataille's sense of the term, though necessary for the exclusionary system of social exchange they validate.[11] But, as Diana Wilson has noted with respect to the "Isla Bárbara" of the *Persiles,* such arrangements do not always display the logic of their own sacrificial violence; on the contrary, covert violence is the mechanism through which they appear as civilized. The Barbaric Isle sustains "a community of isolated males whose 'Law' or ritual idolatry dictates a continual circulation of women. Purchased 'with chunks of gold ore and extremely precious metals' (57), these foreign women are then fetishized as incubators for the horde's potential messiah. This male traffic in women, the text is careful to note, has not *brutalized* the barbarians: whether 'purchased or robbed,' the women are 'well treated by them, who only in this show themselves not to be barbarians' " (57).[12]

Societies of caste tend to interpret the values proper to what they call "civilization" not as historically contingent constructs, but as having the force of nature. Thus Lotario argues that the principles of conjugal honor and cleanliness of blood have a warrant that extends to the creation of woman in Genesis and to the biblical institution of matrimony—all of which are offered as legitimizing principles. What escapes Lotario's notice is that this biblical account, which he adopts as his own, is itself manifestly fleshly. It suggests that the roots of the civilized institution of matrimony used to legitimize the axiology of caste are in the fleshly "birth" of woman from the rib of man, and it presents the two in matrimony as "dos en una carne misma" (two in one flesh):

Cuando Dios crió a nuestro primero padre en el Paraíso terrenal, dice la divina Escritura que infundió Dios sueño en Adán, y que, estando durmiendo, le sacó una costilla del lado siniestro, de la

11. See Bataille, "The Psychological Structure of Fascism," in *Visions of Excess: Selected Writings, 1927–1939,* trans. and ed. Alan Stoekl (Minneapolis: University of Minnesota Press, 1985), 137–60. This complicates the picture of male "traffic" in the love of women presented in Diana de Armas Wilson's study, "Passing the Love of Women: The Intertextuality of *El curioso impertinente,*" *Cervantes* 7 (1987): 9–28.

12. Diana de Armas Wilson, "Cervantes's *Labors of Persiles:* Working (In) the In-Between," in *Literary Theory / Renaissance Texts,* ed. Patricia Parker and David Quint (Baltimore: Johns Hopkins University Press, 1986), 153. The references are to *Los trabajos de Persiles y Sigismunda* (Madrid: Clásicos Castalia, 1969).

cual formó a nuestra madre Eva; y así como Adán despertó y la miró, dijo "Esta es carne de mi carne y hueso de mis huesos." Y Dios dijo: "Por ésta dejará el hombre a su padre y madre, y serán dos en una carne misma." Y entonces fue instituido el divino sacramento del matrimonio, con tales lazos, que sola la muerte puede desatarlos. . . . Y aquí viene que, como la carne de la esposa sea una mesma con la del esposo, las manchas que en ella caen, o los defectos que se procura, redundan en la carne del marido, aunque él no haya dado, como queda dicho, ocasión para aquel daño. . . . Y *como las honras y deshonras del mundo sean todas y nazcan de carne y sangre, y las de la mujer mala sean deste género,* es forzoso que al marido le quepa parte dellas, y sea retenido por deshonrado sin que él lo sepa." (Part 1, chap. 33, pp. 410–11; my emphasis)

(When God created our first father in the earthly paradise, Holy Scripture tells us that He caused a deep sleep to fall on him, and in his sleep took one of the ribs of his left side and created our mother Eve; and when Adam awoke and looked on her, he said: "This is now bone of my bone and flesh of my flesh." And God said: "Therefore shall a man leave his father and his mother, and they shall be one flesh." Then was instituted the divine sacrament of marriage, whose bonds are soluble only by death. . . . Hence it arises that, as the flesh of the wife is one with the flesh of the husband, the blemishes which fall on her or the defects she incurs recoil upon the flesh of the husband, although, as I have said, he may be in no respect the cause of the trouble. . . . Now *as all this world's honors and dishonors spring from flesh and blood, and the bad wife's are of this kind,* part of them must inevitably fall on the husband; and he must be considered dishonored, even though he does not know of it.)

Within a framework like Américo Castro's, the violence of desire in the "Curioso impertinente" tale is to be explained simply as the product of the historical anxieties generated over purity of blood, which are imagined to penetrate directly, but not structurally, into the text. But the anxieties of "El curioso impertinente" outstrip the purely historical and existential frameworks in which critics like Castro have attempted to situate them insofar as they are at once exorbitant, excessive, and hyperbolic. For instance, Lotario warns Anselmo in copious terms about the destruction that he, Lotario, will precipitate: for example, " 'Mira, pues ¡oh Anselmo!, al peligro que te pones en querer turbar al sosiego en que tu buena esposa vive; mira por cuán vana e impertinente curiosidad quieres revolver los humores que ahora están sosegados en el pecho de tu casta esposa; advierte que lo que aventuras a ganar es poco, y que lo que perderás será tanto, que lo dejaré en su punto, porque me faltan palabras para encarecerlo' " (Reflect, then, Anselmo, on the danger you expose yourself to in seeking to disturb your good wife's peace! Consider what vain and foolish curiosity it is that prompts you to stir the passions which now lie quiet in your chaste wife's breast. Be warned that you stand to gain little and to lose so unspeakably much that words fail me to express its value) (Part 1, chap. 33, p. 411). For his part, Anselmo is driven to seek confirmation of facts that he knows already and in advance to be true: " 'deseo que Camila, mi esposa, pase por estas dificultades, y se acrisole y quilate en el fuego de verse requerida y solicitada, y de quien tenga valor para poner en ella sus deseos' " (I want my wife Camila to pass through the ordeal, and be purged and refined in the fire of temptation and solicitation by someone worthy of her) (Part 1, chap. 33, p. 403). In this respect, both Anselmo and Lotario come to resemble the split (Lacanian) subject, who is divided between the *sujet d'énonce* and the *sujet d'énonciation*. To say this much is not to "diagnose" the subject in Lacanian terms as split. Indeed, Anselmo anticipates and thereby nullifies the force of a diagnostic reading of this curious deflection of truth by desire by characterizing his own attempt at self-destruction as a process of contamination, and by comparing his desire for self-defilement to that of a female eating disorder, " '[una] enfermedad que suelen tener algunas mujeres, que se les antoja comer tierra, yeso, carbón y otras cosas peores, aun asquerosas para mirarse, cuanto más para comerse' " (an illness common in women, which makes them long to eat earth, chalk, coal, and other worse things, loathsome to the sight and much more loathsome to the palate) (Part 1, chap. 33, pp. 411–12).[13] What Anselmo here describes as an "illness" (*enfermedad*) of women is at the same time the projection onto Camila of a fear of pollution by food, which may in turn mask an anxiety that the boundaries structuring

---

13. See the fascinating discussion of this passage in Wilson, "Passing the Love of Women."

society may not be as stable as they seem. Julia Kristeva has suggested that food is so often the site of projected fears because of its orality: "when food appears as a polluting object, it does so as oral object only to the extent that orality signifies a boundary of the self's clean and proper body. Food becomes abject only if it is a border between two distinct territories. A boundary between nature and culture, between the human and the nonhuman."[14] While Kristeva notes that food always has the capacity to defile, she offers her most powerful and convincing examples from caste societies ("the Brahmin surrounds his meal and his food with very strict regulations is less pure after eating than before," *Powers of Horror*, 75). Indeed, it is only when we see that the "sacrificial" violence of caste societies is intensified by the tendencies of its members both corporeally and psychically to re-incorporate what has been excluded as alien, ignoble, dishonorable, or base that the "psychoanalytic" significance of the "Curioso impertinente" can be made clear over and above its existential value as an "exemplary" text. Indeed, the exemplary "meaning" of what might be taken as a cautionary tale is overwhelmed by the very exorbitance of the "example" and by the procedures of narrative discontinuity by which it is interpolated into the larger text. As in several of the *Novelas ejemplares*, the "Curioso impertinente" represents an instance in which desire recognizes and reincorporates precisely what it would seem to exclude. What remains for us to investigate are the more general principles by means of which this and other such examples are sutured into Cervantes's text.

✳   ✳   ✳

On the basis of the cases presented thus far it would seem that the "existential" reading of *Don Quijote* to which a simple historicism might lead fails principally in its inability to recognize Cervantes's response to the self-contradictions that seem inherent in any historically situated form of desire. More important than an alignment of the structures of desire with the categories designated by the terms "caste"

14. Julia Kristeva, *Powers of Horror: An Essay on Abjection*, trans. Leon S. Roudiez (New York: Columbia University Press, 1982), 75. Maria Antonia Garcés presents a reading of "El coloquio de los perros" in light of Kristeva's remarks on horror and abjection in her essay "Berganza and the Abject: The Desecration of the Mother," in *Quixotic Desire: Psychoanalytic Perspectives on Cervantes*, ed. Ruth Anthony El Saffar and Diana de Armas Wilson (Ithaca: Cornell University Press, 1993), 292–314.

or "class," it seems, is Cervantes's ability to locate the contradictions of desire both between and within the societies we may call "traditional" and "heroic" or "modern" and "new." As I show in greater detail now, the historical and existential interpretations of Don Quijote tend to neglect the "always already" mediated nature of desire, on which the psychoanalytic understanding of archaeology depends. And insofar as it is through literary mediation that desire displays its complex relationship to an "archaic" past, the purely historical and existentialist interpretations of Don Quijote fail also to come to terms with the modernity of Cervantes's work. Indeed, it would seem inaccurate to say that Don Quijote represents either the absolute failure of the heroic ethic or the achievement of existential or "novelistic" freedom, as Castro has argued. Rather, I suggest that Don Quijote represents a form of post-epic literature in which the concept of an archaic, heroic world as providing an immediate and undifferentiated ground of desire is shown to be self-limiting insofar as it relies on the naive conception of an "original" context of desire and on the possibility of establishing an unmediated relationship to the historical past. In Cervantes's case, the discovery of the prior mediation of historical experience by desire, as shaped by literature and other cultural forms, is articulated through a critique of reading. This is the point of Cervantes's insistence on the mediating function of the romances of chivalry throughout Don Quijote, and it serves to align the exoteric intention of the novel as stated in the famous closing passage of Part 2: "poner en aborrecimiento de los hombres las fingidas y disparatadas historias de los libros de caballerías" (to arouse man's contempt for all fabulous and absurd stories of knight errantry) (Part 2, chap. 74, p. 593) with the mobility of desire displayed throughout the text. More specifically, the Cervantine understanding of our relationship to history as mediated by desire is directed against those modes of reading that would attempt to negate the power of desire through the promise of a direct relationship with the past.[15]

In setting out to imitate the practices of the knights-errant of chivalry, Don Quijote reenacts the drama of modernity's need simultaneously to displace and to assume the cultural authority of the past. The problem of the cultural reproduction of authority—of achieving cultural "matur-

15. On the subject of mediated desire, see René Girard's classic study, Deceit, Desire, and the Novel.

ity" by entering the world of the fathers, while displacing the dominant authority of the past—emerges with particular force during the early modern age, when cultures begin to become particularly conscious of themselves in historical terms.[16] During the European Renaissance, the concept and practice of imitation served as a stabilizing response to the problems generated by the increasing preoccupation with authority and desire in history. At the beginning of *Don Quijote,* Part 1, the as yet unnamed hero adopts the practice of imitation as a means of modeling his desire according to the (textual) examples of his illustrious predecessors. Taken at face value, imitation is designed to stabilize the play of desire and offers a self-projective means of displacing the past:

> le pareció convenible y necesario, así para el aumento de su honra como para el servicio de su república, hacerse caballero andante, y irse por todo el mundo con sus armas y caballo a buscar las aventuras y a ejercitarse en todo aquello que él había leído que los caballeros andantes se ejercitaban, deshaciendo todo género de agravio, y poniéndose en ocasiones y peligros donde, acabándolas, cobrase eterno nombre y fama. (Part 1, chap. 1, pp. 74–75)

> (It appeared to him fitting and necessary, in order to win a greater amount of honor for himself and serve his country at the same time, to become a knight-errant and roam the world on horseback, in a suit of armor; he would go in quest of adventures, by way of putting into practice all that he had read in his books; he would right every manner of wrong, placing himself in situations of the greatest peril such as would redound to the eternal glory of his name.)

If history has the power not only to provide models of action and belief but also to control and demonize the present, then the practice of imitation may be regarded as one way of coming to terms with the

16. See Hans Blumenberg, *The Legitimacy of the Modern Age,* and A. J. Cascardi, "History, Theory, (Post)Modernity," in *After the Future,* ed Gary Shapiro (Albany: State University of New York Press, 1990), 1–16. It might well be argued that the problem of entering the modern age was more intensely felt in the Spain of the Golden Age than elsewhere in Europe because the embeddedness of and cultural attachment to the reigning order of society were particularly deep in Spain.

incalculable power of history by allowing us to recuperate loss in terms of an exemplary discourse; ideally, the past might then be successfully incorporated or absorbed into the present age and the work of "archaeology" might be brought to an end. But as *Don Quijote* abundantly shows, the practice of imitation cannot serve adequately to recuperate losses or to stabilize desire in historical terms. Indeed, in *Don Quijote* the practice of imitation constructs the possibility of a (literary, historical) present as a function of an insatiable desire *for* the past; since this desire cannot conceivably be fulfilled, history has a predominantly disorienting effect. Consider the fact that the objects of Don Quijote's imitations are from the start variable rather than fixed. In the early chapters of Part 1 the hero calls to mind and proposes to imitate the figures of the epic (e.g., the Cid), the fictional heroes of chivalric romance (Amadís de Gaula et al.), as well as figures drawn from the Moorish novel (Rodrigo de Narváez and Abindarráez), and from the ballad tradition (the Marqués de Mantua). This jumbled array—which replicates the confusion of origins surrounding the creation of the Cervantine text itself, with its multiple authors and variants—suggests that the "original" models of Don Quijote's desire have somehow been lost or eclipsed, and that these figures have broken loose from the organizing structure that history once provided. Indeed, it is only through the introduction of the conceptual category of "romance" that this heterogeneous variety of imitative models drawn from the past is later brought under critical control.

According to a critic like Lukács (*Theory of the Novel*), the chivalric romances against which *Don Quijote* was in the first instance a polemic had lost the "necessary transcendent relationship" to the original oneness or "totality" of life predicated of the epic world.[17] But as long as the rise of the novel is seen to depend on the loss of an original totality rather than on the transformation of the idea of such a totality into desire's archaeological "source," we shall be unable to comprehend the mediating function of literary romance. Lukács went on to say of the romances that "their mysterious and fairy-tale like surfaces were bound to degenerate into banal superficiality" (103). I suggest, however, that the "degraded" quality of romance stems from the temptation to restore and repossess "epic" values and thus to refuse to acknowledge as lost

17. Lukács, *Theory of the Novel,* trans. Anna Bostock (Cambridge: MIT Press, 1971), 103.

the proposed objects of desire. Throughout *Don Quijote* Cervantes makes a concerted effort to expose the fantasies of romance as anachronistic or out of place and discontinuous in the disenchanted modern world. As Michael McKeon has argued in connection with the early English novel, the category of "romance" was originally unstable; not only is it possible to detect anti-romance elements within romance, but romance itself passes through a series of seemingly infinite permutations, as the term shifts in emphasis from "heroic" to "amorous."[18] I would say that only in the shift in reading from history to desire could the novel come to be established as a term of categorical opposition to the romance. Indeed, in historicizing the novel McKeon fails to draw the more general conclusion that would seem warranted by the texts at hand; namely, that novelistic or "quixotic" desire is desire in search of a lost or forgotten—not to say "romantic"—object, the effect of which is to transform the "real" world into a series of fantasms or substitute appearances of an "original" that remains inaccessible to consciousness.

In addition, the jumbled array of figures offered as the possible models of Don Quijote's desire introduces an essential discontinuity into the Cervantine text, one that is prefigured by the discontinuities set forth in the prologue to Part 1, which, it bears noting, is itself already, *initially*, discontinuous with the main body of the text; it is this discontinuity that suggests the modernity of Cervantes's stance with respect to the problem of desire itself. As John Lyons has explained in a study of the theory and practice of example in the Renaissance, the discontinuity of example—which may be viewed as a discursive or rhetorical manifestation of the disruptive effects of desire—arises from the fragmentary status of the "original"; that is, from the model's status as a fragment excised from another, perhaps lost, unlocatable, or untotalizable "whole."[19] Indeed, the essential discontinuity implicit in the root concept of *eximere* (to cut out) would suggest that all examples are the sites of a possible, projected, absent, or denied satisfaction; all examples are extracted from one context and placed into another within which they make desire visible by virtue of their own exteriority.

The principal effect of the example is to introduce a series of troubling separations or gaps within the apparently homogeneous contours of

18. Both modes are at work in, among other places in *Don Quijote*, the story of the Captive's relationship with Zoraida (Part 1, chaps. 39–41).

19. John Lyons, *Exemplum: The Rhetoric of Example in Early Modern France and Italy* (Princeton: Princeton University Press, 1989), esp. 31–32.

character and text. In the case of *Don Quijote* these commence with the name of its hero and the forgotten place of his birth. The discontinuity of example applies as well to the textual surface of the (exemplary) work, since a shuttling back and forth between different rhetorical modes or levels of discourse—between "history" and "fiction," "prologue" and "narrative," "fiction" and "theory"—is the way in which the discontinuity that underlies exemplification may be felt as a textual effect. Indeed, it would on even cursory inspection appear that the discontinuities associated with the quixotic principle of exemplification pervade Cervantes's text, which is a sutured work, a "detotalized whole" that seems to be structured principally by such gaps. These range from the rhetorical discontinuities mentioned above to such large-scale discontinuities as are introduced in relation to the genesis of the manuscript and the genealogy of the printed text, as signaled by the break in Don Quijote's adventure with the Vizcaíno in Part 1, chapter 8. The discontinuous quality of Cervantes's text governs as well the procedure of interspersing or intercalating seemingly autonomous narrative segments (e.g., the stories of Fernando and Dorotea, the "Curioso impertinente," and the Captive's tale) within the framework of the larger narrative.

Consider once again the case of the "Curioso impertinente" in this regard. Read in "existential" terms, the point of the story would seem to be that Anselmo comes to recognize, just in time to save himself, that he is ultimately responsible for the destruction of himself, his wife, and his friend. This "existential" point is, however, offset by the sheer exorbitance of the tale and by the Priest's concluding remarks: " 'no me puedo persuadir que esto sea verdad; y si es fingido, fingió mal el autor, porque no se puede imaginar que haya marido tan necio, que quiera hacer *tan costosa experiencia* como Anselmo' " (There is something unconvincing about it. If the author invented it he did it badly, for it is impossible to believe that there could be a husband so stupid as to want to make the *very costly experiment* Anselmo did) (Part 1, chap. 36, p. 324; my emphasis). The case for a purely existential reading of the story is furthermore upset by virtue of the fact that the narrative "staging" of the tale allows Cervantes to highlight a series of coincidental motives and acknowledgments shared by the protagonists of the tale and those who hear it read. We notice this as figures like Cardenio and Dorotea, who listen to the tale, are allowed to see their own abrogation of responsibility and the consequences of that breach refracted in the lives of Anselmo, Lotario, and Camila. As a consequence, the mediated quality of desire at work in the self-representations of Fernando and Dorotea is brought to the fore. Indeed, characters like Fernando, Dorotea, and Anselmo can best be read as repetitions of previously shaped structures of literary desire; it is only when the narratives of these characters are juxtaposed and seen as fragmentary that the rhetorical effect of the interruption of the "Curioso impertinente" by Don Quijote's battle with the wineskins, or the surprising appearance of Luscinda and Fernando at the end of the tale, can be felt. As a result of these and similar interruptions, it becomes impossible to say which elements of the text are "continuous" and which are not.

To return to the specific question of Don Quijote's imitation of examples at the beginning of Part 1: it is customary to think that the novel as a genre requires the assertion of the self qua individual and to believe that self-assertion can only be achieved through the supersession of all relationships to imitative models drawn from the past. This might be an appropriate enough conclusion to draw from the case of a character like Robinson Crusoe, whose narrative begins with his attempted rejection of the authority of the father.[20] But the example of *Don Quijote* would suggest that the eclipse of imitation as a normative practice for containing the force of desire in relation to the past in fact generates a *proliferation* of models, none of which can satisfy the desire that self-assertion demands. Thus in response to a question concerning his identity Don Quijote responds in quasi-epic terms by claiming to appropriate all models of desire for himself: " 'Yo sé quien soy . . . y sé que puedo ser no sólo los que he dicho, sino todos los doce Pares de Francia, y aun todos los nueve de la Fama, pues a todas las hazañas que ellos todos juntos y cada uno de por sí hicieron, se aventajarán las mías' " (I know that I am capable of being not only the characters I have named [e.g., the Cid, Baldovinos, and Abindarráez], but all the Twelve Peers of France and all the Nine Worthies as well, for my exploits are far greater than all the deeds they have done, all together and each by himself) (Part 1, chap. 5, p. 106). Similarly, when confronted with the demand that a work of art imitate and pay homage to preexisting forms, the "author" of *Don Quijote* is counseled to buttress

---

20. Although there is not the space to demonstrate it here, it nonetheless bears noting that Robinson's narrative in the end conforms more closely to the father's law than to the shape of his "modern" desire.

his modernizing efforts by reproducing—more accurately, by excerpting and *citing*—the various modes of discourse that historically have licensed literature, even if these are the occasions of discontinuity and disruption rather that signs of an authentic or legitimate belief in the authority of the past:

> Vengamos ahora a la citación de los autores que los otros libros tienen, que en el vuestro os faltan. El remedio que esto tiene es muy fácil, porque no habéis de hacer otra cosa que buscar un libro que los acote todos, desde la A hasta la Z, como vos decís. Pues ese mismo abecedario pondréis vos en vuestro libro; que, puesto que a la clara se vea la mentira, por la poca necesidad que vos teníades de aprovecharos dellos, no importa nada; y quizá alguno habrá tan simple que crea que de todos os habéis aprovechado en la simple y sencilla historia vuestra; y cuando no sirva de otra cosa, por lo menos servirá aquel largo catálogo de autores a dar de improviso autoridad al libro. (Prologue, Part 1, p. 57)

> (Let us come now to references to authors, which other books contain and yours lacks. The remedy for this is very simple; for you have nothing else to do but look for a book which quotes them all from A to Z, as you say. Then you put this same alphabet into yours. For, granted that the very small need you have to employ them will make your deception transparent, it does not matter a bit; and perhaps there will even be someone silly enough to believe that you have made use of them all in your simple and straightforward story. And if it serves no other purpose, at least that long catalogue of authors will be useful to lend authority to your book at the outset. Besides, nobody will take the trouble to examine whether you follow your authorities or not.)

Indeed, it would not be too much to claim that modern literature begins when the "catalogue of authors" mentioned by Cervantes in the passage above comes to be the heterogeneous site of a fragmented and inevitably unfulfillable desire rather than the model of an "exemplary" relationship to the inheritance of the past.[21]

21. The "formlessness" of the text is reproduced in the claim that this text is similarly

As with the case of Don Quijote's mixed bag of models in Part 1, it is on the basis of a perceived marginality or secondariness with respect to the past that the peculiarly modern nature of desire within *Don Quijote* is made manifest. As I shall explain in the concluding pages of this chapter, Cervantes comes to realize that literature may be historical, that desire may be disruptive, and that the course of literary history may not necessarily be progressive. As a result, the "modernity" of *Don Quijote* must find expression in the spaces already occupied by preexisting forms. Thus when the Cervantine narrator affirms his iconoclastic desire in the famous concluding passage of Part 2, he frames the purpose of his writing with respect to the books of the past, rather than in terms of the desire to shape something radically new—but not because what might be "new" has yet to be invented; his purpose is stated in retrospective terms and so suggests that, strictly speaking, there may be no radically new forms for the modern writer to create. To be sure, Fielding later would claim to have authority over a "new province of writing" (*Tom Jones*, Book 2, chap. 1), but Fielding's *Joseph Andrews* was itself written "in imitation of Mr. Cervantes"; like Cervantes's boast in the prologue to the *Novelas ejemplares* that he was the first in Spanish to "novelize," these assertions of literary modernity can only be carried out through the repetition of preexisting texts.[22]

✳   ✳   ✳

If we think of *Don Quijote* as offering some of the most complex examples of the problem of desire and its literary representation in the modern world, it becomes increasingly clear that Cervantes's novel is both sustained and troubled by the mobile and potentially disruptive nature of desire, but that most conventional methods of reading are designed principally to deaden desire's disorienting effects. Indeed, while an appreciation of the motive force of desire may be central to an understanding of *Don Quijote* in light of the fundamental insights that psychoanalysis provides, readers of the novel often seek to normalize

---

authorless. I refer to the passage in the prologue to Part I, "yo, aunque parezco padre, soy padrastro de don Quijote" (Part 1, p. 50) (I, though in appearance Don Quixote's father, am really his stepfather).

22. Some of the ambiguities of originality in Cervantes have been discussed by John G. Weiger in *The Substance of Cervantes* (Cambridge: Cambridge University Press, 1985), esp. 41–83, and by E. T. Aylward in *Cervantes: Pioneer and Plagiarist* (London: Tamesis Books, 1982).

and control desire by attempting to submit literature to the "higher" authority of a theoretical discourse. The fact of fiction's ultimate inability to redeem desire—or, for that matter, to afford any ultimate justifications of its own status as a secondary, mediated, and therefore potentially degraded world, discontinuous with our own—is the occasion for the inclusion within *Don Quijote* of a seemingly authoritative theoretical discourse. With the theoretical efforts of the Barber and the Canon of Toledo near the conclusion of Part 1 (chaps. 47–48), Cervantes recognizes the temptation to legitimize the literary mediations of desire by passing desire through the crucible of rational judgment. The problem of desire would in this case be "resolved" by an appeal to the discursive norms of unity and verisimilitude of the sort that are invoked earlier by the Priest in order to reduce the ec-centricity (or "impertinence") of the "Curioso impertinente." Yet it seems that despite these efforts a quixotic "remainder" is left to threaten and demonize the achievements of literary theory as represented in Cervantes's text. Indeed, the Canon admits that he has himself attempted to author a perfect romance, taking care nonetheless to discipline himself in the process: " 'guardando en él todos los puntos que he significado' " (observing in it all the points I have mentioned) (p. 567), and Don Quijote provides a particularly extravagant example of the power of desire to overwhelm the efforts of theory in the form of the fantastic adventure of the Caballero del Lago. Consider the following summary of the Canon's reaction to Don Quijote's discourse on the Knight of the Lake: "Admirado quedó el canónigo de los concertados disparates que don Quijote había dicho, del modo con que había pintado la aventura del Caballero del Lago, de la impresión que en él habían hecho las pensadas mentiras de los libros que había leído" (The Canon was astonished at this well-reasoned nonsense of Don Quijote's, at his description of the adventure of the Knight of the Lake, and at the impression made on him by the deliberate lies in the books he had read) (Part 1, chap. 50, p. 588). In short, fiction's attempt to reorient desire by coming to full theoretical consciousness and control of itself may result in the appeal to an independent theoretical discourse, but this appeal is in turn deflected by desire's affective force.

As I want to explain in conclusion, this predicament forms the context surrounding issues that have been recently addressed by the revisionist methods of criticism developed in response to latter-day Barbers, Canons, and Priests—methods that take to heart the insights of contemporary psychoanalysis into the deflections of desire. Revisionism and other "strong forms" of reading attempt to correct the deficiencies of conventional literary history, according to which the imputed status of *Don Quijote* as the founding example of the modern novel derives from the simple rejection of the authority of tradition in establishing aesthetic norms. Ian Watt long ago argued that "previous literary forms had reflected the general tendency of their cultures to make conformity to traditional practice the major test of truth: the plots of classical and renaissance epic, for example, were based on past history or fable, and the merits of the author's treatment were judged largely according to a view of literary decorum derived from the accepted models of the genre. This literary traditionalism was first and foremost challenged by the novel."[23] As a characterization of modern writing, Watt's account might at best provide us with a Cartesian reading of Descartes, who from one point of view attempts to resist the claims of history by arrogating to himself the invention of a new mode of philosophical discourse. Descartes may have hoped that his project of rational self-assertion would serve as a bulwark against the disorienting effects of desire in history and as an absolute defense against the demonic presence of the past. For a figure like Cervantes, by contrast, discourse is always historical, but modern discourse is unique so insofar as it is unable to recover the original referents for our desires, which are themselves literarily and historically defined. In *Don Quixote and the Poetics of the Novel* (1992) Félix Martínez-Bonati discusses the ways in which Cervantes's text outstrips the various preestablished patterns of thought and writing on which it draws.[24] The *Quijote* is, for him, a "transitional form," though the teleology of this transition is indirect, to say the very least: while marking a step toward the "realism" characteristic of one vein of the modern novel, it is also contradicting "the homogeneity of style, the continuity of imaginary region, characteristic of the modern novel" (223).

To be sure, the claims of modern writing as a progressive attempt to contain desire through new ways of form-making may serve as mere covers for a sense of the displacement that stems from the persistence of

23. Watt, *The Rise of the Novel: Studies in Defoe, Richardson, and Fielding* (1957; repr., Berkeley and Los Angeles: University of California Press, 1964), 13.

24. Martínez Bonati, *Don Quixote and the Poetics of the Novel* (Ithaca: Cornell University Press, 1992). Especially interesting is what he calls the "Misdirections from a History of Forms" (223).

a past whose immediate authority has been lost. But all such "modern" form-making must be subordinate to the procedures of "quixotic" forms of reading, which are also iconoclastic, or form-breaking, in their struggles to overcome the past. The result of this tension is a literally infinite and fragmentary form of desire that undermines any view of literary history as forming the stable ground of modernity's relationship to the past. In contrast to their archaic analogues in the canon of sacred texts, works of modern literature can best be seen as responding to an overwhelming accretion of unfulfillable desire in history, which renders the task of autonomy or self-consciousness necessary to the constitution of modernity nearly impossible to achieve.[25] Hence Cervantes's intense but impossible project to "compete with Heliodorus" in the making of the *Persiles*.

As a modern writer, Cervantes is hurled toward the future while the trajectory of his writing is deflected by the stormy accumulation of literary desire in the past. One is reminded in this connection of Walter Benjamin's description of the *angelus novus,* which he sees as advancing toward the future with a visage that remains turned toward the wreckage of the past: "Where we perceive a chain of events, *he* sees one single catastrophe which keeps piling wreckage upon wreckage, and hurls it in front of his feet. The angel would like to stay, awaken the dead, and make whole what has been smashed. But a storm is blowing from Paradise; it has got caught in his wings with such violence that the angel can no longer close them. This storm irresistibly propels him into the future to which his back is turned, while the pile of debris before him grows skyward."[26] Seen in this light, a historical interpretation of *Don Quijote* that measures the possibility of literary and cultural "progress" in terms of the impossibility of a return to the fullness of an archaic past may provide a way to come to terms with the nature of modern desire. Indeed, we might go so far as to think of *Don Quijote* itself as a radically revisionist work. Chapter 8 discusses the further implications

25. In the analysis of one Bloomian critic, "because the secular cannon is never fixed and the 'religion' of humanism never fully revealed, salvation or the achievement of poetic desire remains a salvation for one in which the poets are in a direct and intensely personal competition—the achievement of one detracts from all the others, and the higher the canon elevates the greats of the past, the greater the burden on the poetic future." Jean-Pierre Mileur, *Literary Revisionism and the Burden of Modernity* (Berkeley and Los Angeles: University of California Press, 1985), 130.

26. Benjamin, "Theses on the Philosophy of History," trans. Harry Zohn, in *Illuminations* (New York: Schocken Books, 1969), 257–58.

of this claim in light of the secularization theorem that seems implicit in Lukács's *Theory of the Novel.* For the moment, we can say that one measure of the modernity of Cervantes's text lies in its ability to embarrass any mode of reading that fails to recognize the lost quality of the objects of desire or to acknowledge the always-already-mediated nature of our relationship to the past.

8

Secularization and Literary Self-Assertion in *Don Quijote*

> Yo . . . siempre trabajo y me desvelo
> por parecer que tengo de poeta
> la gracia que no quiso darme el Cielo.
>
> (I . . . am always at work and sleepless,
> so that I might seem to have the poetic
> talent that Heaven did not grant me.)
> —Cervantes, *Viaje del Parnaso*

In *The Theory of the Novel,* Lukács wrote that "the first great novel of world literature stands at the beginning of the time when the Christian God began to forsake the world." "Cervantes," he says, "lived in the period of the last, great and desperate mysticism, the period of a fanatical attempt to renew the dying religion from within; a period of a new view of the world rising up in mystical forms; the last period of truly lived but already disoriented, tentative, sophisticated, occult aspirations." As Lukács went on to say, this was "the period of the demons let loose, a period of great confusion of values in the midst of an as yet unchanged value system. And Cervantes, the faithful Christian and naively loyal patriot, creatively exposed the deepest essence of this demonic problematic: the purest heroism is bound to become grotesque, the strongest faith is bound to become madness, when the ways leading to the transcendental home have become impassible."[1]

The thrust of these passages is to suggest that the beginnings of literary modernity in Cervantes's *Don Quijote* can be understood in terms of the process of secularization. And yet it also seems that the Lukácsean analysis of secularization as it bears on Cervantes's text raises at least as many problems as it resolves. It is not altogether clear how the metaphysical language that we find in *The Theory of the Novel* can allow us to represent the connections between the increasingly secular (not to say prosaic) modes of consciousness typically encountered in the novel and the archaic sources of authority and belief that the novel continues to invoke. Although Lukács clearly intends such connections to be made, it seems that to formulate this issue in terms of the secularized idiom of modernity would lead to the writing of a Whiggish form of literary history, while to express it in the language of belief would be to embark on a quixotic project to restore the cultural authority of the past. This difficulty shows up in the strangely lyrical metaphoricity of Lukács's language, in which phrases like "the demonization of the world" and "the waning of the gods" hover mysteriously between the idiom of historical analysis and the language of religious belief. Yet one is hard-pressed to describe the difficulties posed by *The Theory of the Novel* simply as a language problem; what stands behind them is in fact central to the critical method employed throughout the work, which Lukács describes as "historico-philosophical" in nature and scope. As I take it, a strictly philosophical approach to Cervantes would result in a suppression of the differences between the languages

---

1. Lukács, *Theory of the Novel*, trans. Anna Bostock (Cambridge: MIT Press, 1971), 103–4. In this passage, Lukács's idealizing language borders on the allegorical, as the notion of demonic agency suggests. For a discussion of the demonic in this allegorical sense, see Angus Fletcher, *Allegory: The Theory of A Symbolic Mode* (Ithaca: Cornell University Press, 1964), esp. 41–69. Fletcher emphasizes the role of demonic agents as intermediaries, which links them back to Lukács's understanding of the heroism of the novel as grotesque: "As intermediaries, part man, part god, the daemons were often considered in both pagan and Christian antiquity to the guardians of the human species" (43). Fletcher in turn cites A. D. Nock, *Conversion: The Old and the New in Religion from Alexander the Great to Augustine of Hippo* (London: Oxford University Press, 1933). As will become clear over the course of what follows, the problem in the *Quijote* is not just that Cervantes's hero is "demonic" in any of these specific senses, but that he is haunted, as witnessed by the power that texts have over him. Don Quijote's haunting by these texts argues strongly in favor of the view of literature as a repository of powers once represented and understood in magical and religious terms.

of rational analysis and of belief, and a narrowly historical approach might tempt us to conceive of the division between archaic modes of consciousness and the secular modern world as categorical, definite, and absolute.

The theoretical efforts of more recent critics of the novel, including some Hispanists and Cervantists, have been to inscribe the process of secularization within the dynamics of a still more complex secular dialectic of historical materialism. Jay M. Bernstein has, for instance, argued in *The Philosophy of the Novel* that the Lukács of *The Theory of the Novel* was already a historical-materialist, even though he may not have known it, and that the only way in which the language of metaphysical idealism that pervades *The Theory of the Novel* can make sense is if we transpose it into the discourse of historical materialism, thus interpreting the secularization process reflected in the quixotic tension between "soul" and "world" in terms of the critique of bourgeois culture developed in Lukács's later Marxist works (e.g., *History and Class Consciousness*). But if one believes that a mapping of the *Quijote* onto a materialist grid requires a revisionary reading of Lukács that may betray his own original intentions, and if we nonetheless remain uncomfortable with the language of *The Theory of the Novel,* which speaks of secularization, as in the passages cited above, in the language of "demons" and "gods," then how are we to make sense of the role that Lukács ascribes to Cervantes as the inaugurator of the novel, as standing at the inception of literary modernity in the West?

In what follows here, I follow up Lukács's lead in arguing that the origins of literary modernity as reflected in Cervantes's work may indeed be understood in terms of the process of secularization, but that we must regard "secularization" not just as the result of a change in the patterns of religious belief but as a master-trope for the problem of authority as it is figured within literary history. At the same time I suggest that the process of secularization is not anything happening in culture external to literature, but that literary history itself, as an effort to negotiate between the authorities of the present and those of the past, is the best example of the "secularization" process whose consequences Lukács is attempting to express in the passages cited above. As I explain in greater detail in connection with Cervantes's text, to think of literature in relation to the trope of "secularization" is also to think of the power of modern literature to intuit its own status as both inside and outside of what goes by the names of "theology," "dogma," and "belief." (In *Revolution in Poetic Language,* Kristeva writes that "poetic language and mimesis may appear as an argument complicitous with dogma—we are familiar with religion's use of them—but they may also set in motion what dogma represses. In so doing, they no longer act as instinctual floodgates within the enclosure of the sacred and become instead protestors against its posturing.")[2] At the same time, such a reinterpretation of the secularization process provides a basis for a critique of the suspiciously progressive, self-validating, and self-assertive rhetoric of modernity. When seen as a corrective to modernity's understanding of itself, Cervantes's engagement with the problem of secularization can lead us to a more complex understanding of the dynamics of literature on the threshold of modernity, and eventually to the conclusion that the authority of literature in the modern age is not in fact self-sustaining but represents one consequence of the impossible and unfulfillable (not to say *quixotic*) desire to adapt a prior mode of cultural authority to the purposes and aims of the present age.

I begin by considering two scenes from *Don Quijote* that illustrate the nexus between the secularization process and changes in the patterns of literary "belief." In the first of these, the Priest and the Barber have embarked on their project to cure Don Quijote of his madness and so have disguised themselves in the hopes of convincing him to return to his home. But it turns out that there is a problem with the Priest's disguise. As he and the Barber attempt to exchange places on a mule, the Priest is kicked and falls in a fright "con tan poco cuidado de las barbas, que se le cayeron en el suelo; y como se vio sin ellas, no tuvo otro remedio sino acudir a cubrirse el rostro con ambas manos y a quejarse que le habían derribado las muelas. Don Quijote, como vio todo aquel mazo de barbas, sin quijadas y sin sangre, lejos del rostro del escudero caído, dijo: '¡Vive Dios, que es gran milagro éste!' ¡Las barbas le ha derribado y arrancado del rostro, como si las quitaran a posta!" (with so little care for his beard that it came off. Now when he found that he had lost it he could not think what to do except to clasp both hands hurriedly to his face, and cry out that his jaw was broken. Then, seeing all that mass of beard lying without jaws some distance away from the fallen squire's face, Don Quijote exclaimed: "Good

---

2. Kristeva, *Revolution in Poetic Language,* ed. and trans. Leon Roudiez (New York: Columbia University Press, 1984), 61. This translation is a much abbreviated version of Kristeva's *La Révolution du langage poétique* (Paris: Editions du Seuil, 1974).

Heavens! This is a great miracle! His beard has been ripped from his face as if it had been so designed!"). Seeing that his plot is at risk of being discovered, the Priest then rushes to reattach the beard, "murmurando sobre él unas palabras que dijo que era cierto ensalmo apropiado para pegar barbas como lo verían" (mumbling some words over it, which he said were an infallible charm for refixing beards, as they should see). "Se admiró Don Quijote sobremanera, y rogó al cura que cuando tuviese lugar le enseñase aquel ensalmo; que él entendía que su virtud a más que pegar barbas se debía de estender" (Don Quijote was vastly amazed at this, and begged the priest to teach him the charm when he had the time. For he was convinced that its efficacy must extend beyond the mere refixing of beards).[3]

In the second of my initial examples, we are at Camacho's wedding to Quiteria in Part 2. There, Quiteria's beloved, Basilio, stages his own suicide in the hopes of convincing everyone that she should leave her betrothed Camacho and return to him. Basilio stabs himself with a dagger and falls dead on the ground, or so it seems. When Basilio finds that the prospect of his death has prompted the crowd to agree that Quiteria should marry him, he suddenly rises from his fall, at which the spectators exclaim:

> "¡Milagro, milagro!"
> Pero Basilio replicó:
> "¡No 'milagro, milagro,' sino industria, industria!
> El cura, desatentado y atónito, acudió con ambas manos a tentar la hierba, y halló que la cuchilla había pasado, no por la carne de Basilio, sino por un cañón hueco de hierro que, lleno de sangre, en aquel lugar bien acomodado tenía; preparada la sangre, según después se supo, de modo que no se helase. Finalmente, el cura y Camacho con todos los más circunstantes se tuvieron por burlados y escarnidos. (Part 2, chap. 22, pp. 200–201)

3. I follow the Spanish edition of Luis Murillo (Madrid: Castalia, 1986), here Part 1, chap. 29, pp. 368–69. Translations are based on those of J. M. Cohen (Harmondsworth: Penguin, 1950), here 256. Of the *ensalmo* Covarrubias offers the following gloss: "Cierto modo de curar con oraciones; unas veces solas, otras aplicando juntamente algunos remedios. . . . Dijéronse *ensalmos* porque de ordinario usan de versos del Psalterio, y dellos con las letras iniciativas de letra por verso o por parte hacen unas sortijas, para diversas enfermedades" (in Murillo, 369). Covarrubias notes that these activities should come under the purview of the Inquisition.

("A miracle, a miracle!"

But Basilio answered, "no miracle, no miracle; but a trick, a trick!"

The Priest ran up in confusion and astonishment to feel the wound with both his hands, and found that the knife had not passed through Basilio's flesh and ribs, but through a hollow iron tube, which he had fitted into position, filled with blood so prepared, as it afterwards came out, not to congeal. In fact the priest, Camacho, and all the spectators had been tricked and fooled.)[4]

An investigation of the problem of secularization in *Don Quijote* can, I think, be initiated by these two scenes, which so graphically represent a shift from the seemingly "miraculous" moment in Part 1 when the Priest's beard is removed and subsequently reattached, to the transformation of an apparent "miracle" into a device of human cunning and industry in Part 2. (Needless to say, both of these episodes occur within the fiction's disenchanted world.) But, as will become apparent over the course of what is to follow here, I understand the question of secularization in *Don Quijote* to be far less direct and far less complete than the notion of a linear trajectory away from a belief in the power of miracles and toward a more rationalized view of the world. For one thing, we are already within the framework of "secularization" within the first of the scenes just described insofar as everyone except Don Quijote recognizes that the reattaching of the beard happens by human industry and not as a miracle. (For Don Quijote, the incident is framed in terms of myth and magic, as the beard is reattached by means of a "charm" [*ensalmo*].) But beyond these complexities, which have a direct bearing on the question of the power of fiction to compel belief, the question of secularization involves issues that are of far broader reach than can be indicated by the deflationary impact of these two episodes. I argue that the problem of secularization

---

4. There may well be a resonance of Christ's miracle at the wedding feast at Cana in this episode, though of course the miracles in question are quite different. That biblical episode may in turn have been mediated through Garcilaso's *copla* 7, which, like Cervantes, emphasizes the wonder produced in the audience: "La gente s'espanta toda, / que hablar a todos distes, / que un milagro que hecistes / hubo de ser en la boda; / pienso que habéis de venir, / si vais por ese camino, / a tornar el agua en vino, / como el danzar en reír."

can best be understood not just as the process by which religious practices and belief were eliminated from the world or transformed into their secular correlates; rather, the notion of "secularization" can be taken to involve all of the various ways in which the authority of the past was carried forward, resisted, and transformed as part of the larger process of modernization that took root in the sixteenth and seventeenth centuries. I should also note that this was a particularly complex process in Spain, where writers so often engaged in what we might imagine as a reversal of the secularization process through the rewritings *a lo divino* of decisively secular texts.

＊　＊　＊

The question of secularization as it bears on the interpretation of Cervantes's novel can be approached in terms of a conflict between two versions of cultural history and two versions of the authority on which those histories are founded, which for simplicity I shall call the "humanist" and the "modernist." Whereas modernism represents an attempt to generate a historical orientation for and from itself, humanism reads the past in order to distill a rhetoric of values and a canon to sustain its cultural ideas. Unlike modernist self-assertion, humanism recognizes that it stands in essential need of the tradition as the value-field out of which it arises and to which it ultimately refers. But, to take the figure of *translatio* as an example of the ways in which the humanist version of cultural history was expressed, it seems that humanism also recognizes the belatedness of its intentions as it strives to recuperate the values of the past. Since the tradition is humanism's only resource against the potentially devastating sense of inadequacy that might follow from this fact, however, recourse to the tradition also becomes humanism's contradictory attempt to defend against the consequences of its failure to derive a more certain orientation from history than it can possibly provide. Humanism thus amounts to a demand placed upon cultural history that attempts to derive more from history than it can yield.

If we consider the displacement of the humanist orientation, as it might be exemplified in figures like Petrarch and Montaigne, by the self-assertive gestures of modernizing figures like Descartes and Hobbes, we can begin to understand how modernists attempted to reject the humanist rhetoric in order to secure the autonomy of their own age. The modernist exercise of freedom with respect to history commences for a figure like Descartes with the abandonment of all attachments to the examples of the past: "regarding the opinions to which I had hitherto given credence, I thought that I could not do better than undertake to get rid of them, all at one go, in order to replace them afterwards with better ones, or with the same ones once I had squared them with the standards of reason."[5] Similarly, Hobbes claimed that political science was no older than his own work *De Cive*,[6] and in the *Discourse on Method* Descartes recommended razing the faltering edifice of received opinion for the purpose of building anew.[7]

To be sure, the "overcoming" of the authority of history does not emerge full-blown in the seventeenth century. It was itself provoked by a cultural crisis evident in the efforts of Renaissance writers to assert themselves both by means of and against the example of the ancients. Already for figures like Petrarch, Machiavelli, Montaigne, and of course Cervantes, historical examples were the source of considerable unease, as writers came to discover the anxieties that could follow from the irrecuperable distance between the present and the past.[8] Hobbes attempts to address and overcome this anxiety when he criticizes "men that take their instruction from the authority of books, and not from their own meditation."[9] This is part of Hobbes's wider program of "self-assertion," in which the accomplishments of reason are seen as self-justifying insofar as they reflect the successful actualization of human aims, intentions, and designs (Hobbes: "Good successe is

5. *Discourse on Method*, II, in *The Philosophical Writings of Descartes,* trans. John Cottingham, Robert Stoothoff, and Dugald Murdoch (Cambridge: Cambridge University Press, 1985), 117.

6. Hobbes, *English Works*, ed. William Molesworth (London: John Bohn, 1839) 1:ix.

7. "Admittedly, we never see people pulling down all the houses of a city for the sole purpose of rebuilding them in a different style to make the streets more attractive; but we do see many individuals having their houses pulled down in order to rebuild them, some even being forced to do so when the houses are in danger of falling down and their foundations are insecure" (*Discourse*, I, 117).

8. Karlheinz Stierle provides an illuminating discussion of Montaigne in "L'Histoire comme example, l'example comme histoire," *Poétique* 10 (1972): 176–98. See also Marcel Gutwirth, *Michel de Montaigne ou le pari d'exemplarité* (Montréal: Presses de l'Université de Montréal, 1977), and Michael Wood, "Montaigne and the Mirror of Example," *Philosophy and Literature* 13 (1989): 1–15.

9. See Gary Shapiro, "Reading and Writing in the Text of Hobbes's *Leviathan*," *Journal of the History of Philosophy* 18 (1980): 152. This does not, of course, explain the paradox of the instructive powers that Hobbes claims for his own book.

Power").[10] To explain the success of the modernist response to humanism in terms of the secularization thesis nonetheless exposes the vulnerability of modernist self-assertion on a number of counts. To think of
culture not so much as secular but as *secularized* is dangerous because
it threatens the autonomy of the historiographical perspective of self-
assertion. Indeed, to posit the origins of modernity in a process of
secularization would be to embrace a fundamentally skeptical thesis
with respect to the affirmative claim that the originating sources of
value emanate from the subject in a process of radical self-assertion. For
if modernity were shown to be secularized in some essential way (i.e., if
its specific forms of self-assertion were found to bear within them the
hidden traces of pre-existing modes of action and belief) then the claims
of modern culture to have achieved an unprecedented level of autonomy
would be drastically compromised.

Why is this so? The secularization theorem places at risk modernity's
crucial distinction between the languages of imagination and belief on
the one hand—however tenuous, secondary, or remotely connected to
their origins these may be—and a rational language of criticism on the
other; the latter is embodied not only in philosophy but, as we shall see
in Cervantes, in literary efforts to re-assess the past. Thus for a modernizing historian like Hans Blumenberg the idea of "secularization" as
encountered in the Christian-humanist synthesis said to have been
favored by a writer like Cervantes must be the source of a historical
self-*mis*understanding from which we as moderns have been struggling
to clear free.[11] If the process of "secularization" somehow makes
de-originating figures out of the synthetic humanist transposition of
authority from one epoch or realm to another, then any instance of the
rhetoric of "secularization" would threaten to reveal a breach in the
connections between the secular modes of consciousness represented in
literary institutions like the novel and the archaic paradigms of authority
informing them. Indeed, the greatest threat of the secularization thesis
is that it may reveal a discontinuity in history itself. In Sidney's *Defence
of Poetry* (1595), for instance, the authority of modern writing is always
in competition with a more archaic and powerful conception of poetry,
which it cannot fully reclaim. That more powerful authority was, on

10. Hobbes, *Leviathan,* ed. C. B. Macpherson (Harmondsworth: Penguin, 1968),
part 1, chap. 10, p. 151.
11. Blumenberg, *The Legitimacy of the Modern Age,* trans. Robert M. Wallace
(Cambridge: MIT Press, 1985).

Sidney's account, evident among the Greeks, where poetry was the mask of true "philosophy," and later among the Romans, who recognized poetry as a form of prophetic discourse:

> since the authors of most of our sciences were the Romans, and before them the Greeks, let us stand upon their authorities. but even so far as to see what names they have given unto this now scorned skill. Among the Romans a poet was called *vates,* which is as much as a diviner, foreseer, or prophet, as by his conjoined words *vaticinium* and *vaticinari* is manifest: so heavenly a title did that excellent people bestow upon his heart-ravishing knowledge. And so far were they carried into the admiration thereof, then they thought in the chanceable hitting upon any such verses great foretokens of their following fortunes were placed. . . . Which, although it were a very vain and godless superstition, as also it was to think spirits were commanded by such verses— whereupon this word *charms,* derived of *carmina,* cometh—so yet serveth it to show the great reverence those wits were held in; and altogether not without ground, since both the oracles of Delphos and Sibylla's prophecies were wholly delivered in verse.[12]

The specter of a rupture between one form of authority and another against which Sidney here defends—as he attempts to "think back" from poetry to prophecy, from human industry and causality to miracles, or from genius to grace—threatens the humanist synthesis and leaves the imagination with few creative resources aside from its own somewhat desperate inventiveness.

The difficulty Cervantes faces is roughly equivalent to the one that Sidney betrays in his desire to own the more powerful and authoritative language of the ancients while at the same time asserting his own skepticism about the "magical" powers of verse. In the literary romance, for instance, the problem is that while the marvelous has always served as a marker for that which absolutely exceeds belief, in the early modern age the marvelous increasingly failed to compel assent, while nonetheless continuing to exist—much like Sidney's image of prophetic

---

12. Sidney, *Defence of Poetry,* ed. J. A. Van Dorsten (Oxford: Oxford University Press, 1966), 21–22.

verse—as the object of a modern desire. The effect of the marvelous in a work like the *Persiles* must be produced in a skeptical, critical, and sometimes inattentive audience, for whom the conditions of belief have been lost; but the power of the marvelous within literature (and the power of literature as itself marvelous) continues to be desired just the same. As Periandro's narration of the "muchos y extraños sucesos" (many strange occurrences) of his wanderings begins to outstrip the limits of the "possible" and the "probable" that are expected of a "verdadera historia," he becomes unable to continue in the assumption that his narration will have the desired effects on the beliefs of his audience. But he continues nonetheless to plead for the benevolence *(cortesía)* of his listeners in order to legitimize what he hopes they might have accepted with unskeptical faith, which is to say that the marvelous here is dependent on his listeners' (good) will.[13]

In the *Quijote*, the tension between the authority of the miracle to compel belief in and of itself and the cultivation of belief in an audience by rhetorical means forces us to rewrite the secularization theorem so as to describe the failure of the secular fully to erase the sacred and the inability of the authority of the present to overcome the past. The transformation of an archaic heroic ethos into the substance of "quixotic" dreams whose basis lies neither in the actual world nor in history but in a tradition of texts may be seen as a result of the failure of secularization insofar as the power of that archaic ethos is never categorically and conclusively eclipsed, but survives in such a way as to disorient Cervantes's hero as well as those other characters, like the Barber and the Priest, who seek to reorient Don Quijote to "orthodox" secular ways. Additionally, those forms of reading (and misreading) that are made available through the humanist tradition never become fully transumptive tropes of the original; they remain always haunted, mysteriously possessed and secretly energized by various "demonized" forms of the preceding culture.

This is also to say that, for Cervantes at least, the origins of literary modernity must be located in the failure of the humanist paradigm of cultural history, as reflected in the still more general inability of secular

---

13. Kant makes the "good will" the centerpiece of his moral theory in the *Foundations of the Metaphysics of Morals,* where he begins by saying, quite famously, that "nothing in the world—indeed nothing even beyond the world—can possibly be conceived which could be called good without qualification except a *good will.*" Trans. Lewis White Beck (Indianapolis: Bobbs-Merrill, 1969), 11.

culture fully to subsume its predecessors. As in the prologue of *Don Quijote,* Part 1, the humanist understanding of cultural transmission and continuity (the *translatio studii*) as a fundamentally textual phenomenon argues in favor of the failure of secularization, suggesting also that precisely where secularization fails is in relation to our desire, through (modern) literature, to imagine radically new ends for society and the self. As reflected in the prologue, this "failure" appears as a disorder internal to the humanist desire to transpose and repossess the authority of the past. Thus the prologue's "author" suggests that the modern writer is bound to fail in his attempt to recuperate the sources of value located in the tradition. When confronted with the demand that a great work of art should imitate and pay homage to preexisting authorities, the "author" is counseled to buttress his modernizing efforts by reproducing the authoritative modes of discourse upon which writers traditionally have drawn—including references to canonized figures, learned allusions, and marginal notes—even if these are outmoded and no longer function as truly efficacious cultural signs. Recall the following passage, which we have already had occasion to note.

> Vengamos ahora a la citación de los autores que los otros libros tienen, que en el vuestro os faltan. El remedio que esto tiene es muy fácil, porque no habéis de hacer otra cosa que buscar un libro que los acote todos, desde la A hasta la Z, como vos decís. Pues ese mismo abecedario pondréis vos en vuestro libro; que, puesto que a la clara se vea la mentira, por la poca necesidad que vos teníades de aprovecharos dellos, no importa nada; y quizá uno haya tan simple que crea que de todos os habéis aprovechado en la simple y sencilla historia vuestra; y cuando no sirva de otra cosa, por lo menos servirá aquel largo catálogo de autores a dar de improviso autoridad al libro. Y más, que no habrá quien se ponga a averiguar si los seguistes o no los seguistes, no yéndole nada en ello. (p. 57)

> (Let us come now to references to authors, which other books contain and yours lacks. The remedy for this is very simple; for you have nothing else to do but look for a book which quotes them all from A to Z, as you say. Then you put this same alphabet into yours. For, granted that the very small need you have to employ them will make your deception transparent, it does not matter a bit; and perhaps there will even be someone

silly enough to believe that you have made use of them all in your simple and straightforward story. And if it serves no other purpose, at least that long catalogue of authors will be useful to lend authority to your book at the outset. Besides, nobody will take the trouble to examine whether you follow your authorities or not.)

As this example suggests, the transformation of an imperfect or incomplete secularization process into the dynamics of modern literary history, with its attempt at radical self-assertion, may nonetheless offer a way to *deflect* the implications of inadequacy that the failure of the humanist effort to reappropriate the past might have for culture as a whole. One thinks also of the ambivalent terms in which Cervantes' *Galatea* is judged in chapter 6 of *Don Quijote,* Part 1: "tiene algo de buena invención; propone algo, y no concluye nada: es menester esperar la segunda parte que promete; quizá con la emienda alcanzará del todo la misericordia que ahora se le niega" (it is well conceived in some respects; it proposes something, but concludes nothing: it is necessary to wait for the second part; perhaps with this change it will gain the mercy that so far it has been denied) (pp. 120–21). A passage like this serves both as an admission of weakness and as a defense against it; but perhaps the most interesting fact about it is that Cervantes never completely conceals the devastating implications of the secularization theorem behind the rhetoric of self-assertion that this occasion of self-criticism invites. On the contrary, the conditions of failure, loss, and self-abasement maintain a continuing presence throughout his work. "¿Qué podría engendrar el estéril y mal cultivado ingenio mío," asks the prologue's author, "sino la historia de un hijo seco, avellanado, antojadizo y lleno de pensamientos varios y nunca imaginados de otro alguno, bien como quien se engendró en una cárcel, donde toda incomodidad tiene su asiento y donde todo triste ruido su habitación?" (What could be expected of a sterile and uncultivated wit such as that which I possess if not an offspring that was dried up, shriveled, and eccentric: a story filled with thoughts that never occurred to anyone else, of a sort that might be engendered in a prison where every annoyance has its home and every sorry sound its habitation?) (p. 50). The example of the landed gentleman whose brains have failed from reading too many of the chivalric novels is here transposed into the image of an author whose imagination fails him when called upon to invent an opening for his work, or to place that work with respect to the traditions of the past, and who thus represents himself as unproductive, sterile, abandoned, and alone:

> salgo ahora con todos mis años a cuestas, con un leyenda seca como un esparto, ajena de invención, menguada de estilo, pobre de conceptos y falta de toda erudición y doctrina, sin acotaciones en las márgenes y sin anotaciones en el fin del libro, como veo que están otros libros, aunque sean fabulosos y profanos, tan llenos de sentencias de Aristóteles, de Platón y de toda la caterva de filósofos que admiran a los leyentes y tienen a sus autores por hombres leídos, eruditos y elocuentes. (p. 52)

> (I now appear, burdened by my years, with a tale that is as dry as a weed, bereft of any imagination, meager in style, impoverished in content, and wholly lacking in learning and wisdom, without marginal citations or notes at the end of the book, when other works of this sort, even though they may be fabulous and profane, are so packed with maxims from Aristotle and Plato and the whole learned crowd of philosophers that they fill the reader with admiration and lead him to regard the author as a well read, learned, and eloquent individual.)

The author can only defend against his deficiencies by taking the humanist notion of reading—or of *translatio,* as a form of "misreading"—not just as confirming evidence that no proper work remains for the modern writer to accomplish, but as an ironic basis for the creation of an equally imaginative authorial stance. Indeed, it is through the author's self-projection and doubling as his own "friend," who intervenes in the prologue in order to take up the imaginative slack created by the writer's secondariness with respect to the past, that Cervantes finds a way to fend off the potentially disturbing inferiority, indeed the haunting nothingness, that the modern writer's creative labor threatens to reveal:

> Muchas veces tomé la pluma para escribille [el prólogo], y muchas la dejé, por no saber lo que escribiría; y estando una suspenso, con el papel delante, la pluma en la oreja, el codo en el bufete y la mano en la mejilla, pensando lo que diría, entró a

deshora un amigo mío, gracioso y bien entendido, el cual, viéndome tan imaginativo, me preguntó la causa, y no encbriéndosela yo, le dije que pensaba en el prólogo que había de hacer a la historia de Don Quijote, y que me tenía de suerte que ni quería hacerle, ni menos sacar a luz las hazañas de tan noble caballero. (pp. 51–52)

(Many times I took up my pen and many times I laid it down again, not knowing what to write. On one occasion when I was thus in suspense, paper before me, pen over my ear, elbow on the table, and chin in hand, a very clever friend of mine came in. Seeing me lost in thought, he inquired as to the reason, and I made no effort to conceal from him the fact that my mind was on the preface which I had to write for the story of Don Quijote, and that it was giving me so much trouble that I had just about decided not to write any at all and to abandon entirely the idea of publishing the exploits of so noble a knight.)

To raise the question of secularization in relation to the *Quijote* is thus to ask in more than just a literal way about the relationship between Cervantes as a writer and the Christian God, as Lukács proposed. Similarly, it is to suggest that Américo Castro's understanding of the *Quijote* as "una forma secularizada de espiritualidad religiosa"[14] raises questions about the location of authority as one moves between "sacred" and "secular" forms. It is to pose some fundamental questions relating to the transmission of literary and cultural authority in the early modern age, where the battle between the "old" and the "new" is not limited to the differences between the social regimes of caste and class, but includes the much broader questions of how to honor the past while establishing one's own independence. Likewise, it raises the question of how to defend (modern) literature against the failure of its historical self-assertion. Nowhere in Cervantes are the implications of these issues for the work of the imagination more richly explored than in the scene of "absorptive" reading that opens the *Quijote*. Here the deficit of the modern poetic imagination hinted at in the author's struggles with the writing of the prologue is transformed into the experience of the

14. Castro, "El *Quijote* como una forma secularizada de espiritualidad religiosa," in *Cervantes y los casticismos españoles* (Madrid: Alfaguara, 1966), 90.

principal character's seduction by, and fall into, the text.[15] Although characters like the Barber and the Priest may attempt to invent strategies and advance critical arguments designed to reorient Don Quijote to orthodox ways, Cervantes seems to suggest that nothing in the world can prevent his fall. Indeed, the experience of reading under the conditions of modernity is conveyed not so much in our experience of a fall, but rather, as the leading contemporary theoretician of poetic falls, Harold Bloom, has said, in the disorienting awareness that *we are falling*.[16] What "causes" Alonso Quijano to become overwhelmed by the texts he reads may be interpreted as a function of his inability to defend himself against the power of poetic imagination transmitted by them. Thus while Cervantes objectifies and renders concrete the modern reader's engagement of the literary tradition through Don Quijote's encounter with the chivalric books, the possibility of an imaginative "fall" into the text remains nonetheless a constant possibility, for reader and author as well; it is a reminder of the vulnerability of the modern imagination, or of a weakness of the particular power of resistance on which the reader's own capacity for self-assertion rests.[17]

15. In an essay entitled "The Notion of Blockage in the Literature of the Sublime," Neil Hertz suggests that in Wordsworth's *Prelude,* the episode of the blind beggar keeps Wordsworth from "tumbling into his text." *Psychoanalysis and the Question of the Text,* ed. Geoffrey Hartman (Baltimore: Johns Hopkins University Press, 1978), 84. Jean-Pierre Mileur comments that "the fall into the text is the fall into the community over which the author has no control. The text is at once the means by which imagination and creative identity are manifested and by which the author is appropriated to the community and the tradition, largely on their terms." *Literary Revisionism and the Burden of Modernity* (Berkeley and Los Angeles: University of California Press, 1985), 63.

16. Bloom, *Anxiety of Influence* (New York: Oxford University Press, 1973), 20. Cervantes would be one instance that could be cited to question the claim of George Mariscal that the anxiety of influence is only of "secondary importance" in a discussion of early modern literature, though I find the points Mariscal is making by means of this claim—that a poetry produced for a courtly audience may have been seen as secondary to politics and that the courtly writer may not have aspired to the status of "writer"—to be quite persuasive in the case of Quevedo. See *Contradictory Subjects: Quevedo, Cervantes, and Seventeenth-Century Spanish Culture* (Ithaca: Cornell University Press), 107. Cervantes's interest in the "poetic" fall is itself an instance of the secularization of a theological concept. For Garcilaso's interest in poetic falls (and in the ways in which they may or may not allow the poet to reclaim a lost power), see sonnet 12 ("Si para refrenar este deseo"), where the tercets refer to the myths of Icarus and Phaeton.

17. In psychoanalytic terms, the danger lies in the failure to acquire the capacity for what Winnicott calls "object-use," and thus in remaining at the stage of "object-relating." See "On the 'Use' of an Object," in *Psychoanalytic Explorations,* ed. Clare Winnicott, Ray Shepherd, and Madeleine Davis (Cambridge: Harvard University Press,

Moreover, Don Quijote's fall signals a failure that flies in the face of Cervantes's own historical self-assertions, which he relates to the glories of the Spanish empire and, more specifically, to the glorious heroism of self-sacrifice exemplified while fighting under the imperial flag of Don Juan of Austria at Lepanto, identified in the prologue to the *Novelas ejemplares* as "la más memorable y alta ocasión que vieron los pasados siglos, ni esperan ver los venideros, militando debajo de las vencedoras banderas del hijo del rayo de la guerra, Carlo Quinto, de feliz memoria"[18] (the most memorable and exalted occasion that past centuries have seen or that future ones can expect to see, fighting under the victorious flag of the son of the lightning bolt of war, Charles V, may he rest in peace). Cervantes repeats this very same rhetoric in the prologue to Part 2 of *Don Quijote,* where he speaks of the injury to his hand as having been sustained "en la más alta ocasión que vieron los siglos pasados, los presentes, ni esperan ver los venideros" (p. 33). These assertions represent one side of the ceaselessly contradictory self-estimations, characterized by equal measures of praise and self-deprecation, that we find scattered throughout Cervantes's texts. While Cervantes may for instance boast in the prologue to the *Novelas ejemplares* that he is the first to write novels in Spanish, or that his *Persiles* will compete with Heliodorus, he also doubts his literary authority and prestige, not only in the prologue to the *Quijote* but also in the preface to the *Ocho comedias y entremeses,* where he records the damaging effect of Lope's success on his own theatrical career. "No hallé pájaros en los nidos de antaño" (I found no birds in the nests of yesteryear), he says describing his experience upon returning to works which he had composed decades ago; "quiero decir que no hallé autor que me las pidiese, puesto que sabían que las tenía, y así las arrinconé en un cofre y las consagré y condené al perpetuo silencio. En esta sazón me dijo un librero que él me las comprara si un autor de título no le hubiera dicho que de mi prosa se podía esperar mucho, pero que del

---

1989), 217–46. There, Winnicott describes object use as "more sophisticated" than object relating (227).

18. "Prólogo," *Novelas ejemplares,* ed. Juan Bautista Avalle-Arce (Madrid: Castalia, 1982), 1:63. Cervantes evokes this same rhetoric in the Prologue to Part 2 of *Don Quijote,* where he speaks of the injury to his hand as having been sustained "en la más alta ocasión que vieron los siglos pasados, los presentes, ni esperan ver los venideros." He continues: "Si mis heridas no resplandecen en los ojos de quien las mira, son estimadas, a lo menos, en la estimación de los que saben dónde se cobraron; que el soldado más bien parece muerto en la batalla que libre en la fuga" (33).

verso nada" (I mean I found no managers who wanted them, although they knew I had them. And so, I put them in a trunk, consecrating and condemning them to eternal silence. In good time a bookseller told me he might buy them from me, although a royally licensed stage manager had told him that a good deal could be expected from my prose, but from my poetry, nothing at all).[19]

For a critic like Américo Castro, Cervantes's most problematic self-estimations are best explained in terms of Cervantes's existential retreat into the depths of self-reflection in the face of adverse social circumstances. For example, the assertion made in the prologue to Part 1 that Don Quijote was engendered in jail (a claim echoed in chapter 21 in relation to Ginés de Pasamonte's picaresque autobiography, which is said similarly to have been composed in jail) would have to be seen as a direct reflection of Cervantes's social situation as a converso in Spain, and not as an example of Cervantes's ironic self-reflection on his own creative powers and his place in relation to the literary traditions of the past. For instance, in explaining the genesis of the Quijote's "first author," Cide Hamete, Castro writes that "the Quijote forces one to imagine a long period of retreat on Cervantes' part, a withdrawal into the innermost part of his self, of forced and inconsolable solitude. All possible paths in the surrounding material, moral, and literary worlds were closed to him."[20] Similarly, Castro interprets the claim that the Quijote was engendered in jail as an expression of the creative anguish of Cervantes's spirit: "it is evident to me that the Quijote had to have been conceived in the deepest reclusion of Cervantes' soul, precisely 'where every unhappiness finds its home.' "[21]

And yet this analysis forgets to consider that Cervantes's estimations of his own literary abilities, sometimes veiled or deflected through the voices of his characters, may be the symptoms of a more general literary-historical anxiety. In "El coloquio de los perros," for instance, Berganza tells of four madmen, one of whom is a poet, whose conversations he overheard at the hospital. The poet complains because

19. In Obras completas, ed. Angel Valbuena Prat (Madrid: Aguilar, 1970), 1:210b. Translation from Edwin Honig, Interludes: Miguel de Cervantes (New York: New American Library / Signet, 1964), xxv–xxvi.
20. Castro, "El cómo y el por qué de Cide Hamete Benengeli," in Hacia Cervantes (Madrid: Taurus, 1967), 412.
21. Castro, "Los prólogos al Quijote," in Hacia Cervantes, 264.

habiendo yo guardado lo que Horacio manda en su *Poética,* que no salga a luz la obra que después de compuesta no hayan pasado diez años por ella, y que tenga yo una de veinte años de ocupación y doce de pasante, porque el principio responde al medio y al fin, de manera que constituyen el poema alto, sonoro, heroico, deleitable y sustancioso, y que, con todo esto, no hallo un príncipe a quien dirigirle. Príncipe, digo, que sea inteligente, liberal y magnánimo. ¡Mísera edad y depravado siglo nuestro!

(Having kept to the rules that Horace lays down in his *Ars of Poetry* that one shouldn't publish a work until ten years after it is finished, I have one which took me twenty years to write, not to mention twelve more I had it by me, a work with a vast subject, an admirable and novel plot, dignified lines and entertaining episodes, marvelously balanced, with the beginning matching the middle and the end: so that poem is lofty, tuneful, heroic, pleasing and substantial; yet I can't find a noble patron to whom I can address it. I mean a nobleman who is intelligent, liberal and magnanimous. What a wretched age and century we live in.)[22]

Indeed, precisely because he sees the consequences of all history—including literary history—as bound up with the compensatory ambition of imaginative literature as a source of hope, Cervantes instructs us to read the existential problems of failure and loss in relation to the writer's defenses against his own feared historical fate. What is particularly problematic in Cervantes's way of imagining this dilemma is that in attacking the pretensions of greatness, he also calls into question the "saving power" of literature, which represents its most fundamental compensatory myth. Indeed, literature seems hardly able to avoid the deeply troubling question addressed by poets like Garcilaso and, before him, by Petrarch and the authors of pastoral and elegiac verse: Of what use is poetry in the face of loss and death?[23] In

22. Cervantes, *Novelas ejemplares,* ed. Harry Sieber (Madrid: Cátedra, 1980), 2:335; trans. C. A. Jones, *Cervantes: Exemplary Stories* (Harmondsworth: Penguin, 1972), 248.
23. For a summary of echoes of Garcilaso in Cervantes, see José Manuel Blecua, "Garcilaso y Cervantes" (1948); reprinted in *La poesía de Garcilaso: ensayos críticos,* ed. Elias L. Rivers (Barcelona: Ariel, 1974), 369–79.

Garcilaso's eclogue 1 the shepherd Salicio in essence grants that, no matter how great its powers may be, poetry may be unable to compensate against absence, denial, and loss. I shall return to these verses in my discussion of Garcilaso in the next chapter, but they are worth citing in the present context as well:

> Con mi llorar las piedras enternecen
> su natural dulzura y la quebrantan;
> los árboles parece que s'inclinan;
> las aves que m'escuchan, cuando cantan
> con diferente voz se condolecen
> y mi morir cantando m'adevinan;
>   las fieras que reclinan
> su cuerpo fatigado
> dejan el sosegado
> sueño por escuchar mi llanto triste:
> tú sola contra mí t'endureciste
> (lines 197–207)

(My tears soften and break the natural hardness of the stones; it seems as if the trees bend over; the birds that hear me show sympathy by a change in their voices when they sing, and in their songs they foretell my death; the wild beasts, who recline in their tired bodies, abandon restful sleep to hear my sad lament: you alone have hardened your heart against me.)[24]

Salicio's companion Nemoroso, who confronts a seemingly more final loss in the death of his beloved, attempts to sublimate loss according a vision in which the fruit of transcendence is a new pastoral-poetic space:

> busquemos otro llano
> busquemos otros montes y otros ríos,
> otros valles floridos y sombríos
> donde descanse y siempre pueda verte
>   ante los ojos míos,
> sin miedo y sobresalto de perderte.

24. Garcilaso translations are based on those of Elias Rivers in *Renaissance and Baroque Poetry of Spain* (New York: Scribner, 1966).

(let us seek out other mountains and other rivers, other valleys full of flowers and shade, where I can rest and always see you before my eyes, without the fear of losing you.)

Finally, in eclogue 3 Garcilaso goes on to suggest that it is the very artificiality, indeed the imaginary quality of poetry, that makes it available as the language of secular faith in a world of loss:

> mas con la lengua muerta y fría en la boca
> pienso mover la voz a ti debida.
>
> (lines 11–12)

(even with my tongue dead and cold in my mouth I intend to stir the voice which I owe to you.)

Some of these same issues are raised in relation to the Marcela and Grisóstomo episode of *Don Quijote,* Part 1. In the Marcela and Grisóstomo episode, however, Cervantes transforms the problem of personal loss into an even farther-reaching investigation of literature's power and limits,[25] as Grisóstomo's passing prompts those who survive him to question the power of poetry in the face of death. For Grisóstomo and those who survive his death, literature offers the promise of a means through which the poet can be remembered and thus saved from loss. Indeed, Vivaldo says that his friend's writing will live on, and he implores Ambrosio not to burn Grisóstomo's papers.[26] Grisóstomo, a *pastor culto,* was the son of a rich nobleman, and also a student at Salamanca, who returned from his studies "wise and learned." But his principal fame was as a poet; his name means "silver tongued." (Like his friend Ambrosio, Grisóstomo bears a saintly name; they recall Saint John Chrysostom and Saint Ambrose.) Indeed, what lies at stake in the episode is whether poetry can serve a redemptive function in the secular pastoral world. As the narrator of the episode clearly understands, the power of literature as posited by the pastoral myth lies in its ability to

25. On the subject of limits in relation to language, poetry, and the pastoral in Cervantes, see Mary Gaylord [Randel], "The Language of Limits and the Limits of Language: The Crisis of Poetry in *La Galatea,*" *MLN* 97 (1982): 254–71.

26. The problem of fame, together with the need to be remembered, were issues of constant concern to Cervantes. In chapter 37 of *Don Quijote,* Part 1, the Captive mentions a certain Spanish soldier named "Saavedra, el cual, con haber hecho cosas que quedarán en la memoria de aquellas gentes por muchos años . . ." (486).

transcend loss by means of a sublimation of forces at work in the natural world; the *question* is whether poetry can any longer be successful in such an attempt, or whether its quasi-magical echoes and inscriptions will in fact be transformed into records of that same loss:

> No está muy lejos de aquí un sitio donde hay casi dos docenas de altas hayas, y no hay ninguna que en su lisa corteza no tenga grabado y escrito el nombre de Marcela, y encima de alguna, una corona grabada en el mesmo árbol, como si más claramente dijera su amante que Marcela la lleva y la merece de toda la hermosura humana. Aquí sospira un pastor; allí se queja otro; acullá se oyen amorosas canciones; acá, desesperadas endechas. Cúal hay que pasa todas las horas de la noche sentado al pie de alguna encina o peñasco, y allí, sin plegar los llorosos ojos, embebecido y transportado en sus pensamientos, le halló el sol a la mañana, y cuál hay que, sin dar vado ni tregua a sus sospiros, en mitad del ardor de la más enfadosa siesta del verano, tendido sobre la ardiente arena, envía sus quejas al piadoso cielo. (Part 1, chap. 12, pp. 166–67)

> (Not far from here is a place where there are a couple of dozen tall beeches, and there is not a one of them on whose smooth bark Marcela's name has not been engraved; and above some of these inscriptions you will find a crown, as if by this her lover meant to indicate that she deserved to wear the garland of beauty above all the women on earth. Here a shepherd sighs and there another voices his lament. Now are to be heard amorous ballads, and again despairing songs. One will spend all the hours of the night seated at the foot of some oak or rock without once closing his tearful eyes, and morning sun will find him there, stupefied and lost in thought. Another, without giving truce or respite to his sighs, will lie stretched upon the burning sands in the full heat of the most exhausting summer noontide, sending up his complaint to merciful Heaven.)

The passage recalls the description in Garcilaso's third eclogue of the epitaph for Nemoroso's beloved Elisa that has been inscribed into the trees, and that is subsequently read aloud by one of the nymphs, much as Grisóstomo's *canción* is read after his death: "Elisa soy, en cuyo nombre suena / y se lamenta el monte cavernoso" (I am Elisa, in whose name the cavernous mountains lament and resound) (lines 241–42). As this passage suggests, the pastoral poet's love of nature is inseparable from a deep preoccupation with suffering and loss. But beyond this, it is the imaginative desire to test and move beyond the limiting condition imposed by loss that characterizes the poetic stance in which the power of imaginative desire seems to outweigh any of the ties that may bind the poet to the natural and social worlds. After all, Grisóstomo lives on, like Garcilaso's Elisa, as a function of the poet's voice.

Consider Cardenio's sonnet in *Don Quijote,* Part 1, chapter 23 in this light. Although Cardenio is mad with jealousy and wild with rage at Fernando's deception and Luscinda's apparent betrayal, his sonnet presents him as one who is nonetheless able to achieve good form, as exemplified in this poem's well-balanced and harmonious shape:

> O le falta al Amor conocimiento,
> o le sobra crueldad, o no es mi pena
> igual a la ocasión que me condena
> al género más duro de tormento.
>
> Pero si Amor es dios, es argumento
> que nada ignora, y es razón muy buena
> que un dios no sea cruel. Pues ¿quién ordena
> el terrible dolor que adoro y siento?
>
> Si digo que sois vos, Fili, no acierto;
> que tanto mal en tanto bien no cabe,
> ni me viene del cielo esta rüina.
>
> Presto habré de mirar, que es lo más cierto;
> que al mal de quien la causa no sabe
> milagro es acertar la medicina.
>
> (p. 282)

(Either Love, it would seem, lacks intelligence,
Or else it is over-cruel, or my poor heart
Is all unequal to its painful part,
Condemned to the direst torment there can be.
If love is God, it is certain He
Knows all—that takes no casuistic art—
And He's not cruel. Where, then, does my grief start,
That grief I cherish so persistently?

> To say that it is thou, Phyllis, would be wrong;
> So much of good and ill cannot abide
> In the same body, nor is Heaven to blame.
> One thing I know: I am not here for long;
> He's a sick man who cannot decide
> The nature of his ill or whence it came.)

For Grisóstomo, by contrast, suffering cannot so easily be relieved by the wit and other refinements of verse. For him, loss represents the absolute limit of imagination and expression. His poetry tests itself against this limit, and since it cannot pass beyond it, is turned destructively against nature and itself. Indeed, when viewed in contrast to Cardenio and in light of the pastoral setting of the episode, Grisóstomo's *canción desesperada* raises some fundamental doubts about the power of poetry in relation to the disintegrative forces of history, loss, and death. Whereas the pastoralism of the scene might suggest the image of poetry as a defense against the potentially disorienting consequences of loss, it seems that poetry is bound to be a record of the irrecuperability of that loss: something remains untransformed. Indeed, the *canción desesperada* fails not only to defend against or transform loss; it fails also to fulfill the civilizing and sublimating functions so often imagined for pastoral verse. Grisóstomo's *canción* is a denaturing complaint that serves principally to reinforce the idea of nature as the site of irreducible strife:

> Escucha, pues, y presta atento oído,
> no al concertado son, sino al rüido
> que de lo hondo de mi amargo pecho,
> llevado de un forzoso desvarío,
> por gusto mío sale y tu despecho.
>   El rugir del león, del lobo fiero
> el temeroso aullido, el silbo horrendo
> de escamosa serpiente, el espantable
> baladro de algún monstruo, el agorero
> graznar de la corneja, y el estruendo
> del viento contrastado en mar instable;
> del ya vencido toro el implacable
> bramido, y de la viuda tortolilla
> el sentible arullar; el triste canto

del enviado búho, con el llanto
de toda la infernal negra cuadrilla,
salgan con la doliente ánima fuera,
mezclados en un son, de tal manera,
que se confundan los sentidos todos,
pues la pena cruel que en mí se halla
para contalle pide nuevos modos.

(Part 1, chap. 14, p. 181)

(Then listen, and lend thy attentive ear,
Not well consorted tunes but howling to hear,
That from my bitter bosom's depth takes flight,
And, by constrained raving borne away
Issues forth for mine ease and thy despite.
The lion's raving, and the dreadful cries
Of ravening wolf, and hissing terrible
Of scaly serpent; and the fearful yell
Of some grim monster; and the ominous crow's
Foreboding, sinister caw; the horrible
Sound on the tossing sea of the blustering gale;
The implacable bellow of the new-conquered bull;
The lonely widowed turtle's sobbing moan,
Most mournful, and the dreary night descant
Of the envious owl, commingled with the plaint
Of all the infernal black battalion;
Let all together cry from my aching soul
United in one sound of such sad dole
That all the senses may confounded be,
For my fierce torment needs a manner new
Wherein I may recount my misery.)

In the literary tradition that extends in Golden Age Spain from Garcilaso forward, poetry is supposed to have the power to transform occasions of conflict and loss into experiences of an inestimable, if painful, beauty. Its efficacy is reputed to be nearly miraculous. The canonical point of reference for Grisóstomo's *canción desesperada* would by contrast be Salicio's lament in Garcilaso's first eclogue, where loss reverses and disrupts that power:

¿Qué no s'esperará d'aquí adelante,
por difícil que sea y por incierto,
o qué discordia no será juntada?

. . . .

Materia diste al mundo d'esperanza
d'alcanzar lo imposible y no pensado
y de hacer juntar lo diferente,
dando a quien diste el corazón malvado,
quitándolo de mí con tal mudanza
que siempre sonará de gente en gente.
    La cordera paciente
    con el lobo hambriento
    hará su ajuntamiento,
y con las simples aves sin rüido
harán las bravas sierpes ya su nido,
que mayor diferencia comprehendo
    de ti al que has escogido.
Salid sin duelo, lágrimas, corriendo.
        (lines 141–43, 155–68)

(What can't be expected from now on, no matter how difficult and dubious? What discordant elements will not be joined? . . . You gave the world cause to have hope of achieving the impossible and unthinkable, and of making different things join, by giving your perverse heart to whom you did, taking it away from me with such an abrupt change that the news of it will always resound from nation to nation. The patient lamb with the hungry wolf will join together, and with simple noiseless birds the fierce serpents will not make their nests; for I consider that there is even greater difference between you and the man you have chosen. Flow forth tears, painlessly.)

As a literary heir (or would-be heir) of Garcilaso, Cervantes would recognize that the economy of nature in the pastoral is determined by the irreducible experiences of pleasure and pain, which poetry is in turn charged to transform and "beautify." And yet for a poet like Grisóstomo, schooled as a *pastor culto* in the Renaissance tradition and committed to the idea of poetry as the sublimation of loss and the reconciliation of strife by aesthetic means, there remains the central fact of poetry's failure to fulfill its charge—a failure that is in his case so intensified that the fascination with loss turns the power of poetry against itself. Grisóstomo is in this respect Cervantes's challenge to the received myth of poetry as a source of sublimation and a substitute for transcendence in a secularized world.[27]

For her part, Marcela appears unswervingly confident in her ability to resist and transcend Grisóstomo's irreversible descent into the realm of suffering and loss. She validates her self-chosen solitude under the guise of the poetic ideal of a fusion with the natural world. But this ideal is one that in turn debars her from the social modes of reconciliation on which the pastoral's claims to redemption in a secular world were based:

> Yo nací libre, y para poder vivir libre escogí la soledad de los campos; los árboles destas montañas son mi compañía; las claras aguas destos arroyos son mis espejos; con los árboles y con las aguas comunico mis pensamientos y hermosura. Fuego soy apartado y espada puesta lejos. A los que he enamorado con la vista he desengañado con las palabras; y si los deseos se sustentan con esperanzas, no habiendo yo dado alguna a Grisóstomo, ni a otro alguno, en fin, de ninguno dellos, bien se puede decir que antes le mató su porfía que mi crueldad. (Part 1, chap. 14, pp. 186–87)

> (I was born free, and to live free I chose the solitude of the fields. The trees on these mountains are my companions; the clear

27. Castro's estimation of the Cervantine pastoral is radically different, on several accounts. First, Castro claims that Cervantes is relatively uncritical of the pastoral: "Cervantes no ironiza lo pastoril ni lo toma en broma en el *Quijote,* aunque bien fácil le hubiera sido proyectar cualquier penumbra sobre Marcela—un alma de armiño, presuntuosa de su albura. No cabía hacerlo, sin embargo, porque la maravillosa muchacha descansaba sobre una última intuición de lo humano, en la cual se basa todo el *Quijote:* 'Yo nací libre, y para vivir libre escogí la soledad de los campos' " (*Hacia Cervantes,* 282). Second, and in line with the preceding, Castro associates the pastoral with the revelation of a distinctly "human" intimacy, rather than with a specifically literary problematic: "En el relato pastoril es donde, por primera vez, se muestra el personaje literario como una singularidad estrictamente humana, como expresión de un 'dentro de sí' " (276). Castro recognizes the pastoral's status as a secularized discourse ("lo pastoril es una hijuela laica de la mística religiosa, y opera con el amor humano como Santa Teresa con el divino"), but then subordinates this claim to the assertion that both are examples of an increasingly humanistic mode of discourse: "con un intento similar de traer a expresión las más hondas vivencias, de aquellas que en ciertos casos se han resuelto en armoniosa composición poética" (276). Cervantes's critique of the pastoral has been much discussed by critics, including Javier Herrero in "Arcadia's Inferno: Cervantes' Attack on the Pastoral," *Bulletin of Hispanic Studies* 55 (1978): 289–99.

waters of these streams my mirrors; to the trees and the waters I disclose my thoughts and my beauty. I am the distant fire of the far-off sword. Those whom I have attracted with my eyes I have undeceived with my words; if desires are nourished by hope, as I never gave any to Chrysostom or to any other, it may not justly be said that any man's end was my doing, since it was his persistence rather than my cruelties that killed him.)

Finally, Marcela's rejection of the erotic melancholy characteristic of the pastoral seems to give evidence of a mode of imagination that is directed against the idea of sublimating loss through recourse to the culturing, socializing, and beautifying powers of a poeticized world.

Indeed, the Marcela and Grisóstomo episode would suggest that the procedures of literary sublimation can only confirm the failure of the poetic imagination to absorb the shock created by the discovery that nature is itself the locus of suffering, loss, and death. Moreover, a character like Marcela reveals that the literary mode of discourse that most consistently presses and tests limits—the sublime—is inherently problematic if only because it seeks to establish a superhuman authority upon whose very absence its own power is based. It is thus perhaps no surprise to find that the profound negativity of the discourse of the sublime is so often foreclosed by the modern subject's "foundational" attempts at self-assertion, if only because that assertion rests on the subject's paradoxical rejection of the idea of an identity based on subjection to an alien power or will: " 'tengo riquezas propias, y no codicio las ajenas,' " says Marcela; " 'tengo libre condición, y no gusto de sujetarme' " (I have my own riches, and do not covet those of others; I have a taste for freedom and no wish for subjection) (Part 1, chap. 14, pp. 187–88).[28]

Cervantes returns to these and related issues in the later chapters of Part 2, as Don Quijote revisits the Duke and the Duchess only to see that Altisidora apparently dies and is raised from the dead. The episode brings together both the religious and the literary-historical meanings of "secularization." As Altisidora sees Don Quijote and Sancho, she

---

28. Cf. Castro, who interprets the pastoral as the direct exposition of a personal conscience in Cervantes: "La narración pastoril . . . llega a ser posible cuando el individuo, en busca de conciencia personal, rotas todas sus amarras, se lanza a remar en su propro bote, sin más pertrecho que el de su sola existencia, 'monda y desnuda' " (*Hacia Cervantes*, 277).

cites the following verse from Garcilaso's first eclogue, as if to recall the redemptive function that literature was imagined once to have possessed. She suggests that, through Sancho, Love has "saved" her, and she verbally transforms Don Quijote into a stone-hearted knight: " '¡Oh, más dura que mármol a mis quejas! empedernido caballero' " (Oh, harder than marble to my complaints, you stony-hearted knight!). Both because her words are so obviously citational of Garcilaso's first eclogue,[29] and also because Altisidora's role is a sham, Cervantes makes it clear that poetry has the capacity to save her only from a fictional death, just as the Priest's *ensalmos* have the power to reattach only a fictional beard. Just as her "death" was a function of the belief of those who thought they saw her die, so too her redemption is a function of whatever belief her audience may be able to sustain in the power of "poetic" discourse.

> he estado muerta, o, a lo menos, juzgada por tal de los que me han visto; y si no fuera porque el Amor, condoliéndose de mí, depositó mi remedio en los martirios deste buen escudero, allá me quedara en el otro mundo. (Part 2, chap. 70, p. 565)

> (I lay dead, or at least was held to be so by all who saw me; and were it not that Love took pity on me and entrusted my cure to the sufferings of this good squire, there I should have stayed in the other world. [p. 917])

Early in Part 2 Don Quijote takes Garcilaso's poetry as able to confirm his image of Dulcinea and, thereby, to defend against the demystification of the literary text at the hands of the prosaic world:

> Mal se te acuerdan a ti, ¡oh Sancho!, aquellos versos de nuestro poeta donde nos pinta las labores que hacían allá en sus moradas de cristal aquellas cuatro ninfas que del Tajo amado sacaron las cabezas, y se sentaron a labrar en el prado verde aquellas ricas telas que allí el ingenioso poeta nos describe, que todas eran de oro, sirgo y perlas contestas y tejidas. Y desta manera debía de ser el de mi señora cuando tú la viste. (Part 2, chap. 8, pp. 93–94)

29. Salicio: "'¡Oh, más dura que mármol a mis quejas / y al encendido fuego en que me quemo, / más helada que nieve, Galatea!" (lines 57–59).

(You little remember, Sancho, those verses of our ingenious poet in which he describes to us the tasks which the four nymphs performed in their crystal dwellings, when they raised their heads from their beloved Tagus, and sat in the green meadow to work the rich cloth he there describes, which were all of gold, silk thread and pearls, plainted and interwoven. In such work must my lady have been employed when you saw her. [p. 516])

By Part 2, chapter 70, however, it has been made fully clear that even Don Quijote's faith in the efficacy of literature is in jeopardy. The redemptive powers of poetry are now in an all-out war with "fictions"; and, no matter how sublime, fiction seems weak in that it does not have the ability to guarantee protection against loss and death. As Don Quijote's confidence in his own powers wanes in the concluding chapters of the book, Cervantes turns once again to the pastoral as the mode through which a faith in the efficacious powers of literature might be regained. Only now, the hope is simply that the pastoral might have the power to restore a "literary" faith; it is a substitute for the belief that Don Quijote originally had in the novels of chivalry:

Don Quijote, sin guardar términos ni horas, en aquel mismo punto se apartó a solas con el bachiller y el cura, y en breves razones les contó su vencimiento, y la obligación en que había quedado de no salir de su aldea en un año, la cual pensaba guardar al pie de la letra, sin traspasarla en un átomo, bien así como caballero andante, obligado por la puntualidad y orden de la caballería andante, y que tenía pensado hacerse aquel año pastor, y entretenerse en la soledad de los campos, donde a rienda suelta podía dar vado a sus amorosos pensamientos, ejercitándose en el pastoral y virtuoso ejercicio; y que les suplicaba, si no tenían mucho que hacer y no estaban impedidos en negocios más importantes, quisiesen ser sus compañeros; que él compraría ovejas y ganado suficiente que les diese nombre de pastores; y que les hacía saber que lo más principal de aquel negocio estaba hecho, porque les tenía puesto los nombres, que les vendrían como de molde. Díjole el cura que los dijese. Respondió don Quijote que él se había de llamar *al pastor Quijotiz;* y el bachiller, *el pastor Carrascón;* y el cura, *el pastor Curambro* y Sancho Panza, *el pastor Pancino.* (Part 2, chap. 73, p. 583)

(Without waiting on time or season, Don Quijote took the priest and the Bachelor aside that very moment, and told them in few words of his defeat and the obligation he was under not to leave his village for a year; which he intended to observe to the letter, without infringing on it by an atom, as befitted a knight-errant bound by the rules and order of his profession. He told them also how he intended to turn shepherd for the year, and pass his time in the solitude of the fields, where he could give free rein to his amorous thoughts, whilst occupying himself in that pastoral and virtuous calling. He begged them to be his companions, if they had not much to do and were not prevented by more important business, and said he would buy sufficient sheep and stock to give them the name of shepherds. But, he informed them, the principal part of the business was already done, for he had fixed on names for them which would fit them to a T. The priest asked him for them, and Don Quijote replied that he was to call himself the shepherd Quixotiz, the Bachelor the shepherd Carrascon, the priest the shepherd Curiambro and Sancho Panza the shepherd Panzino.

Even as Don Quijote lies dying in his bed, the pastoral has the force of an imaginative power that Don Quijote's friends attempt to infuse in him. At the very conclusion of the novel, the pastoral is invoked for its ability to revive the dying Don Quijote and to ward off death. But even here, the Bachelor recognizes that the power of the pastoral is inseparable from a literary history in which the modern writer is fated to compete with the accomplishments of poets past (in this case, with Sannazaro):

Estos, creyendo que la pesadumbre de verse vencido y de no ver cumplido su deseo en la libertad y desencanto de Dulcinea le tenía de aquella suerte, por todas las vías posibles procuraban alegrarle, diciéndole el bachiller que se animase y levantase, para comenzar su pastoral ejercicio, para el cual *tenía ya compuesta una égloga, que mal año para cuantas Sannazaro había compuesto,* y que ya tenía comprados de su propio dinero dos famosos perros para guardar el ganado, el uno llamado Barcino, y el otro Butrón, que se los había vendido un ganadero del

Quintanar. Pero no por esto dejaba don Quijote sus tristezas. (Part 2, chap. 74, p. 586; my emphasis)

(All of them believed that grief at his overthrow and the disappointment of his hopes for Dulcinea's deliverance and disenchantment had brought him to this state and tried to cheer him in every possible way. The Bachelor bade him be of good heart, and get up and begin on his pastoral life, for which *he had already composed an eclogue, which would knock out every one Sannazaro had ever written.* He said that he had bought a couple of fine dogs with his own money from a herdsman from Quintanar to guard the flock, one called Barcino and the other Butron. But Don Quijote's dejection persisted all the same.)

If there is no way to avoid the problem of loss, which makes itself evident as the "ground" to which the powers of literature, including those of sublimation, respond, and if there is likewise no hope to escape the "fall" into the entanglements of literary history that Cervantes represents both at the beginning of *Don Quijote,* Part 1, and at the very close of Part 2, there are nonetheless means by which to defend, however unsuccessfully, against some of the more radical consequences of these events; the self-conscious elaboration of these defenses goes a long way toward explaining Cervantes's stance with respect to the problematic status of literature in the (early) modern world. Foremost among the defensive strategies we witness in *Don Quijote* are those of textualization, which offer the means by which the modern imagination, conscious of literature's loss of its effective power, attempts to convert its disturbing deficiencies into something seemingly stable, objective, and real.[30] In the case of the *Quijote,* it seems that by objectifying the

---

30. As is well known, print culture came to play a major role in the eighteenth century's development of new standards of rationality: common sense could claim a normative validity insofar as its objects could be publicly scrutinized. For Kant, for example, the success of the Enlightenment depends crucially on the free circulation of ideas through the press. See "What Is Enlightenment?" in *Kant on History,* ed. Lewis White Beck, trans. Lewis White Beck, Robert E. Anchor, and Emil L. Fackenheim (Indianapolis: Bobbs-Merrill, 1963), esp. 9–10. John Bender and David Wellbery rightly note that "the vehicle that carried Kant's public sphere toward its future of perpetual improvement was the institution of publishing, without which Enlightenment is unthinkable. One need only consider the great publishing enterprises of the period—foremost of all perhaps the *Encyclopédie* of D'Alembert and Diderot—or the expansion of literacy that occurred across the eighteenth century, with its proliferation not only of books but

conditions of imaginative failure and loss Cervantes attempts to secure his identity as a modern writer or, what amounts to the same thing, to gain a critical perspective on the past; he does so by projecting a concrete object, the text, as a defense against the overwhelming prestige, authority, and influence of the past. But as we have already begun to see, the difficulty with an attempt to stabilize the author's identity through the fortifying objectification of the writer's weakened imagination (in the form of the prologue's "friend") is that this defense may not necessarily be able to defend against itself. The text provides an objectivity and a stability that are illusory at best. Indeed, we do not in the end know and cannot decide whether the formation of the quixotic text represents a solution to the problem of a failed poetic imagination overwhelmed by the power and authority of the past, or whether it is a source and symptom of that same problem for the reader, whose subsequent encounters with the tradition are necessarily mediated through texts. Indeed, it could well be said that Cervantes's accomplishment is to have shown how the same literary "defense" against the tradition that may enable the self-assertion of the modern writer cannot produce anything other than figures, personae, tropes, and of course texts, all of which likewise threaten to disorient and overwhelm the reader, who in their presence cannot help being overwhelmed by his own relative weakness with respect to the past.

To be sure, Cervantes has predecessors in this ambiguous strategy of textualization as defense. Already in a work like the *Lazarillo de Tormes* the process of textualization (which assumes the form of letter-writing) is taken as the sign of a coveted maturity, autonomy, and independence. In the *Lazarillo,* the social and historical transition from the fundamentally oral discourse of folktale and proverb to the genre of the written letter, addressed in this instance to "Vuestra Merced," seems to protect and guarantee the author's critical stance precisely when his identity and autonomy are most vulnerable. By allowing Lázaro to speak of the conditions of his own degradation in a double voice, writing collaborates with speech to help ensure the integrity of his self-consciousness and to conceal the facts of his self-abasement and humiliation. For a

---

of learned and moral journals." See "Rhetoricality: The Modernist Return of Rhetoric," in Bender and Wellbery, eds., *The Ends of Rhetoric: History, Theory, Practice* (Stanford: Stanford University Press, 1990), 14–15. See also Robert Darnton, *The Business of Enlightenment: A Publishing History of the Encyclopédie, 1775–1800* (Cambridge: Harvard University Press, 1979).

critic like Francisco Rico, however, these aspects of the *Lazarillo*'s epistolary and autobiographical form are angled toward the successful formation of a rigorously authentic and personal point of view, and this is in turn the basis of the "realism" of work, its claim to literary and novelistic "modernity": "Relativism, whether in epistemology or axiology, is also a form of humanism. . . . Is it not in their attention to the individual that a Cervantes or a Fielding mark out the modern novel? In recognizing subjectivity as a measure of things there is the upsurge of a novelistic impulse, which the anonymous author of the *Lazarillo* could hardly resist. If the *I* is the touchstone of reality, then what could be more realistic than autobiography?"[31] But the *Lazarillo* contains a more subtle play between autobiographical self-assertion and the fundamentally negative experience of self-abasement than this reading can allow. The *Lazarillo* seems to suggest that the writer's precious achievement of an autonomous identity can occur only through his entrance into the world of social masks. Had Lázaro been content simply to expose society's deceits, and to assert himself as the critic of a corrupt world, he might well never have lived to write his story or tell his "truth."

The text's failure to stabilize the subject's identity thus brings with it the need, or the hope, for strategies to reorient the powers transmitted through it. The various critical procedures imagined in Cervantes's text, beginning with the "escrutinio de los libros" in chapter 6 of *Don Quijote,* Part 1, represent such an attempt. Once a text enters the public domain, or acceeds to the roster of canonized works, the expectation is that it may be judged not only according to the desires and needs of its author but according to objective and rational principles as well. Unlike the "private" imaginings of the author (which, we must admit, are never fully private and personal in the way that Castro and others have imagined), the text can be construed as a public object that is open to the pressures of critical judgment. And, unlike the normative judgment of the masses—"el antiguo legislador que llaman vulgo," as Cervantes puts it in the prologue—who in the modern context are increasingly empowered to determine whether an author will succeed or fail,[32] the

31. Rico, *La novela picaresca y el punto de vista* (Barcelona: Seix Barral, 1976), 50, 55.

32. Cervantes addresses this position in the prologue to Part 1, explaining to the (common) reader that he will not bend to "la corriente del uso, ni suplicarte casi con las lágrimas en los ojos, como otros hacen, lector carísimo, que perdones o disimules las

establishment of an autonomous critical discourse promises a "disengaged" assessment of the text.

This is to say that, precisely because the question of authority is so problematic, the development of modern literary history is inconceivable without the parallel emergence of a "science" of interpretation and judgment, such as the Barber and the Priest attempt to initiate in chapter 6 and as the Canon and the Priest pursue in chapters 47–48 of *Don Quijote,* Part 1. Yet, if these examples are to be taken as any measure of such a project's potential success, it would seem that the discourse of criticism remains inextricably entwined with the ambitions and vulnerabilities of literature itself, and is a sign and symptom of literary modernity rather than a solution to the problems of authority it presents. Indeed, since there is nothing to ensure that the critical text will not become the site of yet another imaginary scene of self-assertion against the past, or a defense against loss, the "failures" of modern literature cannot be entirely redeemed, nor the imagination's disconcerting fall from power and grace reversed, by recourse to a literary-critical discourse. Even the Canon admits that he has himself attempted to write a novel of chivalry, and Don Quijote responds to his criticisms with the very powerful story of the Knight of the Lake (Part 1, chap. 50), which leaves the Canon thoroughly astonished and amazed.

One might at best suggest that the process by which history is transformed into a text (or a tradition of texts) constitutes a defense against the past that calls for interpretation, or more exactly, that such a defense initiates a circle of interpretation that can succeed neither in unlocking the "kernel" of the efficacious literary sign nor in fully appropriating the power of what was "originally" imagined in its most authoritative form. Not surprisingly, the secularization process manifests itself in the form of a constant alternation between the equally strong powers of an imaginative remembering and those of a defensive forgetfulness. And, just as in the case of repression it is in failure that the underlying structure of desire is brought into view, so too with secularization it is in the experience of its failure that literary history is suddenly revealed as something worthy of interpretation. This, at least, is the significance I would attribute to the episode of the leaden box

---

faltas que en este mi libro vieres, pues ni eres su pariente ni su amigo, y tienes tu alma en tu cuerpo y tu libre albedrío como el más pintado y estás en tu casa, donde eres señor della, como el rey de sus alcabalas" (51).

that occurs at the very end of *Don Quijote*, Part 1. The discovery of this box serves as a convenient reminder of the question of secularization insofar as it is found in the rubble of a monastery that is in the course of being renovated (Part 1, chap. 52). Moreover, the box contains parchments whose original Gothic letters have not altogether been displaced by the Spanish verses that have been superimposed upon them, thus suggesting that the process of secularization they model has been left imcomplete. And while some of these verses can be read, and are found to contain the epitaphs of Don Quijote, Sancho Panza, Dulcinea, and Rocinante, "los demás, por estar carcomida la letra, se entregaron a un académico para que por conjeturas los declarase" (the rest, as the characters were worm-eaten, were entrusted to a university scholar to decipher) (Part 1, chap. 52, p. 607). They have, in other words, become the imaginary, if not also the anticipatory, objects of the very "sciences" of interpretation whose relationship to the formation of modern culture Cervantes is attempting to decipher.[33]

As I have suggested above, the notion that literature might somehow afford an opportunity for the modern writer to exercise a power of self-assertion must be qualified in Cervantes's case so as to reflect the failure of modern writing either to appropriate or fully to supersede the authority of the past. And yet we have also seen that these apparent "failures" in turn allow Cervantes to circumvent and ironize the rhetoric of self-assertion characteristic of the early modern age. In conclusion, I suggest that the defeat of the myth of the writer's powers at the hands of literary history in turn opens up a new kind of poetic endeavor whose mechanisms are those of compensation and defense, all of which are premised in some measure on the "failure" of the modern imagination in its desire to compete with the past. Cervantes's response to literary history, which defines his particular stance as a modern writer, is to

---

33. Cervantes may be combining at least two references in the image of the leaden box. On the one hand, he seems to be referring to the *tablillas* of the kind mentioned in act 1 of *La Celestina*. According to the *Enciclopedia universal ilustrada*, the *tablilla* was a small tablet or box made of lead that could be inscribed with messages or conjuries and placed at a grave on the belief that the message would then be carried to the underworld by the spirit of the dead person. Olga Lucía Valbuena discusses these boxes in her essay "The Inquisition of Linguistic Sorcery in *La Celestina*," *PMLA* 109 (March 1994), esp. 218 and 222. But Harry Sieber has also suggested to me that Cervantes may also be referring to the so-called *libros plúmbeos,* of the interpretation of their inscriptions, and of the (false) relics and martyrs to which they attested. See Miguel José Hagerty, ed., *Los libros plúmbeos de Sacromonte* (Madrid: Editorial Nacional, 1980).

write within the circle of these defenses, and so rather than redefine literature *tout court*, to redirect its imaginative energies, its weaknesses, and its residual power and so, in the process, to create a new form by questioning the motives of all those who would inherit the past. In this way, the modern writer's stance of lateness or inadequacy represents a way of making space within the tradition that is at least as powerful, and certainly more complex, than that which the rhetoric of self-assertion was able to afford.

9

Instinct and Object:
Subjectivity and Speech-Act in
Garcilaso de la Vega

At various points in the previous chapter we were drawn to Cervantes's engagement with the example of Garcilaso de la Vega as an instance in which the literary imagination is bound intimately to the notion of poetic power. Cervantes associates the problem of history not only with the social structures of caste and class, or with the tensions between "old" and "new," but also with the issues of authority and belief. One of his central concerns is with the role of literature in the transmission of the cultural authority of the past. If his position on this issue is complex this is because he is supremely aware of the demands of (literary) modernity while remaining nonetheless sensitive to the power and prestige of the past. Here, I turn to the earlier historical moment of the fifteenth century in order to present the complementary argument that Garcilaso's verse—which Cervantes recognized as a model for poetic power and prestige—already reflects a deep engagement with the issues that Cervantes rediscovered as fundamental for modern literary history. In Garcilaso, the question of poetic power is situated in a context where Petrarchan forms had acquired a near-hegemonic cultural status but where the power of the heroic Spanish past, whose lyric forms were not at all Petrarchan in nature, remained also to be reckoned with. How can the "creation" of lyric subjectivity, so often claimed as first occurring in Spain in the work of Garcilaso, be understood as a product of these circumstances?

I take as my point of departure for this discussion of Garcilaso the work of William Kerrigan and Gordon Braden, entitled *The Idea of the Renaissance*. Kerrigan and Braden advance the claim that the Petrarchan love lyric can best be approached in terms of an object-relations psychoanalysis that has its basis in Freud's distinction between the ancients and the moderns.[1] They begin their two chapters on Petrarch and the Renaissance lyric with the citation of a late footnote added to the first of Freud's *Three Essays on Sexuality* in which Freud claims that "the most striking distinction between the erotic life of antiquity and our own . . . lies in the fact that the ancients laid the stress upon the instinct itself, whereas we emphasize its object. The ancients glorified the instinct and were prepared on its account to honour even an inferior object; while we despise the instinctual activity in itself, and find excuses for it only in the merits of the object."[2] The immediate context of Freud's remarks is that of sexual aberrations and "unconventional" (e.g., homosexual) object-choices,[3] but Kerrigan and Braden suggest

1. Kerrigan and Braden, *The Idea of the Renaissance* (Baltimore: Johns Hopkins University Press, 1989), 157–218.

2. Freud, *Three Essays on the Theory of Sexuality,* trans. and ed. James Strachey (New York: Basic Books, 1962), 15. Freud goes on to explain "instinct" as follows: "By an 'instinct' is provisionally to be understood the psychical representative of an endosomatic, continuously flowing source of stimulation, as contrasted with a 'stimulus,' which is set up by *single* excitations coming from *without*. The concept of instinct is thus one of those lying on the frontier between the mental and the physical. The simplest and likeliest assumption as to the nature of instincts would seem to be that in itself an instinct is without quality, and, so far as mental life is concerned, is only to be regarded as a measure of the demand made upon the mind for work. What distinguishes the instincts from one another and endows them with specific qualities is their relation to their somatic sources and to their aims. The source of an instinct is a process of excitation occurring in an organ and the immediate aim of the instinct lies in the removal of this organic stimulus." See also Freud's paper on "Instincts and their Vicissitudes" (1915), as well as his *Beyond the Pleasure Principle* (1920) and *The Ego and the Id* (1923).

3. Compare Freud's discussion of the "vicissitudes" of the instincts, including reversal into its opposite, turning back upon the subject, repression, and sublimation, in "Instincts and Their Vicissitudes" (1915).

that the generalization can bear significantly more weight than Freud asked it to carry. In particular, they argue that insofar as the European love-lyric follows Petrarch's example, the entire tradition can be explained in terms of the Freudian account of the way in which the object of desire (specifically in the case of Petrarchan poetry, the feminine "beloved") was constructed during the Renaissance and early modern periods.

As evidence for this claim, Kerrigan and Braden adduce a range of examples from the English, Italian, and French traditions (excluding the Spanish), ranging historically from Petrarch to Milton, in which poets "sing" of a feminine beloved who is the supreme but unattainable goal of all desire. This object of desire, on one level fashioned by the poet in the imagination, is on another level the occasion of the poet's own subjectivity, since it is principally in relation to the separation from or rejection by the desired object that the poet has any power of self-awareness at all. Especially in the poems *in morte,* where Petrarch's beloved is figured as finally departed, and their love not just as unfulfilled but unfulfillable, it seems that the form of subjectivity that is developed in this peculiar attachment to the object of desire is a subjectivity based on a "pre-poetic" loss and that the pain associated with this loss determines poetic subjectivity as a form of subjection to the absent, idealized other. It is the pleasurable pain of this loss that motivates the writing of these poems and, with this, the creation of lyric subjectivity in Petrarch, and it is this model of impossible and unfulfillable (hence inexhaustible) desire that was adopted by many of Petrarch's followers during the Renaissance.

Kerrigan and Braden are nonetheless puzzled by the fact that literary historians and theorists have had considerable difficulty explaining just why Petrarch's lyrics became so central in Western literary culture. Why was it, they ask, that this particular mode of lyric self-consciousness provided a dominant model of literary subjectivity in the West? Why was it that the European lyric's "celebration" of the feminine object of desire began with several centuries of fixation on the unavailability of that object? And why did the creation of poetic subjectivity begin with the fiction of apparent submission to a resistant or unyielding will? One answer to these questions lies in the fact that since "Petrarchism" or the mode of subjectivity it initiates is founded on the mimesis not of an object or of an action but of a desire and a lack, the Petrarchan text allows for the infinite renewal of that desire in the subsequent tradition.

If the fundamental loss that founds Petrarchan subjectivity has played a uniquely productive role over the course of Western literary history, this may well be because the Petrarchan pursuit of the beloved is by definition the search for an object of desire that remains elusive. While any given poem is thus bound to be a false mirror of the object of desire, hence unsatisfactory as the mimesis of an object, "Petrarchan" desire nonetheless remains available to be reinscribed in the subsequent tradition, which constitutes and renews itself around Petrarch's "original" loss. The painful melancholia of this lyric subject thus proves remarkably productive in a literary-historical sense. The impossibility of adequately representing the object is the source of a literary history in which the writer is confronted both with the demand to "imitate" (i.e., repeat and perfect) the model and with the injunction that desire shall remain unfulfilled, that the object shall indeed remain lost. The unfulfillable desire for the beloved is thus transformed by the literary representations of that desire into a form of self-consciousness that never completes or exhausts the original loss.

In his 1975 essay "The Fig Tree and the Laurel," John Freccero described the strategies by which Petrarch effectively foreclosed the efforts of his textual precursors and created himself as poet-lover across the lyric sequence of the *canzoniere*, not only as author of the book but also as the first recipient of the crown of poet laureate for the era of vernacular poetry that followed him.[4] Thomas M. Greene offers the following explanation of the ways in which Petrarch's own literary belatedness became the basis for a new European tradition of lyric self-creation:

> Petrarch precipitated his own personal creative crisis because he made a series of simultaneous discoveries that had been made only fragmentarily before him. It was he who first understood how radically classical antiquity differed from the Christian era; he also saw more clearly than his precursors how the individual traits of a given society at a given moment form a distinctive constellation; he understood more clearly the philological meaning of anachronism. In view of his humanist piety and his literary ambition, these perceptions created a problem that he would

4. Freccero, "The Fig Tree and the Laurel," *Diacritics* 5 (1975): 34–40. See also Roland Greene, *Post-Petrarchism: Origins and Innovations of the Western Lyric Sequence* (Princeton: Princeton University Press, 1991).

bequeath to the generations that followed him: the problem how to write with integrity under the shadow of a prestigious cultural alternative. To be a humanist after Petrarch was not simply to be an archaeologist but to feel an imitative/emulative pressure from a lost source.[5]

For the reasons Greene cites, Petrarch's self-creation was powerful enough to cast the subsequent Western lyric tradition as "post-Petrarchist." As Roland Greene puts in *Post-Petrarchism*, "as soon as a European poet of the 1500s lifts pen to write as a Petrarchan, he or she inevitably becomes a post-Petrarchan, reinventing the idea of a broadly-scaled, self-oriented poetry for present circumstances."[6] The post-Petrarchan tradition thus presents a multilayered display of poetic self-consciousness in which the "original" desire for the lost or unattainable beloved is compounded by the desire to rival Petrarch's *canzoniere* book: the (impossible, unsuccessful) mimesis of desire is rivaled by the imitation *(imitatio)* of the model of a desire founded on lack.[7]

As transmitted throughout Europe, the Petrarchan idiom became one of the most prominent signs of the entrance into the "civilized" culture of the Renaissance. In Spain, where the conduits of Petrarchism were Boscán, Garcilaso, and Herrera, Petrarchism became not so much the "first language" of poetry (a description that might more properly apply to the *romances*) as a code or marker of the entrance into high culture. Petrarchism's repertoire of images came to constitute what Lacan described as a "password" for this code. As Lacan explained, such codes have no meaning in and of themselves; their efficacy is purely symbolic,

5. Greene, *The Light in Troy* (New Haven: Yale University Press, 1983), 29–30.

6. Roland Greene, *Post-Petrarchism*, 3.

7. In Garcilaso this reaches well beyond Petrarch to include Virgil, Ovid, and the mythological tradition as well. Note the fact that in the third eclogue the "contemporary" story of Elisa and Nemoroso (lines 193–264) is set in line with others drawn more or less directly from classical mythology: Orpheus and Eurydice, Daphne and Apollo, Venus and Adonis. Hayward Keniston is one among many who note Garcilaso's indebtedness to Petrarch; but he, like many, confines his comments to questions of style, technique, and theme, leaving the question of language as such aside: "To Petrarch Garcilaso is indebted not merely for his measure, but for his whole artistic technique; Petrarchan is his choice of theme, the analysis of the emotions and the subtle, often too subtle, contrasts; Petrarchan, finally, the spiritual attitude of melancholy, half-bitter, half-tender, in the presence of a love that can never be realized." See Keniston, *Garcilaso de la Vega: A Critical Study of His Life and Works* (New York: Hispanic Society of America, 1922), 189.

and lies in the power they afford to those who are able to move about effectively within them. It is only on this basis that the stock Petrarchan comparisons (e.g., of white teeth to pearls and eyes to the sun) make any sense. As Lacan also suggests, the constitution of a conventional code also has the effect of reducing violence: it brings peace to the "radical hostility of man for his fellows"[8] and thus functions as a reservoir of "objects" in relation to the "instincts" in the way in which Freud suggested is typical of the modern world as opposed to the ancient. According to the later Lacan, however, the price that is exacted for the entrance into any symbolic code or system of representation is castration, which might well explain why it so easily raises anxieties concerning power.

In Spain, not surprisingly, the question of Petrarchism as a sign of literary and cultural modernity was particularly fraught. As the following sonnet of Cristóbal de Castillejo suggests, the entrance into the world of High Renaissance culture in Spain took place in a context in which there were strong historical allegiances on the part of "traditional" poets to indigenous literary ideologies, which were associated with the power and strength of the chivalric past:

> Garcilaso y Boscán siendo llegados
> al lugar donde están los trovadores
> que en esta nuestra lengua y sus primores
> fueron en este siglo señalados,
>   los unos a los otros alterados
> se miran, demudadas las colores,
> temiéndose que fuesen corredores
> o espías o enemigos desmandados;
>   y juzgando primero por el traje,
> pareciéronles ser, como debía,
> gentiles españoles caballeros;
>   y oyéndose hablar nuevo lenguaje,
> mezclado de extranjera poesía,
> con los ojos los miraban de extranjeros.

(Garcilaso and Boscán having come to where the troubadours are, who in our language and its beauties were once famous in

8. Jacques Lacan, "Actes du Congrès de Rome," *Psychanalyse* 1 (1956): 245.

this world, the two groups look at each other in alarm, their colors paling, fearing that they are scouts or spies or renegade enemies; and judging them first by their clothes, they took them to be, as was right, gentle Spanish knights; and hearing them speak a new language, mixed with foreign poetry, they looked at them with the eyes of foreigners.)[9]

Indeed, the invention of lyric subjectivity and the passage into literary modernity in Golden Age Spain had to overcome considerable skepticism about the value of the "new" modes of literary expression when compared with the "old" (i.e., with the poetry of the *cancionero*).[10] And yet the international prestige of the new idiom, when compared with the force of "traditional" culture as represented in the ballads, could not be denied. In the face of Spain's belatedness with respect to Petrarchism, Castillejo's sonnet responds by figuring the troubadours as *forerunners* of Petrarch. Those who speak in the new poetic code are "gentle Spanish knights" ("gentiles caballeros españoles") who carry forward the work of the "original" troubadours (e.g., Ausias March). In this way, Castillejo's sonnet serves to deflect what may have been the deeper fear fueling the literary quarrels over the "new" poetry in Spain: that the practice of imitating Petrarch may indicate a loss or weakening of a more virile form of power associated with the epic and chivalric past.

Before proceeding with this line of argument, however, which will lead us to see subjective self-creation in Garcilaso as the result of an attempt to reclaim the originary power of the poetic speech-act in a way that is neither "traditionally" Spanish nor entirely Petrarchan, it is worthwhile to note that recent critics have proposed other answers to the puzzle that Kerrigan and Braden find in the success of the Petrarchan

9. Text and English prose translation from Elias Rivers, *Renaissance and Baroque Poetry of Spain* (New York: Scribner, 1966), 33. Commentators beginning with El Brocense, and continuing almost to the present, have noted the incorporation of "foreign" locutions in Garcilaso. See Margot Arce de Vázquez, *Garcilaso de la Vega* (Río Piedras: Universidad de Puerto Rico, 1969), 86–100. For the "Spanish roots" of Garcilaso's poetry, see Rafael Lapesa, *La trayectoria poética de Garcilaso*, 2d ed. (Madrid: Revista de Occidente, 1968), 19–71. Lapesa's analysis stresses the influence of Ausias March on Garcilaso.

10. That skepticism continued through the debates on *culteranismo* and *conceptismo*, as Andrée Collard has shown. See Collard, *Nueva poesía: conceptismo, culteranismo en la crítica española* (Madrid and Waltham, Mass.: Castalia and Brandeis University, 1967).

model of desire that proceed by seeing lyric poetry as serving ideological, imperialist, and warlike ends. By breaking down the notion that Petrarchan verse belongs to the private sphere and only epic to the public domain, some critics have pointed to the ways in which lyric verse was instrumental in the formation of colonial elites.[11] According to this view, the separation between the "literary" and the "nonliterary" spheres of discourse in the Renaissance was overshadowed by the increasing desire to reappropriate even the most "private" strategies of self-presentation in the service of much broader, national, cultural ends. This much is suggested by the ways in which humanist modes of literary education, which came to cultivate increasingly complex modes of reading and interpretation, were pressed into service of the state. As Anthony Grafton and Lisa Jardine note, initiation into the more subtle modes of literary language served the interests of those "new élites" who saw the need to build, strengthen, and limit access to their own power-base. This process of initiation was centered in the literature-based programs of the Renaissance Academies, which in their view

> fitted the needs of the new Europe that was taking shape, with its closed governing élites, hereditary offices and strenuous efforts to close off debate on vital political and social questions. It stamped the more prominent members of the new élite with an indelible cultural seal of superiority, it equipped lesser members with fluency and the learned habit of attention to textual detail and offered everyone a model of true culture as something given,

11. See John Beverley, *Against Literature* (Minneapolis: University of Minnesota Press, 1993), 29, and also Roland Greene, "Petrarch Among the Discourses of Imperialism," in *America in European Consciousness, 1493–1750*, ed. Karen Ordahl Kupperman (Chapel Hill: University of North Carolina Press, 1995): "Because of its engagement with such political issues as the distribution of power among agents, the assimilation of difference, and the organization of individual desires into common structures of action and reaction, Petrarchan subjectivity becomes newly immediate in the age of Europe's discovery and administration of the New World. Further, in the first phase of colonization, until about 1600, Petrarchism operates as an original colonial discourse in the Americas, perhaps the first highly conventional language brought over from Europe that adequately expresses colonial experience as a set of relations between individual standpoints, that treats the frustrations as well as the ambitions of Europeans, and that allows Americans the capacity to play out their roles as unwilling (or, at most, deeply ambivalent) participants in someone else's enterprise" (131–32).

absolute, to be mastered, not questioned—and thus fostered in all its initiates a properly docile attitude towards authority.[12]

In the case of Garcilaso, it is widely recognized that not just his poetry but the commentaries on his work written first by Francisco Sánchez de las Brozas ("El Brocense") in 1574 and then, subsequently, by Fernando de Herrera (1580), Tomás Tamayo de Vargas (1622), and José Nicolás de Azara (1765) formed an important element in "humanistic" education in Spain from the Renaissance onward. These commentaries helped establish the fact that to be schooled in the poems of Garcilaso within the context of the Spanish Golden Age provided an introduction to the works of a Spanish "classic," a successful imitator, not only of Petrarch, but of Sannazaro, Ovid, and Virgil, as well as of Dante and Ausias March. It confirmed Nebrija's dictum in his *Grama- 'tica española* of 1492 that "language and Empire go together."[13] What these arguments fail to note, however, is that the case for literature's ideological function in the Renaissance can be made all the more compelling and complex where it can also be shown that imperial politics was itself poetic in some essential way. As we shall see, this is the implicit burden of the introductory stanzas of Garcilaso's first eclogue, which frame the pastoral lyric of unfulfillable desire as a prelude to the poetry of political praise. In the third eclogue, the purpose of pastoral poetry is related to the work of war, as the poet claims his verse was written in moments stolen from Mars: "entre las armas del sangriento Marte, / . . . / hurté de tiempo aquesta breve suma" (from the bloodthirsty arms of Mars, . . . I stole this brief quantity of time) (lines 37–39).[14]

12. Anthony Grafton and Lisa Jardine, *From Humanism to the Humanities: Education and the Liberal Arts in Fifteenth- and Sixteenth-Century Europe* (London: Duckworth, 1986), xiii–xiv.

13. Nebrija writes that "Siempre la lengua fue compañera del imperio; y del tal manera lo siguió, que junta mente començaron, crecieron y florecieron, y después junta fue la caída de entrambos." *Gramática española,* ed. Antonio Quilis (Madrid: Editorial Nacional, 1981), 97. See also the "Arte de poesía castellana" by Nebrija's student Juan del Encina. On this subject see Ignacio Navarrete, *Orphans of Petrarch: Poetry and Theory in the Spanish Renaissance* (Berkeley and Los Angeles: University of California Press, Center for Medieval and Renaissance Studies, 1994).

14. For Garcilaso, I follow the edition of the *Poesías castellanas completas,* ed. Elias Rivers (Madrid: Castalia, 1972). Prose translations have benefited from consultation of those in Rivers, *Renaissance and Baroque Poetry of Spain.*

These verses virtually invite the New Historicist and ideological readings that have increasingly been applied to Renaissance verse. Such readings have called into question the viability of the largely ahistorical, postmodern interpretations of the lyric prevalent throughout the 1980s.[15] But in Garcilaso it turns out that there are ties between the "ideological" and "postmodern" routes of interpretation, or perhaps more accurately phrased, that both paths lead to the discovery that the project of lyric self-creation involves a dramatization of the poet's anxieties concerning the efficacy of his own powers. Both lead us to see in Garcilaso a deep questioning of the fundamental power of the poetic voice. Even a brief comparison of Garcilaso and Shakespeare in light of postmodern readings of Shakespeare can help demonstrate how this is so.

As was best exemplified in works like Joel Fineman's *Shakespeare's Perjured Eye* (1986), postmodern critics took as their point of departure the thesis that Renaissance subjectivity anticipates the postmodern decentering of the self. To be sure, it has often been argued that the complex and sophisticated modes of literary self-consciousness that originated in the European Renaissance were crucial to the development of Western culture. Such arguments have frequently been made in support of claims about the importance of Cervantes's and Shakespeare's texts. In a reading like Fineman's, however, the Renaissance subject is seen as already split by the (post)modern difference between presentation and representation that characterizes postmodern *écriture*. As if in anticipation of the historical questions that might be raised about such a thesis (questions analogous to those that have recently been posed about the relationship between Cervantes and Freud, questions that ask whether Cervantes is a Freudian or Freud a Cervantean),[16] Fineman proposed not just to locate Renaissance subjectivity at the origins of modern self-consciousness or to suggest that postmodern literary theory somehow sheds illuminating light on Shakespeare and the Renaissance lyric. Rather, he advanced a revisionist thesis in which the postmodern discovery of the decentered subject-self was seen as

15. These in turn had displaced the tradition of philological, stylistic, and New Critical readings of the lyric, which had pervaded Hispanism during the previous decades.
16. See, for example, León Grinberg and Juan Francisco Rodriguez, "Cervantes as Cultural Ancestor of Freud," in *Quixotic Desire: Psychoanalytic Perspectives on Cervantes*, ed. Ruth Anthony El Saffar and Diana de Armas Wilson (Ithaca: Cornell University Press, 1993), 23–33.

already contained within Shakespeare's texts. The most interesting examples of Renaissance subjectivity, which can be located in the textual practices of writers like Shakespeare, Cervantes, Montaigne, and Petrarch, would on such a view be the object-causes of our (post)modern desire; postmodern subjectivity articulates and thematizes the principle of difference on which Renaissance writing is founded. Thus Fineman argues that

> it would be possible to trace out in recent theoretical discussion, especially discussion of subjectivity, a development very similar not only to the development that we can discern in Shakespeare's sonnets, as they move from the sonnets addressed to the young man to the sonnets addressed to the dark lady, but similar also to the larger literary development within which we can locate the historical significance of Shakespeare's sonnet sequence as a whole. For example, responding to Husserl's Dantesque phenomenology of *Ideas,* to Husserl's concern with eidetic reduction and a transcendental Ego, Sartre developed a psychology of imagination whose logic and figurality very much resemble the paranoic visionary thematics of at least some of Shakespeare's young man sonnets. . . . Lacan's anamorphic gaze, very different from *le regard* of Sartre or Merleau-Ponty, along with Lacan's account of the way language potentiates and inherits this rupture of the visual imaginary, rather perfectly repeats the formal as well as the thematic logic of Shakespeare's "perjur'd eye." In this context, we can add, it is significant that Derrida's subsequent attempt to rupture Lacan's rupture, Derrida's putatively postsubjective account of supplemental *différance,* seems, from the point of view of Shakespeare's sonnets, nothing but another "increase" that "from fairest creatures we desire" (1), a subjective indeterminacy, that is to say, which is already predetermined, as was Tarquin's rape, by the exigencies of literary life. . . . What Derrida calls "writing," the thematics of the deconstructive "trace" that Derrida associates with *écriture,* is not beyond Shakespeare's sonnets but is instead anticipated and assimilated by them to the theme of language, with the two of these together being opposed to the theme of vision.[17]

17. Joel Fineman, *Shakespeare's Perjured Eye* (Berkeley and Los Angeles: University

I have quoted this passage at length for several reasons. Least interesting (though perhaps most striking) is its historical dislocation of figures like Petrarch and Shakespeare, by virtue of which their experiments with subjectivity appear to be the consequences of a postmodernism they could not possibly have known. More important is the fact that this passage makes a claim not for the importance of the Petrarchan text per se, but, implicitly, for the Petrarchan model, which may equally be anti-Petrarchan (e.g., in a sonnet like Shakespeare's "My mistress' eyes are nothing like the sun"). It thus allows literary history to be imagined as stemming equally from the imitation of models and from the self-conscious resistance to the demands of imitation.[18] Most important of all, however, is that this passage locates subjectivity (whether Renaissance or postmodern) neither in desire nor in its relation to objects, but in the circulation of desire throughout the poetic text in such a way as to shift our attention away from the objectivity of the object toward the ensure of the subject. The model of desire that informs such a view is one that always finds the poem to be a false mirror of the object of desire, and likewise one that always refers back to the subject's failure to be identical with itself. That failure in turn proves the impossibility of locating lyric subjectivity at any original point in literary history. As a response to the "founding fiction" sustained by Petrarch's texts,[19] literary history is most accurately read as the consequence of such impossibilities.

Shakespeare's sonnet 76, for example, conceives the problem of poetic writing in terms of both the impossibility and the need for any enunciation to be an articulation of difference; this need is transformed into the unfulfillable desire to say something new in praise of the beloved:

---

of California Press, 1986), 45–46. Fineman's reading of difference in Shakespeare's sonnets only has its full force when added to Shakespeare's own discovery of the impossibility of identity in the face of his apparent renunciation of difference, as for example in sonnet 105 ("Let not my love be call'd idolatry").

18. Fineman notes that "for all the analogues and precursors that exist for sonnet 130, the poem strikes a reader as more than conventionally anti-Petrarchan for the simple reason that it takes its anti-Petrarchism more seriously than is the custom either in orthodox or in paradoxical praise" (*Shakespeare's Perjured Eye*, 180). Compare Joachim du Bellay's "Contre les pétrarquistes."

19. The term "founding fiction" is Roland Greene's in *Post-Petrarchism* (22–62).

Why is my verse so barren of new pride,
So far from variation or quick change?
Why with the time do I not glance aside
To new-found methods, and to compounds strange?
Why write I still all one, ever the same,
And keep invention in a noted weed,
That every word doth almost tell my name,
Showing their birth, and where they did proceed?
O know, sweet love, I always write of you,
And you and love are still my argument,
So all my best is dressing old words new,
Spending again what is already spent:
   For as the sun is daily new and old,
   So is my love still telling what is told.[20]

The poet's own prior expressions (or those of the tradition as it has been transmitted through him) would seem to define the project of poetic innovation as impossible; but it is this very impossibility that gives the poet something to say ("So all my best is dressing old words new"). Moreover, because what has been already said or written establishes the impossibility of locating the poet's praise of the beloved within the space of his own self-consciousness, it seems that any poem is bound to be a betrayal of that consciousness rather than a mimesis of it. Hence sonnet 115: "Those lines that I before have writ do lie, / Ev'n those that said I could not love you dearer" (lines 1–2). Similarly, sonnet 105 proposes to "leave out difference" in expressing the constancy of love; and yet it concludes with the discovery that difference is built into the very articulation of words like "fair," "kind," and "true," which are not always and everywhere the same:

Let not my love be call'd idolatry,
Nor my beloved as an idol show,
To one, of one, still such, and ever so.
Kind is my love to-day, to-morrow kind,
Still constant in a wondrous excellence,

20. I follow the edition of Stephen Booth, *Shakespeare's Sonnets* (New Haven: Yale University Press, 1977). Booth glosses "noted weed" as "familiar garb," and notes a possible casual pun on the botanical senses of *knot*, meaning "ornamental garden" (*OED*, 7), for "not," and weed.

Therefore my verse, to constancy confin'd,
One thing expressing, leaves out difference.
"Fair," "kind," and "true" is all my argument,
"Fair," "kind," and "true" varying to other words,
And in this change is my invention spent,
Three themes in one, which wondrous scope affords.
    "Fair," "kind," and "true" have often liv'd alone,
    Which three till now kept seat in one.

And yet Fineman's arguments and others like it create at least as many puzzles as they solve, as they fail to put a series of questions regarding the historical and cultural specificity of Renaissance and modern subjectivity fully to rest. One might, for instance, wish to know how the claim for Shakespeare's preeminence in the development of modern subjectivity can be reconciled with the prominence during the Renaissance, outside of England, of alternatives to the Petrarchan model that were not at all Shakespearean.[21] One recent critic has said of Garcilaso that the subject of his poetry is "the prisoner of love we met in Petrarch's text: the lady functions as the source of pain and thus is the other, the object against which the construction of subjectivity takes place,"[22] but the story does not end there. In Garcilaso, the "subject" created in the tension with the unyielding object of desire is one who foregrounds the questions of his own powers of speech. The focus in Garcilaso's verse is thus not the objectivity of the object as a potential vehicle for the satisfaction of desire (or, conversely, the suffering and pain that stems from the absence of the beloved object) but the ability of the subject to create himself out of a series of speech-acts whose ultimate challenge is to establish their own efficacy. In stanza 17 of Garcilaso's first eclogue, for instance, the poet-narrator echoes Virgil's

21. The same question can be raised, more generally, about Renaissance versions of subjectivity that are not Shakespearean. Diana de Armas Wilson, for example, corrects Harold Bloom's claim that while "our map or general theory of the mind may be Freud's" Freud in turn "inherits the representation of mind, at its most subtle and excellent, from Shakespeare," when she argues that "Freud inherited the representation of mind from multiple predecessors, including Cervantes, whose eminent candidacy for this visionary company must now be acknowledged." Wilson, *Allegories of Love: Cervantes's "Persiles and Sigismunda"* (Princeton: Princeton University Press, 1991), 74–75. She cites Bloom from *Ruin the Sacred Truths: Poetry and Belief from the Bible to the Present* (Cambridge: Harvard University Press, 1989), 58.

22. Marsical, *Contradictory Subjects: Quevedo, Cervantes and Seventeenth-Century Spanish Culture* (Ithaca: Cornell University Press, 1991), 120.

eclogue 8 and implores the muses to take up his song where his voice seems to have failed. Garcilaso intensifies his Virgilian source in order to speak a more fundamental fear about the waning power of poetry itself:[23]

> Lo que cantó tras esto Nemoroso
> decildo vos, Piérides, que tanto
>   no puedo yo ni oso,
> que siento enflaquecer mi débil canto.
>   (eclogue 1, lines 235–37)

> (What Nemoroso sang after this
> you tell, Muses, for
> I neither can nor dare to,
> feeling feeble song wane.)

In Garcilaso, poetry is not so much the mimesis of an original scene of object-loss, as a worrying over the loss of the more fundamental poetic power that might compensate for that "original" loss. To a remarkable degree, the hypothetical "if" that opens the ode "Ad Florem Gnidi" remains always in force in Garcilaso's verse, which is to say that Garcilaso's poetry consistently raises the questions of its own status and its force, and that it is within the space opened by these questions that the poetic "I" is constructed:

> Si de mi baja lira
> tanto pudiese el son que en un momento
>   aplacase la ira
>   del animoso viento
> y la furia del mar y el movimiento,
>   y en ásperas montañas
> con el süave canto enterneciese
>   las fieras alimañas,
>   los árboles moviese . . .
> y al son confusamente los trujiese
>   (lines 1–10)

23. Virgil: "haec Damon: vos, quae responderit Alphesiboeus, / dicite Pierides, non omnia possumus omnes" (thus Damon: you tell, Muses, what Alphesiboeus answered, for we cannot all do everything).

(If the sound of my lowly lyre were so powerful that in one
moment it could placate the wrath of the raging wind and the
fury and movement of the sea, and in the rough mountains with
its gentle song it could melt the hearts of the fierce animals, and
could in confusion bring them toward its sound . . .)

Even within the confines of the postmodern reading of the Renaissance lyric, however, one might wish to know what the shift in emphasis
from the beloved as object to an understanding of subjectivity as
founded on the anxiety of the poetic speech-act would imply for Freud's
claims that the overarching difference between the ancients and the
moderns can be located in the latter's interest in objects rather than in
the instincts. What in particular can be said of Spain, where what Freud
names by "instinct" was in certain crucial instances (associated with an
attachment to a historical set of values organized around the notion
"cleanliness of blood") far more explicit in the theater than in the lyric?
(Consider how, in the Spanish Golden Age, the fixation on cleanliness
of blood generates a series of fantasmatic objects, including the image
of the "blood" itself.) If the entrance into cultural and literary modernity
in Golden Age Spain, however contested or fraught, required a transition from social hierarchies determined by the power of the blood to a
social world in which the driving force of the instincts was repressed or
transferred to a more "refined" set of cultural practices, or directed
toward a more "peaceful" set of ends, then what was the price of that
transition and what traces did it leave in Spanish texts?

In recent writing on the question of subject-formation in the Golden
Age, it has been suggested that the lyric provided an arena in which
subjectivity could be constructed relatively free from concerns about
social hierarchy, blood, and caste. Garcilaso is conventionally positioned within this history of cultural modernization. His verse has been
seen as an aesthetic overcoming of violence and as a sublimation of loss
and death into an eroticized form of longing not atypical of the earlier
Italian and Latin pastoral (e.g., Sannazaro and Virgil). George Mariscal,
for instance, has argued that "Garcilaso cultivated the idea of the *alma
bella* who stood apart from traditional hierarchies," and goes on to
suggest that "the speaker's unique identity in the eclogues is articulated
not through blood or clan affiliations but through the community of
shepherds, who imagine a different kind of solidarity founded on the

idea of personal suffering."[24] For some of the same reasons, it has been suggested that Garcilaso presents us with the model of a *centered* subject; especially in critical works like Rafael Lapesa's *La trayectoria poética de Garcilaso;* however, the "centered" view requires a biographical narrative (for which it also supplies the referents) in order to make its case. It is Garcilaso's successors, then, who discover that the center cannot hold. Oreste Macrí, for instance, describes how the subject-center tends to dissolve in the poetry of Herrera, where the lone sufferer of Garcilaso's verse is transformed into a psychologically confused subject who doubts his own projects and abilities.[25] For Mariscal in turn it is in Quevedo rather than in Garcilaso where one can locate "the lack of a center and the relative absence of a stable consciousness within the textual economy of the poem."[26]

The implication of such claims, as I understand them, is that while Garcilaso remains the "founder" and inescapable point of reference for all questions about the formation of poetic subjectivity and literary modernity in Renaissance Spain, it is only in the subsequent, post-Garcilasian tradition that the Spanish lyric subject becomes truly self-conscious and "modern." But this view may not be accurate to Garcilaso's texts, which offer a more complex version of subjectivity than is presupposed by any of these accounts.[27] Garcilasian subjectivity, I suggest, is anchored in the impossibility of making a complete and successful transition from "instincts" to "objects"—which Freud de-

24. George Mariscal discusses this last question in his analysis of Quevedo in *Contradictory Subjects,* 118–19. While arguing that Quevedo's lyric texts were engaged in an ironic distancing from dominant conceptions of the subject, Marsical suggests that in the Spanish Golden Age the Petrarchan lyric was linked to the "relatively repressed ideology of singularity (early modern individualism)" and, as such, was "in conflict with dominant constructions of the subject" (*Contradictory Subjects,* 110).

25. Oreste Macrí, *Fernando de Herrera,* 2d ed. (Madrid: Gredos, 1972), 478. Mariscal describes Herrera's subject as "a wandering lover in search of the center" (*Contradictory Subjects,* 125).

26. *Contradictory Subjects,* 120. Though ultimately rejecting a psychological reading of the poetry in facor of a sociohistorical analysis of the question of subject-formation in Quevedo's lyric poetry, Mariscal quotes Dámaso Alonso's assertion of the psychological distance that separates Quevedo from Petrarch: "Una angustia continuada, arranca esencialiemte, radicalmente, a Quevedo de todo psicologismo petrarquista, lo mismo que le arranca de todos los formalismos postrenacentistas" (A continuous anguish essentially, radically, removes Quevedo from any Petrarchan psychology, just as it removes him from all post-Renaissance formalisms). *Poesía española,* 4th ed. (Madrid: Gredos, 1962), 576; cited in Mariscal, *Contradictory Subjects,* 112.

27. Indeed, one only has to think of the speaker's fundamental disorientation in a

scribes as crucial to the distinction between ancient and modern culture. The impossibility of fully suppressing the instincts, even as they are redefined (and refined) as "passions," in turn leads Garcilaso to posit the peculiar creativity of the instincts, which potentially endows poetry with the power to overcome death.[28]

---

poem like sonnet 12 in order to see the ways in which the "decentered" subject was not an invention of the post-Garcilasian tradition in Spain, but an elaboration of poetic stances available already in Garcilaso:

> Si para refrenar este deseo
> loco, imposible, vano, temeroso,
> y guarecer de un mal tan peligroso,
> que es darme a entender yo lo que no creo.
>   no me aprovecha verme cual me veo,
> o muy aventurado o muy medroso,
> en tanta confusión que nunca oso
> fiar el mal de mí que lo poseo.

> (If, in order to refrain this crazy,
> impossible, vain, fearful desire,
> and to cure an illness so dangerous,
> that I am given to understand what I cannot believe,
>   It's no use for me to see myself as I do,
> either fortunate or fearful,
> in so much confusion that I do not dare
> trust that I possess my own sickness.)

But even here the creation of subjectivity in Garcilaso is dependent not just on the presentation of the confusion caused by desire. It is mediated by Garcilaso's reference in the tercets to the myths of Icarus and Phaeton, whose falls are appropriated as an artistic representation that serves as a mirror—even if as a false, inaccurate, or incomplete mirror—for what the poet feels.

> ¿qué me ha de aprovechar ver la pintura
> d'aquel que con las alas derretidas,
> cayendo, fama y nombre al mar ha dado,
>   y la del que su fuego y su locura
> llora entre aquellas plantas conocidas,
> penas en el agua resfriado?

> (What good would it do to see the picture
> of the one who falling, with his wings melting,
> has given his name and his fame to the sea,
>   and the picture of the one who cries about
> his passion and his madness among those well-known plants,
> his sorrow chilled in the water?)

28. Freud's essay on "Instincts and their Vicissitudes" provides the basis for a tropological theory of the instincts. The various "vicissitudes" (reversal, turning back, repression, and sublimation) all describe what happens to the insticts when they are not

Let us consider, as but one example of the impossibility of fully objectifying desire in Garcilaso, sonnet 31, in which the poet's sense of self is a function of the difference between the passions of love and jealousy, and in which that difference is figured in terms of the poet's anxieties over the question of procreation. While Garcilaso may seem to set aside concerns about the social hierarchies of blood in order to devote himself to the poetry of love, it turns out that those concerns are here rearticulated in a series of equally anxious worries about the ability of the poet to engender anything that would truly resemble himself:

> Dentro en mi alma fue de mí engendrado
> un dulce amor, y de mi sentimiento
> tan aprobado fue su nacimiento
> como de un solo hijo deseado;
>   mas luego d'él nació quien ha estragado
> del todo el amoroso pensamiento;
> en áspero rigor y en gran tormento
> los primeros deleites tornado.
>   ¡Oh cruel nieto, que das vida al padre
> y matas al agüelo!, ¿por qué creces
> tan desconforme a aquél de que has nacido?
>   ¡Oh celoso temor!, ¿a quién pareces?,
> que aun la invidia, tu propia y fiera madre,
> se espanta en ver el monstruo que ha parido.[29]

(A sweet love was engendered in my soul, and its birth was met with such feeling of approval that it was like a cherished only son; but he gave birth to the one who has ruined all my amorous thoughts; this one has turned my first delights into harsh bitter pain and great torment. Oh, cruel grandson, you give the father life and kill the grandfather! Why do you grow so unlike the one from whom you were born? Oh jealous love! Whom do you

---

fully suppressed (recognizing that, for Freud, there is no such thing as the complete "suppression" of the instincts outside death).

29. The linkage between jealousy, as an aberration of desire, and monsters, was common in the baroque, as for example in Calderón's play *El mayor monstruo, los celos*. See Roberto González Echevarría, "Calderón's *La vida es sueño*: Mixed-(Up) Monsters," in *Celestina's Brood: Continuities of the Baroque in Latin American Literature* (Durham: Duke University Press, 1993), 81–113.

resemble? For even your own cruel mother, envy, is frightened to see the monster to which she has given birth.)

At first blush, it seems that what is produced in this poem, the "child of the soul," is the refined and cultured passion of "un dulce amor," the fruit of a cultural convention and, likewise, of conventional (i.e., normative European) culture. However, it turns out that nature is potentially productive insofar as the "natural" tendency of like to engender like runs off the rails. As in Freud's account, the question of the instincts is always the question of one (or more) of their vicissitudes: reversal, turning back, repression, sublimation.[30] The transition from "instinct" to "object" never fully occurs. Moreover, a preoccupation about lineage and filiation, transmuted into the language of love and jealousy, deeply troubles this poem. It is in the space between the first act of engendering that takes place outside of all instinct ("in the soul") and what is subsequently engendered by the offspring that the effect of subjectivity is produced. Specifically, it is the difference between the immaculate conception of the "dulce amor" in the soul and its nearly unrecognizable, monstrous other—the passion of jealous rage—that opens the space in which the subject manifests itself. The poem cannot be read as mimetic of the passions, if only because what they produce fails to be identical with its source in the passions. The "dulce amor" begets an offspring that turns the "father" of desire into a tormented grandfather, and the "mother's" child into a monster. Far from having eliminated the instincts, and far from having put concerns about identity and filiation aside, the poem offers an example of the ways in which the instincts and passions refuse to be fully objectified in the Garcilasian lyric.

As this example suggests, Garcilaso exemplifies a model of literary subjectivity that is incommensurable with the Petrarchan; it is in many ways as complex as the Shakespearean, though significantly different from it. Whereas the Shakespearean reworking of Petrarch leads on Fineman's reading to the deconstruction of the object of desire, or what amounts to the same thing, to the transformation of desire, through the rhetorical play of wit, into *écriture*, Garcilaso's verse takes as its point of departure the impossibility of what Freud described as the passage from "instincts" to "objects." To posit the impossibility of moving

30. See "Instincts and their Vicissitudes" (1915).

completely from the productive and potentially disruptive instincts to the consolidation or deflection of instinctual impulses in objects means that poetry must be regarded as an attempt to appropriate the power and "vicissitudes" of the instincts for creative ends.

※   ※   ※

When seen in the context of what Norbert Elias has described as the "civilizing" process, it is no surprise to find that the Petrarchan idiom, and the Renaissance lyric more broadly, provided a vehicle for the refinement of the instincts during the late Middle Ages and early modern period. But it should not be forgotten that the Petrarchan lyric was itself a development of the work of the troubadours and *Minnesänger,* whose origins among the members of knightly society were never fully eclipsed as this poetry entered the more refined courtly world. According to Elias, the rise and influence of the *Minnesänger* can be explained in terms of the process by which the instincts and drives came under increasing control within the context of the increasingly restricted court circles of medieval and early modern Europe. As Elias suggests, the instincts were never fully eclipsed by polite, courtly behavior. The sword, on Elias's account, still hangs (albeit loosely) at the courtier's side:

> troubadour poetry and service are stamped by the dependent status of their practitioners within a rich social life that was slowly taking on more definite forms. The human relationships and compulsions established here are not as strict and continuous, or as inescapable, as they later become at the larger absolutist courts which are far more thoroughly formed by money relationships. But they already act in the direction of stricter drive-control. Within the restricted court circle, and encouraged above all by the presence of the lady, more peaceful forms of conduct become obligatory. Certainly, this should not be exaggerated; pacification is not nearly so far advanced as later when the absolute monarch could even prohibit duelling. The sword still hangs loosely, and war and feud are close at hand. But the moderation of passions, sublimation, is unmistakable and inevitable in feudal court society.[31]

31. Elias, *Power and Civility* (volume 2 of *The Civilizing Process*), trans. Edmund Jephcott (New York: Pantheon, 1982), 77.

Precisely because they were not fully eclipsed, the instincts remained available to be deployed in the cultural-imperial projects of the early modern age. Consider the image of Garcilaso as the soldier-poet, who in eclogue 3 just as easily takes up the sword as the pen ("tomando ora la espada, ora la pluma," eclogue 3, line 40).[32]

In Garcilaso's first eclogue the poet's pen is likewise "exercised" in praise of the vice-regent of the Spanish colony in Naples, Don Pedro de Toledo, who is said literally to "represent" the god of war, "el fiero Marte":

> Tú, que ganaste obrando
> un nombre en todo el mundo
> y un grado sin segundo,
> agora estés atento sólo y dado
> al ínclito gobierno del estado
> albano, agora vuelto a la otra parte,
> resplandeciente, armado,
> representando en tierra el fiero Marte
> ....
> espera, que en tornando
> a ser restituido
> al ocio ya perdido,
> luego verás ejercitar mi pluma
> por la infinita, innumerable suma
> de tus virtudes y famosas obras
> (eclogue 1, lines 7–14, 21–26)

(You, whose works have earned you renown throughout the world and a rank second to none, whether you are now exclusively in charge of the distinguished direction of the Alban state, or whether you are now turned in another direction, clad in resplendent armor, representing the fierce Mars on earth. . . . Wait, for once you are restored to your lost leisure, you will see

---

32. According to a 1622 comment of Tamayo de Vargas, Garcilaso was unique in having resolved the "ancient division between arms and letters by having ennobled them equally" ("en quien solo se a llegado a concordar la antigua dissensión entre las armas y las letras, por averlas el ennoblecido con igualdad").

my pen at once devoted to recounting the infinite sum of your virtues and famous deeds)

To be sure, there is a dramatic attenuation or "civilizing" of the instincts in a passage like this. The poem is not itself a vehicle of the instincts or a weapon of war, and is not offered to inspire military success, but rather is a substitute for the praise due the one who has successfully waged a military campaign ("*luego* verás ejercitar"). Specifically, it lauds a man who has turned from war to politics. If war is a form of work (*negocio,* line 16), then the poet's leisure (*ocio,* line 23) will allow the hero to see his efforts stamped into the form of a political state. Indeed, the poem could be seen as a synecdoche for the transformation of the warlike instincts into a political object were it not that the shepherds' songs offered in place of that praise call into question the possibility of any such transformation. Both Salicio and Nemoroso define themselves in terms of the struggles that have brought them to grief over the problem of loss: Salicio in terms of his rejection by Galatea, and Nemoroso in terms of the death of Elisa. For each of them, the objectification of grief in the form of song is rendered difficult if not impossible because the object-cause of their suffering is lost. This makes the poem a form of endless labor:

> Nunca pusieran fin al triste lloro
> los pastores, ni fueran acabadas
> las canciones que solo el monte oía
> (lines 408–10)

(The shepherds would never have ended their sad song, nor would the songs that only the mountains heard have come to a close)

Moreover, the poem must confront the fact that the attenuation of the instincts required for the production (and reproduction) of culture in the form of the shepherds' "sweet lament" (*dulce lamentar*) may require the renunciation of the very same powers necessary for its constitution. Accordingly, the thrust of the eclogue is to "read back" from the cultivated verse enjoyed in leisure, through politics, to the work of war, in such a way as to see war as itself poetic. The vice-regent is said to "represent" the god of war by virtue of the mediation of the social-symbolic set of mythological images that mark the work of empire as itself poetic;[33] his military feats, and literature's appropriation of those feats, are mediated by the pre-existing set of figures to which the heroic figure is assimilated.

To the extent that the entrance into civilized culture requires the repression of the warlike instincts, poetry must affirm the difference between the sword and the pen as categorical and complete. The poet is to some degree *obligated* to substitute pastoral poetry for heroic verse. But to the extent that cultural prestige is in fact tied to empire, poetry may need to regain and reappropriate the very thing it would deny. As I have suggested above, this can best be done if war and imperialism are themselves figured as poetic, as in the introductory stanzas of Garcilaso's first eclogue, which frame the pastoral lyric of unfulfillable desire as a prelude to the poetry of military and political praise. Indeed, the entire pastoral drama of love, loss, and death that takes place in the third eclogue, where the powers of poetic language are most severely put to the test, is framed by the shifting of power between the "sword" and the "pen."[34] To say that Garcilaso wishes to substitute the power of the pen for that of the sword is plausible only insofar as he wishes to transform the destructive instincts into creative ones, thereby defeating what Freud famously described as the tendency of all things to work toward death.[35] As becomes clear in relation to sonnet 10 and eclogue 3, the power Garcilaso would reappropriate as the result of these transpositions is the power of figuration itself, which Garcilaso locates in the enunciative power of the voice.

Before turning to those examples, I note that the desire to transform poetry into the articulation of an originally productive power is what lies at stake in the poems of pure praise, of epideixis. These poems begin, as with the cornucopian image of sonnet 21, with the invocation of the object of the poet's praise: "Clarísimo Marqués, en quien

---

33. On myth in Golden Age Spain, see Marcia L. Welles, *Arachne's Tapestry: The Transformation of Myth in Seventeenth-Century Spain* (San Antonio: Trinity University Press, 1986).

34. A similar instability of displacements can be seen in Shakespeare's epideictic sonnets, in which it is sometimes impossible to tell whether the poem directs praise toward the beloved, or whether it is the beloved whose perfection asks to be mirrored in the poem. Because this relationship cannot be decided, it means that the praise is bound to be imperfect and the poem always a false mirror, reflecting accurately neither the beloved nor the poetic self.

35. See "Instincts and their Vicissitudes" and *Beyond the Pleasure Principle*.

derrama / el cielo cuanto bien conoce el mundo" (Noble Marqués, on whom Heaven showers all the good fortune in the world) (lines 1–2). Insofar as that object never achieves an autonomous objectivity, its greatness remains available to be reappropriated as a power of the poetic act. The "object" of the praise is celebrated as unique both in the (divine, Platonic) idea, and also in the making (art, *technē*). The hero is praised for his excellence, and the example is prized for its rarity. But, no matter how unique or exalted, the hero remains a product of the poetic act; as is more graphically evident in the eclogues, the poetry of praise is inescapably a reflection not of the hero but of the poet's powers:

> y en fin, de solo vos formó natura
> una estraña y no vista al mundo idea
> y hizo igual al pensamiento el arte.

(and in the end, nature formed you alone from a rare and never before seen idea and made the art equal to the idea.)

✳ ✳ ✳

In the introductory section of Garcilaso's first eclogue, the link between the sword and the pen underwrites the desire to reclaim an efficacious power for poetry by representing the imperial project as itself poetic. In Garcilaso's amorous verse, the impossibility of fully objectifying desire results in the creation of specially empowered memory-objects,[36] such as the "dulces prendas" (sweet souvenirs) of sonnet 10. In contrast to the public discourse that frames the first eclogue, however, the "dulces prendas" seem to anchor a narrative of private memories. As Susan Stewart writes in *On Longing,* "the souvenir moves history into private time";[37] according to Stewart, this is particularly the case in pre-capitalist economies, where the souvenir is "intimately mapped against the life history of the individual . . . as the material sign of an abstract referent" (139). In the case of Garcilaso's sonnet, however, the narrative is not merely personal; nor does the referent create the absent or

36. There is a tendency for the intermediate or transitional object to take on monstrous proportions, especially in the baroque. It is the source of what Garcilaso names *celos* and Calderón identifies as *monstruos.*

37. Stewart, *On Longing: Narratives of the Miniature, the Gigantic, the Souvenir, the Collection* (1984; repr., Durham: Duke University Press, 1993), 138.

departed beloved as an object of unfulfillable longing. Like the poem itself, the "dulces prendas" perform their creative work in and as memory is brought to voice; in this poem, the voice is that which in principle would have the power to activate memory. The poet's power of re-call is one with the power of his vocative "call" to the "dulces prendas." All the more reason, then, to note that the invocation of the "dulces prendas" reveals the impossibility of attaching the poet's desire to a specific memory-object:

> "¡Oh dulces prendas por mi mal halladas,
> dulces y alegres cuando Dios quería,
> juntas estáis en la memoria mía
> y con ella en mi muerte conjuradas!"
> (lines 1–4)

(Oh sweet souvenirs, discovered to my sorrow, sweet and happy as long as God so willed! You are all together in my memory and conspiring with memory against my life!)

The particular drama of voice in this poem has nonetheless been neglected by most commentators, who seize instead upon the poet's invocation of the "dulces prendas" as an attempt to crystallize his memory of the beloved into an objective form, and so to locate loss in a thing. Readings of the poem beginning with that of El Brocense in 1574 have served to reinforce this effort by assigning a signified to this specific signifier and by setting it within a biographical narrative.[38] El Brocense speculated that the "dulces prendas" may refer to a lock of hair of the beloved ("Parece que habla con unos cabellos de su dama").[39] Here the

38. Such readings confirm the Petrarchan lineage of the Garcilasian text, not for any verbal echoes it may contain, but for the will to read the lyric sequence as the temporal expression of a biographical character in an historical place. Beginning at least with Alessandro Vellutello's 1525 Venice edition of Petrarch's *Rime* (*Il Petrarca con l'espositione d'Alessandro Vellutello*), there has been a consistent tendency to map the Petrarchan lyric onto a specific set of temporal, spatial, and biographical coordinates. Greene's discussion of the poet-Petrarchan tradition contains an analysis of this and related issues. (On character-creation, see *Post-Petrarchism*, 63–108; on space, see 195–96ff.) On the one hand, this tradition tends to fetishize the signified, as in the debates among commentators concerning the exact day and hour on which Petrarch fell in love with Laura; on the other hand, it indicates the resources that the Petrarchan text offers for sustained self-creation. The tradition of Garcilaso criticism repeats many of these tendencies.

39. *Garcilaso de la Vega y sus comentaristas*, ed. Antonio Gallego Morell, 2d ed. (Madrid: Gredos, 1972), 267 (B-12).

biographical narrative carries out the work of signification that the poem either feels unable to complete, or leaves intentionally incomplete. Indeed, it seems that the "dulces prendas" resist the precise determination El Brocense would ascribe to them, and never achieve full objectification within the poem. In his 1622 commentary, Tamayo de Vargas says revealingly of sonnet 10 that "its subject is not any specific thing, but rather any token [*prenda*], imagined or real" ("su sujeto no es cosa señalada, sino cualquiera prenda de voluntad o imaginada o verdadera").[40] Tamayo may have perceived the difficulty involved in assigning a signified to this puzzling signifier, but he failed to understand the problem's source.

Of all the commentaries on this poem, Herrera's (1580) is by far the most interesting in that he noted that the effect of the poet's apostrophic invocation of the "dulces prendas" is equivalent to that of personification, which Herrera calls prosopopeia.[41] Rhetorically, Herrera's description would seem mistaken, for prosopopeia conventionally names the figure whereby something not itself alive is ascribed first a name, subsequently a face, and finally a voice. (As J. Hillis Miller notes, many prosopopeias are also chatachreses: the "eye of a storm"; the "face of a mountain.")[42] In naming this apostrophic invocation of the "dulces

40. *Garcilaso y sus comentaristas*, 602 (T-14). Lapesa acknowledges both the biographical interpretation and the more "liberal" reading in *La trayectoria poética de Garcilaso*. "Generalmente se admite que esta obra, una de las más emocionadas de Garcilaso, fue inspirada por la muerte de Isabel Freyre. Respetaremos la interpretación tradicional, aunque nada obliga a ello; todas las frases del poema pueden explicarse por la presencia de cualquier objeto que, viva o muerta la amada, evocara en el poeta recuerdos de pretéritos días venturosos. Al no mencionar las circunstancias concretas gana amplitud y profundidad la contraposición entre la felicidad perdida y el dolor presente." While Lapesa may be willing to admit that the biographical circumstances here are left imprecise, he does not stop to question the objectivity of the "dulces predas."

41. The figure of prosopopeia has received attention in part due to the influential work of critics like J. Hillis Miller and Paul de Man. See de Man's essay on Rilke in *Allegories of Reading* (New Haven: Yale University Press, 1979), 20–56, and the essays in *The Rhetoric of Romanticism* (New York: Columbia University Press, 1984). See J. Hillis Miller, *Versions of Pygmalion* (Cambridge: Harvard University Press, 1990), especially "Pygmalion's Prosopopeia" (1–12). Jonathan Culler discusses the relationship between apostrophe and voice in his chapter "Apostrophe" in *The Pursuit of Signs* (London: Routledge and Kegan Paul, 1981), 135–54; see esp. 142, where Culler describes apostrophe in relation to "the pure O of undifferentiated voicing." As my discussion of Garcilaso's poem will make clear, the apostrophic "Oh" signifies a power that is only "undifferentiated" insofar as it does not fit easily into a semantic framework.

42. See *Versions of Pygmalion*, 5. On catachresis, see also the section in Derrida's essay "White Mythology" entitled "The Flowers of Rhetoric," in *Margins of Philosophy*, trans. Alan Bass (Chicago: University of Chicago Press, 1982), 246–57, and esp. 255.

prendas" a form of prosopopeia, Herrera modifies its traditional rhetorical meaning, as if to suggest that the figure involves the investment of an inanimate object not necessarily with a face or a voice, but with a power; he implies that what is at issue in the poem is not just the figuration of an object, but a mimesis of the power by means of which figuration occurs. Ultimately, this is the power of *poiesis*, here figured as one with the power to call back a lost object:

> Sírvese aquí de la figura prosopopeia, que los latinos llamaron conformación y nuestra lengua podrá tener por nombre de fingimiento o hechura de persona; la cual contiene en sí mucha dignidad, y es la más vehemente de todas las figuras. Hácese en dos maneras: cuando se introduce persona fingida, como la Fama en Virgilio, la Hambre en el 5, de Ovidio; o casi sacamos del sepulcro y tinieblas de la muerte y Plutón algunos difuntos, y representamos, como si estuviesen vivos y presentes, su acción y palabras. Esta no es figura, sino parte de argumento poético. La otra es cuando no se finge persona por aquel modo, sino por la oración, que se le atribuye.[43]

> (The poet here uses the figure of prosopopeia, which the Latin authors called *conformatio* and which in our language can describe the feigning or fashioning of a person; which in itself carries great dignity, and is the most forceful of all figures. It can be done in two ways: when a fictional person is introduced, such as Fame in Virgil, or Hunger in book 5 of Ovid; or [when] we take some dead figures out of the darkness of death of Pluto's grave and represent their actions and words as if they were alive and present. . . . The other way is when one does not fashion a person in this manner but rather through words which are attributed to him.)

Especially in sonnet 10, but also in the *canciones,* where the concluding apostrophe is often directed to the poem itself, prosopopeia involves not just the attribution of the power of speech to something that is not alive, or, as Herrera would have it, the "feigning" of a person by the attribution of a voice, but the mimesis of a poetic power. The more

---

43. *Anotaciones,* in *Garcilaso y sus comentaristas,* 340 (H-75).

intensely Garcilaso invests in the fiction of such a power, the more one suspects that is designed in order to compensate for the loss of some truly efficacious force. Indeed, the "dulces prendas" perform a function similar to that which Freud attributed to the Moorish king in the *romance* by "Ay de mi Alhama," in which Boabdil receives the news of the fall of the city of Alhama: to deny the very thing that would mark any vulnerability to a diminution of power. In Freud's analysis of the *romance,* Boabdil feels that the loss of Alhama means the end of his rule, and this impels him to treat the news as "*non arrivé*":

> Cartas le fueron venidas
> que Alhama era ganada:
> las cartas echó en el fuego,
> y al mensajero matara.

(Letters had reached him saying that Alhama was taken: he threw the letters in the fire and killed the messenger.)

Freud writes that "it is easy to guess that a further determinant of this behavior of the king was his need to combat a feeling of powerlessness. By burning the letters and having the messenger killed *he was trying to show that his power was still at its full.*"[44]

In Herrera's account of the "dulces prendas" in sonnet 10, prosopopeia is inherently an elevated figure ("contiene en sí mucha dignidad").[45] The "greatness" of its power is akin to the sublime insofar as the object it would conjure up is irretrievably lost.[46] This sublimity is particularly evident in the apostrophic ¡Oh! that goes effectively nowhere, and is not denotative of any object in the strict or literal sense. As a figure with no object, the "¡Oh!" that prefaces the "dulces prendas" refers us to the power at work behind all self-amplifying forms of enunciation on

44. Freud, "A Disturbing Memory on the Acropolis" (1937), in *Character and Culture,* ed. Philip Reiff (New York: Macmillan, 1963), 319; my emphasis.

45. Compare Montaigne on the greatness and power of the imagination in *Essais* I, 21 ("De la Force de l'Imagination"): " '*Fortis imaginatio generat casum,*' disent les clercs. Je suis de ceux qui sentent tres-grand effort de l'imagination" ("*A strong imagination creates the event,*" say the scholars. I am one of those who are very much influenced by the imagination). *The Complete Essays of Montaigne,* trans. Donald M. Frame (1958; repr., Stanford: Stanford University Press, 1976), 68.

46. The formula of a strong passion stirred up in the absence of an object has links that lead to the Kantian understanding of the sublime; see the "Analytic of the Sublime" in the *Critique of Judgment.*

which subjective self-creation depends: the miming of the original speech-act, the divine *fiat,* that the poet would, if possible, appropriate for his own verse, thereby transforming poetry from mere imitation into true *poiesis* (making).[47] In mythological terms, this involves a reenactment of the story of Pygmalion and Galatea, which forms the background for Salicio's lament in eclogue 1.

Still more graphic than the "dulces prendas" as an example of the way in which the poet attempts to objectify his sorrow or loss or to reverse it by means of an efficacious poetic power is sonnet 37, in which the experiences of absence and loss are figured in the form of a howling dog lost in the desert. The howling dog is one of Garcilaso's most impressive images, but also one that is most directly related to the question of poetic power, insofar as it refers back to the origin of the poetic image-object in the conditions of enunciation (in the dog's own inarticulate howling, and in the poet's more "rational" speech):

> A la entrada de un valle, en un desierto
> do nadie atravesba ni se vía,
> vi que con estrañeza un can hacía
> estremos de dolor con desconcierto;
>   ahora suelta el llanto al cielo abierto,
> ora va rastreando por la vía;
> camina, vuelve, para, y todavía
> quedaba desmayado como muerto.
>   Y fue que se apartó de su presencia
> su amo, y no le hallaba, y esto siente:
> mirad hasta dó llega el mal de ausencia.
>   Movióme a compasión ver su accidente;

---

47. Hegel emphasizes the relationship between the divine *fiat* and the sublime: "God is the creator of the Universe. This is the purest expression of the sublime itself. For the first time, that is to say, ideas of procreation and the mere natural generation of things by God vanish and give place to the thought of *creation* by spiritual might and activity. 'God said: Let there be light; and there was light'; this Longinus quoted long ago as in every way a striking example of the sublime. The Lord, the one substance, does proceed to manifestation, but the manner of creation is the purest, even bodiless, ethereal manifestation; it is the word, the manifestation of the thought as the ideal power, and with its command that the existent shall be, the existent is immediately and actually brought into being in silent obedience." Hegel, *Lectures on Aesthetics,* trans T. M. Knox (Oxford: Clarendon Press, 1975), 1:373–74. The reference to Longinus is to *On the Sublime,* ix, 10, quoting Genesis 1:3.

díjele, lastimado: "Ten paciencia,
que yo alcanzo razón, y estoy ausente."

(At the entrance to a valley, in a desert, where no one passed or
was seen, I saw that a dog was making strange and disconcerted
sounds of pain: now he lets loose his cry to the open sky, now he
drags himself along the way; he walks, turns back, stops, and
then falls in a faint as if dead. What happened was that his
master left him, and he couldn't find him, and so he suffers from
this: look what the pain of absence can do. I was moved to
compassion to see his misfortune; I said to him, with pity: "Be
patient, for I can speak, and I am absent [lost]."")

Although Elias Rivers has glossed the phrase "alcanzo razón" of the
final verse as "soy racional" (I am rational),[48] it would seem that
"razón" here means not only "reason" in the more or less Scholastic
sense, but also "speech," for it is only against the raucous "descon-
cierto" of the dog's pain that the poet's more refined (read: less
instinctual) expression of sorrow has the force of a contrast.[49] Here, the
entrance into language ("que yo alcanzo razón") as a means of overcoming the grief of absence is also a way of sublimating the less "civilized"
passions figured in the image of the howling dog.

In this instance, however, sublimation fails because one of the fundamental elements of poetic composition—the image, whose vividness
renders it remarkably objectlike—is itself shown to be a function of the
power of enunciation located in the seemingly less "substantial" poetic
voice. As Julia Kristeva writes, "[mimesis] must posit an object, but this
'object' is merely a result of the drive economy of enunciation."[50] In
other words, voice is the poem's power, the power at work behind the
fashioning of image-objects; the image is a product of it. Indeed, it
would not be too much to say that the poet's final address to the dog
has an effect that is quite the opposite of what Herrera imagined as the
function of prosopopeia in sonnet 10; while the voice calls for the
creation of the dog as an objectification of the poet's own grief, that

48. *Garcilaso de la Vega: Poesías castellanas completas,* 73.
49. Similarly, the phrase "estoy ausente" might be glossed as "I am lost," thus
emphasizing the loss that absence entails.
50. Kristeva, *Revolution in Poetic Language,* trans. Leon S. Roudiez (New York:
Columbia University Press, 1984), 57.

voice also de-creates the image-object insofar as it shows it to be dependent upon the poetic voice. Moreover, that voice is not itself a true presence in the poem; it is given together with the poet's absence ("que yo alcanzo razón, y estoy ausente") (I can speak, and I am absent [lost]). It is this absence that in turn leads us to raise questions about the efficacy of words of consolation offered to a dog by a poet who is not himself present in what he speaks. Thus if this sonnet is meant to help relieve the poet's grief by dramatizing the power he has to console the howling dog, and if the sonnet's refined and "rational" speech is meant to emblematize the ways in which the poet has overcome the suffering that afflicts the dog, then the power of poetic enunciation is undermined by the poem's concluding line, in which absence appears to be the very condition of poetic speech.[51]

In the third eclogue and in sonnet 11 (which are closely related), we encounter a complex attempt to work back from the poetic "object" to the fantasy of a natural world in which the instincts were themselves originally poetic in the creative sense. In both poems we see a complex movement that takes us beyond the desire to create an object, and also beyond a mimesis of the process or power by which objects are made, to a moment in which the process of artifactual creation is referred back to nature as the primary locus of all desire (hence also of death). In these poems Garcilaso explores the possibility of a lyric form of self-creation grounded in a movement toward a world whose processes can themselves be read as poetic.

In sonnet 11, Garcilaso conjures up the image of nymphs who inhabit a structure that, like poetry under ideal conditions, is figured as well-formed—as hard, objective, and seemingly real: "contentas habitáis en las moradas / de relucientes piedras fabricadas / y en columnas de vidrio sostenidas" (you live happily in your mansions made of gleaming stones, supported by crystal columns) (lines 2–4). And yet these nymphs are creatures of the water, and so are one with the poet's tears of grief; their brilliant edifice of stone is the purified monument erected on the ground of his grief. In his sympathetic relationship with the nymphs the poet is himself dissolved into water, but whether this is the "object" of the river or his own grief remains undecidable on the basis of anything in

---

51. A striking instance of speech from absence—in this case from the poet's death—is found in eclogue 3, where he says he will sing his beloved's praises, "con la lengua muerta y fría en la boca" (even with my tongue dead and cold in my mouth) (line 11).

the poem: "o no podréis de lástima escucharme, / o convertido en agua aquí llorando / podréis allá despacio consolarme" (either you will be too sorry to listen to me, or else, changed into water by weeping here, you'll have plenty of water to console me down there) (lines 13–14). The nymphs mirror the poet's grief, but that mirror is water, which both is and is not the poet's grief. As these verses suggest, poetic subjectivity in Garcilaso is not the effect of the displacement of the negativity of desire through writing, or even of the creation of a "subject-effect" as the consequence of such displacement, but rather is the result of the dramatic impossibility of objectifying desire.

Along with what I have been calling the "mirror" of water in this poem,[52] Salicio in eclogue 1 is a good example of someone who is deluded by the belief that the image of desire counts as an objectification of it. In his case, the result leads to an identification with the image of his grief, that is, to narcissism:

> No soy, pues, bien mirado,
> tan disforme ni feo,
> que aun agora me veo
> en esta agua que corre clara y pura,
> y cierto no trocara mi figura
> con ese que de mí s'está riendo;
> ¡trocara mi ventura!
>
> (lines 175–81)

(Seen clearly, I am neither misshapen nor ugly, for I see myself now in this water that runs clear and pure, and I certainly would not exchange my looks with him who is laughing at me now; but I would exchange my fortune!)

What takes place in eclogue 3 involves a recognition of the impossibility of objectivizing desire, coupled with a far more subtle deflection of the narcissism that the project of poetic self-creation inevitably raises. What we find in this eclogue is the sublimation of the instincts coupled with a displacement of those sublimated instincts back onto a "nature" that is itself imagined as civilized and refined. The instincts remain

---

52. Compare the "river of tears" that punctuates Salicio's lament in eclogue 1: "Salid sin duelo, lágrimas, corriendo" (flow forth tears, painlessly).

recoverable in the artifacts and activities of culture, which are centrally those of poetic making, of mimesis; but the instincts also remain improved by work. Just like the nymphs of sonnet 11, who are engaged in a subtle and complex form of work in the weaving of tapestries—"tejiendo las telas delicadas, / agora unas con otras apartadas / contándoos los amores y las vidas" (weaving delicate tapestries, gathered in little groups telling each other of your loves and lives)—so too the nymphs of eclogue 3 are involved in a complex and advanced form of artificing. As Rivers showed in his elegant study of the "pastoral paradox" of natural art,[53] everything that happens in the tapestries of this eclogue is allegorical or emblematic of some aspect of literary or rhetorical art: the "convenía" and the "delicado estilo" of stanza 14 are quite literally poetic; the "varia tinta" of stanza 15 suggest the rhetorical colors and adornments; the stories of Filódoce in stanza 16 and of Eurídice in stanza 17 are referred to as "figuradas."[54] Moreover, the materials used in weaving the nymphs' tapestries—the dyes made from the seashells, the golden threads from the Tagus—suggest that the formation of the poetic object is a consolidation or crystallization of work.[55] Unlike in the poetic theory of Philip Sidney, however, where the poet's work is to transform the "brazen world" into the "golden world," Garcilaso sees the natural world as already sublimated by the powers of art: what is conventionally understood as "poetry" is elaborated upon a nature whose constitutive forces and elements (e.g., the "beautiful death" of a shepherdess or the "golden threads" that are used to weave a tapestry) are already poetic.

If Garcilaso can imagine nature as the site of a truly original poetic activity, then one might wonder why the tapestries of the third eclogue do not succeed in creating an object that is immune to the effects of time, desire, death, and decay. Similarly, one might wonder why the poetic speech-act does not succeed in returning the beloved. As noted above, the story of Pygmalion and Galatea forms the background for Salicio's lament in eclogue 1; but Salicio's lament refers explicitly to the

53. Rivers, "The Pastoral Paradox of Natural Art," *MLN* 77 (1962): 130–44; reprinted as "La paradoja pastoril del arte natural" in *La poesía de Garcilaso: Ensayos críticos,* ed. Rivers (Barcelona: Ariel, 1974), 285–308.

54. Compare the use of "figurado" in stanza 18 and the "artificio" of Dinámene in stanza 19. Climene uses "destreza y maña" and refers to the colors as "matizando" in stanza 22.

55. The tapestry of the last nymph, who depicts the tragic love of Nemoroso and Elisa, is described as a form of labor and of work ("la labor de su sotil trabajo," line 195).

failures of poetic figuration when confronted with the fact of a resistant will. Salicio's song is powerful enough to soften stones and to bend trees,[56] but he remains unable to change Galatea's heart:

> Con mi llorar las piedras enternecen
> su natural dureza y la quebrantan;
> los árboles parece que s'inclinan;
> las aves que m'escuchan, cuando cantan,
> con diferente voz se condolecen
> y mi morir cantando m'adevinan
>
> (lines 197–202)

(My tears soften and break the natural hardness of the stones; it seems as if the trees bend over; the birds that hear me show sympathy by a change in their voices when they sing, and in their songs they foretell my death)

> tú sola contra mí t'endureciste
>
> (line 207)

(you alone have hardened your heart against me)

> ¡Oh más dura que mármol a mis quejas
> y al encendido fuego en que me quemo
> más helada que nieve, Galatea!
>
> (lines 57–59)

(Oh, harder than marble against my complaints, and colder than snow against the blazing fire in which I burn, Galatea!)

In eclogue 3, the question of the power of poetic verse is framed in the tapestry of Nemoroso and Elisa, which depicts the "ninfa degollada"; she in turn is compared to "el blanco cisne cuando pierde / la dulce vida

---

56. In the reference to the softening of the stones, Garcilaso recalls Ovid's *Metamorphoses*, 1:400–403. Compare Nemoroso's account of the power of Severo in eclogue 2: "Acuérdaseme bien que en la ribera / de Tormes le hallé solo, cantando / tan dulce que *una piedra enterneciera*" (I remember that I found him alone on the shores of the Tormes, singing so sweetly that a stone would have been softened) (lines 1098–1100; my emphasis).

entre la hierba verde" (the white swan when it loses its life among the green grasses) (lines 231–32). And yet, the dead Elisa's epitaph is inscribed on trees, which, when read, causes them to "speak." As in sonnet 37, this is poetic speech whose very condition of possibility is the speaker's absence ("que yo alcanzo razón, y estoy ausente"). The scriptural signifier here is the source less of a poetic reflexivity than of the fantasy of a poetry that would be powerful enough to be victorious over death. Unlike Nemoroso's transcendental vision at the conclusion of eclogue 1, such a vision is of poetry puissant enough to endow nature itself with the power of speech. These verses dramatize the fantasy of mastery over the creative powers that drive figuration in the first place:

> . . . en la corteza
> de un álamo unas letras escribía
> como epitafio de la ninfa bella,
> que hablaban ansí por parte della:
>   "Elisa soy, en cuyo nombre suena
> y se lamenta el monte cavernoso,
> testigo del dolor y grave pena
> en que por mí se aflige Nemoroso
> y llama 'Elisa'; 'Elisa' a boca llena
> responde el Tajo, y lleva presuroso
> al mar de Lusitania el nombre mío,
> donde será escuchado, y yo lo fío."
> (lines 237–48)

(On the bark of a poplar were written some letters, as an epitaph of the beautiful nymph, which spoke thus on her behalf: "I am Elisa, in whose name the cavernous mountains lament and resound, witness to the pain and deep sorrow with which on my account Nemoroso suffers and calls out 'Elisa'; 'Elisa' responds the full-throated Tagus, and swiftly carries my name to the Lusitanian sea, where it will be heard, I do believe.")

The figure of Elisa's epitaph inscribed on the trees is a compelling and dramatic instance of the prosopopeia that Herrera attributed to the "dulces prendas" in sonnet 10. In both these instances, the power of poetry is located not just in the imitation or figuration of an object, but in the figuration of a power that would be able to animate objects. As such, it provides a way of imagining the instincts not merely as recoverable from objects, but as the source of the power informing them. And yet, as the "tag" line would seem to suggest ("y yo lo fío"), the poet himself must have considerable doubts about the power of his own verse to transmit such creative powers; if not, he would be unlikely to incorporate such an assertion of secular, poetic faith so explicitly into his poem.

Indeed, eclogue 3 is clear that the fantasy of a truly efficacious speech-act is powerless to defeat the image of the shepherdess's death. Why can the power of the poetic speech-act not be truly efficacious, and how does Garcilaso's project of poetic self-creation succeed in spite of this fact? Garcilaso's general debt to Petrarch may provide a point of orientation for answering such a question, but it cannot itself be the response. In eclogue 1, the problem of the limits of the poetic speech-act is resolved in the form of a transcendent pastoral space in which Nemoroso and his beloved Elisa will be reunited.

> busquemos otro llano
> busquemos otros montes y otros ríos,
> otros valles floridos y sombríos
> donde descanse y siempre pueda verte
> ante los ojos míos,
> sin miedo y sobresalto de perderte
> (lines 402–7)

(let us look for another meadow, other mountains and rivers, other valleys full of flowers and shade where I can rest and always see you before my eyes, without the fear and shock of losing you)

But even here the fantasy of the recovery of the beloved through the powers of the poetic imagination is undercut by the ending of the poem, in which the shepherds quietly disappear from view:

> su ganado llevando,
> se fueron recogiendo paso a paso.
> (lines 420–21)

(gathering their flock, they gradually withdrew step by step.)

The unraveling of the poetic fantasy is even more emphatic in eclogue 3, where the attempt to reclaim the beloved has been at once more explicit and direct (in the mimesis of the absent Elisa's voice, as contained in her epitaph), and subject to a more complex series of mediations (in the displacement of the poet's desires onto the shepherds, the nymphs, and their tapestries). The poem concludes with what Freud described as the counterpart to the "normal" trajectory of desire that seeks satisfaction; namely, the turning of a failed or frustrated desire destructively back upon itself.[57] The poem ends with the deconstruction of the fictional scene, as the shepherds depart and the nymphs disappear beneath the waves:

> Esto cantó Tireno, y esto Alcino
> le respondió, y habiendo ya acabado
> el dulce son, siguiendo su camino
> con paso un poco más apresurado;
> siendo a las ninfas ya el rumor vecino,
> juntas s'arrojan por el agua a nado,
> y de la blanca espuma que movieron
> las cristalinas ondas se cubrieron.
>
> (lines 369–76)

(This is what Tirreno sang, and this Alcino answered, and having finished their sweet song, they went on their way with a slightly swifter step; when their sound almost reached the nymphs, the latter plunged themselves in the water to swim, and the crystalline waves were covered up with the white foam they made.)

In Garcilaso, the impossibility of crystallizing desire in the form of a durable object serves to provide a set of terms against which claims for the power of poetic discourse can be tested and proved, and it is this testing and proving that establish the conditions of possibility for the success and failure of the poet's project of self-creation. Garcilaso is indeed skeptical about claims for a speech-act that would result in the

---

57. In "Instincts and their Vicissitudes" this leads Freud to postulate the proximity of love and hate. Elsewhere, Freud speculates that something within the sexual instincts themselves may impede their full satisfaction. See "The Most Prevalent Form of Degradation in Erotic Life," in *Standard Edition of the Complete Psychological Works of Sigmund Freud* (London: Hogarth Press, 1953–64), 11:188–89.

supreme fiction of the satisfaction of desire in the lyric. But this skepticism in turn endows his own poetic self-creation with a compelling rhetorical force.[58] Perhaps even more emphatically than in Petrarch, the success of this rhetoric depends upon a beloved who escapes the poet's and his surrogates' powers; it relies upon the dramatization of a prosopopeia that fails to animate its object. It is precisely this failure that opens a space in which the more daring project of lyric self-creation as a form of objectless enunciation can be put forth; it is here that the modernity of Garcilaso's effort is unmistakably marked. As we have already seen in our discussion of the mechanisms of social control in Counter-Reformation Spain and of the development of the discourse of "taste" (*gusto*) in Gracián, the availability of something like the inward voice of the lyric, minus Garcilaso's deep doubts about its ultimate efficacy, proved to be essential for the social construction of the subject-self in early modern Spain.

58. None of the commentators makes any reference to the phrase "y yo lo fío" (eclogue 3, line 248), which seems the most obvious (and, for that reason, the least convincing) of the instances in which Garcilaso asserts the success of his project by having one of his poetic "voices" simply claim it. This would be one instance in which the rhetorical compulsion of the poems fails to conceal itself adequately in the play of speech-acts.

10

Reason and Romance

At various points in the preceding chapters I have suggested that some of the most important literature of the Spanish Golden Age can be interpreted against the backdrop of a process of historical change, in which a highly stratified and hierarchical social structure was weakened, contested, and displaced by one where identifications and evaluations were no longer made according to the principles of lineage and caste, but rather were shaped according to what would eventually be called the values of social class. At the same, we have seen a series of resistances to this shift, as dramatists like Lope de Vega, Guillén de Castro, and Calderón de la Barca attempted to marshal the energies of the theater for the *asujétissement* of subjects within the absolutist state. We have also seen how, when faced with the *comedia*'s response to modernizing social change, Cervantes sought to subvert its values by dislocating the principles of identity and desire so essential to the project of subject-formation in the old social order. In *Don Quijote,* the conflict between two historically distinct social regimes is interlaced with a more general critique of culture's encounter with the past; here, literature plays a crucial role in de-sedimenting those conflicts and in dislocating the subject from the social and political structures that would bind it in advance.

In the process of this complex negotiation between present and past, Cervantes suggests that the verse of Garcilaso de la Vega may occupy a position analogous to (and perhaps even more forceful than) that of the romances of chivalry. The parallelism between romance and lyric is not altogether surprising. Since lyric and romance both depend upon a psychology of affective identification, and since Cervantes is both attracted to and wary of all such mechanisms, he takes great pains not just to criticize the lyric and the romance in terms of the criteria that Aristotelian poetics and rhetorical theory provide (e.g., plausibility or "verisimilitude"), or to regard the power of the marvelous as obsolete, but to resituate the marvelous and the closely related question of literary belief within the framework of the social, where it can be rhetorically understood. As we shall see in this final chapter, the *Persiles* continues to explore the questions, already broached in *Don Quijote,* of whether and how one can articulate a stance that would bind the members of society *überhaupt.* Central to Cervantes's attempt in the *Persiles* to establish the symbolic basis for a new moral discourse is the reinstatement of romance within a world otherwise subject to historical change. As we shall see, it is not only the Greek or Byzantine model that is central to this effort, but the attempt to adapt the response of wonder associated with the ancient romance to new social conditions and, in the wondrous moment, to recover the moral function of the truly efficacious sign.

To be sure, Cervantes's attempt to rewrite romance in the *Persiles* must be considered in light of his ambivalent dealings with the plot structures and identificatory mechanisms of romance in *Don Quijote.* Consider the Captive's tale in *Don Quijote,* Part 1, which offers a good example of Cervantes's critique of the psychology of identification that underwrites romance. I shall return to this episode below, but even at a glance it can be seen that the story of the Captive denies the reader the pleasure of finding the identificatory expectations of romance fulfilled. On the surface, the story of the Captive's escape from Algiers with Zoraida appears to be a prototypical romance, with the Captive's escape and Zoraida's return with him to the land of the "true (Christian) faith" serving as strong, identity-conferring developments at the level of plot. And yet on closer inspection it can be seen that the romance ending cannot be achieved without incurring substantial losses. Unlike the figure of Ana Félix of *Don Quijote,* Part 2, who is reconciled with her father as he returns from exile to Spain, Zoraida's return to Spain occurs at the expense of her father, whom she is forced to abandon. And rather than re-assume an identity that was hers "originally," from birth, Zoraida's passage to Spain allows her to assume an identity that came to her in the form of a substitute or second nature, since Christianity was not by birthright her faith, but an acquired set of beliefs. In this and other ways, the story of the Captive and Zoraida represents the triumph of culture over nature; so too it is the story of the loss of nature (and of the father) and their substitution by a series of culturally conditioned beliefs that are communicated and, in this case, rendered contingent, during the course of the romance.

In the *Persiles,* however, Cervantes goes substantially beyond the critique and subversion of romance to what he regards as a still more progressive position that once again incorporates romance. (His development in this respect is not unlike Shakespeare's passage from tragedy to romance.) Specifically, the *Persiles* adapts the form of romance to goals that are still more progressive than those that the *Quijote* had outlined. Some of the recent *Persiles* scholarship has begun to bear this out. In *Allegories of Love,* for instance, Diana Wilson has shown how Cervantes wishes to leave behind "barbaric" conceptions of love and human relationship in order to shape a more integrative social space that can only be regarded as progressive with respect to the old régime.[1] She argues that in the *Persiles* Cervantes undertakes a new kind of generic thinking, and also a new kind of thinking about gender that favors the androgyne and that allows for the tempering of the idealism of Quixotic desire by bodying forth the image of woman as a term of difference, rather than as a simple antithesis to the masculine imaginary. If this is indeed the case, then it will be no surprise to see that the *Persiles* also represents a literary thinking that adapts romance to ends that complement, rather than contravene, the novelistic purposes of the *Quijote.*

---

1. Diana Wilson, *Allegories of Love: Cervantes's "Persiles and Sigismunda"* (Princeton: Princeton University Press, 1991).

Here, I would suggest that Cervantes's turn to romance can be understood as his further way of dealing with problems that he thought a genre like the *comedia* systematically failed to confront. One of these is the problem that Max Weber described as the "disenchantment" of the world, which involves the loss of faith in magical powers and auratic presences. Since a loss of an underlying faith in the essential, sustaining goodness of nature was no doubt part of the process of "disenchantment," it is no surprise to find that in returning to romance Cervantes also turns to the problem of morality. In addition, Cervantes's confrontation with the problem that Weber later describes in terms of "disenchantment" may also be taken to explain why Cervantes turns so often (e.g., in the Maese Pedro episode in *Don Quijote,* or in *El retablo de las maravillas*) to criticize theater's quasi-magical effects. He sees theater as a potentially dangerous "substitute" for nature, as a form of representation that rushes in to fill the gaps created by the gradual disenchantment of the world with an affectively grounded and politically powerful force. If Cervantes's task in the *Quijote* is to expose the fact that the world is indeed disenchanted, and to call into question all false and illegitimate uses of the marvelous (a fact that is confirmed in, among many other places, the critique in the *escrutinio de los libros* of the intervention of "Sabia Felicia" in Jorge de Montemayor's *Diana* in Part 1,[2] and in the staged or rigged quality of the "fantastic" episodes of Part 2), then in the *Persiles* he takes it as his task to explore what it might mean to "re-enchant" the world, all the while recognizing that the prospect for a return to nature in its original, enchanted state is an illusory dream.

* * *

To focus this discussion, I begin with a passage on the problem of disenchantment that occurs near the conclusion of Marx's 1857 "Introduction to a Critique of Political Economy," where Marx questions the

2. Speaking of books of "poesía" as opposed to books of "caballería," the Cura says "comenzamos por *La Diana,* de Montemayor, soy de parecer que no se queme, sino que se le quite todo aquello que trata de la Sabia Felicia y de la agua encantada." *El Ingenioso hidalgo Don Quijote de la Mancha,* ed. Luis Murillo (Madrid: Castalia, 1986), Part 1, chap. 6, p. 118. The philosophical foundations of the rejection of the deus ex machina solution can be found in Alonso López Pinciano's *Philosophía antigua poética* (Madrid: Biblioteca de Antiguos Libros Hispánicos, 1953), 2:87–88. On Cervantes's interest in the critique and legitimation of the marvelous in romance, see Alban Forcione, *Cervantes, Aristotle, and the "Persiles"* (Princeton: Princeton University Press, 1970).

relationship of Greek art to modern times in terms of the transformation of myth:

> Is the view of nature and of social relations on which the Greek imagination and hence Greek [mythology] is based possible with self-acting mule spindles and railways with locomotives and electrical telegraphs? What chance has Vulcan against Roberts & Co., Jupiter against the lightning-rod and Hermes against the Crédit Mobilier? All mythology overcomes and dominates and shapes the forces of nature in the imagination and by the imagination; it therefore vanishes with the advent of real mastery over them. What becomes of Fama alongside Printing House Square? . . . Is Achilles possible with powder and lead? Or the *Iliad* with the printing press, not to mention the printing machine? Do not the song and the saga and the muse necessarily come to an end with the printer's bar, hence do not the necessary conditions of epic poetry vanish?[3]

In this passage and in the discussion surrounding it, Marx encounters not just the phenomenon of the loss of myth, but the more interesting problem of the impossibility of its full erasure. The evidence for this, as Marx goes on to say, lies in the idealizations we continue to make. As Marx explains, the problem posed by Greek art in relation to modern times is not just that the conditions necessary for its production have been transformed or eclipsed, or that the power of myth has been displaced by the forms of what Walter Benjamin would later call "mechanical reproduction" in art. Marx's greater concern is that we continue to derive pleasure from Greek art, and moreover that we tend to elevate and idealize it as representative of artistic value *tout court:* "The difficulty we are confronted with is not," Marx says, "that of understanding how Greek art and epic poetry are associated with certain forms of social development"; those questions could be answered, we might suppose, through an analysis of the conditions of social and material production of precisely the sort that the "Introduction" seeks to analyze. "The greater difficulty," Marx goes on to say, "is that they still give us aesthetic pleasure and are in certain respects regarded as a

---

3. Marx, *Grundrisse: Foundations of the Critique of Political Economy,* trans. Martin Nicolaus (Harmondsworth: Penguin, 1973), 110–11.

standard and unattainable ideal." The problem is not just that the weight of the past remains inescapable, but that we take it as the basis of our idealizations.

Recent work in literary history and theory has gone a considerable distance in helping us to answer Marx's question, but in the process has modified his claims in ways more sensitive both to the authority of the past and to the desires of those who come later to admire and compete with it. Thinking of Cervantes's case, one need only mention how recent investigations of the humanist reappropriation of the "classics" during the Renaissance have shown how questions about what it meant to be "historical" and what it meant to be "modern" open up possibilities of reading in which the status of the model or "master" text is dependent not upon any of its intrinsic features but rather upon the desire of those who follow "after the fact"—including the desire to compensate for their own belatedness by defending against the past. Scholarship has continued to recognize that the process of cultural transformation in the Renaissance (pre)figures the dynamics of modern literary history, which inaugurates an impossible desire to compete with the most exemplary models of the past.[4] Here, the way was prepared by works like Edgar Wind's *Pagan Mysteries of the Renaissance* and Jean Seznec's *La Survivance des dieux antiques,* though not with the revisionist perspective of contemporary criticism. In Seznec's view, the Renaissance reinterpretation of pagan myth represents the restoration and recovery of the substance and meaning of myth, which had been displaced from its antique form: "Not for a moment is there any question of 'resurrection,' " Seznec writes; this is because "Hercules had never died, any more than Mars or Perseus. As concepts and as names, at least, they had survived tenaciously in the memory of man. It was their appearance alone which had vanished, Perseus living on in his Turkish disguise and Mars as a knight of chivalry. . . . In spite of long periods of eclipse, [the classical form of myth] survived during the Middle Ages—as a memory maintained and revived at certain privileged epochs."[5]

4. For Harold Bloom, this begins in English literature with Milton. However, more recent work has seen a not unrelated dynamic in the history of Petrarchism. See Margaret W. Ferguson, *Trials of Desire: Renaissance Defenses of Poetry* (New Haven: Yale University Press, 1983), and Roland Greene, *Post-Petrarchism* (Princeton University Press, 1991).

5. Seznec, *The Survival of the Pagan Gods,* trans. Barbara F. Sessions (1940; repr., Princeton: Princeton University Press, 1972), 211.

To establish a given body of works (e.g., "Greek art") as representing a transhistorical ideal relies on a belief in the existence of an abstract and autonomous category of value, one very closely aligned with the notion of value as such. To view works of art as detached from the historical and social conditions surrounding their production is to view art as what Marx calls a "simple abstraction."[6] Abstractions have a certain validity whose importance in helping us conceptualize and categorize the world cannot be denied. But the nature of an abstraction is such that it contradicts or denies the historical reality of that which it categorizes or represents. Thus the true historical difference between "ancient" and "modern" art according to Marx is lost as a result of our attempts to regard ancient art as exemplary in any strong evaluative or moral sense; rather, its importance is to be found in the fact that ancient art is, by virtue of its natural or unmediated incorporation into the social and material circumstances surrounding its production, a pre-aesthetic or "unintentionally artistic" phenomenon: "Greek art presupposes Greek mythology, in other words that natural and social phenomena are already assimilated in an *unintentionally artistic manner* by the imagination of the people" (*Grundrisse,* 110). But it is precisely this fact that will remain invisible to us as long as we continue to assimilate ancient tragedy and epic to the categories of "art," "aesthetics," or "literature" as we know them in the modern world. "Modern" art—by which Marx means the autonomous art of the "disenchanted" world—presupposes its independence from other social processes, and this can only be achieved within the context of social rationalization. And yet, as the carrying-forward of the marvelous in literary romance suggests, that process of rationalization was never complete, and the "legitimate" use of the marvelous in romance places wonder in the service of aims that are not strictly literary, but political and moral as well.[7]

Whereas Marx understood the process of rationalization as occurring primarily at the level of productive forces, I argue that it takes place across a variety of cultural and discursive spheres and that it remained decisively incomplete. (It is the incompleteness of the process of rational-

6. Marx's discussion of the concept of abstraction can be found in the introduction to the *Gundrisse* (1857–58).

7. The problem of legitimizing the marvelous is, at the same time, the problem of legitimizing fiction. Among the many useful studies of this topic in the Renaissance, William Nelson's *Fact or Fiction: The Dilemma of the Renaissance Storyteller* (Cambridge: Harvard University Press, 1973), provides a brief but cogent account.

ization that enabled the past to continue to exert a pressure upon the present age, and that likewise makes the notion of a radical modernity, wholly discontinuous with the past, something of a self-serving myth.) A justification and a program for "rationalization" are visible in the philosophical work of writers like Bacon, Descartes, and Hobbes, who seek to redefine the world in accordance with the powers of reason. Their notion of "reason" serves to reinforce the subject's powers of intellectual autonomy and control by drastically eliminating the conditions for astonishment or surprise necessary for the wonder of romance: "Because the principal cause of fear is surprise," writes Descartes, "there is no better way to avoid it than to exercise forethought and prepare oneself for any eventuality, anxiety about which may cause it."[8] Descartes seeks to domesticate wonder by removing wonder from the natural world: "we wonder only at what appears to us as unusual and extraordinary; and something can appear so only because we have been ignorant of it, or perhaps because it differs from things we have known (this difference being what makes us call it 'extraordinary'). . . . The other passions may serve to make us take note of things which appear good or evil, but we feel only wonder at things which merely appear unusual. So we see that people who are not naturally inclined to wonder are usually very ignorant" (*Passions of the Soul*, 354–55). But I suggest also that the "rationalization" process is visible in the regularization of the category of the literary romance, one of the purposes of which was to sanction and preserve a legitimate and exemplary use of the marvelous within the modern, "disenchanted" world. Moreover, if we commonly conceive of the process of cultural rationalization as a necessary condition of modernization, then I would also propose a revision of the modernization paradigm itself, which would enable us to "read back" into romance, epic, and indeed myth itself a tendency toward rationalization that is more archaic than any so far described. For, as Marx says, myth itself "subdues, controls and fashions" the forces of nature through the imagination.[9]

---

8. *The Passions of the Soul,* in *The Philosophical Writings,* trans. John Cottingham, Robert Stoothoff, and Dugald Murdoch (Cambridge: Cambridge University Press, 1985), 1:392.

9. Marx's thesis had a powerful effect on Horkheimer and Adorno in *Dialectic of Enlightenment;* see especially the treatment of myth in the essay "The Concept of Enlightenment" in *Dialectic of Enlightenment,* trans. John Cumming (New York: Continuum, 1972), 3–42.

My attempt to situate Cervantes's *Persiles* and certain of the *Novelas ejemplares* with respect to a local and historically specific cultural model of the global paradigm of modernization that would be valid for seventeenth-century Spain leads to two interrelated claims. The first is that the rise and regularization of the category of romance in contrast to the emergent (and largely untheorized) category of "novel" parallels a distinction between the moral and the ethical orders of discourse. The division between the moral and the ethical is visible in the establishment of the (ethical) categories of right and wrong, grounded in human freedom, as distinct from but not necessarily opposed to the values of absolute good and evil. The point to be made about the rationalized world is not so much that its moral order has collapsed, or that moral discourse was definitively displaced by ethical rationalism, but rather that as measures of human action these categories came to be set apart. The second claim is that the *Persiles* represents not a reactionary or conservative effort, as many earlier critics have taken it to be, but a vanguard attempt that rejects the return to the old moral order that others in early modern Spain (especially as represented in the *comedia*) were interested in sustaining. Indeed, the shape of the *comedia* as a genre is explicitly seen as insufficient to define the action of the *Persiles*. Consider as but one example of this the fact that as their journey proceeds through Spain Periandro and Auristela meet a poet who wants to find the appropriate backdrop for a play about their trials and tribulations, "por venirle a la imaginación un grandísimo deseo de componer de todos ellos una comedia; pero no acertaba en qué nombre le pondría: si le llamaría comedia, o tragedia, o tragicomedia" (because there entered his mind the great desire to write a play about all of them; but he could not hit upon the appropriate name to give it: whether to call it a comedy, or tragedy, or tragicomedy).[10] In the *Persiles*, Cervantes is searching for a genre appropriate to his boldly progressive attempt to speak in a new moral voice, the possibility of which he attempts to locate in the model of the Greek romance.

※　※　※

10. I cite the *Persiles* according to Cervantes, *Obras completas*, vol. 2, ed. Angel Valbuena Prat (Madrid: Aguilar, 1970), here book 3, chap. 2, p. 1894b. Further references will be incorporated into the text. Translations draw directly on the work of Celia Weller and Clark Colahan, trans., *The Trials of Persiles and Sigismunda: A Northern Story* (Berkeley and Los Angeles: University of California Press, 1989).

I want to proceed by recalling some of Américo Castro's pronouncements about the *Persiles,* all of which seem to terminate in some form
of self-contradiction, and all of which conclude by disparaging the work
that Cervantes considered to be his masterpiece, which is seen to fail in
comparison with the novelistic discourse of *Don Quijote.*[11] In an essay
first published in 1948, for instance, Castro advanced the view that
Cervantes's later writing is overwhelmingly determined by Cervantes's
return to a conservative social and aesthetic stance after the ambitiously
modern, critically "experimental" writing of *Don Quijote,* and especially of *Don Quijote,* Part 1. Following this argument, the popular
success of *Don Quijote* in 1605, reinforced by its cordial reception
among church and state officials, bears directly on both the moral and
political character of Cervantes's next published works. Cervantes's
later works are in this light seen to represent the experience of one who
had come to feel himself a member of the privileged "inner circles" of
social and political power: "Cervantes, después de fracasar una y otra
vez en su aspiración a ser persona importante y de primera linea, da
ahora otro paso al frente y se arroja a proponer dechados de ejemplaridad a los más altos entre sus compatriotas. . . . El escritor, al fin
glorioso, se sentía dentro, no fuera, del círculo moral de los más altos y
significativos personajes en la España de entonces" (After failing more
than once to fulfill his aspiration to be a person of importance and of
the first rank, Cervantes now takes another step towards the front and
begins to issue standards of exemplarity to the highest among his
compatriots. . . . The writer, at long last glorious, sees himself within,
and no longer outside the moral circle of the highest and most important
figures of Spain at the time).[12] The literary ambition surrounding the
Persiles announced in the preface to the *Novelas ejemplares* (the boast
of a "libro que se atreve a competir con Heliodoro" [a book that dares
to compete with Heliodorus]) and Cervantes's description of it in the
Viaje del Parnaso (Part 4) as "el gran *Persiles*" (the great *Persiles*) must
on this view be of a piece with Cervantes's new social alignments, for
as Castro claims, not implausibly, the aspiration to moral authority and

    11. For a more detailed discussion of the material contained in the next paragraphs,
see A. J. Cascardi, "Cervantes's Exemplary Subjects," in *Cervantes's "Exemplary Novels" and the Adventure of Writing,* ed. Michael Nerlich and Nicholas Spadaccini,
Hispanic Issues 6 (Minneapolis: Prisma Institute, 1989), 49–71.
    12. Castro, "La ejemplaridad de las *Novelas ejemplares,*" in *Hacia Cervantes* (Ma-
drid: Taurus, 1967), 462, 466.

literary prestige presupposes the ability to speak in a universal voice, to legislate for and command the respect of all: "Moralizar desde arriba requiere contar con alguien que considere respetable al moralista y sentirse importante en algún modo dentro del escenario social" (to moralize from on high requires that one count on someone who considers the moralist respectable and on feeling oneself important in some way within the social scene).[13]

And yet the success reflected in Cervantes's later works is not without serious drawbacks for what Castro and others have regarded as most valuable in Cervantes's writing. If the literary ambition evidenced in the *Persiles* was to go to illustrate a series of moral truths whose veracity could be presented as universally valid, and as knowable in advance, then the ethical purpose disclosed in the subjective irony and existential experimentalism of *Don Quijote* (and especially in Part 1) would have to be retracted. In contrast to the *Persiles,* the achievement of the *Quijote* was to call into question a series of traditional beliefs about human purposes, values, and ends in favor of an ethical view of life in which the purpose of existence could not be ascertained in advance of its "novelistic" elaboration. Our position as agents of value in the world is in novelistic terms derived from the fact that any "world," any framework of values, must be regarded as socially, historically, and perhaps most important of all *narratively* conditioned and produced, rather than taken as given a priori and in advance. The problematization of authority and of point of view in the *Quijote* may be taken as the formal signs, the generic markers, of this conditioning and production. Seen in this light, the *Persiles* might indeed seem to represent a rejection of Cervantes's progressive ethical stance in favor of a view of life in which the subject faces the anxieties of existence only to be resituated within a reassuring framework of fixed essences, social hierarchies, and universal moral truths. Like the characters of Cervantes's "idealistic" exemplary novels, Persiles and Sigismunda are seen to gain their moral victories at the expense of subjective selfhood. They do not, on Castro's account, "create themselves," for they are not in possession of "selves" to create; each of them follows a preordained course, which in their paradigmatic case leads through a voyage of chaste love to marriage in the Eternal City.[14] "El escritor rebelde se hace, en cierto modo, un

13. "La ejemplaridad," 466.
14. "No se hacen a sí mismos, no poseen un *sí mismo,* van adonde 'les han dicho' que

mesurado conservador" ("La ejemplaridad," 466) (The rebellious writer becomes, in a certain way, a restrained conservative).

Castro's position reflects a series of apparent discrepancies within Cervantes's writing that others have attempted to resolve by recourse to the hypothesis of "two Cervantes" or by the thesis of a progression with Cervantes's work from novel to romance.[15] For instance, Marthe Robert claims that the *Persiles* is Cervantes's return to chivalric romance: "After symbolically burning the chivalric romances he struggled to renounce, Cervantes began again and died writing a last chivalric work."[16] And yet this argument raises a number of questions that cannot so easily be resolved: given the critique of romance articulated in the *Quijote*, what can explain Cervantes's attempt to recuperate the romance as modeled in Heliodorus's Byzantine work? And given the constitution of the (novelistic) subject in terms of the ethics of autonomy and freedom, what can explain the additional need to define the self as *subject to* the authoritative commands of a universal moral discourse? This point is particularly important in Cervantes's case; it was just such a process of subjection, so often modeled in the *comedia*'s adherence to an archaic or absolutist law, that he so often sought to resist. If we assume with Castro and those who most closely follow him, including Gilman,[17] that the principal achievement of the novel lies in the development, through narrative, of an ethics of subjective freedom, then what can explain the subject's will to be positioned as *subject to* universal moral demands?

Castro's attempt to locate the origins of a novelistic ethos in *Don Quijote* was part of his larger effort to reverse the claims made in *El pensamiento de Cervantes,* where Cervantes was characterized as an artist whose love for universal harmonies and whose aspiration to "good form" were the reflections of a presiding faith in human rationality: "Cervantes pugna por descubrir el módulo que rija la vida de los seres desde fuera a dentro, a manera de ley o norma . . . ; salirse de la norma, errar en la conducta o en el pensar son resultados de no

---

tienen que ir, a que los casen en Roma, y sean buenos y santos padres de familia" ("La ejemplaridad," 471).

15. See, for example, Cesare de Lollis, *Cervantes Reazionario* (Roma: Fratelli Treves, 1924), and Ruth El Saffar, *Novel to Romance* (Baltimore: Johns Hopkins University Press, 1974).

16. Marthe Robert, *The Old and the New: From Don Quijote to Kafka,* trans. Carol Cosman (Berkeley and Los Angeles: University of California Press, 1977), 3.

17. See Gilman's *The Novel According to Cervantes* (Berkeley and Los Angeles: University of California Press, 1989).

comprender, de no colocarse en la inclinación necesaria para que el destello de lo real llegue debidamente a nuestra retina. En el fondo, Cervantes está impregnado del amor a lo razonable" (Cervantes battles to discover the measure that rules the life of human beings from outside inward, as a law or norm; . . . to depart from the norm, to err in conduct or thought are the result of not thinking, of not inclining oneself as one ought in order for the sparkle of the real to reach our retina. At bottom, Cervantes is steeped in a love for what is reasonable) (43). Rejecting the assumptions of his earlier work, Castro came to valorize the ethical perspectivism of *Don Quijote* at the expense of the moral vision of the *Persiles* and the romance-like *Novelas*.

In contrast to Castro, however, who sees Cervantes's later attempt to speak from a moral point of view as a renunciation of the ethical stance adopted in *Don Quijote,* and therefore as reflecting a social and political conservatism, I propose that the impulse to transcend the ethics of subjective freedom is aligned to an ambitiously *progressive* attempt on Cervantes's part, not inconsistent with the literary objectives of the *Persiles* and certain of the *Novelas ejemplares,* as forms of romance, to project the self as the ideal or exemplary subject of universal moral commands. Nicholas Spadaccini and Jenaro Talens write for instance that "if *Don Quijote* represents the exploration of [human] experience in its concrete nature and in certain sociohistorical parameters, *Persiles* would be its abstraction beyond all conditioning, transforming that experience into a purely symbolic dimension. *Persiles* thus begins where *Don Quijote* leaves off, and is its culmination."[18] In the course of this project, Cervantes rejects conservative efforts to situate the self in relation to the dominant social order through an idealist reshaping of the past or through the resurrection of an archaic symbolic law, as the demands of honor require, or in the enforcement of the power of the absolutist state. And whereas some have interpreted the discrepancies

18. *Through the Shattering Glass: Cervantes and the Self-Made World* (Minneapolis: University of Minnesota Press, 1993), 164. They go on to say that "within this interpretive scheme, however ambitious *Persiles* may have been, a universalizing intention supposedly led it toward an abstraction of all narrative elements. The characters are all destined to be one-dimensional and artificial, transparent symbols of universal validity. Persiles and Sigismunda would stand as the perfect Christian lovers, Rosamunda would represent lasciviousness, and Clotaldo slander. The completeness of the *Persiles* as a novel was sacrificed to ideological expression. This interpretation undoubtedly leads toward the finding in *Persiles* of the most radical manifestation of the spirit of the Counter-Reformation" (164).

between *Don Quijote* and the *Persiles* as the sign of a contradiction somehow to be resolved, I suggest that the apparent generic tension within Cervantes's writing, like the distinctions between the ethical and the moral orders of discourse, are reflections of a division that is itself embedded within the novel and that may be identified as internal to the formation of the modern subject itself. On the one hand, the subject wishes to be ethically free, but on the other hand it wishes to be bound by a universal moral law.[19]

This more complex understanding of the relationship between the ethical and the moral may provide the basis for questioning the idea of a categorical distinction between "novel" and "romance": on the one hand, the subject attempts to secure for itself the grounds of ethical freedom consistent with the (novelistic) representation of the world as objective, rational, and real; on the other, the subject seeks to transcend mere representations in the (romance-like) projection of a reconciled totality, a universal, moral community of mankind, whose claims can be secured beyond purely "subjective" grounds.[20] As exemplified by *Don Quijote*, the novel embodies the paradox of rationalization outlined by both Weber and Marx; namely, that while reality is rendered ever more "rational," values are displaced to an ever more distant and abstract realm. While a rationalized world may in principle be more accessible to domination and control, the subject finds it increasingly difficult to assume a posture of conviction or otherwise to relate beliefs and values to the world. As we can see in the figure of Don Quijote, the archaic heroic ethos, as reflected in a belief in an act's intrinsic and self-justifying worth, is transformed into a species of quixotism, or is forced to yield to the idealizing pressures of romance in its "bad" (abstract) form, which is lacking in verisimilitude and which Cervantes must accordingly seek to "purify."

At the same time, Cervantes allows us to see that what Weber meant by the "disenchantment" of the world takes the form of an erasure of authentic wonder. This is especially true of the aesthetic effects produced

19. This paradox is the cornerstone of Kant's moral philosophy, in which only an *absolutely* free will can also be morally bound.

20. In contrast to Avalle-Arce, who sees the *Persiles* as an instance of the "architradicional presupuesto metafísico de la cadena y escala ontológicas" (arch-traditional metaphysical assumption of the ladder and chain of being), I would caution that the unity conveyed by the "great chain of being" cannot be taken for granted in the *Persiles*, which confronts transgression in as direct a form as cannibalism; on the contrary, it must be *produced*.

in *Don Quijote,* Part 2, in which Cervantes thinks through the proper use and the limits of wonder. In addition to the episode at Camacho's wedding (Part 2, chap. 21) when Basilio appears to be revived from death, consider the episodes of the *mono adivino* and the *cabeza encantada,* where Cervantes demonstrates the pointlessness of attributing supernatural powers to the things of nature. The process of disenchantment is necessary if the "natural fallacy" that attributes an inherent goodness and power to things of nature is in turn to be laid to rest. And yet the desire for belief in such a nature and in such supernatural powers remains in place all the same, just as the desire for romance and for *admiratio* remain intact. Indeed, if this were not the case there would be no possibility of transferring that desire to Basilio's "audience," who believes him, just as there would be no possibility of Don Quijote's believing in the staged fiction of Maese Pedro's puppet show. The same holds true for the appearance of Merlín at the ducal castle. Part of the rationalizing "disenchantment" of the world is the process whereby the belief in magical causes disappears and is replaced by an "enlightened" understanding of cause and effect. Still, there is a place for Merlín in this world, within the artificially staged (i.e., fictional) reality of the ducal castle, where it is dependent on an audience's willingness to believe what he says. Merlín says that Sancho must administer himself three thousand lashes if Dulcinea is to be disenchanted, but what matters is not whether Merlín's pronouncement can in fact be verified, or whether there is any connection between the three thousand lashes and the "disenchantment" of Dulcinea, but whether Sancho can be convinced to comply with Merlín's command.

In a very suggestive interpretation of the aesthetic response of *admiratio* as it enters into these and other incidents in the *Quijote,* George Mariscal has suggested that wonder at the marvelous must be understood not only in contrast to the credibility or rationality of the real (*lo verosímil*), but also in relation to laughter, which corresponds to neither term. Laughter, which is one response to the marvelous in *Don Quijote,* and which does not fit easily into either category, is the intermediate and indeterminate effect that is produced when the effect of wonder fails to hit the mark, or perhaps more accurately in the case of *Don Quijote,* when the desire for wonder persists in the face of the knowledge that it can no longer be the effect of an original encounter with nature. Tempered by laughter, wonder is a fully socialized response that stands in place of the awe and respect that might have been felt in the experience of knowing something wholly new and different.[21] Perhaps not knowing whether the *Quijote* is indeed a romance (or a novel, or just what British Hispanists would drily call a "funny book"),[22] the narrator says that Don Quijote's deeds should be met *either* with laughter or wonder: "Los sucesos de Don Quijote, o se han de celebrar con admiración, o con risa" (Don Quijote's adventures must be honored with wonder or with laughter) (Part 2, chap. 44, p. 368).[23]

But, as Mariscal suggests, wonder may also have had a role in the creation of a new class of subjects in seventeenth-century Spain, for certain groups were positioned in such a way as to be able to register its effects. "It is an improper (that is, ethically empty) or artistically ineffective use of spectacle that produces nothing more than laughter—as Altisidora's 'funeral' provokes Don Quijote's mirth. This idea also begins to explain the almost (?) total lack of humor in an otherwise surprise- and wonder-filled text such as *Persiles y Sigismunda*."[24] While Cervantes may have used laughter in the creation of the modern, novelistic subject, completion of the process of subject-formation would

21. Compare Kant, who says that "we do not, and cannot, find in ourselves the slightest effect on the feeling of pleasure from the coincidence of perceptions with the laws in accordance with the universal concepts of nature (the Categories), since in their case understanding necessarily follows the bent of its own nature without ulterior aim. But, while this is so, the discovery, on the other hand, that two or more empirical heterogeneous laws of nature are allied under one principle that embraces them both, is the ground of a very appreciable pleasure, often even of admiration, and such, too, as does not wear off even though we are already familiar enough with its object. It is true that we no longer notice any decided pleasure in the comprehensibility of nature, or in the unity of its divisions into genera and species, without which the empirical concepts, that afford us our knowledge of nature in its particular laws, would not be possible. Still it is certain that the pleasure appeared in due course, and only by reason of the most ordinary experience being impossible without it, has it become gradually fused with simple cognition, and no longer arrests particular attention. Something, then, that makes us attentive in our estimate of nature to its finality for our understanding . . . is required, in order that, on meeting with success, pleasure may be felt in this their accord with our cognitive faculty." *Critique of Judgment,* trans. James Creed Meredith (Oxford: Clarendon Press, 1952), 27–28.

22. See Peter Russell, "*Don Quijote* as a Funny Book," *Modern Language Review* 64 (1969): 312–26. See also Daniel Eisenberg, "Teaching *Don Quijote* as a Funny Book," in *Approaches to Teaching Cervantes' "Don Quijote,"* ed. Richard Bjornson (New York: Modern Language Association, 1984), 62–68.

23. I owe this reference to George Mariscal, *Contradictory Subjects: Quevedo, Cervantes, and Seventeenth-Century Spanish Culture* (Ithaca: Cornell University Press, 1991), 195.

24. George Mariscal, *Contradictory Subjects,* 196. Mariscal's critique of the British interpretation of the *Quijote* as principally a "funny book" (195–96) is especially apt.

require a realignment of the effects of wonder with the goals of moral suasion. No doubt, Cervantes seems to see (e.g., in relation to the episodes that occur with the Duke and the Duchess) that what Mariscal calls "aristocratic arrogance" and the lack of "refinement" of the lower classes precluded such a possibility: If "aristocratic arrogance precluded the proper use of *admiratio* and the lack of refinement attributed to the subordinate classes led only to stupefied astonishment, then the morally salutary effects of wonder were available primarily to an educated elite located somewhere in the middle of the social field. The subject positions of such groups were not necessarily fixed by the category of blood or determined by strictly economic factors. . . . Wonder was the first and most important step in the ethical refashioning and repositioning of this peculiarly modern individual" (*Contradictory Subjects*, 196–97).

*   *   *

Within the fabric of the *Quijote,* the possibility of interpreting wonder as a response to the "true signs" of nature is problematized first in the narrative of Zoraida and the Captive and later in the story of Ana Félix and Ricote. Of all the intercalated tales incorporated into Part 1, the story of the Captive's bold and daring escape from captivity seems to represents romance in the form of a "pure adventure" narrative. It is paired with the story of Zoraida's flight with him to the land of "true faith." Throughout the tale, it appears that Cervantes is rewriting the romance genre, in part by emphasizing the contingency of the social and religious customs that come into play as the Captive and Zoraida attempt to communicate with each other. The story accepts as a point of departure the absolute separation between Christianity and Islam.[25] But Cervantes proceeds at once to break down the absolutism of this separation as part of an apparent attempt to "soften" the monological vision of romance. He introduces a linguistic mediator to negotiate the cultural space between the Captive and Zoraida and he draws attention to the heteroglot speech of Zoraida's father: "me dijo en lengua . . . que ni es morisca, ni castellana, ni de otra nación alguna, sino una mezcla de todas las lenguas" (he spoke to me in a language that is neither moorish, nor castilian, nor that of any other nation, but rather a

25. The ability of the Captain and Zoraida to communicate by a series of gestures and material signs poses the question of what separates and what binds these cultures.

mixture of all tongues) (Part 1, chap. 41, p. 496). Perhaps most impressively of all, he has it that her "natural" faith in Islam was in fact displaced by a belief in Christianity that was taught to her by her nursemaid. It is this second, culturally acquired faith to which she is "returned" when the two are saved from pirates and finally reach Christian land. Unlike conventional romance, where the "return" is often to the point of an original departure, to a "first culture," or to a hidden but true identity, here the return is to an adopted faith, to a foreign land, and to an assumed identity. Rather than assert a faith in a truth that lies absolutely beyond the contingencies of culture and language, the episode is in fact a counterromance that reinforces the ethical perspectivism of the novel.

The narrative of Ana Félix and Ricote in part 2 appears to contravene known historical facts in order to resolve or reverse many of the issues laid out in the Captive's story. (Cervantes has it that the two receive vice-regal protection against the edicts expelling the *moriscos* from Spain, which hardly seems plausible, but then one of the main points of the story has to do with the narrative's power to imagine against the facts.) Like the earlier romance, this narrative raises the issue of the role of belief in relation to cultural identity. In this case, however, both the female protagonist Ana and her betrothed Don Gregorio are disguised in the clothes of the opposite gender. And, unlike the story of the Captive, there is a convincing reconciliation between Ana and her father.[26] Here, the recognition is a resounding confirmation of identity: "¡Oh Ana Félix, desdichada hija mía! Yo soy tu padre Ricote, que volvía a buscarte por no poder vivir sin ti, que eres mi alma" (Oh, Ana Félix, my unhappy daughter! I am your father Ricote, returned to seek you, for I cannot live without you, who are my soul) (Part 2, chap. 63, p. 529).[27] And perhaps most revealing of all, the recognition of Ricote and his daughter is paralleled by the return of a series of estranged or "alienated" signs to their natural referents. As Ricote explains,

> Yo salí de mi patria a buscar en reinos estraños quien nos albergase y recogiese, y habiéndole hallado en Alemania, volví

26. In the case of Zoraida and her father, Agi Morato first condemns his daughter, then at the very last minute pardons her.

27. *The Adventures of Don Quijote*, trans. J. M. Cohen (Harmondsworth: Penguin Books, 1950), 885; further references will be incorporated into the text. The passage contains an important pun on *Félix/feliz* (fortunate, happy) and *desdichada* (unlucky, unfortunate).

en este hábito de peregrino, en compañía de otros alemanes, a buscar mi hija y a desenterrar muchas riquezas que dejé escondidas. *No hallé a mi hija; hallé el tesoro, que conmigo traigo, y agora, por el estraño rodeo que habéis visto, he hallado el tesoro que más me enriquece, que es a mi querida hija.* (Part 2, chap. 63, p. 530; my emphasis)

(I left my country to seek some place in foreign parts to shelter us and take us in, and when I found it in Germany I came back in this pilgrim's habit with other Germans, to look for my daughter and dig up the great riches I had left buried. *I did not find my daughter, though I did find my treasure, which I have with me. But now by the strange turn you have seen I have found a treasure which makes me still richer, my beloved daughter.*) (p. 886; my emphasis)

And yet we would do well to point out that just as there is no recuperation of authentic "wonder" as a truly first form of knowledge here, but only a re-cognition, so too there is never a complete and final renaturalization of the sign. In the passage above, for instance, it is not that the "signs" become substitutes for Ana; rather, it would be more accurate to say that Ana becomes another sign, a *tesoro* that resembles (to the point of metonymic identity) the signs that previously stood in her place, marking her identity in her absence. The "coincidence" of the signifier and the signified confirms identity and sparks the wonder of recognition, but this is principally the recognition of the way in which the sign fits into its place in a signifying chain. It holds the promise that there may exist signs that truly bind, but it does not allow for an escape from the world of signs. Accordingly, what needs to be addressed are the possibilities for the circulation and exchange of signs within the context of romance and the prospects for discovering a system of binding signs that would not be indebted to the symbolic law of the heroic past.

＊   ＊   ＊

The rise and regularization of the category of romance may be related to a more encompassing social transformation in which the structure and values of the "traditional" world were subjected to the modernizing pressures I have described in earlier chapters: a culture in which interpersonal relations had been determined largely by kinship ties and bloodlines, in which actions were evaluated according to an archaic heroic ethos, with its characteristic demands for honor and revenge, and in which social relations had become sedimented into near-static hierarchies, was confronted with a series of relatively more "modern" conditions whose organizing principle was that of free exchange and in which the self was displaced across social lines with greater mobility.[28] In an essay entitled "Symbolic Exchange and Death" Jean Baudrillard proposed a distinction between *caste* societies (whether archaic or feudal) and *class* societies that helps articulate this shift in terms of the function of signs. Caste societies are structures in which social assignation tends to be both hierarchical and absolute, in which social mobility is in principle nil, and in which any attempt to cross these boundaries would constitute an act of transgression.[29] In contrast stands the horizontally differentiated world of free exchange, marked by unbounded signs, which constitutes the context for the exercise of subjective freedom and, by implication, for novelistic self-creation, but which also has the potential to create a vertiginous multiplication of signs, no one of which can be taken as original or as truly binding in any strong sense: "this multiplication of signs no longer bears any connection with the bound sign of restricted circulation. It is the counterfeit of it, not by virtue of having denatured some 'original.' . . . No longer discriminating (but only competitive), relieved of all barriers, universally available, the modern sign nevertheless simulates necessity by offering itself as a determinate link to the world" ("Symbolic Exchange," 136).

For our purposes, the crucial point of Baudrillard's thesis is that the passage from the world of caste relations and heroic signs to the world of the free production of signs by no means eliminates the nostalgia for the assurance offered by the archaic or "bounded" sign. On the contrary, this desire is intensified, even if it is displaced onto such categories as history, which so often in the Golden Age represents the real in its constitution as the "always anterior" (i.e., archaic) sign, or onto moral-

---

28. See Chapter 1.
29. In caste societies, Baudrillard writes that "social assignation is total, social mobility nil. In these societies, signs are shielded by a prohibition that assures their absolute clarity: each sign refers unequivocally to a (particular) situation and a level of status." See "Symbolic Exchange," in *Selected Writings*, ed. Mark Poster (Stanford: Stanford University Press, 1988), 136.

ity, which becomes a locus of the desire for the universally binding sign. In the *romancero*, the *libros de caballerías*, and most of all the Lopean *comedia*, where the demands of history are often aligned with those of morality, we witness the overwhelming power of the symbolic social order that had been in force as recently as the previous century.[30] It might well have been tempting to think that such an order could be revived, and it would not be too much to suggest that the Lopean *comedia* depends for its success on precisely the attraction of this possibility, but as Baudrillard warns, we have also to keep in mind that this was a world of restricted signs, and therefore *cruel* and unyielding in its demands: "If we start yearning nostalgically . . . for a revitalized 'symbolic order,' we should have no illusions. Such an order once existed, but it was composed of ferocious hierarchies; the transparency of signs goes hand in hand with their cruelty" ("Symbolic Exchange," 136).

Given, moreover, the historical impossibility of a return to the old symbolic regime, the problem that Cervantes confronts is that of how to establish the authority of the signs that bind. It is the basis of his social and ethical concerns, and his response to this demand sets his work apart from other founding figures of the early modern age. In thinkers like Descartes, Bacon, Hobbes, and Locke, reason is empowered to redefine the "natural" meaning of signs and so to establish and make legitimate its self-chosen ends. This power supplies the subject with a basis for ethical action; but a rationalist ethics, which turns on distinctions between right and wrong for freely choosing agents, proves insufficient to satisfy the demand for a universally binding sign and the authority it provides—more accurately, it asks the subject itself to provide such a law, which is masked (e.g., in Kant) as a form of moral "freedom." Thus Baudrillard notes that "the modern sign dreams of the sign anterior to it and fervently desires, in its reference to the real, to rediscover some binding obligation. But it finds only a *reason:* a referential reason, the real—the 'natural' on which it will feed. This

---

30. Vicente Lloréns wrote of "la atracción por el mundo señorial y guerrero que el Estado moderno, con su organización burocrática, con sus ejércitos permanentes y mercenarios, había destruído un siglo antes. ¿Se trata, quizá, de una reacción contra la nueva sociedad, como la del romántico inglés frente a la revolución industrial de su tiempo? Lo cierto es que se glorifica el pasado medieval en vez de la poderosa monarquía contemporanea." "La intención del 'Quijote,' " in *Literatura, historia, política* (Madrid: Revista de Occidente, 1967), 213.

lifeline of designation, however, is no more than a simulacrum of symbolic obligation. It produces only neutral values, those that exchange among each other in an objective world" ("Symbolic Exchange," 136).

For a thinker like Descartes, the collapse of the archaic symbolic order is figured as a crisis of personal identity that is "resolved" by a dramatic reorganization of the order of signs. Yet the result of the Cartesian solution (one that becomes more pronounced in Kant) is a division *within* the subject between the transcendental ego and empirical self. In Cervantes's works this same problem has been "resolved" by critics in terms of a division within "literary" discourse between novelistic narration, with its ethos of subjective irony and the characteristic anxieties that this generates, and the "romantic" desire for participation in a universal community of mankind through willing submission to binding laws.[31] In romance, this results in the affirmation of a universally transcendent "human nature" that admits of only local variations or individual differences in quality or kind:

> las almas todas son iguales, y de una misma masa en sus principios criadas y formadas por su Hacedor, y según la caja y temperamento del cuerpo donde las encierra, así parecen ellas más o menos discretas, y atienden y se aficionan a saber las ciencias, artes o habilidades a que las estrellas más las inclinan. (*Persiles,* book 1, chap. 18, p. 1819a)

> (all souls are equal and have their origins in the same material, created and shaped by their Maker. Depending on the form and temperament of the body that encloses them, they seem more or less intelligent and show aptitude for and take pleasure in learning the sciences, arts, or skills toward which the stars most incline them.)

Indeed, the very structure of the *Persiles* as a romance seems designed to illustrate the principle that despite the contingencies of time and chance and the fluctuations of fortune, there exists a transcendental plane on which our individual differences can be reconciled and the vagaries of our fortunes justified. As such it goes to show that rational-

31. In either case, the Cervantean or the Cartesian, the crisis in "exemplary" discourse is precipitated by the "precession" of the model (Baudrillard's term) as a short-circuiting of the project of identification. See Baudrillard, "Simulacra," in *Selected Writings,* 175.

ization does not necessarily mean the absolute loss of transcendence, but rather a displacement of the objects to which our idealizations and desires attach and a relocation of the sources from which moral authority is drawn. And just as this does not amount to a "negation" of the novel's subjective freedom, but a sublation of it, the moral is not in any way a contradiction of the ethical. Rather, it would be more accurate to say that the moral is that which, within the sphere of an increasingly modernized (read: novelistic) world, seeks to transcend the ethical in the projection of an unassailable authority and uncontested principles of belief. The appeals to virtue, beauty, and truth announced on various occasions in the *Persiles* thus amount to a *supersession* of the ethical, rather than a *cancellation* of the novelistic ethos established in the *Quijote,* by an appeal to universal moral claims. To take but one case in point, consider the process of aesthetic and moral "purification" of Sigismunda announced at the conclusion of the work: "hermosa era Sigismunda *antes de su desgracia,* pero *hermosísima estaba después de haber caído en ella;* que tal vez los accidentes del dolor suelen acrecentar la belleza" (Sigismunda was beautiful before this misfortune befell her, but after it she was extremely so; often one of the side effects of pain is that it increases beauty) (book 4, chap. 14, p. 1988a; my emphasis).

In contrast to the ethical, the moment of the moral is produced when the freely acting (novelistic) subject is brought willingly to submit to some more powerful source of social and cultural authority, which is identified with a supreme and unassailable good.[32] While a novel like *Don Quijote* may issue in a discovery of the burdens of subjective freedom—a condition that leads Lukács to posit irony as the novel's highest possible achievement—the subject in the idealizing *novelas* and the *Persiles* is unified against all odds: a semblance of transcendence is produced in a world held already to be disenchanted, through a synthetic process that works at the level of plot, the crucial moments of which draw importantly on the effects of wonder. These include a series of trials and "fortunate" reversals, the dramatic drawing together of the various adventures, and finally the disclosure of the ultimate coherence of disparate signs, in conformity with the patterns of the Byzantine romance. At one point in book 4 of the *Persiles,* this synthetic process is marked in the illusion of converging lines: "Parece que el bien y el mal

---

32. It is in the identification of the subject with the supreme good, rather than in the subjection to such an overwhelming power, that marks the avoidance of the sublime.

distan tan poco el uno al otro, que son como dos líneas concurrentes, que, aunque parten de apartados y diferentes principios, acaban en un punto" (It seems good and bad fortune are separated from each other by so little space that they're like two convergent lines; even though they begin at different and distant points, they come together at the same place) (book 4, chap. 12, p. 1983a). At another moment, this synthesis is ascribed to the powers of agency of the quasi-allegorical "fortune," which retains its double meaning as (good) luck and as chance, but which has been desecularized in such a way that it can claim the power of Heaven as its own: "que estas mudanzas tan extrañas caen debajo del poder de aquella que comúnmente se llama Fortuna, que no es otra cosa sino un firme disponer del Cielo" (for these reverses fell with the strange power commonly called Fortune, but which is nothing less than Heaven's unwavering plan) (book 4, chap. 14, p. 1988a). Whereas the order of exemplary signs established by the old symbolic regime would meet the demands of a moral law through the sacrificial logic of violent revenge, the *Persiles* and the romantic *novelas* aim to produce what are essentially new conditions for moral discourse. These do not depend on a sublimation of those sacrificial demands through an idealist reshaping of the past, but require instead the projection of a reconciled community of mankind. And whereas the theoretical discussions of romance contained within the novel seek to bridge the gap between seeming and being, as between "ought" and "is," Cervantean romance seeks to widen these gaps, which become the privileged sites at which this idealizing projection takes place. When measured by Cervantes's "novelistic" achievement, Cervantean romance becomes not a retraction or a return, but a boldly progressive step, an attempt on the part of the writer to represent a binding morality that subjective freedom could not itself provide. To be sure, it must be said that the impulse, through the moral functions of the marvelous, to represent such a truly binding morality is itself historically, socially, and politically produced, that this projection must contend with the regulatory power of an absolutist state. And yet the central point remains intact. Cervantean romance discloses the excesses of "heroic" emulation and the sacrificial demands of the old symbolic regime. In contrast to the archaic moral law, which still survived in the Golden Age in the form of preoccupations over questions of honor, the idealizing romance promises redemption through submission to the demands of a universally binding law in the form of a reconciled community of mankind.

* * *

That Cervantes may have understood the function of narrative romance as involving a critique of the *comedia* and, more broadly, of the closed society and traditional values on which it was based, can be gleaned from his own critical adaptation of the honor/jealousy plot in *El celoso extremeño* and "El curioso impertinente" in *Don Quijote;* in both instances we find that a typical "honor plot" is somehow deflected or derailed. Consider first the economy of jealousy and desire at work in *El curioso impertinente.* On the one hand, we see that while Anselmo and Lotario attempt to establish Camila as a paragon of virtue, she is the sacrificial victim of the exclusionary logic of a caste society. But we also see that the violence in this story stems from the rivalry between Anselmo and Lotario, "los dos amigos," neither of whom has been able to establish himself as superior to the other:

> Eran solteros, mozos de una misma edad y de unas mismas costumbres; todo lo cual era bastante causa a que los dos con recíproca amistad se correspondiesen. Bien es verdad que el Anselmo era algo más inclinado a los pasatiempos amorosos que el Lotario, al cual llevaban tras sí los de la caza; pero cuando se ofrecía, dejaba Anselmo de acudir a sus gustos, por seguir los de Lotario, y Lotario dejaba los suyos, por acudir a los de Anselmo; y desta manera, andaban tan a una sus voluntades, que no había concertado reloj que así lo anduviese. (*Don Quijote,* Part 1, chap. 33, p. 399)

> (They were bachelors, lads of the same age and the same habits, which was sufficient reason for the affection that united them. It is true that Anselmo was rather more inclined to affairs of the heart than was Lotario, who was fonder of hunting. But when the occasion arose, Anselmo would give up his pleasures to take part in Lothario's, and Lothario his to follow Anselmo's. Their minds, in fact, worked in such unison that no clock could keep better time.) (p. 282)

If this exemplary friendship is in fact the cover for a more deeply seated rivalry between the two friends, then Anselmo's effort to involve Lotario in a plot to test and "prove" Camila must be explained not only in terms of his desire to certify her fidelity (and his own honor) beyond the shadow of a doubt, but to establish his superiority over Lotario. Indeed, these figures give us a glimpse into the darkly competitive underside of a social world whose roots lie in a homosocial bond of sublimated (male) desire requiring the circulation and sacrifice of women as objects of exchange among men.[33]

As *El curioso impertinente* and dramatic works like *El médico de su honra* show, the jealous suspicions that reveal this mechanism of desire require sacrificial violence if the moral law of a caste society is to be upheld. Seen from the modern, "rational," subject's point of view, however, these facts would be repressed or denied. Suspicions are the source of illusions that must be rationally controlled, for they impede the modernizing project to constitute the self through a process of free and reasoned inquiry into the "true nature of things." Thus Sir Francis Bacon describes suspicions as "bats amongst birds, they ever fly by twilight. Certainly they are to be repressed, or at least well guarded: for they cloud the mind. . . . *They dispose kings to tyranny, husbands to jealousy, wise men to irresolution and melancholy*"; "Suspicions that the mind of itself gathers are but buzzes; but suspicions that are artificially nourished, and put into men's heads by the tales and whisperings of others, have stings. Certainly, *the best mean to clear the way in this same wood of suspicions, is frankly to communicate them with the party that he suspects; for thereby he shall be sure to know more of the truth than he did before;* and withal shall make that party more circumspect not to give further cause of suspicion" (*Essays* 86, 87; my emphasis). As Hans Blumenberg has suggested, the success of the subject in securing a world that is both rational and real depends on the transformation of "natural" suspicions and curiosities into a "scientific" inquiry into the relationship between causes and their effects.

By contrast, consider Carrizales, the jealous protagonist of *El celoso extremeño*.[34] It would appear that the jealous Extremaduran's house, with its windowless walls and single master key, reflects a social order in which signs are organized into closed hierarchies, their threateningly productive "mobility" closely contained. Jealousy drives Carrizales to

33. Here we enter what Juliet MacCannell has aptly called the "regime of the brother." See her volume of that title (New York: Methuen, 1991).

34. I am dealing with the final version of the text, rather than with the earlier one brought to light in the Porras manuscript, which offers significant differences.

various forms of excess that attempt to mask the more fundamental fact of constraint:

> [Leonora] pasaba el tiempo con su dueña, doncellas y esclavas, y ellas, por pasarle mejor, dieron en ser golosas, y pocos días se pasaban sin hacer mil cosas a quien la miel y el azucar hacen sabrosas. Sobrábales para esto en grande abundancia lo que habían menester, y no menos sobraba en su amo la voluntad de dárselo, pareciéndole que con ello las tenía entretenidas y ocupadas, sin tener lugar dónde ponerse a pensar en su encerramiento. . . . sólo se desvelaba en traer regalos a su esposa y en acordarle le pidiese todos cuantos le viniesen al pensamiento, que de todos sería servido. (182–83)

> ([Leonora] spent her days with her duenna, maids, and slaves who, to pass the time more agreeably, indulged their fondness for sweets, and hardly a day went by that they did not prepare a thousand dishes with honey and sugar. They had all of this they needed, thanks to the abundance which reigned in the house, and their master was only too happy to give then all they wanted, for it now seemed to him that in this way he kept them busy and contented, without occasion to think of their confinement. . . . He missed no opportunity to shower his wife with gifts and to urge her to ask for anything she fancied, for whatever she wanted was hers for the asking.)

Carrizales's reason for marrying corresponds to his desire to secure his lineage and guarantee his standing at the origin of a signifying chain. But this is also to say that his jealousy is rooted in anxieties concerning his status as a signifying subject: "Quisiera tener a quien dejar sus bienes después de sus días, y con este deseo *tomaba el pulso a su fortaleza, y parecíale que aun podía llevar la carga del matrimonio*" (What he wanted was someone to whom to leave his worldly goods when his end came, and with this in mind *he took stock of his abilities, and it seemed to him that he could still carry the burden of marriage*) (179; my emphasis). Insofar as his claims of virility are used to mask a fear of impotence,[35] Carrizales proceeds to reproduce himself in Leo-

---

35. A comparison could easily be made with "El curioso impertinente" of the *Quijote*. Compare my discussion in *The Bounds of Reason: Cervantes, Dostoevsky, Flaubert* (New York: Columbia University Press, 1986), 244ff.

nora, to fashion her in his image and likeness ("Encerraréla y haréla a
mis mañas, y con esto no tendrá otra condición que aquella que yo la
enseñaré." (I shall wed her, shut her up, and mold her to my ways, and
thus she will conform completely to my teachings) (179). Carrizales's
jealous suspicions may be read as a natural inclination or "passion" of
the soul. And yet when considered in relation to the signified, to the
designated "object" of signs, jealousy is a passion that is never "natural"
but always in excess, hence without grounds: "De su natural condición
era el más celoso hombre del mundo, aun sin estar casado, pues con
solo la imaginación de serlo le comenzaban a ofender los celos, a fatigar
las sospechas y a sobresaltar las imaginaciones" (he was by nature the
most jealous man in the world, even though unmarried, and the mere
thought of entering into wedlock aroused his jealous instincts, and
supicions began to harass him and prey on his imagination) (179).
"Apenas dio el sí de esposo, cuando de golpe le embistió un tropel de
rabiosos celos, y comenzó sin causa alguna a temblar y a tener mayores
cuidados que jamás había tenido" (No sooner had he said "I do" than
he was seized by the most violent jealousy, without the slightest grounds
for it, and began to quake and be more troubled than ever before in his
whole life) (180).[36]

To balance and control this exorbitant jealousy, the requirements of
the typical "honor plot" would lead us to expect a reassertion of the
(moral) law through the uncovering of the scandal and the enactment
of a sacrificial rite of revenge (compare Baudrillard: "The denunciation
of scandal always pays homage to the law" ["Simulacra," 173]). Indeed,
Carrizales is drawn toward the obligatory vengeance we might expect
of a *comedia* hero but, perhaps not surprisingly given the intimations of
his possible impotence, he fails to execute his plan:

> tomara la venganza que aquella grande maldad requería si se
> hallara con armas para poder tomarla; y así, determinó volverse
> a su aposento a tomar una daga, y volver a sacar las manchas de

36. If jealousy begins as a reflection of the potential for excess within a restricted
economy of signs, the subject will depend for its constitution as a self-certifying,
autonomous individual on the containment of this passion within rational bounds. Thus
for Descartes jealousy is transformed into the expression of a failure to respect reason's
commands. According to the *Passions of the Soul*, "[jealousy] does not result so much
from the strength of the reasons which make us believe we may lose the good, as from
the high esteem in which we hold it. This causes us to examine the slightest grounds for
doubt, and to regard them as very considerable reasons" (*Passions of the Soul*, 389).

su honra con sangre de sus dos enemigos, y aun con toda aquella de toda la gente de su casa. Con esta determinación honrosa y necesaria volvió, con el mismo silencio y recato que había venido, a su estancia, donde le apretó el corazón tanto el dolor y la angustia que, sin ser poderoso a otra cosa, se dejó caer desmayado sobre el lecho. (214–15)

(he would have wreaked the vengeance that great affront demanded if he had a weapon at hand. He made up his mind to seek a dagger in his room and return to cleanse the stains on his honor with the blood of his two enemies, and even with that of his entire household. Having taken this honorable and imperative decision he returned to his room, with the same precaution and silence with which he had come, but his grief and his distress so clutched at his heart that he fell fainting on his bed without being able to do a thing.)

The closural patterns worked out in the *comedia* as a genre would have provided a familiar enough resolution for Cervantes's "exemplary" text. Instead, we find in the published version of the story that Carrizales offers freedom to his wife and is himself destroyed:

La venganza que pienso tomar de esta afrenta no es ni ha de ser de las que ordinariamente suelen tomarse, pues quiero que, así como yo fui extremado en lo que hice, así sea la venganza que tomare, tomándola de mí mismo como del más culpado en este delito. . . . Yo fui él que, como el gusano de seda, me fabriqué la casa donde muriese, y a ti no te culpo, ¡oh niña mal aconsejada . . . ! [M]andaré doblar la dote de Leonora y le rogaré que después de mis días, que serán breves, disponga su voluntad, pues lo podrá hacer sin fuerza, a casarse con aquel mozo, a quien nunca ofendieron las canas de este lastimado viejo (pp. 218–19)

(The vengeance I plan to take for this affront is not that which is ordinarily employed; for just as I was extreme in what I did, I wish my revenge to be of the same nature, wreaking it upon myself, as the person most responsible for this crime. . . . Like the silkworm, I myself fabricated the house in which I shall die,

and I do not blame you, misguided child . . . ! I shall double
Leonora's dowry, and ask her, when my days are over, which
will be very soon, to consent of her own free will to marry
that youth, whom the grey hairs of this unfortunate old man
never offended.)

Indeed, *El celoso extremeño* refuses to demand the categorical obedience and respect that are definitive of the old moral law. In contrast to
the *comedia,* where the outrages of violent vengeance are sublimated as
the *vulgo* enthusiastically submits itself to a higher law, the conclusion
of Cervantes's *novela* is fraught with an awareness of the ethical
dilemmas that freedom entails: "Yo quedé con el deseo de llegar al fin
de este suceso, ejemplo y espejo de lo poco que hay que fiar de llaves,
tornos y paredes *cuando queda la voluntad libre*" (I was left with the
desire to reach the end of this story, an example and mirror of how little
trust can be put in keys, turnstiles, and walls *when the will is left free*)
(220; my emphasis). In confronting the self-destructive violence and
excess of the old symbolic regime, Cervantes's characters come to
experience the ethical demands that freedom makes, and yet they fail to
find the happiness that so many *comedia* heroes appear to find. In the
published text, Carrizales renounces vengeance but fails to escape the
pattern of self-destructive violence; Loyasa in despair seeks refuge in
the Indies, thus repeating the familiar pattern of Carrizales's youth;
Leonora is consigned to a life of monastic exile; and Leonora's parents
find but a modicum of consolation in their sorrow. Cervantes may reject
the sacrificial demands of the old symbolic law, yet his characters are
unable to satisfy their hearts' desires. Apparently, it seems that neither
freedom from the old symbolic structures, nor a positive assertion of
the subjective will can in themselves guarantee happiness. As I suggest
in conclusion, this is the additional function served by Cervantean
romance: the achievement of happiness, to be pursued through the
"transvaluation" of the old symbolic regime and the dispensation of a
new (moral) law.

Of all Cervantes's stories, it is *La fuerza de la sangre* that most
emphatically underscores such a process. In this instance the heroine of
the story, Leocadia, ends up falling in love with and marrying the man
who at the beginning of the story was her rapist. Indeed, the injury to
Leocadia's honor is righted in a way that would have been impossible
to imagine without a radical revision of the symbolic social code that

envisions justice in terms of revenge. Indeed, this particular text can be read as Cervantes's most explicit engagement with and critique of that symbolic code. It is a story not only of personal transformation but of social change—of the transformation of one social code into another. Textually, this transformation is motivated in two ways: first, through the religious sign, the crucifix that had belonged to Leocadia's rapist Rodolfo; and second through the human fruit of their violent encounter, the son Luisico whom Leocadia recognizes after a separation of some seven years. Through these events Cervantes faces a central question raised by the persistence of romance in an increasingly disenchanted world: whether, and how, recognition in purely human terms (in *La fuerza de la sangre,* the recognition of Luisico's face) could be read as having the same effect as the miraculous sign. Answering this question was the task for which the *Persiles* was designed.

*   *   *

Whereas the order of signs established by the old symbolic regime was often forced to establish the demands of a moral law through the sacrificial logic of violent revenge (of the kind we see in certain plays by dramatists like Juan de la Cueva, Guillén de Castro, Lope de Vega, and Calderón), the *Persiles* by contrast seeks to establish what is essentially a new law, together with new conditions for moral discourse. These do not depend, as in the *comedia,* on a sublimation of those sacrificial demands through an idealist reshaping of the past, nor do they depend, as in the novel, on the distancing effects of laughter and on the generic institutionalization of an ironic point of view; they require instead the projection of a reconciled community of mankind where differences are not fully erased. "Reconciliation" in the *Persiles* does not respect the sacrificial demands of revenge; this is emphatically *not* the "force of the blood" that is shed at Maximino's death in the closing pages of the work, whose passing serves to preclude the most violent possible outcome of the kind of rivalry we see in the case of "the two friends" (i.e., fratricide). By avoiding fratricide, which may be thought of as the violent extreme to which a society of "equals" may be drawn, Maximino is in a position to bear witness to virtuous heroes for generations to come: " 'Sean testigos de este casamiento la sangre que estáis derramando y los amigos que te rodean' " (Let the witness of this marriage be the blood you're shedding and the friends who surround you) (book

4, chap. 14, p. 1988b). Moreover, the creation of the truly moral community is marked by the intervention of nearly miraculous signs, which reestablish the grounds of belief. Indeed, it could be said that these signs mark the wish for compelling, irrefusable conditions of belief in an otherwise "disenchanted" world, which become the privileged sites at which its idealizing projection and universal reconciliation take place.

The difficulty Cervantes faces is that while the marvelous element of romance has always served as a marker for that which absolutely exceeds belief, in the early modern age the marvelous increasingly failed to compel general assent.[37] The effect of the marvelous in a work like the *Persiles* must be produced in a skeptical, critical, and sometimes divided audience, one that has nearly lost the conditions of belief.[38]

37. Three hundred years after Cervantes, Henry James confronts this same problem in his well-known statement on romance in the "Preface" to *The American*:

> The only *general* attribute of projected romance that I can see, the only one that fits all its cases, is the fact of the kind of experience with which it deals—experience liberated, so to speak; experience disengaged, disembroiled, disencumbered, exempt from the conditions that we usually know to attach to it and, if we wish so to put the matter, drag upon it, in a particular interest, of the inconvenience of a *related,* a measurable state, a state subject to all our vulgar communities. The greatest intensity may so be arrived at evidently—when the sacrifice of community, of the "related" sides of situations, has not been too rash. It must to this end not flagrantly betray itself; we must even be kept if possible, for our illusion, from suspecting any sacrifice at all. The balloon of experience is in fact of course tied the earth, and under that necessity we wing, thanks to a rope of remarkable length, in the more or less commodious car of the imagination; but it is by the rope we know where we are, and from the moment that cable is cut we are at large and unrelated: we only swing apart from the globe—though remaining as exhilarated, naturally, as we like, especially when all goes well. The art of the romancer is, "for the fun of it," insidiously to cut the cable, to cut it without our detecting him.

Among James's literary influences in this passage, Renaissance sources are prominent; Sidney's comment on the marvelous in the *Defence of Poetry* (1595) is among the most important: "Only the poet, disdaining to be tied to any such subjection [to nature], lifted up with the vigour of his own invention, doth grow in effect another nature, in making things either better than nature bringeth forth, or, quite anew, forms such as never were in nature, as the Heroes, Demigods, Cyclops, Chimeras, Furies, and such like: so as he goeth hand in hand with nature, not enclosed within the narrow warrant of her gifts, but freely ranging only within the zodiac of his own wit." *A Defence of Poetry*, ed. J. A. Van Dorsten (Oxford: Oxford University Press, 1966), 23–24.

38. In this, Cervantes begins to confront the problem that nagged the Enlightenment. See, for example, David Hume's essay *Of Miracles* (1748). Hume is equally suspicious of what Lucretius calls the "avidum genus auricularum" (race eager for hearsay), and is cautious about the "gazing populace" ready to "receive greedily, without examination,

Thus as Periandro's narration of the "muchos y extraños sucesos" (many strange occurrences) of his wanderings begins to outstrip the limits of the "possible" and the "probable" that are expected of a "verdadera historia," he becomes unable to continue in the assumption that his narration will have the desired effects on the beliefs of his audience. Periandro must instead plead for the benevolence (*cortesía*) of his listeners in order to legitimize what he hopes they might have accepted with unskeptical faith, which is to say that the marvelous here is dependent on a category of the ethical (i.e., goodwill):[39]

> ¡Caso extraño, y que ha menester que la cortesía ayude a darle crédito! (book 2, chap. 13, p. 1865a)

> (A strange case, indeed, and one that requires a courteous listener to be believed!)

> No es nada lo que hasta aquí he dicho . . . porque, a lo que resta por dezir, falta entendimiento que lo perciba, y aun cortesías que lo crean. (book 2, chap. 16, p. 1873a–b)[40]

> (You haven't heard anything yet . . . for what remains to be said requires your intelligence to get a clear picture of it, not to mention your courtesy to believe it.)

> Lo que en la isla nos sucedió ya lo sabéis, y con esto, y con lo que a mi hermana le queda por decir, quedaréis satisfechos de casi todo aquello que acertare a pediros el deseo en la certeza de nuestros sucesos. (Part 2, chap. 21, p. 1887a)

---

whatever soothes superstition, and promotes wonder." *Of Miracles,* ed. Anthony Flew (LaSalle, Ill.: Open Court, 1985), 49.

39. Kant makes the "good will" the centerpiece of his ethical theory in the *Foundations of the Metaphysics of Morals,* where he says, famously, that "nothing in the world—indeed nothing even beyond the world—can possibly be conceived which could be called good without qualification except a *good will.*" Trans. Lewis White Beck (Indianapolis: Bobbs-Merrill, 1969), 11.

40. Compare Mauricio's response to the doubts that Auristela herself expresses ("De tal manera . . . ha contado su sueño mi hermano, que me iba haciendo dudar si era verdad o no lo que decía"): "Estas son fuerzas de la imaginación en quien suelen representarse las cosas con tanta vehemencia, que se aprehenden de la memoria, de manera que quedan en ella, siendo mentiras, como si fueran verdades" (book 2, chap. 16, p. 1874a).

(You all already know what happened to us on the island, and with this and what my sister has left to say, you will be satisfied regarding almost everything you could possibly wish to know about the truth of what has happened to us.)

The marvelous continues to aspire to the status of that which no one could refuse, and in this sense is the locus of moral suasion. But these rhetorical pleas, no less than the attempts at the theoretical legitimation of the marvelous in the *Quijote*, indicate that whatever morality may be emergent from the marvels of romance must be seen as contingent on the "archaic" process of disenchantment mentioned above.

Nonetheless, the impulse to imagine a truly moral community depends for its success on a suppression of the fact that both the Byzantine romance and the poetic theories invoked in order to justify its "marvelous" elements are themselves historical, and that these forms reveal the effects of a prior "disenchantment," of a "rationalization" process relative to which the early modern critique of romance would have to seem at best secondary or derived. Indeed, it seems that what makes Cervantes's progressive vision of human relations possible is a concealment of the fact that the Byzantine romance is a belated mode of mythmaking, whose sporadic revival (and subsequent critique) within the late Renaissance and early modern age attests to the formation of an autonomous category of "literary" works, rather than a return to mythical origins. The regularization of romance, which depends on the prior separation of literary and nonliterary modes of discourse, is in turn a condition of possibility for the emergence of the novel as a form of anti-romance that, in Cervantes's case at least, cannot entirely break its ties with romance. At the same time, Marx's 1857 "Introduction" cited above suggests that a tendency toward the rationalization and regularization of experience is itself archaic, and may be counted as one of the original functions of myth. Not unlike myth, romance submits the contingencies of experience to the ordering powers of an episodic and linear narrative form, which at one level is full of surprises and at another level is cyclical and repetitive. The viability of a form that is at once marvelous and repetitive is a function of the fact that romance exists within a world that had already been "disenchanted;"[41] for this

---

41. For an elaboration of related views, see Patricia Parker, *Inescapable Romance* (Princeton: Princeton University Press, 1979).

reason it requires the elaboration of a self-conscious rhetoric and a "theory" in order to legitimize its effects. (It is precisely the legitimation of romance that most recent literary theory, in its re-engagement with history, has sought so strongly to resist.) In Cervantes, the self-consciousness of romance is one of the unavoidable traces left by history—whose essence is inseparable from the process of disenchantment—in what has often been perceived as his most a-historical work. It goes to show that even in its alliance with romance, the attempt to speak in a new moral voice is a project that occurs within the framework of a historical world.

Index